OPINIONS FROM THE NEW GLASWEGIANS

"You shouldn't try to describe people like that. It's wrong to stereotype." B *"Glasgow people*
more often." D *"There are old men who sit on the benches and drink "Old England" almost*
know about anyone else but my next door neighbour's a pain in the neck." B *"The people in*
nice people." C *"I would miss Glasgow because of the friendliness and kindness of the peop*
my friends, they run about mental, smashing fire alarms and that. I don't like that. Sometimes they annoy me." C *"A Glaswegian is a person who comes from Glasgow."* B *"Some of them are caring."* B *"Anything happens to someone outside, my mother's always out to help them with covers and that. No one else does it, just my mother."* A *"They've always got shopping bags."* B *"They have to pay the Poll Tax."* A *"Most of them are travelling people."* B *"There's a man who runs a shop up where I stay,who's always getting robbed and he keeps a big machete under his till now."* A *"Glaswegians are funny if they want to be funny."* D *"People set fire to the bins. The bins get melted."* A *"If they've got enough money, they can be funny."* D *"They talk in slang."* A *"The way we are isn't changing."* D *"They're better than people in the rest of Scotland."* A *There are loads of people who light fires in Glasgow"* C *"Most of them try to get on with each other most of the time."* A *"They watch too much T.V."* D *"They're happy most of the time."* A

"Glasgow Green is the people's Green, they shouldn't build on it. They should make it something for everybody." E *"There'll be a lot faster trains and hover wheelchairs."* B *"They should make the council houses look better out at the front instead of just glum veranda after veranda."* B *"The pensioners should get on the buses for nothing. So should everyone else."* A *"I might have to go away from Glasgow if the goverment in England didn't change."* B *"We're trying. I think if we try, we can do it. Make it better."* C *"That new hospital – that's trying – that's saving people's lives."* C *"Probably then a Lada will be like a Lamborghini and everyone will like it."* B *"In a long time, if people don't stop buying aerosols and things that aren't ozone friendly, Glasgow won't be here."* B *"I would still stay in Castlemilk, because I don't think I could get used to living anywhere else."* A *"I hope I'll stay in Glasgow"* A *"I want to go to America, but I haven't got enough money to."* A *"They're trying to change Glasgow into a snobby place."* A *"Pensioners and folk on the Social should get more money.* A *"There should be free hotels where the homeless can go. They should turn the old, wasted buildings into places for children and old people to go."* E *"They should make a big funfair and keep it here."* A *"They should do what they can and tidy it up."* C *"All the big houses getting built up the town for snobs and that, aren't giving anyone else a chance."* A *"We should bring in computer systems and get rid of all the teachers."* C

"Sandyhill used to be a dump but now it's beautiful – it's lovely." C *"There's a lot of syringes down the stanks round here."* E *"Prince Charles came to see our house when it had got renovated and they sent a sniffer dog first. We thought it would be a big alsation, but it was just a wee spaniel and it bashed its head off the wardrobe."* A *"I like Glasgow because the S.E.C.C. is in Glasgow and I wouldn't have been able to see Status Quo if there hadn't been an S.E.C.C."* D *"We're getting decanted – that's no good."* A *"See Glasgow Airport? I don't think that's where it should be – away out there."* C *"The Parkhead Forge is good."* A *"A bull once escaped from the meat market. It was all shaved because they were getting ready to kill it and it just flew past. I asked my mum what it was."* C *"Where we are, you can smell the sewers. Everyone keeps the windows shut."* E *"I would like to stay in the flats round George's Square. They're really nice flats."* B *"In that Briggait Centre, they were selling jumpers for £150. Just a jumper. As if someone would just walk in and buy them like that."* A *"The Garden Festival should have stayed. It was brilliant."* C

United Kingdom in 1989

THE WORDS AND THE STONES

Glasgow's Glasgow: The Words and The Stones
Copyright © The Words and The Stones
All rights reserved

First published in the United Kingdom in 1990
published by
THE WORDS AND THE STONES
152 Bath Street, Glasgow G2 4TB
ISBN No: 0-9515837-0-0

No part of this book may be reproduced or transmitted in any form or by any means without the permission in writing from the publishers, except by a reviewer who wishes to quote brief passages in connection with a review written about this book for insertion in a broadcast, magazine or newspaper.

British Library Cataloguing in Publication Data
Glasgow's Glasgow: The Words and The Stones
1. Scotland. Strathclyde Region. Glasgow, history
I. Title
941.443

Design by James Hutcheson and Paul Keir, Edinburgh
Typeset in Garamond by Hewer Text Composition Services, Edinburgh
Colour separation by Creative Colour Reproduction, Glasgow
Printed in the United Kingdom by Butler and Tanner, Frome, Somerset

This book has been made possible by financial resources
provided by Glasgow District Council

Contents

CONTENTS

Glasgow Family from the 1950s.

"Since our meeting, I have spent some time developing initial ideas about an exhibition which might be relevant for the events to be held in 1990. I attach a copy of my suggestions, at present with the working title '*Glasgow – The Words and the Stones*'.

I would appreciate it greatly if you would discuss this idea with Robert Palmer and Neil Wallace.

The idea is in tune with the initial submission for U.K. nomination. It is an idea for a major exhibition based on European Themes; it is capable of taking on the mood of a Biennale or Dokumenta event; it could be used to seed the renovation of a building in the city . . . while there is no doubt that given the investment of time and money, it could be a major visual arts event of international standing.

What is however different about this suggestion, is the challenge of the concept itself. Previous exhibitions such as that on the 1920s held in Berlin in 1977, or the Medici show in Florence, or even more city orientated ones such as those in Berlin in 1984 and 1987, have not really attempted to synthesise the 'invisible' city of literature (*The Words*) with the 'visible' city of architecture and urban space (*The Stones*). In the past, books and objects have been set out in cases like dead leather with little or no association for the visitor with drawings, models or photographs. The challenge inherent in the proposed idea is to do justice to the people and history of Glasgow by composing a series of twelve spaces constructed today and notable in their own terms, which synthesise the 'inner' and 'outer' urban experience of Glasgow."

Letter from Doug Clelland to Harry Diamond. July 9, 1987.

Bellahouston Park Empire Exhibition of 1938 – "Tait's Tower".

Preface

THE WORDS AND THE STONES

North End of the Old Bridge of Glasgow – 1776 – James Brown.

Map of Glasgow 1773 Charles Ross.

It is one thing to say something and quite another to do it.

During travels to Europe in the 1970s and Eighties, the visitor to the main European Exhibitions was offered attendant publications. In most cases these flagship catalogues were of flagstone dimensions. After publication they enjoyed a long and undisturbed shelf life.

It is palpably inadequate to describe *Glasgow's Glasgow* as an exhibition. Equally, I have never conceived the event's main publication as a catalogue: Glasgow is not captured so easily. In as much as the event is complex and plural, so too the book.

The development of *Glasgow's Glasgow* and this publication have been formed by many people. A comprehensive, monolithic history was neither possible nor even desirable. No-one – whether in museums or universities – has exclusive rights to the past. I wished to open up the project to a range of contributors and to find a character and structure which would enable them to describe the view from their vantage point.

Glasgow's Glasgow became a practical proposition in May 1987, but this book began to acquire substance a year later, in June, when Carl MacDougall joined the project. Since then, our diverse group has unravelled many themes. Among these, I have found seven particularly intriguing.

Steam boat on the Clyde near Dumbarton – 1818 William Daniell.

Map of the Town of Glasgow and Country Seven Miles Round – 1795 – Thomas Richardson.

THE PLACE

From its shape and character at the time of the Reformation, (see page 46), little major physical change occurred to the town until the 18th century despite the passing of some thirty generations of people.

Glasgow comes into some kind of focus for us as a recognisable place roughly two centuries ago. In the *Ross* map of 1773 we can find the place east of the centre of today's Glasgow. *SIGILLIUM CIVITATIS GLASGUENSIS* (Seal of the City of Glasgow) endorses the image. What was then a complete, densely built town, is now a gradually improving quarter of Glasgow. In many European cities the historic core has been successfully developed; Glasgow Cross awaits its turn.

It is during these years that some of our "first team" were about. In 1776 Adam Smith created his *Wealth of Nations* drawing on his experience in Glasgow, and James Watt, twelve years before, had his brainwave on the Laigh Green which would change Glasgow and the world. Yet when we consider for a moment the *James Brown* drawing of 1776, there is little hint of the great changes in the making. At the bottom of "Stock Wall" street there is a gate, a bridge and a ford no chance a boat of any size up there. We are presented with a city which is hard working and lively enough, but still rural.

Claremont Terrace with Woodlands Terrace in back – 1852 – unknown.

Two decades on, the *Richardson* map shows all the names we know today. The grid is marching outwards from George Square (unseen in the *Brown* map of 22 years earlier) and the countryside is dotted with big houses. The trees and animals are being evicted. The river now looks significant – three bridges instead of one now span it – yet the Clyde is still without industry.

Watt's discovery was applied. The *Daniell* painting is of Dumbarton and of a single powered vessel among the sail boats it would render obsolete. Glasgow was inventing Port Glasgow and deepening the river to bring sea to town.

Mill Lade at Kelvinbridge looking to Hillhead – 1852 – unknown.

St Vincent Crescent in the 1850s, attributed to Robert Carrick. The Crescent was designed by Alexander Kirkland.

Industrial development followed, but Glasgow was no more able to exercise radical political control over its impact than any other European city. Immigrants flowed in. The city, throughout the 19th century, grew, and grew more dense. The two paintings from 1852 show the westwards expansion. *St Vincent Crescent* is on a

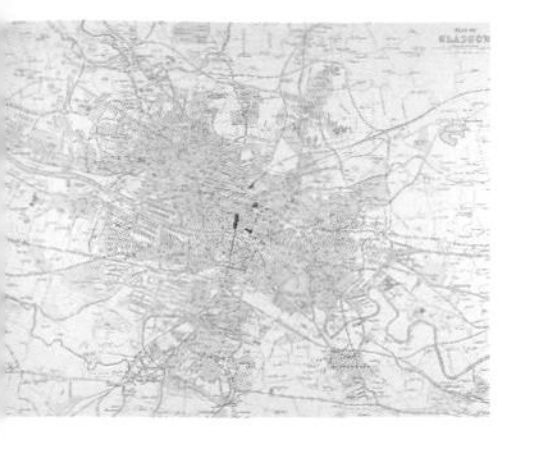
Bartholemew Map of Glasgow – 1917.

Calton Entry – 1881 – David Small.

scale equal with any equivalent elsewhere – a big development done well. To the east, the old Town Centre and the East End of that time became more and more squalid. The painting by *Small* of the Calton describes another Glasgow – a poor and unsanitary place.

The *Bartholemew* map of 1917 is of Glasgow as workshop, making everything and sending it everywhere. The hamlets and houses of the *Richardson* map are now densely packed with streets and factories; the sea has come from the west and coal and ore from the east. The sky is ablaze. The exhausting, dangerous industries consume people as well as raw materials. The story is ablaze.

Blyth captures a quiet moment in the tenement city. The faces are reflective; there is no man in this family. Today Glasgow is recorded more obsessively than ever as new forces shake and shape the place.

Tenement Family – 1948 – Robert Henderson-Blyth.

THE PEOPLE

Places are made by their people, although a lot of nice places challenge this view. The words devised for our coat of arms tell us something about our forefathers. They hedge their bets in a way we like to think of as modern.

Here's the fish that never swam!

Women at Work at "Lyle's" sugar factory – Greenock.

Mungo's miracle is simultaneously commemorated and denied. These are the phrases of a people who are ready for anything; they have needed to be. Most recently, with the collapse of the industrial economy during this century, Glasgow has left many people with no hope of work. The *Wilkie* is from the last century and is of human despair away from the city. People like these probably left their homes and moved to Glasgow where work could be had. Yet within three generations, that employment was being lost. "Distraining for rent" became a phenomenon of the city itself and many have recounted its effects.

Distraining for Rent – 1815 – David Wilkie.

Women, apart from tending families and homes, knew heavy labour and light pay. After 1914 – when the war required its supply of men to be killed and ordnance with which to kill – Glaswegians were not to be distrained by Factors without a fight. Women expanded the domestic role until it even included the fundamental struggle known as the "Rent Strikes". The plain but political idea of fairness, a haunting presence down the centuries, continued to be pursued.

Agit prop cart at the time of the Rent Strikes – 1915.

The Edinburgh trial of those Glaswegians who wished to make a new society after 1918 is a watershed. Britain remained what it had been since 1707 and, conversely, British politics has never had a true cutting edge since. Despite improving social welfare conditions during this century, Glasgow, after 1919 and this trial, went downhill fast. Industrial productivity dwindled away and for a long time all we made in its place were feeble attempts to conceal the damage.

Old woman chatting.

Glasgow people have faced up to enormous odds. Not here the silky smooth way of history. Instead there has been a compulsory experiment with non-tradition, but ironically lots of stories about past exploits: a city that can cancel itself and yet still find a laugh. No wonder things happened here, and are happening once again.

The Trial of Brennan, Ebury, Gallacher, Hopkins, Kirkwood and Shinwell in Edinburgh – 1919.

SPARKS

They have flown, but those of industrial friction have gone. Glasgow, however, has always been a place where ideas are sparked off, where the past turns abruptly into the future.

The *Hearne* is an exercise in archaeology: a recording of two institutions of religion, one passed away long before, the other well into decline. The *Boerhaave Portrait* on the other hand, shows a man of vital modernity, the type of person Glasgow was once enthralled by.

We have spoken of Smith and Watt, but what of Black, Cullen, Hunter, Hutcheson, Reid and Simson? They are remembered in the world and forgotten in Glasgow.

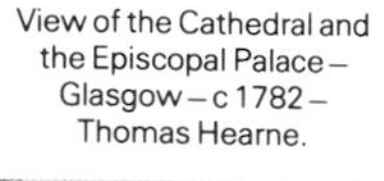
View of the Cathedral and the Episcopal Palace – Glasgow – c 1782 – Thomas Hearne.

Hermann Boerhaave: The innovative teacher of medicine, based in Leiden in the early 18th Century, taught many Glasgow students.

A View of Glasgow from the South East – mid 18th Century – R Paul Eleve.

View taken from the West of the Cathedral Church of Glasgow – mid 18th Century – R Paul Eleve.

Then we hear Taggart growl "In Glasgow we do not put people on pedestals." Scepticism has its uses, but this city has been too contemptuous of new dreams and ideas. Many of our people have been driven away, looking not for a pedestal, but at least for a more optimistic climate.

The engraving of the church by *Eleve* is an image of a world, in the mid-1700s, which is ending. The hay stacks will soon be Cathedral Street, the Cathedral will soon become what it is today, a fine cold place for minority interests. *Eleve's* view from the east includes the first Glasgow Bridge, the eight spires and the old town which is soon to become squalid. It also shows the use of the countryside and the uncontrolled flow of the Clyde – shallow and, like the Nile, capable of flooding in a country however, that does not lack rain.

The Stockwell Bridge – 1850 – Thomas Fairbairn.

Ingram Street – 1830 – unknown.

This world is as static as our own, as static as static can be, which is only a world however that calls on us to change it. Glaswegians have always sought to do that. But what has changed?

Copernicus changed everything by *demoting* the significance of the Earth. He moved things forward by negating a previous belief. Glaswegians are good at that.

As the Cathedral dropped in value and Glasgow Cross no longer was the meeting of routes, the town changed. The *Fairbairn* of 1850 is still of a rural river and a fine town, but Ingram Street and West George Street twenty years before, show a new city of classical simplicity spreading west. The grid of streets and civilised life swept over the hills as if they were flat. The Calton festered, and Glasgow divided.

Everything moved west; at least, like Glasgow University, everything that was meant to mean anything.

It is this city, before the huge factories came, that bred ideas and intellectual sparks.

Today, in the manner of Copernicus, we need to creatively deny Glasgow its previous role and become convinced of the truth of its relegated status in industry. Without the friction of change the sparks will not fly.

Main Street Gorbals looking north 1868 Annan.

West George Street – 1830 – unknown

INNOVATION

Not long after the *Fairbairn* and just across the bridge to the south, Gorbals was home to many immigrants. The Rue Mouffetard in Paris is today still a museum of that kind of street, with its people and its smells a universe away from the primness of West George Street. Glasgow was crucible and many men and women made things which were new and, by being new, swept the board.

The people of ideas a century before became the people of practical ideas: Beardmore, Bell, Elder, Kelvin, Lister, Napier and Robertson.

More softly, people sent each other postcards which they chose to draw and paint themselves. The cause was not the absence of a card shop, but a commitment to actually creating the small gestures of life.

Glasgow has struggled painfully to make the 20th century as much its own as the industries of the 19th century *were* its own: the building of the R34 which crossed and recrossed the Atlantic; the Bennie Railplane, a prototypical "bullet" train . . . the Hillman Imp . . .

Hand painted postcard by Alan Mainds sent to Miss E Lever in 1902.

The R34 at home, Atlantic Crossing 1919 – Inchinnan.

LABOUR

The place, the people, the sparks of innovation which made Glasgow relatively attractive for over a million to live there until the 1960s – everything comes down to jobs and labour, play and dreams.

Having work is the mainstay of the Glaswegian and if that work means something to the world then so be it . . . if it does not, equally . . . so be it. There is a feeling abroad today, that despite the improvement we witness, Glasgow will never work at its best again. That is a mentality that is worth challenging, because the mainstay of a city is to know that it is at the forefront of what it can be. Glasgow has not merely pulled itself back from the brink, but is beginning to see a growing self-respect among its people.

The Bennie Railplane – 1939 – Milngavie.

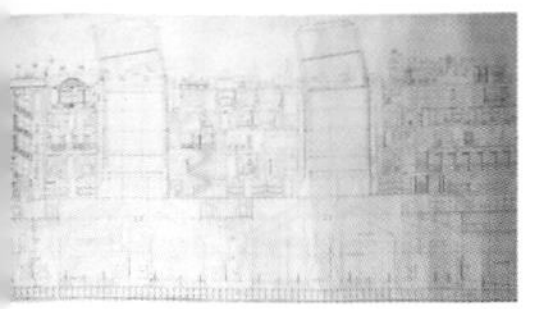

Cross section through the *Lusitania*.

Glasgow Green – 1960.

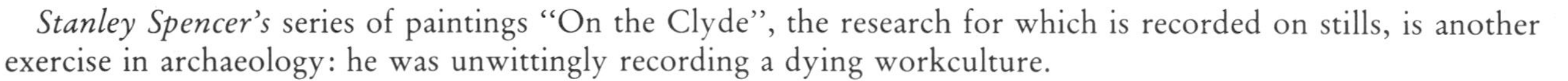

Stanley Spencer's series of paintings "On the Clyde", the research for which is recorded on stills, is another exercise in archaeology: he was unwittingly recording a dying workculture.

This workculture is long gone, but it *was* an incredible Glasgow phenomenon. This was the wealthiest place of them all as it made huge things and squeezed the juices out of its working people.

The *Stewart Steam Hammer* or the cross sectional drawing through the *Lusitania*'s guts are two images from an infinity of industrial achievements which kept people at work and shaped the Glaswegian's attitudes. The rest of the world was simply Glasgow's periphery.

The smoke from the chimneys blackened people and stones, legitimised our vengeance on the past. We demolished not only buildings, though, but also the economic vigour which had once been associated with them. And all the bosses managed, one way or another, to escape the demise of the community.

On the Clyde – 1944–45 – Stanley Spencer at work.

Postcard to Miss Lever, 1902.

PLAY

Glasgow Airport thrives. The city's people want to travel . . . they work hard at all that. Equally to "play" on home ground, in Glasgow, is to change everyday life and the work by humour and creative self mockery. It is as hard and as skilful as work, but requires different skills. It is, however, not yet play.

The scene in *Glasgow Green* from the 1960s is typical: relaxation and play feature only marginal alterations in the normal flow of life.

The *postcard* of 1902 shows people taking their lives in their hands to play. The Broomielaw of yesterday was the airport of today. Yet without knowing it, the pleasure seekers off "doon the watter" did more for the Glasgow conurbation economy than their sun loving grandchildren of today. Pleasure and work were conjoined. This hints at future possibilities. The child unhappy with his load was, after the slog, happier than he ever expected to be, "continents" away, twenty miles from home. That's the way it all worked when it worked.

Today, Glasgow is at the centre of a region full of wonderful natural resources and pleasure spots – except that our knowledge of the Costas makes it cold and wet for us nowadays. Yet gradually Glaswegians like Berliners or Milanese, will realise that it is only by making this wonderful wet bit of the globe work that we will play again so well.

A "Stewart of Glasgow" steam hammer.

Child with Suitcases, 1954.

UTOPIA

Because we have not been able to make it all work as it did, since the carpet was whipped from under our feet, Glaswegians have been susceptible to glib ideas of modern development. We have yearned fatally for solutions as instant as our coffee – find the favourite blend – buy it from a foreign producer – pour on some water – add milk – and stir to perfection.

After the demise of Glasgow's independent resolve at the Edinburgh Trial of 1919, we adopted others' patterns of life. Before that, Glasgow's expansion west had left an old city which received no funds: it rotted and the people of it, with it.

The *Molendinar* became an open sewer. The "Dear Green Place", over-populated since the map of 1773, killed people very dead. Glasgow and Glaswegians made slums.

So far as health is concerned, water from *Loch Katrine* sprang to our aid and then the Trossachs became a playground: the robust solution to an ill became an unforeseen asset. Glasgow was like that; the world learned from that; Glasgow needs to relearn that.

And then along came Bruce.

Since 1942, popular organs such as the *Picture Post*, had projected a new Britain. It needed "heroes" and each city required its own. Glasgow had Robert Bruce.

Chimneys rather than Church Towers. Glasgow at the end of its most recent dream.

Seaside near Glasgow.

Surge of fresh water.

His conclusive achievement was to consciously forget all that Glasgow had been. He wanted a different place, people, sparks, innovation, labour and play. He wanted to consume what the outside world had made – the ideal places of the 1920s and 1930s were created in France and Germany – rather than make the solutions here in Glasgow.

The results are clear. A new place with all meaning removed - mum, dad, kids, friends, community, the lot. And what had engendered all this barbarity? In simple terms, the city which had been made in the prosperity of the 19th century was still the same place in the grinding poverty and deprivation of the post 1918 world. The end of the Second World War and the euphoria of a new Labour Party-led social order demanded that Bruce's world be made.

We tried – harder than anyone else west of the Elbe – but it failed. Even recently, little utopias like the Garden Festival, have bloomed and gone . . . never believed in sufficiently to stay; no matter howw loved.

Glasgow today is a funny old place. We nibble again at the world which actually does things, but we only nibble. The bigger appetite, the confidence to choose and swallow the consequences, is stirring though. Perhaps we will once more find the confidence to act aggressively – to bite.

WHY WE GOT THE IMPROVEMENT TRUST ACT 1866
THE SLUM DEATH ROLL

1832	Deaths from Cholera	2842	average %	46
1837	Typhus	2180		41
1847		4346		56
1849	Cholera	3772		35
1853-4		3885		42
1864	Typhus	1183		41
1865		1177		30.5 *

* This average for ten years until 1874 when many slums were demolished and much Sanitary work done.

The results of the sanitary conditions in the "Dear Green Place" – The Improvement Trust Act of 1866.

THE BOOK

This has been a journey to the point I began with. The concept and talk turned into action when Carl MacDDougall began work, yet the variety of contributions should be set out clearly (and alphabetically).

Martin Bellamy *Content Research*, Elspeth Campbell *Typing*, Lynn Cochrane *Content Research*, Douglas Clelland *Concept and Interpretation*, Morag Cross *Content Research and Picture Research*, Joe Fisher *Contents Reader*, Andy Gibb *Contents Reader*, John Hewer *Typesetter*, Jim Hutcheson and Paul Keir *Graphic Designers*, Linsey Irvine *Typing and Indexing*, Carl MacDougall *Writing the core text, and insert invitations*, Annette MacMillan *Typing*, Kevin McCarra *Editor*, Francis McKee *Content Research and Interpretation*, Jill Paton *Content Research, Photographic Research and Picture Editor*, Maggie Pettigrew *Typing*, Ian Rae *Publication Management*, Hamish Whyte *Contents Reader*, Sarah Wiscombe *Publication Management*

The Molendinar as an open sewer.

Trossachs Pier, Loch Katrine, 1902.

And what else? The contributors of the inserts, the many people who have permitted us to illustrate the book, the captionists, the cartoonists . . . I could go on, but cannot.

When asked, as I have been, about who among the team helped to score the goals, I have no answer. A co-operative, non-profit making work like this does not need to answer such a question. Rather this is a work for Glasgow, about Glasgow, by Glaswegians in 1990.

Doug Clelland

Bruce Plan – view of the city centre – from *The First Planning Report* March 1945.

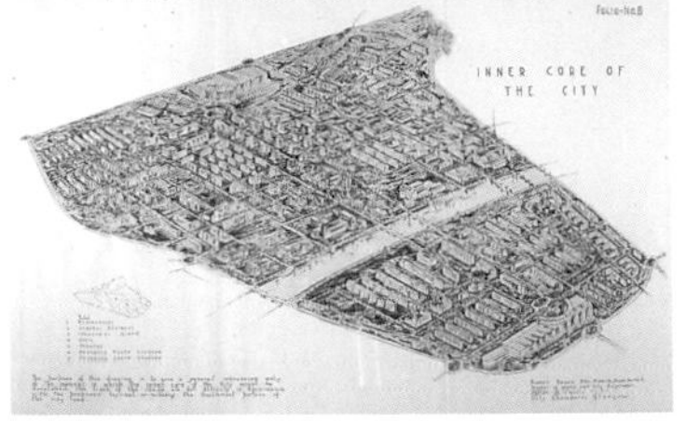

Bruce Plan – plan of the city centre.

The "little utopia" of the Garden Festival.

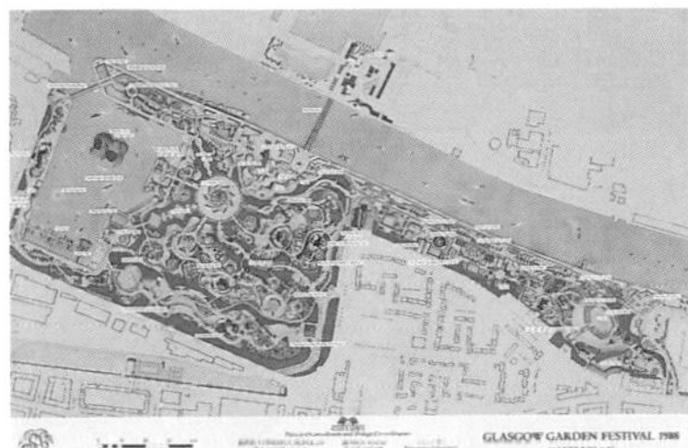

The venue for Glasgow's Glasgow prior to reclamation.

Prologue

AND ANOTHER THING

Glasgow has been seriously out of order for 800 years, as long as we've had the Fair.[1] It is the birthplace of the Industrial Revolution, antiseptic surgery, the raincoat, Ian Brady and the Boys' Brigade.

It is currently home for three orchestras, two chamber orchestras, an opera company, one internationally famous theatre company and at the last count 18 others. It also houses what has been called "one of the most remarkable assemblages of works of art ever brought together by one man.".[2]

Mary, Queen of Scots, fought her last battle here, Bonnie Prince Charlie met his mistress and Robert Burns bought Jean Armour's wedding dress.[3]

One district contains what is believed to be the oldest European site of continuous worship,[4] and St Valentine's bones are here.[5]

"Wee Willie Winkie" was written here,[6] and *The Wealth of Nations* was planned here. Robert Service was educated here,[7] so too was the first Director General of the BBC, then plain John Reith. He bullied a schoolboy called John Logie Baird; they met later in life, though neither forgot their early encounter. Albert Einstein lectured us on Relativity[8] and a Glaswegian founded McGill University.

"James McGill", founder of the McGill University, by Louis J Dulongpre.

We have the second oldest Chamber of Commerce in the world, the only Doge's Palace outside Venice, and the only sea-going paddle steamer in the world.

We built the first column to Nelson, the first memorial to Sir Walter Scott, had the first cable underground system and gas lit streets. We placed great faith in the tramcar, had the world's first municipal tramway system, the world's longest track, at 238 and a half miles, and the world's busiest junction.

We have "the most astonishing piece of earthenware ever made",[9] the largest public reference library in Europe, the biggest indoor market in Europe and Europe's first temperance meeting was held here. This was the northern limit of the Roman Empire. Presbyteries

1. See Page 37 **2.** Peter Wilson, Foreword to Richard Marks, **Burrell**, 1983. **3.** Letter to Robert McIndoe, Horn's Land, Virginia Street, August 5, 1788. **4.** See Page 18. **5.** St Valentine's relics are supposed to be resting in St Francis RC Church, Gorbals. **6.** William Miller, "The Laureate of the Nursery", was born in the Briggait in 1810. **7.** See Page 96. **8.** On June 20, 1933. **9.** A.M. Doak and A Young, **Glasgow At A Glance**, 1965, Item 119. See Page 190.

Princes Square, Buchanan Street, symbol of localised affluence in the new Glasgow.

were named here, giving the world Presbyterianism. Mr Anderson's Polytechnic was the world's first department store[1] and Glasgow is currently the third biggest shopping centre in Britain. We boast a gents' outfitters which stocks more suits than any other.[2]

Per head of population, we have more parklands than any other European city. We have a population of around 725,130,[3] of whom 17.7 per cent are under 14 and 19.4 per cent are over 60; 401,000 people are employed here; 22.6 per cent of Strathclyde Region's labour force were looking for work in April 1989. Glasgow has 40 parks covering 3,325 acres. We have our own herds of Highland cattle, Clydesdale horses, sheep and deer.

Glasgow has a total land area of almost 49,000 acres, has a housing stock of 304,668, is on the same latitude as Moscow and until recently, our rainfall averaged between 37 and 40 inches per year, with temperatures ranging between −18 and 30 degrees Centigrade. The Gulf Stream that laps the shores of the Atlantic, the hills to the north and south-west and a prevailing westerly wind give us a moderate climate.

Glasgow is the only city in the world to have its own dictionary, claimed as the best selling Scottish paperback ever.[4] To stand at a bus stop in this city is to invite conversation.

The Mitchell Library, stone-cleaned and floodlit, by night.

1. John Anderson, "The Universal Provider", opened his Argyle Street store in 1845. **2.** The claim of Slater Menswear in Howard Street. **3.** **City Profile, Facts and Figures about Glasgow**, 1985, and **Strathclyde Social Trends No. 2**, October, 1989. **4.** Michael Munro, **The Patter**, 1985.

Prologue

AND ANOTHER THING

"The Barras" by Bet Low.

Stethaconthus, whose mouth is at the front of its head. Every detail has been preserved, down to its last meal.

Chapter One

THE WATER'S EDGE

Whereas various Portions of the City of Glasgow are so built, and the Buildings thereon are so densely inhabited, as to be highly injurious to the moral and physical Welfare of the Inhabitants, and many of the thoroughfares are narrow, circuitous, and inconvenient, and it would be of public and local Advantage if various Houses and Buildings were taken down, and those portions of the said City reconstituted, and new Streets were constructed in and through various Parts of said City, and several of the existing Streets altered and widened and diverted, and that in connexion with the Reconstruction of these portions of the City Provision was made for Dwellings for the Labouring Classes who may be misplaced in consequence thereof.

The Minute Book of Trustees under the Glasgow Improvements Act, 1866.

History is a matter of tides. We look to the waters for early signs of life.

Glasgow's first citizens were ferocious. Three hundred and twenty-five million years ago sharks were swimming around Bearsden, a dormitory town on the north-western edge of the city, whose name is a trap for unwary news readers. Beside a stream in the middle of a housing estate, in the spring of 1982, a Youth Opportunities team unearthed *stethaconthus*, the oldest shark ever found and the best preserved member of its family.

There were also eleven examples of a previously unrecorded type of fossilised fish, several varieties of shrimp, shells and even a giant fish louse. The abundance and distinctiveness still attract palaeontologists from all over the world.

The story of Glasgow is often written in water. In its frozen form it shaped the very look of the place. The Clyde Valley is floored with Highland boulders which prove the way the ice moved. Drumlins were moulded in the glacial drift and they have controlled Glasgow's topography and town planning ever since.

The glaciers left other remains. Mammoth, reindeer and Irish elk were scattered around the valley and traces of the woolly rhinoceros were found in the gravels at Bishopbriggs.

It is generally believed that just as the 1866 City Improvement Act was later to obliterate much of the medieval archaeological evidence, so the post-Glacial seas removed all traces of previous settlements. Pockets of medieval Glasgow avoided the Improvement and a number of pre-historic axe and arrow heads and dug-out canoes survived to be discovered. They raise some interesting problems.

One was found a quarter of a mile away from the Clyde and 26 feet above sea level at high tide. It was resting "on pure sea sand", which according to the Edinburgh Antiquarian Robert Chambers, proved that "the Firth of Clyde was a sea, several miles wide at Glasgow, covering the site of the lower districts of the city,

A fossilised fish from the Mesozoic Period, the time of the dinosaurs and flying reptiles.

The founder of the Victoria Park Fossil Grove in the midst of his discoveries in 1904.

One of Govan's hog-backed stones.

"Govan on the Clyde". A watercolour by William Simpson, painted in 1842, with Govan Parish Church in the background and the mouth of the River Kelvin on the right.

and receiving the waters of the river not lower than Bothwell Bridge".[1]

Dug-out canoes from other locations, including Stockwell Street, the Drygate, London Road, Glasgow Cross and Springfield Quay, produced more conundrums. The first came to light when they were excavating for the foundations of St. Enoch Church in 1780. It carried a Neolithic axe "of beautifully polished dark green stone"[2] and is almost certainly over 4,000 years old. Other axes have been found elsewhere in Glasgow.

In 1780, Glasgow's population was 43,000; by 1850, 359,000. During this period of expansion 17 canoes were found. Twelve were discovered when they widened the Clyde. Some had been paddled, some rowed, some had seats and others none. One was made of cork, although Spain is the nearest cork growing country. Another was built with a keel and ribs.

When these early examples of Clyde shipbuilding were being sailed, Gilmorehill, Garnethill and Garngad were islands in a valley of water that stretched from the Cathkin and Gleniffer Braes to the Campsies; John Street, Montrose Street and North Frederick Street were part of the estuary embankment; George Square and Argyle Street were under water.

Predictably, we find evidence of civilisations more readily comprehensible to us on the margins of the rivers. When the Vikings came up the Clyde, Govan was a natural harbour for their longships. Five hog-backed stones in Govan's Old Parish Churchyard may mark the graves of Viking warriors.

Our earliest structures are sepulchral monuments, the cist cemeteries at Victoria Park, Greenoakhill at Mount Vernon and Springhill Farm, Baillieston. At Shields Farm, Govan, they found a Neolithic henge. Govan also has what many believe to be Glasgow's oldest, most important religious site. Its Old Parish Church has been a site of continuous worship for more than 2,000 years.[3] This was hallowed ground for successive Britons, Gaels, Vikings, Normans and Scots, who have left a collection of monuments. The circular shape of the graveyard is an indication of its antiquity.

The Govan name first appears in the 12th century under a variety of spellings, such as Gwffane or Gouffane, and is assumed to have been derived from the Welsh and Gaelic meaning Smith, or Land of the Smiths. When the Romans arrived in Strathclyde, the tribes were armed with splendid swords, dirks and spears and the ancient Celts worshipped Goban, their God of the Forge.

At some point between 1126 and 1138, King David granted the lands of Guven to the Church of St Kentigern in Glasgu. The

DUG-OUT CANOES

One of the largest portable artefacts that has come down to us from prehistoric and early historic times in western Scotland is the oaken log-boat or dug-out canoe. Several were found in the mud of the river Clyde when the docks were being excavated in the 19th century. Many more have turned up in the lochs of the south-western counties, occasionally associated with the Iron Age and Dark Age dwellings known as crannogs.

The dug-out canoe required relatively advanced technology; it has to be hollowed out laboriously with fire and with a hafted axe or adze, and such tools – of flint or stone – were probably not available more than a few thousand years ago.

There are two kinds in Scotland – the single-piece craft (in which bow and stern are of uncut cross sections of the log) and those with a separate stern board. In the latter, more developed form the stern board is set into a groove and presumably made watertight with resin. The earliest log canoes must have been paddled but the Hunterian Museum has one from the Clyde which is 6.2 metres long and up to 95cm wide; it has traces of foundations for seats and holes for four or five rowlocks in the tops of the sides. It was doubtless an early ferry, used when the river was wider and shallower than at present. Its age might be about 1,000 years: a more primitive, single piece boat from Loch Doon in Ayrshire, also in the Hunterian, has been dated by radiocarbon to the middle of the first millennium AD.

Euan W MacKie

1. Robert Chambers, **Raised Beaches**, quoted in **St Mungo's Bells**, 1888. See also Chambers, **Ancient Sea Margins**, 1848. 2. **Transactions of the Glasgow Archaeological Society**, 1883. 3. **Old Govan Club Transactions**, 1914–39.

Glasgow from the south-east, 1693.

territory extended across the river, covering Partick and Hyndland, with the River Kelvin as its farthest boundary. Govan was the first point where the Clyde could be forded. Stepping stones crossed the river till 1768, when the Clyde was dredged and deepened to allow ships into the heart of Glasgow.

Sir James D Marwick, Town Clerk of Glasgow, wrote a detailed account of *The River Clyde and The Harbour of Glasgow*. It is a small addition to the catalogue of literature covering our fight against nature. "Previous to the latter half of the 18th century the Clyde was practically what nature had made it", said Sir James, "and was so shallow as to admit of the passage only of boats and small vessels".[1]

In 1597, such craft "engaged in carrying wine, probably from France, and other commodities, probably timber and wool from the Highlands".[2] None of these boats could get beyond Dumbarton or Dumbuck Ford. The boats lay in the middle of the river till their cargoes were carried ashore by porters and loaded onto horses for the trip to Glasgow.

A Town Council minute of October 14, 1609, however, talks of the "pier and port at the Brumelaw".[3] In April, 1600, King James VI and his Privy Council had authorised the Council to improve the channel of the river. On May 28, the Council ordered the master of works to begin "the casting of the water". Four men and an Englishman named Smyth set about it.

Glasgow's trade had grown so that by 1667, the town had its first register of ships. The Council also approached Dumbarton to become the city port, but that burgh feared "the great influx of mariners and others" would raise the price of food.[4]

So, in January and February, 1668 Glasgow Town Council acquired from Sir Patrick Maxwell of Newark at a price of 12,000 merks a feu of 13 acres opposite Dumbarton. From December 23, 1669, when the agreement was ratified by Parliament, in Edinburgh, the town of Port Glasgow was built, a harbour was constructed and Scotland's first graving dock and new town were completed.

Goods were unloaded at Port Glasgow and shipped up river on smaller boats. On November 30, 1768, John Golborne, an engineer from Chester, told Glasgow Town Council what they already knew. The river was in a state of nature.

A year later, with James Watt's approval, Golborne devised a series of jetties, to make the river navigable from Dumbuck Ford to Glasgow Bridge. He said he could make the river six feet ten inches deep and 300 feet wide. By 1775, the river was seven feet

Port Glasgow.

CRANNOGS AND BROCHS

Later in the Iron Age – in the two centuries before the Romans arrived (in 79 AD) – massive roundhouses began to be built. These were individual family dwellings, quite different to hillforts, almost certainly belonging to tribal chiefs and sub-chiefs.

The crannog is a form of wooden roundhouse which was built on piles and on a brushwood platform on an artificial island in a loch. At least three have been found in the Clyde, downstream from the city. Dumbuck was explored in the 19th century but the site was unfortunately "salted" with fakes; the crannog at Langbank yielded an unusual bone comb carved with a curvilinear Celtic pattern and that at Erskine produced a rotary quern stone.

The broch was a two storeyed wooden structure protected by a massive round drystone tower with an ingenious double or galleried wall. A stone stair ran up between the two walls and through each gallery in turn. One broch – Leckie near Gargunnock in the Forth valley – was excavated during the 1970s. This broch was built during the first Roman occupation in the mid-Eighties AD. It is so close to the Imperial frontier that it was probably put up by an ally of Rome.

Later Leckie was violently destroyed and the broch was demolished; so abrupt was the destruction that many of the possessions of the last owners remained inside. Exhibited in the Hunterian Museum, they give us an unique glimpse of a wealthy Iron Age family. They were both farmers and warriors; among many iron artefacts Leckie produced swords and spears but also a pair of wool shears and a spade.

Euan W MacKie

1. Marwick, The River Clyde and the Harbour of Glasgow, 1898. **2.** ibid. **3.** Extracts from the Records of the Burgh of Glasgow, 1573–1642. **4.** George MacGregor, The History of Glasgow, 1881.

THE GEOGRAPHY OF GLASGOW (PHYSICAL LANDSCAPE)

The Clyde Valley is a facet of the western portion of the great Midland Valley of Scotland, floored with Old Red Sandstone measures which outcrop in the Menteith Hills. Overlying these measures are sedimentary rocks of the Carboniferous Series, once rich in coal and Blackband ironstone, relics of the swampy environment. Igneous rocks of the Carboniferous Series complete the picture, with their exposed volcanic vents and resistant lava flows providing the high ground of the Campsie, Kilpatrick and Renfrew Hills.

The hard rock measures and their surface drainage were altered and overlain by glacial action. In the Devensian glaciation which ended over 10,000 years ago, ice from the Highlands reached Glasgow by way of the Gareloch, Loch Lomond and Strathblane Gap. Ice blocked the flow of the Clyde to the sea, forming an extensive lake, about 33 yards deep, in the Clyde Basin. When the ice advanced eastward, it moulded the sands, silts and gravels of portions of the lake bottom into a swarm of drumlins.

Melting of the ice around 13,000 years ago raised sea levels and flooded the old lake bed, laying down extensive deposits of silts and clays. As the land was freed from the weight of the great ice mass, it rose elastically, gradually exposing a series of gently-sloping terraces, visible today from the smaller terraces such as Ramshorn and Meadowflats, on which George Square and much of the Central Business District lie, to the broad agricultural acres of the Renfrewshire embayment. The Clyde flowed westward, through a gap in the lava plateaus, to its broad estuary.

Andrew Gibb

eight inches deep, so the Council gave him a £1,500 bonus and a silver cup, as well as £100 for his son.

Thomas Telford moved the jetties and built a series of parallel dykes. The river was still inadequate in 1812 when Henry Bell brought steamship sailing to the Clyde. The *Comet* drew only four feet of water, but had to leave both Glasgow and Greenock at high tide to avoid being grounded.

Bell's enterprise had its origins in trials conducted two dozen years before. It was in 1788 that William Symington travelled across Dalswinton Loch, Dumfriesshire, at five miles an hour. The event was watched by Robert Burns, who might have had a sail in the boat, which was fitted with an atmospheric engine and two hulls. A year later, he built a bigger version which travelled the Forth and Clyde Canal at seven miles an hour, but it wasn't till 1801 that Symington managed to construct the first paddle steamship for practical use.

The *Charlotte Dundas* towed barges along the Forth and Clyde Canal till the complaints about damage being done by her wash saw her beached and abandoned. Henry Bell heard about the boat and got permission to examine her. In 1811, he persuaded John Wood and Company of Port Glasgow to build the *Comet*, which was the first steamship to sail in open waters.

The early trials were off the Helensburgh coast and Bell was soon advertising steam sailings between Glasgow, Greenock and Helensburgh "for passengers only", who travelled amongst velvet sofas, curtains, gilt mirrors and a library.[1] She made the journey three times a week and took four hours to travel from Glasgow to Greenock.

Ten years after the *Comet* was launched, nearly 50 steamboats had been built on the Clyde. In their heyday, they outclassed the world. The shipbuilding industry had arrived and through all its transitions, Glasgow led the way. By the outbreak of the First World War, Clyde yards were building almost half the world's shipping tonnage.

The early steam engines were of little economic value since they used too much fuel and most of the steam was wasted. While taking a Sunday stroll through Glasgow Green in 1765, James Watt first thought of condensing the steam in a separate vessel so the cylinder could remain hot.[2] This made the engine run continuously, was much safer and used less fuel.

The first steam engines built from Watt's ideas pumped water from the Cornish mines, but were quickly adapted for wider use. Cotton mills then employed water power, but soon changed to

A partial section of the *Charlotte Dundas*.

Doon the Watter for Easter, April 4, 1933.

A pen and wash drawing of Clyde Street, looking west towards the Broomielaw, attributed to Robert Carrick around 1850.

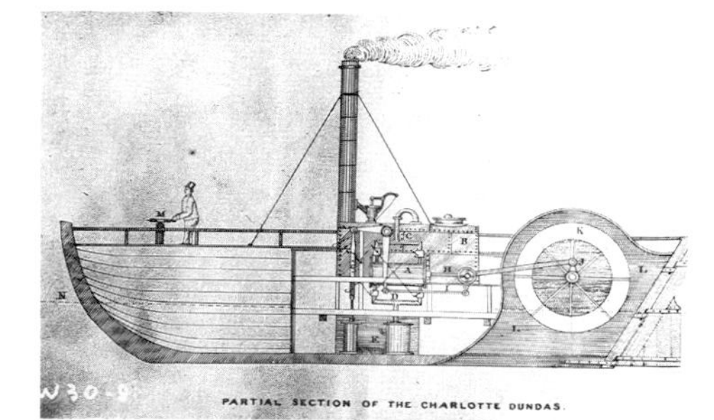

1. **Glasgow Chronicle**, August 12, 1814. 2. A stone marks the spot where the idea struck him.

THE CLYDE STEAMERS

The effects of early steam transport on the Firth of Clyde area were similar socially and economically to the wide availability of cheap air travel some 150 years later. By the 1840s and Fifties the main Clyde resorts had their own steamship piers (Brodick had to wait until 1872); they were followed by a rush of holiday villas as the well-to-do established summer quarters well away from the fire and pestilence. Increasing speed and elegance of the steamers also made possible the day-trip or excursion from the Broomielaw or Greenock, bringing to its full glory the century that was the Clyde's golden summer.

Its origins lay in the 44–foot wooden-hulled *Comet* with her incongruous 25–foot smokepipe and four makeshift paddlewheels – the world's very first commercial passenger steamboat. The sole sea-going survivor, *SS Waverley*, was built by A & J Inglis in 1947.

Once the railway companies were permitted to operate their own fleets in the 1890s there was intense competition on the Arran route. For Bute and beyond the North British Railway developed Craigendoran as its base on the north shore.

The last war, when Clyde steamers were used for mine-sweeping and other duties, reduced the fleets to a pitiful level and railway nationalisation and the growth in car ownership ensured that they never recovered.

Waverley is the only remnant of the glorious years of Clyde paddle-steaming. There is also the *Rob Roy* on Loch Katrine, but the water she plies is drinkable. For the experience of steam power over salt water, grown men and children keep going back to the *Waverley*.

Simon Berry

steam. From Henry Bell's *Comet* to the coming of the railways, steam driven paddle boats were the most popular form of travel. The early ships were made of wood, but Glasgow had a plentiful supply of iron ore nearby, so her inventors experimented with iron ships.

The first iron boat in Scotland, the *Vulcan*, was built on the banks of the Monkland Canal, in 1818. The construction of this vessel was so revolutionary, that the same principles are largely still in use today. The *Margery* was the first steamboat to sail the Thames and first to cross the English Channel. The first vessel to steam across the Atlantic was built in Leith, but her engines came from Glasgow.[1]

The shipyards were originally sited up river, but continuous dredging kept the waters clear and by 1839, Govan's first shipyard was opened.

This site was taken over a year later by the man who was to become known as the father of Clyde Shipbuilding, Robert Napier. By the end of the 19th century, 21 shipbuilding companies had been based in Govan. Alexander Stephen arrived from Aberdeen, Randolph and Elder left Napier to set up on their own, bought a riverside estate and laid it out as a shipyard which eventually acquired the name of the site, Fairfield.

The Cunard Company, the Government and P & O gave them orders, but Glasgow soon had lines of her own such as the City Line, the Clan Line and the Donaldson Line.

There was a brief boom following the First World War when owners were anxious to replace what they had lost, but by then foreign customers had yards of their own and British owners found it cheaper to buy from them. Clydeside never got over the Depression. The rusty hull of Order Number 534 hung unfinished over Clydebank for more than two years. When she was launched as the *Queen Mary*, the end was nigh, the cost in human terms incalculable.

Steam-powered water travel opened up the river to Glaswegians who would never have seen much further than their own street. This created a market for men like William Harriston. His *The Steam Boat Traveller's Remembrancer* squeezes out a rhyme or two, while offering some colourful but questionable information.[2]

The metrical journey down river takes us past the Erskine Ferry.

> Near by there's an old Roman Bridge,
> That stands from destruction quite free,
> What man who had leisure, could grudge
> An hour, this old Fabric to see

The Glasgow based Anchor Line sailed between Glasgow and New York every week.

The Clyde built PS Industry, whose engines survived the boat's submersion at Bowling.

The Queen Mary on the Clyde.

1. The **P.S. Sirius** took 18 days ten hours to sail from Cork to New York.
2. Glasgow, 1824, "Printed by W. Lang, 59, Nelson Street, for the Author, and Sold at his House, 22, Saracen's Lane."

Roman men's, women's and children's shoes found at the Bar Hill Fort near Twechar.

The Romans introduced Scotland to money and built a wall across the waist of the country. The Drygate is thought to be Glasgow's oldest street and the Romans marched along it in the 1st century AD. For many, those footsteps constitute Clydeside's first intimations of urban life.

The Antonine Wall marks the north-western frontier of the Roman Empire. It may not be the best preserved Roman ruin, but it must surely be one of the most important because this is as far as they came. It was 37 miles long and ran from Bo'ness on the river Forth to Old Kilpatrick on the Clyde, a route later followed by the Forth and Clyde Canal and the Glasgow-Edinburgh railway line.

Work began around AD 142 on the orders of the Emperor Antoninus Pius, who was Hadrian's adopted son. For more than 1800 years it has survived as the most striking evidence of the Roman occupation in Scotland, as well as an impressive piece of engineering. It was 14 feet wide and made of stone with a ten feet high turf superstructure and a timber frame on top. There was a twelve feet wide defensive ditch on the northern side, a cobbled road to the south and forts every couple of miles or so. There are 16 known forts along the frontier.

The wall must have puzzled and frightened the wooden hut dwellers who lived to the north and perhaps the forts increased their sense of helplessness. These were rectangular with red tiled roofs and glass windows, bath houses and a primitive flushing toilet. This was Roman society adapted to suit the climate.

More foundation remains than structure, since our landscape was entirely changed by the Industrial Revolution. One part of the wall now straddles a golf course and others have been ploughed. Bits tangled with the Forth and Clyde Canal or the Glasgow–Edinburgh railway line. Another section is a rubbish dump and the wall peters out in some folks' gardens. Roads and motorways move across it.

Often there is only a rickle of stones or the ditch that followed the north of the wall, though most of its line can be seen from the air. Distance slabs were put to use. Some were built into houses as decoration and others were simply abandoned, though most were collected and preserved by William Dunlop when he was Principal of Glasgow University between 1694 and 1700.[1]

The Bridgeness Slab, which marked the eastern end of the Antonine Wall, was unearthed in three pieces by "a man wishing to enlarge his kailyard".[2]

GLASGOW'S SHIPBUILDERS

The main focus for the early shipbuilders who established Glasgow's reputation was at Lancefield and Govan. David Napier (1821) and Robert Napier, his cousin (1836) set up businesses which became the training grounds for many of the most famous of Glasgow's shipbuilders. David Tod and John MacGregor managed David Napier's Lancefield works, and then set up on their own as engineers in 1834, and as shipbuilders in 1836. James Thomson and his brother, George, also worked at Lancefield and then established J & G Thomson at Mavisbank in 1847, moving later to their new yard at Clydebank in 1870. David Elder and his son, John, and Charles Randolph, who founded Randolph & Elder at Govan (later Fairfield) also worked with the Napiers, as did many others.

The Lancefield-Kelvinhaugh, Govan and Meadowside complex, attracted other famous builders like Alexander Stephen & Sons, Kelvinhaugh (1851–70), Linthouse (1870–1968) and A & J Inglis at Anderston (1847–62), and Pointhouse (1862–1962). Further downstream at Whiteinch and Scotstoun was another concentration of famous builders like Barclay Curle & Co, beginning with John Barclay in 1818 at Stobcross, Charles Connel (1861–1965), who built only cargo boats, and a distinguished latecomer from London, Sir Alfred Yarrow, in 1906.

The Glasgow builders virtually all began as partnerships and family firms, and families remained in control even when they took limited liability form. The founders all trained in engineering shops or shipyards as apprentices before setting up on their own; their sons and other family members were also put to apprenticeships. To a large extent the great Clyde shipbuilders were men of practical experience rather than of extensive theoretical training.

Anthony Slaven

1. All but the Bridgeness and Summerston distance slabs are in the Hunterian Museum, Glasgow University. **2.** In April, 1868, and now in the Royal Museum of Scotland.

GLASGOW'S ROMANS

The Romans first arrived in the Clyde valley in the later Seventies of the first century AD, having invaded southern Scotland under the leadership of Julius Agricola, governor of Rome's British province. Scotland was occupied and garrisoned up to the edge of the Highlands; but the legions soon withdrew.

A second attempt to include Scotland in the Roman Empire was made in the reign of Antoninus Pius from 142 AD onwards. The army returned and this time built the Antonine Wall. Numerous finds of sculpture, ironwork, glassware, leatherwork and pottery give us a picture of life on Rome's northern boundary. The Wall served as the frontier of the Roman province of Britannia until it was abandoned in favour of Hadrian's Wall around 165 AD, by which time the Roman episode in Scotland's past was effectively over.

No Roman fort has ever been identified within Glasgow itself, contrary to popular tradition, though a good site would be at Yorkhill, where Roman finds were made long ago at the junction between the Clyde and the Kelvin, on high ground now occupied by the Queen Mother's Hospital. Certainly a Roman road ran along the river's north bank from Bothwell to Old Kilpatrick, and a fine pottery bowl was found on Glasgow Green in 1876. It is now in the People's Palace Museum.

Lawrence Keppie

A distance slab from the Antonine Wall.

SAINT MUNGO, *by* Craig Forrester.

Chapter Two

THE PREACHING OF THE WORD

According to Mungo's biographer Jocelyn, Abbot of Furness Abbey in Lancashire, the saint's last day on Earth was January 13, 603. According to the Book of Saints, written by the Benedictines, he died while taking a bath. He bequeathed a set of images to his city.

The fish was first. It appeared erect on Bishop William Wyschard's seal in 1270 and was joined by the bird in 1271 on the emblem of his nephew, Bishop Robert Wishart. A later seal of Wishart's has the tree, or the branch of a tree, with the fish and the bird. The bell first appears in 1321 on the privy seal of the Chapter of Glasgow, whose later seal, used from 1488 to 1540, was also the first to show all the symbols together. They appeared in something like their present arrangement in 1647 on a seal "maid by directioune of the toune".[1]

Glasgow had no official armorial bearings up to the middle of the 19th century, when three official seals were used and the magistrates asked Mr. Andrew Macgeorge, a writer and authority on the subject, to design an official crest for the City. His design was approved on a petition dated October 25, 1866. His motto, Let Glasgow Flourish, was a reduction from Let Glasgow Flourish by the Preaching of the Word, which itself was a curtailment of the text on the Tron Church Bell, cast in 1631: *Lord let Glasgow flourish through the preaching of Thy word and praising Thy name.*[2]

Nowadays, we are perhaps more attached to the jingle which commemorates the miracles of St Mungo:

> Here's the tree that never grew,
> Here's the bird that never flew,
> Here's the bell that never rang,
> Here's the fish that never swam.

The history of Scotland has either been reduced to hagiography or a recitation of failure and the Mungo myth places Glasgow's

Glasgow's coat of arms from the Clayslap Mills, Partick.

1. Andrew MacGeorge, **Old Glasgow**, 1880. 2. J Gordon (ed.), **Glasghu Facies**, 1872.

GLASGOW'S EARLY CHRISTIAN SETTLEMENTS

Although it is accepted that Christianity was present in Strathclyde during the 5th century, and that by the end of the 6th century a monastery had been founded by Kentigern (d. AD 612) on a site said to have been a cemetery consecrated by St Ninian and given to Kentigern by Rhydderch ap Tudwal, King of Strathclyde, whose first bishop Kentigern became, there is no contemporary documentary evidence to confirm this acceptance. After the death of Kentigern, with the exception of the name of a possible bishop in the 8th century, there is a gap in the episcopal succession until a recorded reference to three bishops during the 11th century.

The evidence concerning Kentigern comes from two much later "lives of St Kentigern", one written in the 12th and the other in the early 13th centuries. However, allowing for the hagiography in both, it has been shown that these two "lives" had relied on an earlier "life", now lost. This earlier "life" might have helped to establish or continue an already existing cult of St Kentigern. It is unfortunate also that at the present time there is no archaeological evidence from the ecclesiastical site for early settlement.

In addition to legend and place names (Kilpatrick, Kilmacolm and Kilbride preface a saint's name with the Gaelic *cill*, or church), there is , more tellingly, material evidence of early Christian settlement in the Glasgow area. Sculptured memorial stones from the 7th to early 12th centuries are to be found in Inchinnan, Kilmahew and, most notably, Govan.

Alistair R Gordon

origins in fairyland. Current myths say something about where we come from, as well as a little about where we are going. The Red Clydeside myth says we always were a workers' city; the myth of freemasonry links our past to the Bible and to Egypt; religious myths lock us into constant conflict; the myth that we were poor, but happy, sentimentalises and trivialises hardship; the hard man myth glorifies violence; and so on. The Glasgow's Miles Better campaign is cunning nonsense, based on the same wilful ignorance as the myth that the Art Galleries were constructed back to front, that Lewis's Argyle Street store is built on a lake, that the village of Grahamston survives intact beneath Central Station or that Glasgow University Library is sliding downhill because architects forgot to allow for the weight of the books. What we need is a demythology.

Our contemporary myths are open to a variety of interpretations which should encourage us to take another look at tradition. It might be seen as a series of images which appear and disappear, full of creative possibilities. The very images themselves must alter in the light of fresh evidence.

The 17th century embraced scientific perception. This was simply a new way of looking, a change in perspective, a new set of superstitions and beliefs to supersede the old. The new myths were blessed with scientific efficacy and established reliable procedures.

Now there was the Doctor as God, the Scientist as Hero, or the Myth of the Magic Bullet, which is still with us as we search for a drug to cure AIDS and the worst of our ills. This leads to the professionalisation of the health services and the rise of the hospital.

Dr James Graham came to Glasgow in 1783. The advertisement declared him "President of the Council of Health, sole Proprietor and principal Director of the Temple of Health in Pall Mall, London".[1] Gone were the days of Godbold's Vegetable Balsam, the Elixir of Life, Cornwell's Oriental Vegetable Cordial, Oldbridge's Balm of Columbia, Parr's Life Pills, Rowland's Kalydor and Morrison's Pills from the British College of Health. Graham was a superior sort of quack. He claimed his treatments prevented patients from dying and brought people into life who, but for his wonderful skills and the potency of his potions, would never have breathed at all.

The earth bath cured all diseases. His clients were stripped naked, placed on a glass stool, electrified, rubbed down with silken towels, buried up to the mouth in an earth pit for half an hour, dug out, cleaned, rubbed down and sent away rejoicing.

HANS CHRISTIAN ANDERSEN AND ANNA MARY LIVINGSTONE

"I do like your fairy tales so much that I would like to go and see you but I cannot do that so I thought I would write to you when Papa comes home from Africa I will ask him to take me to see you". So, in 1869 began a remarkable correspondence, continued over five years, between young Anna Mary Livingstone, daughter of the explorer, and Hans Christian Andersen. On the envelope she had written merely "Hans Andersen, Denmark".

His short reply was in Danish but luckily he also enclosed a translation. Her next letter went unanswered, but after describing a visit to the pantomime in Glasgow's Theatre Royal and enclosing "a little flower from Scotland just to let you know that I love you so much" he responded.

In their subsequent letters they exchanged many small gifts. The description of her Hebridean holidays were accompanied by seaweed and lucky greenstones. He in turn sent her pictures and fairytales.

Once, after a relation gave her a present of a sovereign she put half towards a casket for Stanley who had just returned from Africa. She then wrote to Andersen "I have heard that there have been dreadful floods in Denmark, I willingly give the other ten shillings for the relief of the people".

Despite their wishes the two never met. In her last letter Anna Mary describes how "instead of going the places I fully intended with Papa, I was obliged to take the sad journey to see him buried in Westminster Abbey".

Martin Bellamy

1. Roy Porter, "Sex and the Singular Man: the Seminal Ideas of James Graham". **Studies on Voltaire and the Eighteenth Century**, 1984.

"A Cure for Corns". A contemporary medical opinion from *The Northern Looking Glass.*

An 18th century quack on stage with his assistants.

William Cullen (1710-90), one of the great teachers of his age.

The *pièce de résistance* was the Temple of Health and Electric Bed, which Senex, the journalist and antiquarian Robert Reid, describes in some detail, coyly adding: "It is inconceivable how much curiosity was excited at this period in Glasgow, to find the names of any lodgers who had availed themselves of the benefits to be derived from the application of Doctor Graham's electric system; but notwithstanding of the most prying vigilance on the part of hundreds of our population, the Doctor managed his affairs so dexterously, that the public could never, with any degree of certainty, fix upon the names of any personages who had taken up their lodgings in the Temple of Health and Electric Bed".[1]

Robert Dreghorn, alias Bob Dragon, the ugliest man in Glasgow, tried harder than most. He walked the street outside Graham's house watching to see who came and went, but even he was disappointed.

Graham went to Edinburgh, where he appeared "to have caused a greater stir amongst the inhabitants of Auld Reekie than he did amongst us sober west-country folks".[2] He was jailed in the Tolbooth on August 6, 1783, because he "had been publishing lascivious and indecent advertisements and delivering wanton and improper lectures in the City".[3] He was also jailed in Dublin, Chester, Liverpool, Manchester and Norwich and banned from lecturing in Newcastle and Gateshead for pretty much the same thing.

James Graham had been born in Edinburgh in 1745. He was the son of a saddler who studied medicine at Edinburgh University, with tutors such as Joseph Black and William Cullen, though it appears he never graduated. He married in 1770, settled in Pontefract, emigrated to America where, subsidised by Shelley's grandfather, he practised physic, met Benjamin Franklin and was converted to the medical applications of electricity.

His half-voodoo, half-science mixture of showbiz and fakery, could only have existed in the 18th century. People were confounded by electricity. It was the invincible force that had been sought throughout the ages – a power to transform lives.

In the Introduction to her novel *Frankenstein*, Mary Shelley recalls her husband and Byron discussing "the principle of life" and "the experiments of Doctor Erasmus Darwin".[4] Darwin had placed a piece of vermicelli in a glass case and moved the pasta by charging an electrical current through the case. Mary Shelley speculated that, "Perhaps a corpse would be reanimated; galvanism had given token of such things: perhaps the component parts of a creature might be manufactured, brought together, and endued with vital warmth".[5]

JOSEPH BLACK (1728–99)

A founder of modern chemistry, Joseph Black was born in France. His father was an expatriate Belfast wine merchant, and his mother the daughter of an Aberdonian, also in the Bordeaux wine trade. Training as a Doctor in Glasgow, Black was inspired by the chemistry lectures of William Cullen.

In 1756 Black was appointed to Cullen's post at Glasgow. He spent ten years there, before returning to Edinburgh to be Professor of Chemistry. The major scientific achievement of this period were his studies of the nature of heat. He demonstrated that a precise quantity of heat was required to change a substance from its solid to its liquid state – one crucial experiment had to wait until December 1761 for ice to be available. Black coined the term "latent" heat, for this, and with collaborators and pupils measured experimentally the different heat capacities of different substances – "specific" heat.

Black insisted that careful controlled experiment was the key to advancing chemical knowledge, and was consulted on chemical problems in industries as diverse as bleaching, brewing, tar distillation and iron manufacture.

The convivial but otherworldly Black was once charged by members of a dining club to find a suitable meeting place. He booked a room in a vintner's shop close to the University, discovering months later that he had been inviting his friends to meet weekly in an Edinburgh bordello. A parsimonious bachelor, he is reputed to have weighed the guineas with which his students paid their class fees. He amassed a tidy fortune, being worth more than £20,000 when he died in December 1799.

D.J. Bryden

1. ibid. **2.** ibid. **3.** ibid. **4.** From the Standard Novels edition; Introduction written 1831. **5.** ibid.

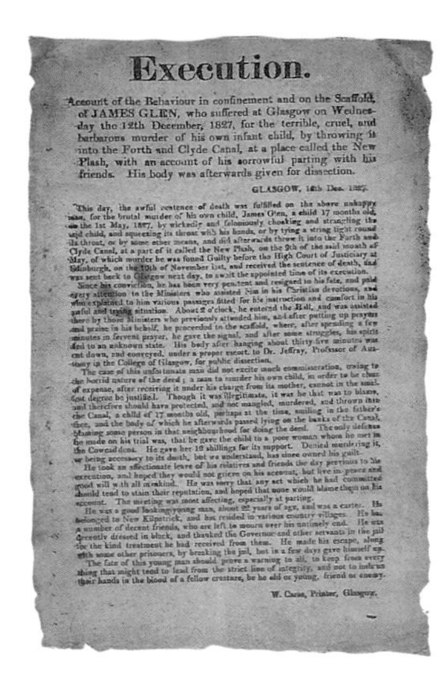

Execution.

Account of the Behaviour in confinement and on the Scaffold, of JAMES GLEN, who suffered at Glasgow on Wednesday the 12th December, 1827, for the terrible, cruel, and barbarous murder of his own infant child, by throwing it into the Forth and Clyde Canal, at a place called the New Plash, with an account of his sorrowful parting with his friends. His body was afterwards given for dissection.

GLASGOW, 12th Dec. 1827.

This day, the awful sentence of death was fulfilled on the above unhappy man, for the brutal murder of his own child, James Glen, a child 17 months old, on the 1st May, 1827, by wickedly and feloniously choking and strangling the said child, and squeezing its throat with his hands, or by tying a string tight round its throat, or by some other means, and did afterwards throw it into the Forth and Clyde Canal, at a part of it called the New Plash, on the 9th of the said month of May, of which murder he was found Guilty before the High Court of Justiciary at Edinburgh, on the 19th of November last, and received the sentence of death, and was sent back to Glasgow next day, to await the appointed time of its execution.

Since his conviction, he has been very penitent and resigned to his fate, and paid every attention to the Ministers who assisted him in his Christian devotions, and who explained to him various passages fitted for his instruction and comfort in his awful and trying situation. About 2 o'clock, he entered the Hall, and was assisted there by those Ministers who previously attended him, and after putting up prayers and praise in his behalf, he proceeded to the scaffold, where, after spending a few minutes in fervent prayer, he gave the signal, and after some struggles, his spirit fled to an unknown state. His body after hanging about thirty-five minutes was cut down, and conveyed, under a proper escort, to Dr. Jeffray, Professor of Anatomy in the College of Glasgow, for public dissection.

The case of this unfortunate man did not excite much commiseration, owing to the horrid nature of the deed; a man to murder his own child, in order to be clear of expense, after receiving it under his charge from its mother, cannot in the smallest degree be justified. Though it was illegitimate, it was he that was to blame, and therefore should have protected, and not mangled, murdered, and thrown into the Canal, a child of 17 months old, perhaps at the time, smiling in the father's face, and the body of which he afterwards passed lying on the banks of the Canal, blaming some person in that neighbourhood for doing the deed. The only defence he made on his trial was, that he gave the child to a poor woman whom he met in the Cowcaddens. He gave her 12 shillings for its support. Denied murdering it, or being accessary to its death, but we understand, has since owned his guilt.

He took an affectionate leave of his relatives and friends the day previous to his execution, and hoped they would not grieve on his account, but live in peace and good will with all mankind. He was sorry that any act which he had committed should tend to stain their reputation, and hoped that none would blame them on his account. The meeting was most affecting, especially at parting.

He was a good looking young man, about 22 years of age, and was a carter. He belonged to New Kilpatrick, and has resided in various country villages. He has a number of decent friends, who are left to mourn over his untimely end. He was decently dressed in black, and thanked the Governor and other servants in the jail for the kind treatment he had received from them. He made his escape, along with some other prisoners, by breaking the jail, but in a few days gave himself up.

The fate of this young man should prove a warning to all, to keep from every thing that might tend to lead from the strict line of integrity, and not to imbrue their hands in the blood of a fellow creature, be he old or young, friend or enemy.

W. Carse, Printer, Glasgow.

Contemporary mass media account of a popular event.

Matthew Clydesdale appeared before Glasgow Circuit Court on October 3, 1818. Clydesdale was 35 years old and charged with murdering Alexander Love, an 80 year old retired miner, with his own pick axe at Laigh Drumgelloch in New Monkland, Lanarkshire.

The jury took minutes to reach their verdict. Lord Gillies sentenced Clydesdale to death, stating that his body should be given to James Jeffrey, Professor of Anatomy at Glasgow University, for dissection.

A large crowd gathered to watch Clydesdale breathe what they thought would be his last. And at five past three in the afternoon of November 4, 1818, the platform fell. His body was left hanging for an hour, as a warning to others and to make sure he was dead.

There were cheers when the corpse arrived at the College, where Jeffrey and Andrew Ure, Professor of Natural Philosophy at the Andersonian Institute, had their apparatus set up for the experiment.

Peter Mackenzie's account of what happened next was first published almost 50 years after the event but was accepted and repeated as fact. Clydesdale was seated in an armchair. Parts of his body were attached to a galvanic battery and an air tube was stuck up his nose. When the battery was connected and the bellows were working, Mackenzie tells us Clydesdale's chest "immediately heaved! – he drew breath!".[1]

His tongue moved and his eyes opened widely. Then, "he stared, apparently in astonishment, around him; while his head, arms and legs (at the same time, also) actually moved; and we declare he made a feeble attempt as if to rise from the chair".

Clydesdale does rise. And Mackenzie spares us none of the details. "The thrill ran round the excited and crowded room, that his neck had not been dislocated on the gibbet, and that he had now actually come to life again through the extraordinary operation of that galvanic battery! At this sudden, startling, and most unexpected sight, some of the students screamed out with horror; not a few of them fainted on the spot; others of a sterner class clapped their hands as if in exultation at the triumph of the galvanic battery! Certain it is that the professor himself and his assistants stood amazed with some of their own experiments; and ere the lapse of a minute or two Dr Jeffrey pulled out his unerring *lancet* and plunged it into the jugular vein of the culprit, who instantly fell down upon the floor like a slaughtered ox on the blow of the butcher!".[2]

The December 1987 issue of the *Strathclyde Guardian and Newsbeat* published an article by Alex Young, a sergeant at

An 18th century magnetometer made by John Crichton of Glasgow.

SERIAL MURDERS

More murders are committed in Glasgow than any other Scottish city and each has its circle of impact, its anger and grief. The serial murderer stands apart, finding perverse pleasure in the act, and on mercifully rare occasions a single killer will hold a whole city in fear.

Dr Edward William Pritchard simply enjoyed murder. An untiring self publicist, he compensated for his lack of conventional qualifications with smooth talking and a winning bedside manner. He probably burned his maid to death in 1863, but he was finally convicted of gradually poisoning his wife and her mother in 1865. Nearly 100,000 attended Glasgow's last public hanging to see Pritchard swing.

Peter Manuel was a small time burglar and rapist, but he wanted to make history. Manuel had to murder at least seven times before the world gave him the attention he felt he deserved. His threat had kept Glasgow and Lanarkshire besieged for nearly two years.

Manuel was unique in conducting his own defence, including the interrogation of a man whose family he had murdered. But, unable to resist showing police how clever he had been, Manuel had already made a full confession. In May 1958, he was sentenced to hang.

Ten years later, the nightmare of serial murder returned. His portrait was everywhere and more than 5,000 suspects were interviewed, but the man they called Bible John was never caught.

All three victims were attractive young women, found beaten and strangled after nights spent dancing in the Barrowland Ballroom. Only one man knows why or if the killings stopped. Glasgow could only be grateful when 1970 brought in a year without Bible John.

Alison Kennedy

1. Peter Mackenzie, **Reminiscences of Glasgow and the West of Scotland**, Vol. II., 1866. **2.** ibid.

GLASGOW BROADSIDES

Until the advent of the popular press in the middle of the 19th century, broadsides (or broadsheets) – sheets of flimsy paper printed on one side and sold for a penny or a halfpenny – were the poor person's newspaper. Every town had its cheap printers (in Glasgow men like Thomas Duncan, William Carse and John Muir) who churned out these "factsheets" to be hawked in the streets.

All human life was there: topical events of home and abroad, legal and political statements, ballads, advertisements (for shops, auctions, plays, freak shows etc). Their purpose was to amuse and inform but as often as not the broadsides catered to the demand for scandal and sensation; and like the modern tabloid press couched their accounts in moralistic terms.

Their staple diet was murders and executions ("nothing beats a stunning good murder" as a London patter merchant said to Henry Mayhew), frequently printing a condemned prisoner's (often invented) last words, usually ones of repentance and admonition. Though gory and grisly, the broadsides were not without a certain gallows humour.

David Wylie, executed in 1823 for house-breaking: "the drop fell and the world closed over this unfortunate victim of dissipation and vice. Wylie was a native of Paisley, about 17 years of age. It is a singular circumstance that he was at one time employed in the rope-making business." And James Dick, about to be hanged in 1792 for murdering his wife, exhorted the spectators "to beware of bad women and drunkenness, and likewise wives not to give their husbands bad words when they came home perhaps the worse for liquor".

Hamish Whyte

Ayr Police Office, which tells a different story.[1] It looked at the evidence from contemporary accounts of the experiment, and came to a totally different conclusion.

Five weeks after the event Andrew Ure read his version of the experiment to the Glasgow Literary Society. Edited extracts were later published in the *Journal of Science and Arts*.[2] His account of the five experiments are similar to Mackenzie's, up to a point. In the third experiment the nerve above the left eyebrow was exposed and the second terminal was inserted in Clydesdale's heel. Expressions of rage, horror, despair, anguish and ghastly smiles passed over the murderer's face, which caused some spectators to leave and one gentleman to faint. There is no mention of a standing ovation. No unerring lancet and no butcher's blow either. A newspaper report follows Ure's story.[3]

Perhaps Mackenzie's description drew on decades of popular exaggeration. The city still lives by word of mouth, but the old motto meant the Word of God, and for that we have to look to The Book. Glasgow's oldest book is the *Liber Pontificalis*, the pontifical book of Glasgow Cathedral, which lists and describes the proper procedures to be used in ecclesiastical ceremonies. It is unlikely to have been generated here, but was probably designed around 1190 for the diocese of Canterbury and subsequently adapted for use in Glasgow.

Protestants saw the Word, the World and God as one and the same and emphasised a personal rather than doctrinal interpretation of the Bible, which further allowed them to view the world as an amalgam of signs and signatures which could be decoded and read in the light of Calvinistic theology. The printing revolution in Europe reinforced this approach, making The Word more accessible to a larger number of people and therefore turning a personal interpretation of God into a common assumption.

Glasgow's first printer was George Anderson. The magistrates gave him an annual salary and compensated his move from Edinburgh. In 1638, after James VI's episcopal reorganisation was overturned by a General Assembly held in Glasgow Cathedral, Anderson published Glasgow's first book: *The Protestation of the Generall Assemblie of the Church, and of the noblemen, barons, gentlemen, borrowes, ministers and commons; subscribers of the Covenant, lately renewed, made in the high Kirk, and at the Mercate Crosse of Glasgow; the 28, and 29, of November 1638.*[4]

Robert Sanders styled himself Printer to the city when Anderson's son went back to be Edinburgh's Printer to the city and the College. His edition of the New Testament was so inaccurate that the Privy

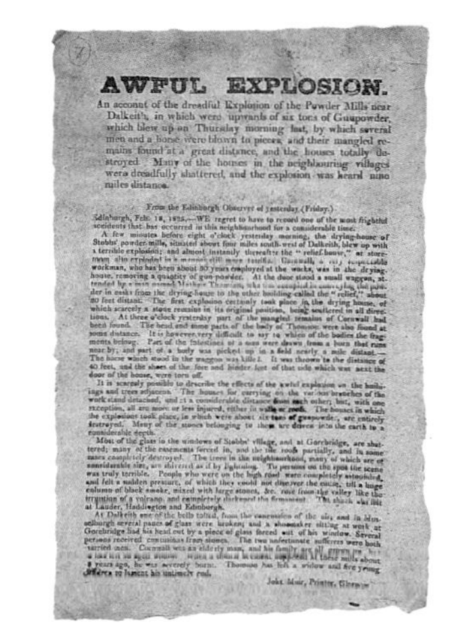

AWFUL EXPLOSION.

An account of the dreadful Explosion of the Powder Mills near Dalkeith, in which were upwards of six tons of Gunpowder, which blew up on Thursday morning last, by which several men and a horse were blown to pieces, and their mangled remains found at a great distance, and the houses totally destroyed. Many of the houses in the neighbouring villages were dreadfully shattered, and the explosion was heard nine miles distance.

From the Edinburgh Observer of yesterday (Friday.)

Edinburgh, Feb. 18, 1825.—WE regret to have to record one of the most frightful accidents that has occurred in this neighbourhood for a considerable time.

A few minutes before eight o'clock yesterday morning, the drying-house of Stobbs' powder-mills, situated about four miles south-west of Dalkeith, blew up with a terrible explosion; and almost instantly thereafter the "relief-house," or store-room also exploded [illegible] Cornwall, a very respectable workman, who has been about 30 years employed at the works, was in the drying-house, removing a quantity of gun-powder. At the door stood a small waggon, attended by a man named Mathew Thomson, who was occupied in conveying the powder in casks from the drying-house to the other building called the "relief," about 80 feet distant. The first explosion certainly took place in the drying house, of which scarcely a stone remains in its original position, being scattered in all directions. At three o'clock yesterday part of the mangled remains of Cornwall had been found. The head and some parts of the body of Thomson were also found at some distance. It is however very difficult to say to which of the bodies the fragments belong. Part of the intestines of a man were drawn from a burn that runs near by; and part of a body was picked up in a field nearly a mile distant.—The horse which stood in the waggon was killed. It was thrown to the distance of 40 feet, and the shoes of the fore and hinder feet of that side which was next the door of the house, were torn off.

It is scarcely possible to describe the effects of the awful explosion on the buildings and trees adjacent. The houses for carrying on the various branches of the work stand detached, and at a considerable distance from each other; but, with one exception, all are more or less injured, either in walls or roofs. The houses in which the explosions took place, in which were about six tons of gunpowder, are entirely destroyed. Many of the stones belonging to them are driven into the earth to a considerable depth.

Most of the glass in the windows of Stobbs' village, and at Gorebridge, are shattered; many of the casements forced in, and the tile roofs partially, and in some cases completely destroyed. The trees in the neighbourhood, many of which are of considerable size, are shivered as if by lightning. To persons on the spot the scene was truly terrible. People who were on the high road were completely astonished, and felt a sudden pressure, of which they could not discover the cause, till a huge column of black smoke, mixed with large stones, &c. rose from the valley like the irruption of a volcano, and completely darkened the firmament. The shock was felt at Lauder, Haddington and Edinburgh.

At Dalkeith one of the bells tolled, from the concussion of the air, and in Musselburgh several panes of glass were broken; and a shoemaker sitting at work at Gorebridge had his head cut by a piece of glass forced out of his window. Several persons received contusions from stones. The two unfortunate sufferers were both married men. Cornwall was an elderly man, and his family are all grown up, [illegible] 8 years ago, he was severely burnt. Thomson has left a widow and five young children to lament his untimely end.

John Muir, Printer, Glasgow

Broadsheet from early 19th century.

1978 [Barlinnie Prison] 3.14 a.m. I've been wakened for over an hour, am irritable and restless. The Radio Clyde disc jockey is speaking to people in their homes via telephone. I get the atmosphere of home parties from it. Pop music is blasting in my ears and I marvel at radio and how it must comfort lonely people. It's almost as though it's reassuring me I'm not alone. 3.55 a.m. One of these days I won't be 'still here'. It's amazing how difficult I find it to think of myself being anywhere else.

Jimmy Boyle, The Pain of Confinement, *Canongate, 1984.*

1. An in-house magazine for Strathclyde policemen. 2. Vol. 6, 1819. 3. **Glasgow Chronicle**, Thursday, November 5, 1818. 4. George MacGregor, **The History of Glasgow**, 1881.

JAMES "PARAFFIN" YOUNG
(1811–83)

The father of the Scottish oil industry, James Young was born in Glasgow in 1811. Trained in his father's joinery, Young's education also included the chemistry lectures of Thomas Graham at Anderson's University. In 1832 he became Graham's assistant. Through him, Young's skills as an analyst became known to the industrial and scientific community.

While working in England Young set up his own company to exploit a natural oil seepage in a Derbyshire mine, refining the raw oil to produce lubricating oil, lamp oil and naphtha. The spring ran dry in 1851, but Young had been experimenting with the production of oil from the distillation of coal and patented his process in 1850.

An old Glasgow friend sent Young a sample of cannel coal, from the Torbanehill Mine near Bathgate. This was found to yield good qualities of oil. Young and his partners moved to West Lothian to ensure supplies, and established a works to produce oils and other by-products. Before supplies of the coal ran down, he turned his attention to the nearby oil shales.

In 1865 James Young bought out his partners and established Young's Paraffin Light and Mineral Oil Company. Young's new company continued to dominate the rapidly expanding Scottish oil shale industry, though within a few years the founder had sold his shares – realising at least £400,000.

His patronage of Anderson's University included endowment of a chair in technical chemistry (1870) and erection of a chemical laboratory. Young also provided substantial financial support for an old Glasgow friend, the explorer and missionary David Livingstone.

D.J. Bryden.

Council ordered all copies to be returned, but three months later young Anderson issued a revised Testament with a new title page and became His Majesty's Sole Printer in Scotland.

Sanders was the only printer in the West of Scotland and Anderson felt the monopoly of bibles should be his, but again the Privy Council decreed that every printer in Scotland had an equal right to print the New Testament and Psalm Book in an English Roman typeface. Sanders did more. He took the city's motto to heart with an output that consistently focused on religious affairs. *A Dialogue Between a Popish Priest, and an English Protestant* was one of his titles and a small selection gives an idea of his firm's output:[1] *A Pick-tooth for the Pope, or The Packman's Paternoster; Witchcraft Proven, Arraign'd and Condemn'd in its Professions and Marks*; and *The Spiritual Merchant, or The Art of Merchandising Spiritualised.*[2]

Eighteenth century Glasgow printers raised the standard to an art, as a new spirit dominated The Book in Glasgow. The Enlightenment brought a secular desire for prosperity and empire.

Robert Urie published books by contemporary British authors which reflected the new emphasis on an economic state where consumerism dictated policy. This trend could even be seen in the production of the books themselves, for Glasgow's most famous printers of this time were the Foulis Brothers, who produced a series of high quality, mainly Classical texts. Urie's work rivalled the Foulis's in its artistry and his main difference lay in the choice of published titles. The Foulis Brothers were more closely allied to the University and matched the scholarship and presentation of any Continental printer.

The 19th century industrialisation brought collectors of books, as of everything else, including James "Paraffin" Young of Anderson's University, the man who invented the oil industry.[3] He left a large and valuable collection of early chemical texts which complemented Professor Ferguson's equally large collection and library of alchemical and magical texts. Glasgow antiquarians collected masses of printed material on all aspects of Glasgow life as well as the world's biggest collection of emblem books.

There was also an extension of the ways to describe a City in a book.[4] Nathaniel Jones had printed his *Directory or Useful Pocket Companion for the Year 1787, with an Introduction, and Notes of Old Glasgow Celebrities.* This early Glasgow Directory, which described itself as "an alphabetical list of the names and places of abode of the merchants, manufacturers, traders and shopkeepers in and about the City of Glasgow, compiled as accurately as the time limited would admit". Glasgow subsequently grew so aware

The Yenangyaung Oilfield, Burma, part of the Glasgow based Burmah Oil Company's extensive interests. The Burmah Oil Company was founded by David Sime Cargill in 1886.

An artist's impression of the *Beatrice A* Oil Platform in the North Sea.

1. Andrew MacGeorge in **Old Glasgow** dates Sanders' Almanacs from 1667. **2.** Then, as now, publishers knew their market. See **Robert Sanders the Elder Bibliography**, 1914. **3.** Now part of the Strathclyde University Archives. **4.** The first Glasgow directory was published by John Tait in 1783.

of itself and its manufacturing past, that a facsimile of this directory, reprinted in 1868, outsold the contemporary editions.

Philanthropic and workers' movements developed throughout the 19th century, drawing on the continuing Glasgow desire for self-education. From the church Sunday schools to the ILP's socialist variety, a strong campaign urging the value of The Book was waged throughout the city. Education for its own sake was valued and an increasing use of illustration in books made in Glasgow must surely have stemmed from this movement. Decoration was obviously a primary consideration, as people wanted their books to be as attractive as possible in as many ways as possible, but printers pioneered a theme that would dominate 19th century Glasgow; they attempted to combine art and education, as others would attempt to combine entertainment and education. The beautifully produced miniature hieroglyphic Bibles can be traced back to the Continental illustrated emblematic Bible, and one printer cites Comenius' schoolroom text *Orbis Pictus* as his original inspiration.

Such efforts by Glasgow printers may well be the source of the modern cross-fertilisation between textual and visual arts we still find in the City. Our contemporary writers often illustrate their own work and in many cases attempt to integrate illustration as part of the text.[1] Those who do not illustrate directly, have definite ideas as to how their work should be illustrated and many contemporary Glasgow painters use texts as a recurring image.

Of course the very fact that we have two volumes of a dictionary as defining guides to the way we speak, gives us another way to look on The Book. Glasgow has always stressed its oral culture and it is not difficult to see The Book as an elitist intrusion or a parasite upon the body of our freewheeling, improvisational dialect.

In the beginning The Word was a code, a cipher, a symbol, a means of entry into secret societies, freemasonry, the guilds and clubs of which Glasgow became and remains extremely fond.

GLASGOW PUBLISHERS

Among the many Glasgow publishers of the 19th century – names like John Tweed, James Lumsden and David Bryce – two stand out: Collins and Blackie.

William Collins (1789–1853) was an evangelistic cotton mill clerk with a pedagogic bent: from organizing classes for fellow workers, opening a private school and conducting Sunday schools, he went into publishing. The opportunity to teach and preach to not just a few souls in a classroom but the whole world through the medium of print was afforded by his friend the Rev Thomas Chalmers, who in 1819 co-financed the business and wrote its first best sellers (like *The Christian and Civic Economy of Large Towns*). Only recently has Collins lost its independence as a family firm (to the Murdoch Group), but it is still one of the largest general publishers, producing a diverse range of print, from diaries to dictionaries, classics to cookbooks. It still retains a presence in Scotland (reference books at Bishopbriggs) – and a strong religious list, with William Barclay perhaps the modern Thomas Chalmers, although best sellers are now Alistair MacLean and Agatha Christie.

One of the reasons for Collins's success was his control of production – he owned the presses that printed his books. Another successful Glasgow publisher to follow a similar path was John Blackie (1782–1874), a weaver turned bookseller and publisher who began business ten years before Collins and who also realised the value of printing as well as publishing – his books were produced at his well known Villafield printing works. Blackie also published religious works but it is probably for their children's books and Annuals, with their bright pictorial covers, that they are best known.

Hamish Whyte

John Blackie, founder of the firm.

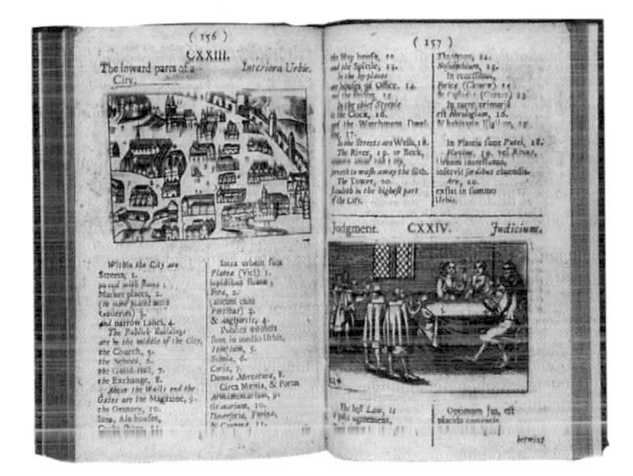

(156)
CXXIII.
The Inward parts of a City.
Interiora Urbis.
(157)
Judgment.
CXXIV.
Judicium.

From Comenius, *Orbis Pictus*.

A Blackie's Children's Annual from the Twenties.

1. Alasdair Gray and John Byrne are the best known examples.

SAMUEL HUNTER (1769–1839)

Samuel Hunter who ran the *Glasgow Herald* from 1803 to 1837 was one of those rare editors who are as well known as their paper itself; the kind of larger-than-life character that Glasgow takes to its heart. He was born in Stoneykirk, Wigtownshire, a son of the manse. After attending Glasgow University he served in Ireland as a surgeon and then as a captain in the North Lowland Fencibles. About the turn of the century he returned to Glasgow, where be became a great favourite of society, noted, as John Strang elegantly says, "not more for his wit and good humour, than for his innate principles of honour and gentlemanly deportment".

The deportment was needed: six feet tall and weighing 18 stone, he took up two inside seats in the coach when he travelled to Edinburgh. A Tory of the old school he was admired even by his political opponents. In the *Herald* he steered a middle course, pleasing both Whig and Tory readers, but speaking up on broad issues or when he thought Glasgow's interests were being threatened. His editorials, according to Peter Mackenzie of *The Reformers Gazette* were "pretty clear, sharp, and explicit".

His extra-curricular exploits were just as notable: whether as Town Councillor and Magistrate, commander of the Gentlemen sharpshooters (addressing them from a pulpit during the famous "Wet Wednesday" of the 1820 "Insurrection"), or as a stalwart of the Hodge Podge Club. He was perhaps the nearest Glasgow ever came to having a Dr Johnson figure.

Hamish Whyte

A Comic History of Glasgow. One of 19th century publisher James Lumsden's typically colourful covers.

Chapter Two

THE PREACHING OF THE WORD

A detail from a frieze in the Scottish National Portrait Gallery. Painted by William Brassey Hole in 1898, it shows an inspirational list of Scots.

Stained glass windows of St Mungo and the Cathedral. Salvaged from a Wellington Street building.

Chapter Three
CHURCH AND STATE

This medieval image of St Mungo, from a pillar in Cologne Cathedral, is the earliest surviving representation of him.

A fanciful tale, recounted with great seriousness, says Glasgow derived its name from an incident in which an old carter tried to get a load of glass up High Street in the snow. The horse slipped on the ice and, as the cart slid backwards, the man jumped clear, shouting, "Let the glass go, but save my horse". Why the city was then called Glasgow, rather than Save My Horse, was not explained.

The most commonly acceptable explanation comes from the Gaelic: *Glas*, meaning Green and *Ghu*, meaning Dear. So that Glasgow means the Dear Green Place.

Various attempts have been made to impose an ecclesiastical meaning, as well as origin, to Glasgow's name. Not surprisingly, the most popular theories are those which link it to the city's patron saint, Mungo.

The cult of St Mungo enhanced the Cathedral's importance and one account of how the city got its name adds to the Brythonic Celtic version of Mungo's other name, Cunotegernus the prefix *Glas*, meaning Church, forming *Glas-cu*, the Church of Kentigern, which in time has been hardened into Glasgow.

The church founded by St Kentigern was of the Celtic monastic type, where a community of priests and laymen lived under the rule of a bishop whose influence extended across the whole of Strathclyde.

The Celtic church expanded throughout the country in the 6th and 7th centuries, and following the Synod of Whitby in 663, both the Bishop of Durham and the Bishop of York claimed Strathclyde.

Then the area was attacked by Picts, Scots, Angles and Norsemen. Dumbarton was both burned and sacked. Edmund of Wessex overran Strathclyde, transferred it to Malcolm who lost it to Owain the Bald. When he died in 1018, Strathclyde was absorbed into the Kingdom of Scotland under Malcolm Canmore. And so began the long fight to maintain and consolidate the territory. Glasgow

"Glasgow Cathedral" by Martha Brown.

I see the chosen missionaries go
from Mungo's burning centre, to and fro.
North into Shetland and the Orkneys, North
even to Norway, living for Christ's sake
and planted there grow churches in their wake.
I see the old Saint peer with dimming eyes
from his green hill to question the blown skies
afraid for that small barque that cleaves the mists
taking away his young evangelists.

From Dorothy S Walton, "The Hidden Stream"

THE EARLY CHRISTIAN MONUMENTS AT GOVAN

The graveyard at Govan Old Parish Church is the one site within the City of Glasgow District which has yielded material evidence for Early Christian settlement. This evidence is a collection of over 40 sculptured memorial stones – a sarcophagus, two cross-shafts, two cross-slabs, five hogback tombstones and a large number of recumbent grave-markers. At the time of the demolition of the pre-Reformation church in 1762, two further sarcophagi were in existence. The stones date from the early 10th to the early 12th century.

Whatever the early history of the site may have been, it is clear from the evidence of the surviving material that, by the early 10th century, Govan was a major ecclesiastical centre. This collection of Early Christian stones is one of the finest in Scotland. The decorative work on them indicates that the Govan craftsmen were familiar with motifs and interlace patterns from other sources. The hunting scene in one panel of the sarcophagus and the two horsemen, one on a cross-shaft, the other on a cross-slab, clearly derive from Pictish work. Anglian, Irish and Norse influences are also to be seen in the Govan monuments.

Of particular note are the five hogback tombstones. The inspiration for, and origin of, this type of grave-marker must be Viking. The Govan examples, though late, show considerable similarity to those in Cumbria where there was an existing Scandinavian tradition in the 9th century. This suggests considerable maritime communication with Cumbria. Alternately, people of Scandinavian origin or descent living near at hand must have held positions of importance to justify such grave-markers.

Alistair R Gordon

was at the heart of a politically unstable region in a fledgling kingdom whose military, political and ethnic difficulties did little to ease a complex religious situation in which rival ecclesiastical factions claimed the area. It is therefore reasonable to assume that the recognition of Glasgow as an ecclesiastical centre and the cultivation of the Kentigern myth were for political rather than religious considerations, since they bestowed a unifying identity.

Glasgow's monastery was, like all the others, a centre of education and learning. It offered hospitality to pilgrims and travellers and was responsible for the pastoral care of its parishioners. Members of the community embarked upon missionary work throughout the kingdom, making difficult and hazardous journeys, teaching and preaching often to other religious communities in the holy places which were spreading across the country.

The responsibility for establishing a diocese in Glasgow belongs to King David I, whose reign marks the beginning of new order for church and state. He added seven burghs to the eleven that already existed. All were on crown lands, near a royal residence and therefore probably also close to a royal court of justice. Some were beside his abbeys.

Glasgow was obviously of special interest. One of the first things David did, as Earl of Cumbria, was to form a bishopric and from then until the Reformation, Glasgow was second only to St Andrews as a site of ecclesiastical importance in Scotland. The king ordered documents to be searched and old men questioned about what lands had belonged to the church and, as well as ordering their restoration, he gave some land of his own.

He installed his former tutor, John Achaius, later his chancellor and credited with introducing the thistle into Scotland from France,[1] as Bishop of Glasgow, consecrated by Pope Paschal II in person. It is reasonable to assume that this papal intervention was because of the long running dispute with York. Achaius' consecration was conditional upon his accepting canonical obedience from York. He was reminded more than once of this promise and Pope Innocent II had to write to the Archbishop of Canterbury asking him to excommunicate the Bishop of Glasgow. Achaius however, had David's support and spent a lot of time away from Glasgow, travelling as the king's chancellor across the kingdom. He was buried in Jedburgh Abbey.

One of John Achaius' first duties as Bishop of Glasgow, was to take stock of the lands and possessions belonging to the church in what became known as The Inquest of David, the earliest known document relating to Glasgow and one of the few pre-Reformation

SEE NATURE

The female sparrowhawk shot across my path trailing a tattered and battered blue tit in one claw. On the same day I watched sunlight filtering through the pinions and tail feathers of a hovering kestrel. Wonderful glimpses of wild life; but not in the wild. The sparrowhawk was dashing to a nest somewhere in the grounds of Glasgow University, and the kestrel wheeled and soared above the roar of traffic on the Great Western Road.

The wild life highways into the city are the rivers and canals, the woods, parks and gardens, the railway embankments, and, more recently, the motorway verges. These lead the wild creatures to the higher temperatures and easy pickings of our throwaway society. No sensible fox will hunt itself ragged, having discovered abandoned sandwiches, potato crisps, Chinese take-aways and fish suppers. Predators thrive on an abundance of rats, mice, sparrows and starlings, and a passing peregrine falcon has been known to ca' the heid aff an innocent street pigeon unused to such gangsterism. Kingfishers and herons have been seen on the Kelvin and Clyde, and the black and white Carts have an abundance of wildlife.

Keep your eyes raised as you walk in the city, and, like an artist friend of mine, you could see the facade of a building covered in superb waxwings. On the other hand, you could walk into a clump of giant hogweed and develop a nasty skin rash. See Glasgow, See Nature.

Jimmie Macgregor

1. Another Achaius, King of the Picts, is further supposed to have founded the Order of the Thistle in 810 AD.

"A View Taken From the North of the Cathedral Church of Glasgow" by R Paul Eleve.

[1] pieces to have survived. The amanuensis appears to have been unusually expert in drafting the narrative, for the document shows Achaius' political skills. In a formula that gave little scope for embellishment, he manages to pack in the founding of the see, the election of the first bishop, the advent of Earl David and the restoration of the bishopric, which is the dominant note of the narrative.

The Inquest of David has been credited with laying the foundations of the modern Glasgow, for from it grew the Cathedral and from the Cathedral grew the schools and the university, the town and the trade. Among the lands it named are Partick, Rutherglen and Govan.

Nothing of the original church remains, but Achaius built the first stone Cathedral on the site in honour of God and St Mary, with the high altar immediately over the supposed tomb of St Mungo. He spent 20 years erecting a Cathedral, which was dedicated on July 7, 1136, with the king in attendance.

Achaius' Cathedral was destroyed by fire as was its successor, but in 1174 Bishop Jocelyn began work on a new Cathedral. He had been Abbot of Melrose and started on the new Glasgow Cathedral as soon as he took office. He inaugurated the present stone building and commissioned from Jocelyn of Furness Abbey the official biography of St Mungo.

The York problem had dragged on, but in 1175, Pope Alexander [2] III called Glasgow "our special daughter of the Roman church, without any intermediary" and the following year the privilege was extended across the country. This was eventually confirmed in 1192, though Whithorn continued to accept the authority of York till the middle of the 14th century.

Jocelyn was a friend of the king and somewhere between 1175 and 1178, William the Lion signed a charter creating Glasgow a burgh. In 1190 he signed another, allowing them to hold a fair for eight days "from the octaves of the apostles Peter and Paul" beginning on July 7. This was later confirmed in a charter dated 1211, which also ordered that the king's peace be kept during the time of the Fair, with a fine of 180 cows for manslaughter.

Glasgow Fair was a great event; it attracted people from all over the country for business, entertainment and devotion. Ordinary trade was suspended, games and sports were held, firstly at the Wyndheid, where Rottenrow meets the High Street, then at the Water Port at the foot of Stockwell Street, later Glasgow Green, then Vinegar Hill and finally the Green once again.

One historian says craftsmen came from Selkirk, "Guid-burghers

The 16th century Rental Book for the Diocese of Glasgow, one of the town records removed by Archbishop Beaton.

GLASGOW – EARLY URBANISATION

"The road which leads from the High Church to the Market Cross." Thus is High Street described in an early charter. Glasgow was unusual in having these *two* focal points of development, and in the changing relationship and influence of Cathedral and Cross – not just as town centres linked by High Street, but in political and social terms as Church and Burgh – we have a large part of the story of early Glasgow.

The beginnings of the town, as such, were surely around the Cathedral. If no substantial settlement existed before, then the building and servicing of a great church would have ensured one. But this high, uneven ground was not a suitable site for a thriving town – it must have been difficult enough to accommodate a cathedral.

And so appears the second centre of Glasgow – the Cross. While the building plots of the Cathedral precincts are irregular and spontaneous, the town around the cross has all the signs of a planned development. This became the heart of Glasgow as a burgh of craftsmen and merchants while the Cathedral precincts remained the heart of ecclesiastical wealth and influence until the Reformation.

Even by the Reformation there was undeveloped wasteland between the "upper" and "lower" towns. Nevertheless, however distinct these "districts" appear to have been, no distinct names – such as "nether town" or "new town" – appear to have been used for them. Both Cathedral and Cross, whatever their differences, had claim to the heart of Glasgow.

Donald M Farmer

1. MacGregor quotes it in full, "preserved in the Ancient Chartulary of Glasgow". **2.** **Glasgow Episcopal Register** I, No. 38.

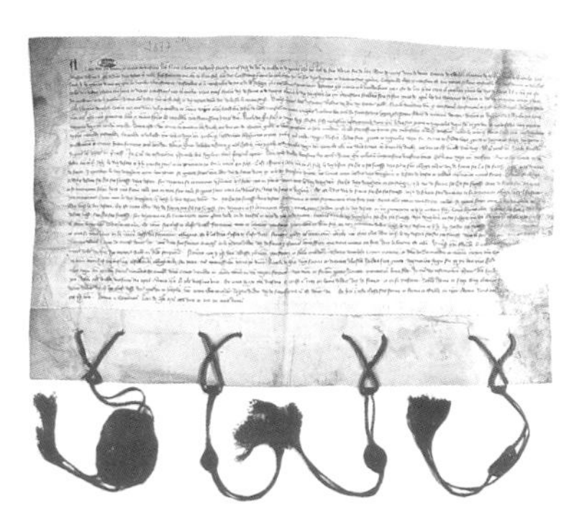

Treaty of 1326 between Robert the Bruce and King Charles "le Bel" of France. The four seals are of the ambassadors who negotiated the accord, including Twynham, Canon of Glasgow.

from Dumbarton, Solway fishers, shepherds from the Forest, Nithsdale yeomen, squires of Carrick, Clydesdale knights, the lordly abbots of Jedburgh and Crossraguel, Highland chiefs from the Lennox and Border moss troopers from the Liddell and the Esk".

Because of the Fair, Alexander II forbade Rutherglen's magistrates from taking tolls from anyone going to Glasgow. In 1243, he also granted Glasgow men full liberty to buy and sell in Argyll, Lennox and throughout the whole kingdom. Dumbarton had been created a burgh in 1221 and tried to ban Glasgow's merchants from entering the town, but Glasgow's trade was already expanding.

In the Middle Ages, a career in the church was a ready ladder to advance the able. The higher clergy formed a literate élite throughout Medieval Europe. Their services were valued by the state and the higher offices of the church were seen as a fitting reward for those who had served their monarch. A goodly proportion of Glasgow's bishops held secular positions.

Church and state were intertwined in Robert Wishart, who played an active role in the troubles that followed the death of King Alexander III, who fell from his horse in Kinghorn in 1286.

When Alexander reeled from the saddle, the throne of Scotland went to Margaret, Maid of Norway. When he was buried in Dunfermline Abbey, there was little enthusiasm for the child queen. A pair of the nation's guardians, Bishop Robert Wishart of Glasgow and Bishop William Fraser of St Andrews, sent two priests to Margaret's great uncle King Edward of England, asking for guidance and favour. Edward had recently brought the Welsh to heel. From the emissaries' visit, until Robert Bruce defeated him at the Battle of Bannockburn, his bloody attempts to win control of the country north of the border earned him the nickname, The Hammer of the Scots.

Wishart apparently took an oath of allegiance to King Edward, who gave the bishop 50 oaks from Ettrick Forest to build a tower for Glasgow Cathedral after attending the thanksgiving service. The trees, it is said, were used as battering rams to hammer the way into Edward's fortress at Kirkintilloch.

Although shrewd enough to survive, Wishart was also committed. Robert Bruce was 31 when he dragged John Comyn the Red from the altar of Greyfriars church in Dumfries and murdered him in the aisles. Thereafter, the fight for Scotland's independence became a fight for Bruce to preserve his own liberty. Wishart invited him to Glasgow. Bruce asked for absolution and Wishart agreed, then preached a rousing sermon of support from the pulpit.

GLASGOW CATHEDRAL

Glasgow Cathedral, which apart from its tower is almost entirely a product of the 13th century, is the most complete piece of medieval architecture in Scotland.

Mungo is traditionally said to have chosen the site for his church in about 600. The diocese was re-established by the future David I in 1114. A surviving fragment suggests the Cathedral, consecrated in 1136, was a simple structure with fine painted decoration. Bishop Jocelyn's extension of it was unfinished at his death in 1199.

Building was re-started to a fresh design in the early 13th century, when the nave was laid out to its present plan, but around the 1240s there was yet another change. Bishop Bondington redirected the effort back to the eastern limb of the building, in order to provide a more fitting setting for the high altar, the shrine of St Kentigern and the choir of the canons who staffed the Cathedral. Because of the slope of the land all of this was elevated above a crypt of wonderful spatial complexity. Work had progressed as far as the transepts (cross arms) by the 1260s, and the unfinished nave (western limb) was completed in the later decades of the century.

In the course of the work there were several changes of designer. The mason who designed the choir was probably trained in the workshops of northern England, while the man who completed the nave was evidently aware of work in the English west country. But these changes in no way detract from the Cathedral's serene unity of appearance.

Richard Fawcett

Royal robes and a banner were supposedly made from Wishart's vestments and on March 27, 1306, Palm Sunday and five weeks after the Red Comyn's murder, he crowned Robert Bruce King of Scotland at Scone.

Edward put a price on his head and when Wishart was captured after a siege at Cupar Castle, the English King is supposed to have said he was as pleased as if Bruce had been taken. After Bannockburn, Bruce was able to dictate his own peace terms. His first demand was that all Scots held captive in the south should be allowed home. The Bishop of Glasgow returned with Bruce's wife and daughter. He was blind.

Wishart died in November 1316, and is buried near Mungo between the altars of St Peter and St Andrew, at the east end of the Cathedral.

The head of his effigy was destroyed during the Reformation.

A 15th century alabaster panel, named "Betrayal"

A bagpipe playing angel from the 15th century

An early stained glass indication of literacy.

THE HANSEATIC LEAGUE

A "Hanse" was an association which organised the flow of trade between cities. The origins of the system lay in guilds such as those of Valenciennes and St Omer, established around 1100 AD for importing wool, amalgamated by the mid-12th century into the Hanses of Bruges and Ypres.

At one time the League numbered 160 towns together with numerous agencies scatted across Europe from Bergen in the North to Bruges in the south, and from London in the west to Novgorod in the east. The Hanseatic fleet dominated North Sea and Baltic trade in salt, cloth, wax and grain, and sailed to Iceland in search of fish. By the 15th century, however, countries on the periphery of the League's core territories were developing their own independent maritime economies.

Scotland was involved in the League's trading system at least from the time of William Wallace, who wrote in 1297 to the burgesses of Lubeck and Hamburg. Scottish settlers and factors were active in these towns, as well as Danzig and Konigsberg, while Hanse factors operated in Glasgow, Aberdeen, Dunbar and Leith. The real growth of Scottish trade and influence was in the 16th and 17th centuries, when Hanseatic power had weakened. "Jeens Wilz", a Glasgow merchant, was reported operating at Middleburg as early as 1552, while later in the century the progressive desalinisation of the Baltic with the consequent loss of its herring stocks proved a boon to the fishers, curers and merchants of the Clyde, who sold barrelled salt herring through Baltic ports in enormous and highly lucrative quantities.

Andrew Gibb

"The Trial of William Wallace at Westminster" by Maclise.

Chapter Four
FOGS OF PREJUDICE

"View of the Bridgegate", engraved by Joseph Swan around 1827 by which time it had "fallen exceedingly from its former dignity".

It is in this cathedral that part of the scene of Rob Roy is laid. This was my first experience in cathedrals. It was a new thing to me altogether, and as I walked along under the old buttresses and battlements without, and looked into the bewildering labyrinths of architecture within, I saw that, with silence and solitude to help the impression, the old building might become a strong part of one's inner life. A grave-yard crowded with flat stones lies all around it. A deep ravine separates it from another cemetery on an opposite eminence, rustling with dark pines. A little brook murmurs with its slender voice between.

From Harriet Beecher Stowe, Sunny Memories of Foreign Lands, *1854.*

The two classes of burgesses, craftsmen and merchants, have their own anthem, "The Molendinar", subtitled "The Burgess Song of Glasgow". Copyrighted in 1925, it was written by the Rev Robert MacOmish with music by George Henry Martin.

The fourth and penultimate verse records Glasgow's pride in its Cathedral.

> Saint Mungo slept with the good and just,
> And they raised a shrine above his dust;
> Years passed; and o'er the sainted dead
> A great cathedral reared its head
> With awe the people gazed and thought
> No structure could be finer,
> When Mass was sung and the censer swung
> On the banks of the Molendinar.

The story goes that the craftsmen of Glasgow saved the building from the marauders of the Reformation who were about to put it to the torch, as they had every other mainland cathedral in Scotland. Other accounts feature a single man, Provost Thomas Crawford of Jordanhill, rebuking the reformers. "Ding down the kirk if you have a mind, but not till you have built as good a one to take the place of it".

There was a movement to demolish the Cathedral, led by Andrew Melville, Glasgow University's first principal after the Reformation. He and other ministers wanted to use the stones to build smaller churches around the town, because only superstitious people frequented the Cathedral, which was too big anyway and no-one could hear the preacher.

We learn of the matter primarily from Archbishop John Spottiswoode's *History of the Church of Scotland*, which has

Andrew Melville, acknowledged "light and leader" of the "Schools and Kirk in Scotland".

"Nothing Without Labour", a Victorian moral emblem.

"Preaching of John Knox Before the Lords of the Congregation" by David Wilkie.

1. George Eyre Todd, **History of Glasgow**, 1931.

been referred to as "especially valuable on account of its author being a prominent actor in the many important events he puts on record".[1]

Spottiswoode was Glasgow's first Episcopal archbishop. He was born in Mid-Calder where his father was parish minister. He had a brilliant early career at Glasgow University and when his father died, he too became Mid-Calder's minister. He was at this time a strong Presbyterian, but mellowed towards episcopacy, the king's religion. The conversion happened around 1595. Rumour had it that Spottiswoode was a clype, carrying stories of the Edinburgh ministry's private meetings back to the King.[2]

He was the Duke of Lennox's chaplain on a trip to France and this ensured he was thought of as episcopalian, since he had both been to Paris and discussed matters with English bishops in London. He certainly entered heartily into the royal desire to establish the episcopacy in Scotland.

When James was on his way to London to be crowned King of England in 1603, he heard of Archbishop Beaton's death and immediately appointed Spottiswoode, who was accompanying the King to London, to the vacant see. The revenues from Glasgow were not what they were, though Spottiswoode is credited with restoring the coffers to something approaching their former glory.

Prosperity, of course, had secular roots. The merchants saw themselves as socially superior. They used their brains, rather than their hands, and the wealth they generated was good for everyone. Where would medieval society have been without the merchants who alone saw beyond the parochial and used it to their advantage? Their activities created an international perspective and ended the medieval world's insular security.

Craftsmen were the socially inferior half of the burgess class. Though they had existed from earliest times in Scottish burghs, it wasn't until the middle of the 15th century that they organised themselves into guilds. By 1600, both Edinburgh and Glasgow had 14 incorporated trades, Dundee had nine, Perth eight, while Stirling and Aberdeen had seven.[3]

The craft was analogous to the merchant guild and its purpose was precisely the same: to uphold the rights of a small group of privileged citizens against the majority.

In 1536 Glasgow's metal workers petitioned for permission to establish an Incorporation of Hammermen because of the "great hurt and damage" honest blacksmiths, lorimers, saddlers, goldsmiths, bucklemakers, armourers and the like were suffering from unqualified men. Their first rule was that no-one could set up a

MEDIEVAL BUILDINGS IN GLASGOW

Most of Glasgow's finest medieval buildings would have been associated with the Church. Clustered around the Cathedral were the residences of its clergy, including the Castle of the bishop, the fine manses of the canons and the lesser houses of the vicars who acted as substitutes for the canons. Of these, we know something of the Bishop's Castle both from early views and from recent excavations, which show a fortified wall, defended by a strong gatehouse, enclosing a massive tower house and other buildings.

Some of the canons' manses also survived long enough for us to know a little of their appearance, and one of these is still represented by the house known as "Provand's Lordship". That building was, however, probably first built not as a manse but for the hospital of St Nicholas, which was founded by Bishop Durisdeer in the mid-15th century. The chapel of that hospital was also recorded before its destruction in 1808, and it appears that its chancel was a typcially Scottish late Gothic structure, with a polygonal east end as the setting for the main altar.

One of Glasgow's finest churches, apart from the Cathedral, must have been that of the Dominican friars, which was later absorbed into the university precinct. A view engraved before its destruction in 1670 suggest its rectangular shape masked a building of some complexity. Of the appearance of other churches we can only obtain tantalising hints from buildings in the surrounding area, such as Paisley Abbey, Bothwell Collegiate Church and the fragments of Rutherglen Parish Church.

Richard Fawcett

ARMS AND ARMOUR IN GLASGOW

A certain Johne Hamilton, "steil bonet maker", is recorded working in Glasgow in 1577. The following year he was fined and ordered to pay eight shillings damages "for troublans done be him to Jonet Barde in first casting ane chandeler at hir and thaireftir dinging and dowping of hir to the greit effusion of hir blude . . ."

During the 17th and 18th centuries, Glasgow established a reputation as an arms manufacturing centre, producing the distinctive all metal pistols, usually in steel but sometimes in brass, and the basket hilted broadswords popular with both Lowlander and Highland clansmen alike. The so called claymore, or "twa handit sword" with sloping cross and quatrefoil quillons was a favourite weapon of the Highlanders during the 16th and 17th centuries, but gave way to the more convenient basket hilted sword.

Evidently Glasgow also had a reputation for the quality of its targes (wooden shields covered by cowhide, decorated with brass studs). In 1562, Mary Queen of Scots remarked that she longed to be a man "to lie all night in the fields, or to walk upon the causeway with a pack or knapschall (steel bonnet), a Glasgow buckler and a broadsword". Comparatively few genuine targes remain today, as the vicissitudes of the Scottish climate led to many simply rotting away. James Boswell in his *Journal of a Tour to the Hebrides with Samuel Johnson*, recorded how in 1773 "there is hardly a target now to be found in the Highlands. After the disarming act they made them serve as covers to their buttermilk barrels, a kind of change like beating spears into pruning hooks".

The Baron of Earlshall

1. John Prebble, **The Lion in the North**, 1971. **2.** ibid. **3.** See John Harvey, **Mediaeval Craftsmen**, 1973.

"Portrait of James VI" attributed to Adrian Vanson

George and Thomas Hutcheson, the Hutcheson Brothers who founded the hospital and school.

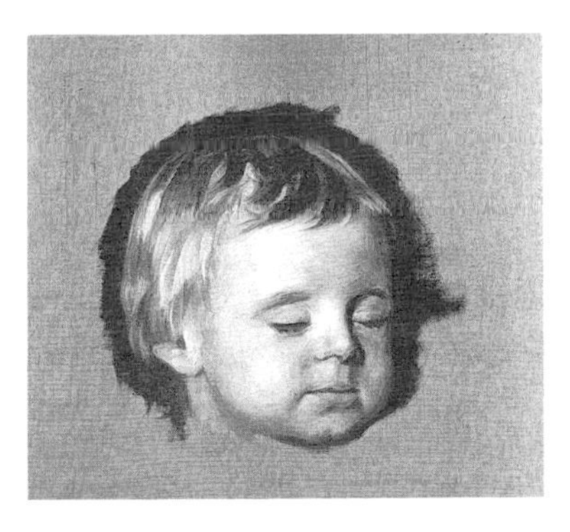

"Sketch of a Dead Child" by Allan Ramsay.

metalware booth in the town unless he was a member of the craft and had been "examined and found qualified to work by three of the best masters". They subsequently seemed to spend much of their time tracking down and banishing practitioners of "dishonest work", preventing hammermen from the Gorbals flooding their market and stopping merchants from employing private smiths.

In general, however, those merchants encountered few hindrances. Indeed, only town burgesses were freemen. Everyone else, including affluent householders belonging to the literate classes, chamberlains who administered the nobility's town houses, advocates and lawyers were unfree. Many were granted an honorary freedom of the burgh, given burgess rights and privileges. Respectable widows also came into this group. Many of them kept lodging houses, though not all of those lodging houses were respectable.

The underprivileged poor, most of the population, had no rights, and left no records. Some were servants, drovers, hawkers, carters; elsewhere they were fishermen and seamen. The poorest widows sold ale. Some sold water, others milk. There was also a criminal class: prostitutes, cutpurses, footpads, vagabonds and thieves of all sorts.

Needless to say, there was no sanitation. Filth was thrown into the open street to be washed away or remain as mud. The stench of a medieval city carried with it the threat of the plague. Life was close to destitution. The infirm and the elderly displayed their sores and deformities and begged for alms. When a harvest failed and grain had to be imported from Poland or Ireland, it was the children in the vennels who died first.

Although existence was fragile it could still be pursued with vigour. Glasgow's first recorded riot was a tame affair, but it had serious consequences. It was a riot of burgesses, which had begun with a sitting of the burgh court on June 4, 1574. John Pollock had threatened James Anderson, an officer who was pursuing him in connection with an alleged disturbance. A certain Andrew Stewart objected to Pollock's arrest and was himself taken into custody.

Other burgesses stood surety for them and that appeared to be that; until June 11, when "Johne Pollok, cowper, Eduard Pollok, skynner, and Hectour Dunlop, wrycht, burgessis of Glasgow" took arms against the provost, bailies and townsfolk of the city, contrary to their burgess oaths. The provost and bailies sentenced that their freedoms be "cryit doun be ane officair vpone ane mercate daye on the cors; and als ar ordanit to be retenit in firmance in the heych tolbuyth, aye and quhill thai fynd cautioune to mak amendis and repentance to the kirk for breking of thair aithis,[1]

GLASGOW'S HOSPITALS

Lagging half a century behind their Edinburgh counterparts, the citizens of Glasgow did not respond to the movement to provide public hospitals for the "sick poor" until 1787, when the urgings of the University and the unrest amongst their workforces convinced the local textile magnates to start raising funds. Planned by Robert Adam – currently in town to design the Trades' House in Glassford Street – and situated on the site of the present building, the original Glasgow Royal Infirmary had beds for just over 100 patients. As the only hospital available to Glasgow and the surrounding communities, the Royal drew patients from a wide catchment area and treated a far greater range of illnesses than any modern general hospital when it finally opened in 1791.

The burden on the GRI eased with the opening of the Glasgow Asylum for Lunatics (now Gartnavel Royal Hospital) in 1814 and the establishment of the Glasgow Eye Infirmary ten years later. Other specialist hospitals were erected in the second half of the 19th century, as were the rival Western (1874) and Victoria (1890) Infirmaries. The remainder of the existing network of hospitals – the former fever and poor law institutions – resulted from the efforts of the local authorities and parochial boards, and was virtually completed before the 1911 National Insurance Act.

With the passage of time, a number of specialist units have closed and others have undergone a considerable change of function. So long as the names live on, however, Glasgow will be reminded of the visionaries who laid the foundations of hospital medicine in the city.

Derek A Dow

1. George MacGregor, **History of Glasgow**, 1881.

George Buchanan, the only layman ever appointed Moderator of the General Assembly of the Church of Scotland, in 1567, when Mary, Queen of Scots, was deposed as monarch.

and to fulfill sick iniunctiones as the kirk will devys for the samyn".[1]

In July of that year the magistrates found it necessary to advise every booth-holder to have "ane halbert, jak and steil bonnet" ready just in case. The sense of upheaval was, to some degree, a result of the Reformation whose tensions could still be felt.

The practices and structure which were eventually adopted by the post-Reformation church owe much to Andrew Melville, a scholar of European reputation. He came back to Scotland after six years exile in Geneva and,in 1574, was appointed Principal of Glasgow University.

Melville was a stabler and subtler character than Knox, with a far more refined and polished intellect. The historian John Prebble describes him as "a product of the reform movement rather than a founder of it". He was a creative inspiration, largely remembered for calling His Majesty James VI of Scotland "God's sillie vassal",[2] reminding the King we are all God's subjects and that even a king was a commoner in the eyes of Christ.

His achievement, if such it be, was the *Second Book of Discipline* of 1578, which was eventually accepted by the General Assembly of the Church of Scotland. The Kirk's power came directly from God, it said and built an authority based upon Scripture and outwith the state. The church should be devoted to its ministers, its organisation and its obligations to the poor.

Everyone was subject to its guidance in matters of conscience and religion, so the General Assembly of the Church of Scotland raised itself above the monarchy, the nobility, the populace and parliament, creating a rival government. More powerful and influential, it had a greater effect on Scottish life and literature, the arts and fabric of our country than any secular authority. It is the foundation and sustenance of all the myths by which we are known across the world, and the means by which we address and understand ourselves. It was neither benevolent or wrong. In its fight against the Antichrist fear, pain and humiliation were the roads to salvation. No-one was immune and the brotherhood of man it promised destroyed individual freedom.

Religion therefore had its uses, and if T.C. Smout's assertion that the modern world began with the Reformation is true, then surely[3] this is nowhere more evident than in the use of religion as a means of social control. The continuing and maintained divisions which polarise sections of our society and city are rooted here.

The local laird had his own pew in kirk, bought and paid for, used by himself, his family and friends, often with a retiring room

Thomas Rickman's elevation drawing of St David's Ramshorn Kirk, which he designed in 1824.

REFORMATION ANTI-WOMEN LAWS

On January 24, 1681 seven Edinburgh women were hanged for concealing their pregnancies. This was a fairly everyday occurrence in post-reformation Lowland Scotland, when being unmarried and pregnant was a criminal offence under Presbyterian law.

In some respects, however, women in Lowland Scotland were better treated under the Presbyterian law than they had been under the previous Roman Catholic laws, where they could not even enter church without covering their faces, but it was to prove a different kind of anti-female régime.

Laws, which still apply though now in disuse, were passed prohibiting women from trying to entice men by using false bosoms, wigs, bums and make-up, or even "profane walking". For some transgressions the penalty was death, particularly for adultery though this did not apply to married men who had been unfairly "tempted".

In 1690 an Act was passed making women who had tried to conceal their pregnancies guilty of murder if the child was born dead or could not be found. Professor Gordon in his book *The Criminal Law of Scotland* explains: "It appears that during the 1680s there were a large number of cases of murder of newly born children by their mothers".

In 1809 the offence was changed to concealment of pregnancy and given a maximum sentence of two years' imprisonment. It is still an offence under Scottish law, though since 1967 abortion itself has been legal in specified circumstances.

Eveline Hunter

1. Ibid. **2.** John Prebble, op. cit. **3.** T.C. Smout, **A History of the Scottish People, 1560–1830**, 1969.

THOMAS CHALMERS (1760–1847)

The evangelical minister, the Rev Dr Thomas Chalmers, was born in Anstruther and educated at St Andrews University. His first charge was Kilmany, Fife, but owing to the efforts of future publisher William Collins who had been profoundly affected by Chalmers's preaching, he was translated to the Tron Kirk of Glasgow in 1815. In 1819 he was translated to St John's, a new parish in the East End, endowed by the Town Council. Here he set about putting into practice his theories on reorganizing the old parochial system, to improve schooling and provide better welfare for the poor – much needed at this particularly bad period of depression.

Despite his initial feelings about Glasgow ("a desolation of heart") he vigorously took up this challenge to practical Christianity. He divided St John's into 25 districts, known as proportions, each with 40–100 families and with its own deacon and elder ("agents") to look after it; other agencies included Sabbath schools. He was as energetic in writing as he was in church and public affairs: a prolific correspondent, firing off his illegible "little billets" in all directions, and constantly publishing (his scientific, economic and theological works occupy 34 volumes).

Worn out by his labours, in 1823 he accepted the Chair of Moral Philosophy at St Andrews, returning to Glasgow 20 years later to preach the opening sermon at the Assembly of the Free Church, in whose founding he had been the leading light. Chalmers' oratory enraptured Glasgow. When he gave his farewell discourse at St John's troops had to be called in to control the crowds. "Oh!" he exclaimed. "I never can forget the city of so many Christian and kind-hearted men."

Hamish Whyte

off-stage where he could rest from the endless sermons. The minister bowed to the laird and his family when they arrived in church.

The sabbath started at six o'clock on a Saturday night and lasted for 24 hours. It was a good source of revenue from the fines imposed on those who broke laws designed to make them holy. Basically, there was no nothing; neither music, singing, dancing, markets, commerce, gambling, theatre, sports or drinking. Fines were imposed on anyone caught working and little was allowed except staying indoors or attending church, where a parishioner was expected to await the arrival of the minister.

Souls and their salvation were paramount and nothing was too severe for transgressors. Obscene, degrading punishments were imposed, because the righteous believed they were necessary to secure the sinner soul. Humiliation was commonplace. Irons, imprisonment, stocks and branks were in daily use against slanderers, scolders or those who criticised the church and its teachings, the actions of the unco guid.

Glasgow's branks are in the People's Palace, a padlocked iron helmet with a flat triangular piece which fitted into the victim's mouth, depressing the tongue.

Worst of all was fornication, sin of the body. *The First Book of Discipline* actually recommended death for adulterers, though that was seldom carried out. The cutty stool and the pillar were the customary punishments, with Robert Burns being the best known offender. The stool was inside the church and the pillar outside, so the humiliation was complete.

Needless to say, most of the folk thus humiliated were poor. Scotland's nobility have been renowned for their bastards, the amount and the cheek of them, yet few were charged with shagging. Lesser souls were forced to wear paper crowns describing their sins and walk barefoot to a public whipping cross. Scourge and the branks, stocks and the stool of repentance, banishment, burning and the ducking pond in the name of the Lord and the furtherance of Gentle Jesus and his Kingdom on Earth.

"A Prospect of the Entry into the Blackfriars Church, Glasgow, March 1, 1756".

APPRENTICE RUN OFF

On Wednesday the 28th, ult. JOHN McCONNELL, apprentice to Jonathan Tomlinson, weaver, Calton, left his work. He is about nine years of age, four feet high, fair hair and fair complexion. Had on an old blue jacket and a pair of new corduroy calshes, but neither shoes, stockings nor hat.

Any person who will bring the said Boy to his Master, will receive HALF-A-GUINEA of Reward; and those who employ him after this intimation, will be prosecuted with the utmost rigour.

Glasgow Courier, *December 15, 1804.*

Juvenile delinquency board.

Key for Glasgow gallows.

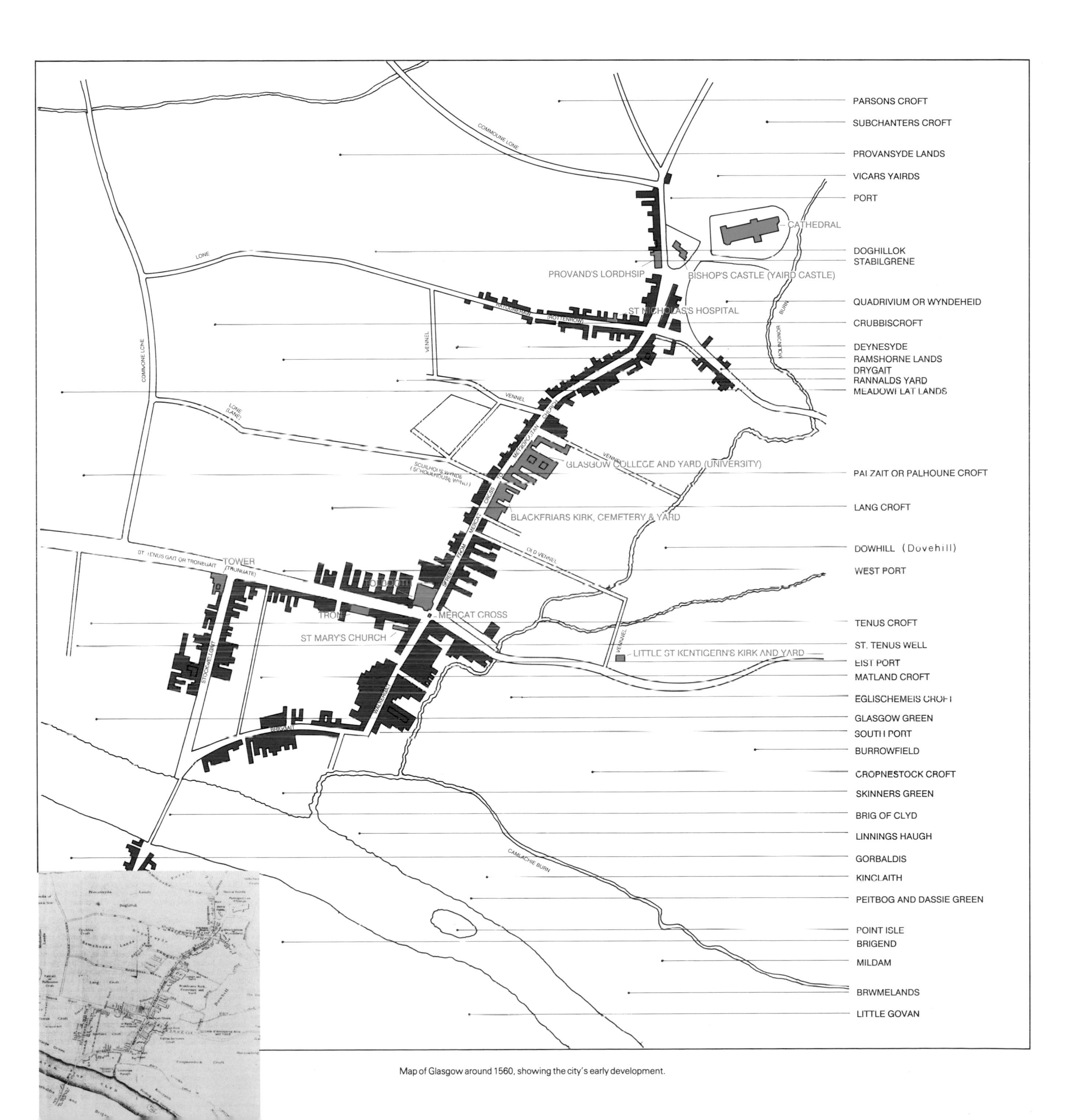

Map of Glasgow around 1560, showing the city's early development.

"Saturday Matinee Queue" by Joan Eardley.

Chapter Five

ENTERTAINMENT

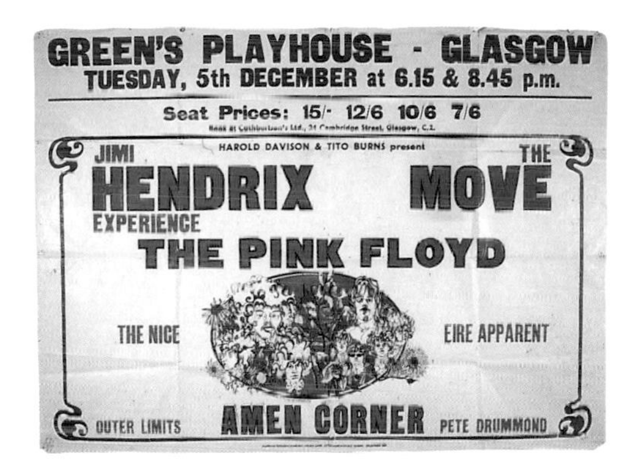

A late Sixties poster for a Green's Playhouse concert.

Who would believe humour and human dignity, reason and a sense of proportion could survive? Yet folksong is Scotland's and Glasgow's greatest music. It is undervalued because people hear only its birdsong ease and not the concealed artistry.

By its very nature, the Reformation obliterated the chance that any composers of church, or any other type of formal music, would appear in Scotland. In countries where the sterner practices of John Calvin were followed, music was seen as a worldly distraction and anything but the simplest settings were banned.

Scotland rejected accompanied singing. A precentor led the congregation by singing the opening lines of a psalm or metric paraphrase, which the congregation then followed. This style of musical worship is still favoured in the Free Kirk today.

"Unity Theatre" by Bet Low.

In their desire for purity, the church even banned the organ. Glasgow's appetite for music was resilient, and a kist o'whistles built by James Watt (now in the People's Palace), was the cause of some dispute starting in the church and eventually enveloping the entire city.

In 1805 Dr William Ritchie was appointed minister of St Andrew's Parish Church, which was the kirk of Glasgow Town Council. In one of the outer rooms, he discovered the organ made by a former member of his congregation, Watt, when working up the road at Glasgow University in the High Street.

Dr Ritchie liked the idea of music in his kirk and allowed the instrument to be used during choir practice. In 1806, the congregation presented a petition to the Town Council asking that they be allowed to remove certain seats from the church to allow the organ's use in public worship. It was accompanied by a letter from Ritchie, which said that were the request granted, "our Heritors, Magistrates of one of the first commercial cities of Europe, will thus give new evidence to mankind that the genius

GLASGOW SONGSHEETS – 19th CENTURY

Bemoaning the loss of the chap-books and broadsides of the "Salt-market Literature" was almost as frequent a feature of 19th century autobiography as deploring the disappearance of traditional songs or children's games. In fact, both the little unsewn 24–page story-books and the single song-sheets flourished for most of the century. In the 1820s Francis Orr and Sons, who published a series of 150 chapbooks, also advertised "Ballads, both eight pages and slips, a large assortment embracing all the old and most popular of the new songs". Thirty years later, three new firms specialising in song sheets were just starting, in St Andrew's Lane, King Street (City) and King Street (Calton), none of them far from the Saltmarket origins of the genre.

These also printed all the old songs and many of the new ones, some specially written for the sheets. In The Poet's Box, Matthew Leitch's little shop in St Andrew's Lane, you could have songs written to order for any occasion. The old songs included ballads such as "Barbara Allan" and "The Golden Glove", but in 1854 they were still publishing songs about Bonnie Prince Charlie and Napoleon, and about the martyrs of Bonnymuir – Baird, Hardie and Wilson. For indeed the local element was a strong selling point, as was the topical. So alongside the national hits like "The Battle of Inkerman", you would have songs about Sabbath-breaking steamers on the Clyde. With the publishers boasting "Upwards of 5,000 titles" few subjects remained untouched.

Adam McNaughtan

of commerce is not the contracted spirit of hostility to the liberal arts, but the enlivening sun of science, dispelling, in its progress, the gloomy fogs of prejudice that have too long benumbed the energies and untuned the feelings of our country".[1]

The Lord Provost, Magistrates and Town Council weren't interested. They refused the application, but the organ was moved into the church anyway and kept under a green baize cover. During the afternoon service on August 23, 1807, the organist from the Episcopalian church down the road, played, while the congregation sang the final psalm.

This outrageous act was the talk of Glasgow and bitter controversy enveloped the country. Finally, the Glasgow presbytery announced that organ music was "contrary to the law of the land, and to the law and constitution of the Established Church," and prohibited it in all churches and chapels within their bounds.

The organ was removed and sold to a music dealer who improved it by adding pipes to the front. Bailie McLellan, whose collection of paintings formed the nucleus of Glasgow Art Galleries, having previously been shown in the galleries he built to house them, bought the Watt organ around the time the kirk session of St Andrews was disposing of a lectern with a finely carved eagle at its head because it was too fancy.

Scotland has no formal tradition in music, or painting. Folk song was the natural expression for a people denied a voice in any other way. Indeed, Scotland's relatively backward position in most of the arts is directly attributable to the Kirk's steadfast concern for the nation's immortal soul. The church's hierarchy hated theatre. The ministers' fear of drama's potential for expressing dissent and criticism and disseminating ideas never relaxed. Sir David Lindsay's *Ane Satyre of the Thrie Estaitis*, actually favourable to the Reforming spirit, had lampooned the existing order and presented a powerful argument for spiritual reform, but bigotry held every type of creative expression by the throat and the great promise of Lindsay's fine play was never developed.

The destructions of the Reformation removed much of what records there were of Glasgow's medieval festivals and religious drama. Plays with themes such as the Creation or the Fall of Man were performed in Perth from the 15th century to the Reformation, and it is unlikely that Glasgow would have lacked them.

In 1596, the Provost, Bailies and Council had ordained that a "Fast be keeped both dayes of the Communion, and that the Lord's day be not profaned with pastimes and playes".[2]

They had even gone so far as to decree, on April 24, 1595, that "the

GLASGOW CITIZENS THEATRE

"A Citizens' theatre in the fullest sense of the term", was promised to subscribers to the Glasgow Repertory Theatre in 1909. Over 30 years later, Scots dramatist, James Bridie borrowed the phrase for his new company. Bridie's play, *Holy Isle*, was the inaugural production of the Citizens' Company at the Athenaeum Theatre in October 1943.

Two years later, the Company found a permanent home in the Royal Princess's Theatre in the Gorbals. They were central to Tyrone Guthrie's famous production of *Ane Satyre of the Thrie Estaitis* at the 1948 Edinburgh International Festival.

Under Bridie, who died in 1951, the programme was composed of a mixture of classics and new Scottish plays. But, by the beginning of the Sixties, the Citizens' was virtually indistinguishable from any other good provincial rep. The advent of the Seventies found it in a parlous state. Box-Office receipts and critical esteem had fallen alarmingly.

Then Giles Havergal, formerly director of Watford Palace Theatre, was appointed as Artistic Director, and William Taylor, a lawyer and former Labour Councillor, became Chairman of the Board, This partnership has lasted for 21 years. Havergal, in conjunction with designer/director, Philip Prowse, and playwright, dramaturg, director, Robert David Macdonald, transformed the Citizens' into a theatre of international reputation. The underlying philosophy of this "discotheque of a theatre" has at its core a quest to explore and define the relationship between art and life, actor and audience, illusion and reality, reflection and image.

Jan McDonald

1. Jack House, **The Heart of Glasgow**, 1965. 2. **Extracts from the Records of the Burgh of Glasgow, 1573–1642.**

"No Mean City", a watercolour, painted in 1939 by Osborne Henry Mavor, otherwise known as James Bridie.

drum is to go throu the Town discharging bickerings on Sunday, or playes, either by young or old", or in simpler terms – no fun.[1]

And in 1603, the year of the first Union, no-one was allowed to travel to Rutherglen on a Sunday "to see vain playes". This was renewed in 1607 and in 1612.

Plays, guisings and the like were constantly being censured, especially around Christmas and May-day. Indeed in 1609, there were to be "no playes, nor guisings, nor pypings, nor drinking nor any superstitious exercise to be used the dayes following Yuil". Citizens were ordered to address their repentance for "putting on of man's cloths, and a man for putting on of woman's cloths". Minstrels were barred, as were fools and strong and idle beggars. Football survived. There was a folk custom of playing the game in the churchyard or through the town at shrovetide.

Ane Satyre of the Thrie Estaitis ends in music, Diligence making a speech to the "Famous people" of his audience:

> Now let ilk man his way avance:
> Let sum ga drink and sum ga dance.
> Menstrell, blaw up ane brawll of France;
> Let se quha hobbils best!
> For I will rin, incontinent,
> To the tavern or ever I stent,
> And pray to God Omnipotent
> To send you all gude rest.[2]

And the cast exit dancing.

Medieval man playing the organ.

Dancing was banned. It was seen as a form of sorcery, a triumph of flesh over spirit. And though offenders were punished with the pillory, stocks and so on, they never entirely suppressed the nation's love of music and dance, though they presumably believed they could. Musicians had been maintained at the Burghs' expense throughout Scotland.

Glasgow was something of a musical centre. From the beginning of the 16th century, the harp, fiddle, lute, organ, monocord, the taubron "the clarescha, the drone and the schalmis" were used and[3] enjoyed in the town. The King's Lord High Treasurer has entries for "a lute with the case, and a dozen strings bought in Glasgow and sent with Troilus to the King's Grace at Inveraray".[4] A diarist tells of a musical coterie. At the beginning of the 17th century he visited "a gentillman's house in the town wha enterteined maist expert singars and players and brought upe all his berns thairin".

Sir David Lindsay. His play was performed before James V in 1540. After the show, the King told his chancellor, Gavin Dunbar, Bishop of Glasgow, to mend his ways.

GLASGOW ROCK (1955–75)

Setting what would prove to be an inescapable transatlantic tone, Fifties skiffle stalwarts the Kinning Park Ramblers named themselves after the North Carolina Ramblers. Most Glasgow rock'n'rollers have ever wanted to be from somewhere else, sadly all-too-few managing to accommodate where they really come from. Thus in 1956 Lonnie Donegan took the Rock Island Line from Iowa into the US charts, likewise the destination of Chas McDevitt and Nancy Whiskey's Freight Train (written by a North Carolinan). In the Sixties Lulu added Glasgow raucousness to the Isley Brothers' Motown Shout: Al Stewart tried to be a wispier Bob Dylan; the Poets sought black roots R & B credibility; brave Maggie Bell ploughed a primeval Mississippi cottonfield blues furrow; the Marmalade adopted Paisley kaftans in an attempt to sound San Franciscan. Originally billed as "Scotland's Tommy Steele", Alex Harvey bestrode all the eras, taking the best bits from them: skiffle, R & B, big-band soul, Hamburg beat boom, Hair flower power, cabaret. In his ultimate mid-Seventies incarnation, as focal point of the Sensational Alex Harvey Band, he was uniquely and truly Glaswegian: the leader of the toughest, wittiest, wisest, sharpest, most humane gang. Of the street and for the kids, Harvey broadcast a message of repsonsible urban pride that welded comic book depth and simplicity to the directness of spray-can graffiti. No-one before or since has been so rock'n'roll – cool and daftly anarchic – and so Glasgow (warm and practically anarchic).

David Belcher

1. ibid. 2. Sir David Lindsay, **Ane Satyre of the Thrie Estaitis**, ed. Roderick Lyall, 1989. 3. **Extracts from the Records of the Burgh of Glasgow, 1573–1642.** 4. Entries from the **Accounts of the Lord High Treasurer**.

Burning of the Adelphi theatre on November 22, 1848. The wind carried embers as far as George Square.

Early theatre was like a Variety bill, with tumblers, jugglers, acrobats, singers, dancers, tight-rope walkers and a "pantomime entertainment" fitted in at the end; and the place to see it was Burrell's Close, off Duke Street.

Burrell was a dancing master who was lured to Glasgow in 1738 by a Council subsidy of £20 a year. His predecessor, Glasgow's first dancing master, John Smith, had to behave soberly and could allow "no promiscuous dancing of young men and young women together".[1] God knows what they did; and even though it was socially acceptable to be seen at these events, so few people went that the city fathers had to bribe Burrell to stay.

The first real theatre was a wooden shed, propped against an old wall of the Bishop's Palace beside the Cathedral. The audience turned up in their sedan chairs, with servants to protect them against those calling for hell's fires and damnation to be the lot of whoever entered Satan's Playhouse. This theatre lasted until the most famous evangelist of the day, George Whitefield came to Glasgow. Whitefield knew what sinful places theatres were, having been an actor himself and called upon Gabriel to smite those who frequented with the Devil.

Glasgow was without a theatre until some of the town's hardier souls decided to put up a stone building, but no one would sell or rent the ground. They were forced to go outside the city boundaries and eventually persuaded John Millar of Grahamston to sell them part of the site now occupied by the Central Station. Millar demanded an exhorbitant price. "If I am to risk my soul," he said, "I am entitled to be well paid for it."[2]

The opening production in the spring of 1764 was to have featured Mrs Bellamy, the most famous actress of her day, who had been in Edinburgh, packing them in, while dodging her London creditors. The night before the theatre opened, a Methodist preacher told a crowd at Anderston Cross that he dreamed he was in hell where Lucifer was drinking a toast to John Millar; the theatre was burned down before it opened.

Mrs Bellamy was a lady of spirit. She borrowed curtains, dresses and chairs from sympathisers and called the actors to a rehearsal at her digs in the Black Bull Inn. While carpenters were rigging up a stage, an announcement was made at Glasgow Cross that Mrs Bellamy would appear that night, "in the comedy of The Citizen and the farce of The Mock Doctor."[3]

It was a triumph; and even though the town guard had to accompany her sedan between the Black Bull and the theatre for the rest of her stay, she not only drew crowds, but also managed

THEATRE FIRES

The drama of Glasgow's theatres has not been confined to the stage performances. In 1721 the magistrates and town council, "considering that the allowing of publick balls, shows, comedies and other plays or diversions, where acted in houses belonging to the town, and particularly in the Grammar Schooll house, hes occasioned great disturbance in the citie", prohibited these "excepting such plays as are acted by the boys of the school, and have relation to their learning".

The disturbances did not cease when private buildings were used, although the Reverend George Whitefield denied that his followers committed any violent act against the theatre of 1753. The owners, he reported, rolled up their roof and decamped when they heard of the feelings that had been raised against them. There was no question about the destruction wreaked by protestors at the Alston Street "Concert Hall" in 1764; building, props and costumes were burned. The protest was a different one in 1845 when John Henry Anderson erected his City Theatre. Sixty thousand citizens signed a petition against this permanent structure on Glasgow Green. Small wonder that its destruction by fire was viewed by Anderson with suspicion.

Accidental fire has been a frequent visitor to Glasgow's halls. The fact that both the Dunlop Street and Queen Street theatres were destroyed in association with the pantomime *Bluebeard* was not allowed to start a tradition of ill-luck, for it was with that piece that The Metropole sucessfully opened in 1897.

Adam McNaughtan

1. Extracts from the Records of the Burgh of Glasgow, 1708–1738. **2.** Quoted in C Stewart Black, **Glasgow's Story**, undated. **3.** Walter Baynham, **The Glasgow Stage**, 1892.

Early 17th century firemen.

to borrow enough to discharge her debts. The Black Bull Inn also played host to performing animals, giants, dwarfs and other musical novelties. It was one of the earliest music hall venues in Glasgow.

In 1763 Mr Boverick presented his Miniature Curiosities at the Mason's Arms in the Trongate. Attractions included a wide range of remarkable miniatures, such as "a pair of steel scissors weighing but the sixteenth part of a grain which will cut a large horse-hair; 36 dozen of well-fashioned silver spoons in a pepper corn, and still room for several dozens more." [1] Mr Boverick could also boast the inevitable succession of testimonials from European persons of note and nobility.

During the 18th century, Glasgow offered a great many performing animals, including pigs, dogs, cats who could play the dulcimer with their paws, and a tortoise which had been specially trained to "fetch and carry articles". Programmes were also enlivened with conjuring, whistling and a variety of other musical performances.

Early outlets for music hall fell into three categories. At first there were the pubs. In one case in Sauchiehall Street it was necessary to erect a barrier between the gentlemen of the audience and the ladies of the cast.

The Penny Geggies were sited largely around Glasgow Green and the Saltmarket and these portable poor folks' theatres offered a varied bill of comedy, circus, sideshow and high drama. Mr Mumford's Penny Geggie Company was a particular favourite, producing such classics as *Rob Roy*. Mumford appears to have enjoyed a wee refreshment and was occasionally good natured enough to provide his audience with a temperance lecture, using himself as an example of the horrifying effects of the demon drink. His cast contained an artist of probably unique talents, Mr Johnnie Parry, who specialised in falling from high objects. Mountain top deaths were arranged to allow him to show off his remarkable muscular control. He would stagger in his death throes, relax his body totally and bounce down the side of the artificial cliff to roars of approval from the audience. He could frequently be persuaded to perform an encore.

Eventually there were auditoriums of a more formal nature. The first brick theatre on Glasgow Green was the Hibernian Theatre in Greendyke Street, built in 1849 by a Mr Calvert and sited "immediately to the east of the Episcopal Chapel and adjoining the Model Lodging-Houses for the working classes." [2] Music hall artists eventually found their way, via pantomime, into the early permanent theatre buildings such as the Adelphi and the City, both of which were on the Green and both of which were destroyed by fire.

Advertisement for the Princess's Theatre in Main Street, Gorbals which became the Citizens in 1945.

KEEK SHOWS AND PENNY GEGGIES

It used to be quite common in Glasgow to be told to "shut your geggie" instead of "shut your mouth". Geggies or more usually penny geggies, were portable theatres made of wood and canvas which performed rough and ready versions of Shakespeare, melodrama and Scottish plays – admission one penny. They were part of the popular entertainment of Glasgow for much of the 19th century and were erected wherever there was space in the city centre. The most famous, Mumford's, founded in 1835 by a drunken Englishman, which stood at the corner of Saltmarket and Greendyke Street wasn't really a geggie at all as it was permanent.

The geggies had a very free and easy relationship with their audiences. Some actors like Geordie Henderson of Mumford's would even repeat their death scenes if requested. At busy times the geggies could perform *Richard III* 20 times in seven hours. On less frantic occasions the company could produce Macbeth "in five 'LONG' acts" on a Friday night, though that, with the added attraction of a coal brazier to keep the audience warm, would cost you tuppence.

Keek shows, a catch-all name which could describe menageries, freak-shows, panoramas, waxworks or a "wizard in kilts" were, like the geggies, a feature of Glasgow Fair and usually clustered around the Green. Unkind souls were heard to say that the hairy lady was really a bear with a shaved face and that the "Bosjesmans" advertised as "primitive African tribesmen", were Irishmen dressed in skins and furs and speaking Gaelic. But the last laugh was with the showmen who persuaded 96,000 people at a penny a time to see these "tribesmen".

Alasdair Cameron

1. Glasgow Journal, August 4, 1763. **2.** Senex, Glasgow Past and Present, 1851.

Will Fyffe, Dundonian author of "I Belong to Glasgow".

From the first, Glasgow attracted the great names of vaudeville to theatres which appear to have been less than safe. Most of Glasgow's 19th century theatres were destroyed by fire, sometimes with an appalling loss of life, as in the case of the Dunlop Street Theatre. In the days when lighting was provided by naked flames, theatre buildings were particularly prone to fire, because they are usually filled with dry wood, highly inflammable canvas cloth and rope, with their stages positioned below fly towers which acted as enormous chimneys, creating a vast proscenium fireplace.

Glasgow was the starting ground for Harry Lauder and Stan Laurel alike and produced its own great names; like Liverpool it has become famous for comedians who, until the great Billy Connolly, found they could make a comfortable living in Scotland and ignore audiences south of the Border who, allegedly, could not understand their accents. We got our own back with the Glasgow Empire, graveyard of the great, a byword for disaster amongst English comics. According to Ken Dodd, "The trouble with Freud is he never played the Glasgow Empire Saturday night." [1]

George Green's Travelling Cinematograph, one of the first to take moving pictures across Scotland.

The amazing things about Glasgow's comedians is that the best of them coexisted with the cinema and reached their height at a time when Glasgow was Cinema City. Tommy Lorne, Will Fyffe, Frank and Doris Droy, Dave Willis, Tommy Morgan and as many again filled their theatres twice nightly, six nights a week, competing with and often beating the best Hollywood could provide.

There used to be more than 130 picture halls in Glasgow. In its heyday there were more cinemas per head of population in Glasgow than in any other city outside the United States. At the top of Renfield Street, Green's Playhouse was the biggest cinema in Europe, seating 4,200. The ABC, the biggest cinema chain in the country, was started in Glasgow. [2]

Moving pictures were first shown in fairgrounds and the early picture halls were converted theatres, just as many of today's bingo halls used to be cinemas. For more than 50 years, a night at the pictures was Glasgow's main form of entertainment and throughout the Thirties, Forties and Fifties, the cinema was as much a part of small communities throughout the country as the pub or the Post Office.

Glasgow's first picture hall was Pringle's Picture Palace on Sauchiehall Street. Mr Pringle opened his doors in 1907, when films were shown in any hall large enough to make it pay. Corporation halls were favourite venues, but films were still shown at fairgrounds and were used as an interval attraction in the music halls.

Mr Pringle showed films only and his idea caught on. Three years

Charlie Chaplin with George Green's son, Fred, in Hollywood.

GLASGOW PANTOMIME

Glasgow can fairly be called the Pantomime Centre of the World. I have seen many pantomimes (particularly those in London) but never any up to the standard of Glasgow's. A great deal of this pre-eminence is due to the Royal Princess's Theatre in the Gorbals. The building is now the Citizens' Theatre, which still runs a pantomime in season, but one quite different from its predecessors.

The first Princess's pantomimes were written and produced by the theatre owner, Rich Walden. He was followed by Harry McKelvie, who introduced the famous 13–letter titles because, so it's said, his own name had 13 letters in it and that brought him luck. His pantomimes were entirely Scottish and the chorus numbered 100. The first two rows were professional chorus girls from London, but the 80 girls behind them were local lassies who were taught basic steps and told to sing the choruses very loudly.

The principal boy and one or two members of the cast were English and one Sassenach performer said it was the only pantomime he knew where you started wearing a fur coat and ended the season wearing a straw basher.

Another long runner was the Queen's at Glasgow Cross, which was even more local than the Princess's. I recall a season when, out of eleven theatres, ten were presenting pantomimes, all successful.

The world records for pantomime runs were held by Glasgow theatres, one for full-length, the other for twice-nightly shows. Glasgow was, indeed, pantomime daft.

Jack House

1. The Oxford Dictionary of Quotations. 2. T Louden, The Cinemas of Cinema City, 1983.

JOHN MAXWELL (died 1941)

The mass popular appeal of the new "moving pictures" in the 1900s was not long in attracting the attention of the business community. One of the first and most successful of the entrepreneurs to enter the industry on a purely commercial basis was John Maxwell.

As senior partner in the city's legal firm of Maxwell, Hodgson and Co he began to acquire existing "kinemas" and build new properties in the early years of the First World War. By 1916 he had formed, with exhibitors James Wright and Jimmy Milne, Scottish Cinema and Variety Theatres, a company that was, in 1928, to become Associated British Cinemas (ABC). With the creation of this fledgling organisation, Maxwell broke new ground, consolidating a small group of cinemas that would have more bargaining power with the film renters. The circuit went from strength to strength, expanding its interests south of the Border.

The success of cinema owning depended very largely on getting the best films. By the early 1930s, Maxwell had brought under his control not only an impressive circuit of cinemas in most of the major towns in Britain, but had acquired the means of producing and distributing the films to these outlets. With British International Pictures' studios at Elstree, control of renting company Wardour Films, and distribution run by Pathe and the American First National Company, he created the first camera-to-screen combination in the history of the industry, ensuring for his cinemas a steady supply of product and for the studios a guaranteed outlet for their films.

Janet McBain

later Glasgow had its first custom built cinema, The Electric Theatre at Charing Cross, which advertised itself as "the new wonder of the day". It was so popular that days after it opened, the owners put an advert in the papers apologising for turning away so many would-be customers.

In 1912, the Vitagraph opened along the road. It became the King's, the Newscine, the Tatler and latterly the Curzon-Classic, which until recently was Glasgow's oldest operating cinema. When it exhausted the market for so-called adult pictures, it became a disco.

The oldest operating cinema in Glasgow is the Grand Central, which was one of two city picture halls built in 1916. The Grand Central seated 750 people and was built in the middle of a warehouse. In its early days it had its own orchestra, but popularity waned during the Fifties. The cinema closed in 1966 and lay derelict until 1973 when it reopened as the Classic-Grand. Now part of the Cannon chain, it seems to attract the audiences who found the Curzon-Classic so enjoyable.

Cranston's, later the Classic, Cinema was opened in 1916 as an additional attraction for the customers of Miss Cranston's Tearooms. The hall in Renfield Street originally seated 850, but was converted into three separate cinemas, with a main theatre, the old cartoon theatre and a smaller cinema upstairs. The building was gutted by fire in 1981 and has been empty ever since.

It seems no building was safe from the cinema boom. Any auditorium was likely to be converted into a picture hall. Music halls were particularly suitable and one of Glasgow's oldest music halls became the Grand Cinema in Cowcaddens. It switched to films in 1916 and over 1,700 people could be seated in a stalls-only auditorium which suddenly sloped as it neared the screen. No-one knows why, since neither the architect nor the owners provided an explanation, but the slope is as well remembered as any film shown at the Grand.

The Regal in Sauchiehall Street had previously been the site of an Ice Skating Palace, Hengler's Circus and the Waldorf *Palais de Dance*. It was also the ABC's main house in the West of Scotland.

John Maxwell, who had started showing films in Corporation halls, pioneered Associated British Cinemas. At their height, they had 342 picture halls in practically every town in Britain. Their policy was to open the same film in two locations and they took great care to make sure those were at the opposite ends of the town. Their main Glasgow theatres were the Regal and the Coliseum.

The Queen's Enlarger – a magic lantern from the early years of the century – plus lens.

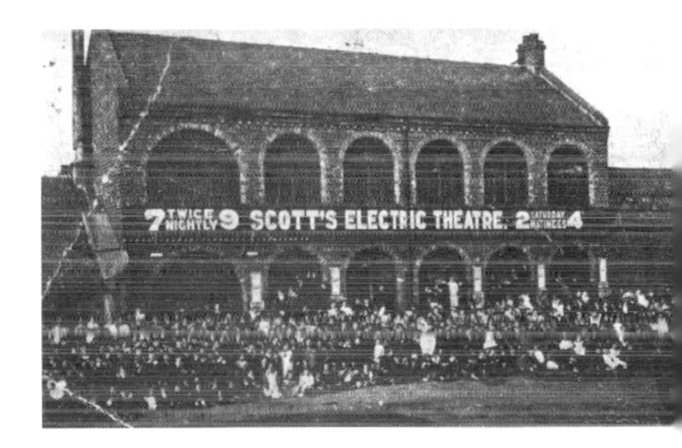

Scott's Electric Theatre, a converted wine works in the East End of Glasgow.

Mr Cosmo, George Singleton's puppet mascot.

The Coliseum was a music hall which showed films between the turns. It was converted into a cinema in 1925 and four years later, became the first Glasgow cinema to be fitted with sound. When they showed Al Jolson in *The Jazz Singer*, the queues reportedly stretched for miles. It transferred to the Regal and ran for weeks, though the record run belonged to Charlie Chaplin's *City Lights*.

Glasgow was never short of cinema entrepreneurs. The Singleton circuit was standardised by the name Vogue, with picture halls in Riddrie, Govan, Possil, Cathcart, Cardonald and Knightswood. The company still survives and runs the first four Vogues as bingo halls. Their specialist cinema, the Cosmo, whose logo included a globe of the world and the bowler hatted Mr Cosmo on every advert, survives as the Glasgow Film Theatre.

The Cosmo was unique in Glasgow as a venue for foreign language and art films. It was opened in the dark years before the Second World War, when its failure was commonly predicted. Between them, Singleton and his manager Charles Oakley,[1] proved that a friendly responsive cinema showing quality British, American and Continental films could pay its way. The building, designed by James McKissack and W. J. Anderson, is an interesting piece of Thirties architecture, with suitable cosmopolitan influences.

Popular pastimes have a long, and sometimes dark history. Superstition, sorcery, magic and witchcraft were the staple ingredients of the medieval world's wonders. The Church had utilised the pagan, pre-Christian festivals; had even fashioned them into their own image, yet the beliefs around the festivals persisted, as ingrained as dancing.

Burning for the sin of heresy was not only a punishment and a salvation combined, it was also a public entertainment; though victims were spared if they made full confessions, which were extracted by hanging the accused from prison walls with weighted feet, tearing their flesh and piercing their tongues, often while their children were forced to attend. Because Glasgow was an important religious centre, the excesses of the Reformation featured as prominently here as anywhere.

Glasgow's importance increased with its population, or *vice versa* and as it did, so did the importance of its presbytery. They obviously considered themselves to be of some consequence. Like most revolutionaries, they wanted the course of their revolution plotted, and there hardly seems to be anything too incidental to be excluded.

According to a decree of December 20, 1591, no one in Glasgow could be married until they had the consent of both parents, could

GLASGOW AS CINEMA CITY

Glaswegians' appetite for moving pictures is legendary within the industry. From the earliest days of the fairground bioscope shows at the Carnival ground in the Gallowgate, the population clamoured for more. Hastily converted skating rinks, theatres and churches were employed to show "the pictures".

As cinema became more respectable and attracted the attention of commercial interests the "picture palaces", purpose-built cinemas, began to spring up. One could have afternoon tea whilst watching the latest Hollywood weepie at the La Scala in Sauchiehall Street or, if you preferred to watch without the sounds of teaspoons clinking in saucers, the orchestra at the Vitagraph further along the street was deemed one of the finest in Glasgow.

The culmination of the rapid growth in cinema provision in the city, which at over 130 screens once boasted more cinemas per head of population than any other city in the UK, was heralded by the construction of Green's Playhouse in Renfield Street. At its opening in 1927, it was the largest cinema in Europe, seating 4,200 with provision for many more in the Geneva Tea Rooms, and upstairs in the rooftop ballroom.

The historical loyalty to the pictures on Clydeside is still evident today with UCI's multi-screen Clydebank 10 exceeding all box-office expectations. It is perhaps fitting that "Cinema City" should also boast one of the oldest surviving cinemas in the UK, the Hillhead Salon, refurbished to the standards of the Nineties, but still resplendent as a monument to the pioneering days of "the pictures".

Janet McBain

One of Singleton's Vogue cinemas, at Govan, in 1938.

The Paragon Cinema, a converted synagogue in Cumberland Street, Gorbals, which closed in 1955.

1. Oakley is also author of **The Second City**, 1946 **Arts and Crafts**

repeat the ten commandments, the articles of faith and the Lord's Prayer. Those who could not were not only single, but liable to censure. Six days after the deed was drawn up, flushed with the new law and desirous to find an example, they banned a wedding till the groom could perform the necessary tasks. When a fine of ten merks was paid, the banns were read.

The Cosmo Cinema by Andrew MacKenzie Delt.

THE LOST CHURCHES

The saddest losses of all in post-war Glasgow have been churches. Strangely enough, despite the fierce independence of many religious bodies, church and local authorities seem to have been unaware of the historical and architectural importance of their buildings, and rarely has there been a public outcry against the destruction of what were obviously important works of art.

The Park Church was an early example of a building in the new "High Church" manner, with many notable works of art contained within it. After some years of acrimonious debate it was demolished in 1969. As a compromise its tower was retained beside an office block of hideous mediocrity.

Anderston Parish Church was another tragic loss. Built in 1864–65, its Venetian Gothic style in the Ruskin tradition lent a certain exotic enchantment to the west end of St Vincent Street. Its interior, in bright primary colours, came as a surprise to those unprepared for this early experiment in improving both architecture and ceremonial.

The list is endless. St John's Parish Church, erected for the great Dr Chalmers in the impoverished East End – the Catholic Apostolic Church in McAslin Street, designed by the great Augustus Welby Pugin – Renfield Free Church at the corner of Bath Street and Elmbank Street, with its splendid octagonal tower – and Pollokshields Trinity Church, with an interior containing stained-glass, marble and woodwork unsurpassed in the city. And still the vandalism goes on – only look at the disintegrating hulk of Langside Hill Church at Battle Place.

Frank Worsdall

DOON THE WATTER, *by* Malky McCormick.

Chapter Five
ENTERTAINMENT

Partick wedding.

Model of the Temple of Solomon. A central symbol of freemasonry.

Chapter Six

ARTS AND CRAFTS

Newes from Scotland.

that hee did worke it by the Diuell, without whom it could neuer haue bæne so sufficientlye effected: and therupon, the name of the said Doctor Fien (who was but a very yong man) began to grow so common among the people of Scotland, that he was secretlye nominated for a notable Cuniurer.

Newes From Scotland tells the story of John Cunningham who supposedly plotted James VI's destruction at North Berwick Kirk with 100 other witches.

Andrew Brown wrote the third history of Glasgow, published in 1795. In it he claimed an alleged witch named Aitken came to Glasgow and accused several innocent women, or women who were subsequently considered innocent. They were burned "through the credulity of John Cooper, one of the ministers of the city". [1]

Women had a bad time of it. There are few examples of men being burned as sorcerers, though we may suppose it happened. Because of the Fall, the Garden of Eden and the Devil's known liking for women, it was assumed they would be more susceptible to his charms and advances. Most of the efforts to eradicate the Devil and his ways from Scottish life resulted in torturing women.

The Devil was the most potent symbol of the Reformation. The belief persisted; the tap root of Scottish mystery, magic and superstition is so deep that the sensibility prevailed when the rest of the 17th century was embracing science and mocking superstition.

George Sinclair was Professor of Experimental Philosophy at Glasgow University and author of a tract entitled *Satans Invisible World Discovered: Or, A choice Collection of Relations anent Devils, Spirits, Witches and Apparitions.* [2]

"Relation 1 Touching the Troubles which Sir George Maxwel of Pollok met with from the Devil and his Haggs" tells of Sir George of Pollok House falling seriously ill. Medical attention fails, but a young, dumb girl reveals that he is the victim of witchcraft. Eventually, a witch named Jennet Mathie and her two children, John and Annabil Stewart, are identified as the culprits and Sir George recovers.

Annabil Stewart testified that "in Harvest last, the Devil in the shape of a black man, had come to her Mothers house, and required the Deponent to give herself up to him," promising "any thing that was good". Annabil got a new coat and name; the Devil called her Annippy, having nipped her arm, which was sore for half an hour.

Sir George MacKenzie's *Law and Custom of Scotland in Matters Criminal*, published in 1678, shows the recently introduced practice of hanging witches, which gradually replaced burning.

1. Andrew Brown, History of Glasgow, 1795.
2. Published in "Pollok, 24 June, 1684"

The Devil lay with her in the bed, "under the Cloaths. That she found him cold. That thereafter he placed her nearest to himself." The black man had cloven feet and was present when an effigy was made.

Annabil is reprieved, but her mother is sentenced to be burnt at the stake. We are told that, in the meantime, both she, and her brother John, "did seriously exhort their Mother to confession, and with tears did Annabil put her in mind of the many Meetings she had with the Devil in her own house, and that a summers day would not be sufficient to relate what passages she had seen between the Devil and her. But nothing could prevail with her obdured and hardned heart.

"It is to be noted, the dumb Girle, whose name was Jennet Douglas doth now speak, not very distinctly, yet so as she may be understood, and is a Person that most wonderfully discovers things past, and doth also understand the Latine Tongue which she never learned". [1] Devil worship still flourishes on the fringes. An occult bookshop recently opened in Glasgow. [2]

Umberto Eco tells us that, "looking at the Middle Ages, means looking at our infancy, in the same way that a doctor, to understand our present state of health, asks us about our childhood, or in the same way that the psychoanalyst, to understand our present neuroses, makes a careful investigation of the primal scene." [3]

In addition to the supernatural, other medieval obsessions linger in the contemporary mind. Today we are obsessed with our bodies and our health. It was commonly assumed that the Scots had little to show for themselves in the arts of cooking. Yet Glasgow was an important market for fish and vegetables from the earliest time and by today's standards, diets were healthy. Common folk lived on oatcakes, peas and beans, and though fish was a fairly common dish, bread was sometimes a luxury. Meat was scarce and reserved for the gentry, who drank wine. Poor folk supped ale.

The oft-quoted Englishman Fynes Moryson, who travelled Scotland in 1598, gave life to the notion that Scottish cooking wasn't up to much. His remarks suggest he did not understand the customs and economy of the country, pretty well expecting what he was used to. "He was like a man", says the writer Annette Hope, "who, surrounded with good strawberries, raspberries and currants, complains that the peaches are sour and the oranges bitter". [4]

Contemporary with Moryson are reports that "surfeits killed more than sword and knife" and medical counsels of the time were largely directed against the perils of overeating.

A wee bit down the social scale from him were those who

ANTI-WOMEN LAWS

Until 1920 women in Scotland were in the position of minors throughout their lives, firstly under the guardianship of their fathers and then, if they married, under the guardianship of their husbands. This was justified, according to Baron Hume, by "obvious and sufficient reasons – to keep her free of the bustle and business of the world, which is not her sphere".

Several statutes were passed last century to give women more control over their own financial affairs but it was not until 1920 that the husband's right to administer his wife's estate was completely abolished. It was 1973 before women could become legal guardians of their own children. Even as late as 1986 husbands of women aged under 18 were their legal guardians, though married men under 18 were not considered minors.

It was not until 1976 that a husband's right to sue his wife's lover for damages was abolished, and the husband's right to decide what would be the marital home was not removed until as late as 1986, at the same time as other antiquated laws such as breach of promise for engagements were abolished.

Yet the past is also to some extend the present. Although married women now have equal rights in law and greater legal protection against violence, a recent *World in Action* study found that 44 per cent of married women interviewed in Scotland said they had been beaten by their husbands. The UK figure was 28 per cent. More than a third – 35 per cent – said they had been raped by their husbands.

Eveline Hunter

"A GUDE CAUSE MAKS A STRONG ARM"

1867 is a good starting point for Scottish Women's struggle for the vote. In that year John Stuart Mill, who was to publish his treatise *On the Subjection of Women* in 1869, proposed as an amendment to the Franchise Bill, then being debated in the House of Commons, that the word "person" should be substituted for the word "man". It was soundly defeated.

Many women, subsequently became converts to the campaigns of either the Women's Social and Political Union or the Women's Freedom League. The suffrage movement in Scotland received remarkable public support from male organisations. No less than 33 Town Councils, including Edinburgh, Glasgow and Dundee passed resolutions between 1910 and 1913 supporting women's suffrage. The Convention of Royal Burghs followed suit.

But the Government was unmoved and by 1913 the Scottish WSPU had launched a policy of disruption and violence. They started by destroying the contents of pillar boxes and then continued with arson. The authorities resorted to forcible feeding for women in prison on hunger strike. When the prisoners became too weak to stand any more they were released under the "Cat and Mouse" Act of 1913.

By the summer of 1914 suffragettes and government had reached an impasse. In these circumstances the outbreak of war in August came as something of a relief to both parties. Within weeks the Government was encouraging women to enter factory, farm and shipyard, to undertake heavy work for which they had previously been regarded as too frail. Within months barriers had fallen like ninepins.

The Representation of the People Act, the thin edge of the wedge, which granted the vote to some women over the age of 30 years was passed in January 1918.

Olive Checkland

1. ibid. **2.** Witchcraft stories make a fairly regular appearance in the local press, soothsayers abound and fringe bookshops usually have a selection of occult publications.
3. Umberto Eco, "The Return of the Middle Ages" in **Travels in Hyperreality**, 1986. **4.** Annette Hope, **A Caledonian Feast**, 1987.

Sixteenth century prints of Scottish men, women and soldiers as seen by an anonymous French traveller, artist and poet.

A silver cup donated to the University of Copenhagen by King James VI in 1590.

[1] "in cities also have wheaten bread, which for the most part was bought by Courtiers, Gentlemen and the best sort of Citizens". The King's Commission decree of 1602 regulated the diet of masters and students at Glasgow University. The masters' dinner consisted of white bread and good ale, a choice of soups, broth, kail or skink, a piece of boiled mutton and another of fresh or salted beef according to the season, two roasts, one of veal or mutton, the other of chicken, rabbit or pigeons. Students had oat bread, a dish of pease or broth, a dish of beef and a quart of ale between four. On meatless days, both groups got eggs and fish.

Forks were unknown and if there was a shortage of plates, slices of bread were used to hold the food. Pewter dishes and spoons were in common use, as were old wooden trenchers. Knives were seldom mentioned in household inventories since it was the custom for men to use those they carried around for general use. Food was brought to the mouth by the hand and politeness required only three fingers (the index, middle and thumb) be used. Cups and glasses were held in the same way and towels were provided. Each had their own napkin.

Maister Adam Colquhoun died at his house in Glasgow in February, 1542. He was described as an "ordinary Scottish priest", though he was a canon of Glasgow Cathedral and "persone of Stobo". The Stobo Manse was at the top of the Drygate.

The Glasgow chapter consisted of 32 canons or prebendaries with Stobo amongst the most desirable. The benefice brought in 2,000 merks a year.

A full description of his possessions survives, from which we can form a tolerably clear picture of what must have been a remarkable house. For Maister Adam was not short of this world's gear.

The bed he died on was richly carved, of wood and decorated with gold. The mattress had 140 lbs of feather down; sheets and pillows were of holland cloth, covered by a pair of fine fustian blankets. To ensure the parson's slumber, damask curtains "of divers hewis, fassit with silk and knoppit with gold" surrounded the bed, a covering of rich velvet, lined with fustian, stretched across his person and was spread with a blue mantle.

Panels of arras work hung round the walls, designed with foliage and flowers, varied with squirrels, monkeys or little rabbits disappearing into their burrows, "portraiture of huntsman, hawk and hound", scriptural scenes, or a secular romance. There were twelve varied panels, low toned tapestries, a large chandelier with tall white candles, an oak settle, a carved oak press, boxes of wood and silver for storing valuables, a silver water pot, sponge, rubber,

TRAVELLERS IN GLASGOW

[2] Cromwell came to Glasgow in 1650. When Pepys arrived with the Duke of York in 1662, the diarist thought it "a very extraordinary town for beauty and trade". Thomas de Quincey lived from 1841 to 1843 at 39 Renfield Street, and from January to October 1847 at 112 Rottenrow. Hans Andersen and Thackeray paid fleeting visits.

Dickens was delighted with his reception in 1847, when he came to open the old Athenaeum in Ingram Street. He gave readings in 1861, 1868 and 1869, the last time complaining of "the confounded mists from the Highlands and smoke from the factories . . . rains as it never does anywhere else". Conrad came seeking marine employment in 1898, while experiencing a temporary writer's block. He stayed with Dr John MacIntyre at 174 Bath Street, [3] watching his host demonstrate Röntgen rays on a screen by showing "the ribs and backbone" of the young Neil Munro.

Mendelssohn stayed on his return from his Highland tour in 1829. Paganini appeared twice during the 1830s. The 29 year old Liszt played in 1841, the dying Chopin in 1848, when the *Glasgow Herald* thought his music "frequently unintelligible." Caruso sang, causing "an epidemic" of enthusiasm in 1909 and had himself fitted for "Highland costume". Mrs Bellamy, Mrs Siddons, Mrs Jordan Kean and Sir Henry Irving trod the Glasgow boards. Balloonist Lunardi ascended from Glasgow in 1785, Blondin balanced his tightrope in 1861 and The Beatles arrived in 1964. Peel became Lord Rector of the University in 1837, Palmerston received the Freedom of the City in 1853, Gladstone in 1865.

Maurice Lindsay

1. ibid. **2.** ibid.
3. J Warrack, "The Wealth of the Church: A Pre-Reformation Manse" in **Domestic Life in Scotland**, 1920.

THE
CONSTITUTIONS
OF THE
FREE-MASONS.
CONTAINING THE
Hiſtory, Charges, Regulations, &c.
of that moſt Ancient and Right
Worſhipful *FRATERNITY.*

For the Uſe of the LODGES.

LONDON:
Printed by WILLIAM HUNTER, for JOHN SENEX at the *Globe*, and JOHN HOOKE at the *Flower-de-luce* over-against *St. Dunſtan's Church*, in *Fleet-ſtreet*.

In the Year of Maſonry —— 5723
Anno Domini —— —— 1723

Title page and frontispiece of the *Constitution of the Freemasons*, printed in London in 1723.

combs, and the parson's pet, a parrot. There was an enormous quantity of jewellery, crosses, rings and chains made from gold and sapphires, valued at hundreds of pounds.

There were no clerical vestments, but the Parson of Stobo was distinguishable by his silk clothes, damask shirts, sable furs, velvet shoes, golden pins, buttons and a silver toothpick in a bag at his waist.

Holland cloths surrounded the altar. There were gold and silver sacred vessels and a silver cushion for the "mess buke", hand-penned in black and red Gothic lettering, illuminated with rich colours and golden foils. There was also a substantial library of holy and secular books, similarly made.

There were 40 separate silver vessels, silver bottles, silver carving knives and a fork, used for eating fruit. The cupboard abounded in silver plate and the kitchen, though fairly bare of furniture, was crammed with utensils, pots, jars, bottles and plates; oven and bakehouse paraphernalia; brewing requisites; a barn of wheat, oats, "beir", pease and hay, eight carcasses of salted beef, eight dozen salmon, forty bolls of meal, eight dozen Loch Fyne herring, six stone of butter, 22lbs of cheese and eight loads of coal.

The stable accoutrements were of silver, wood and velvet. He had a fully carved suit of armour and swords. His sport was archery. He had silken dog leads and silver studded collars. Maister Adam also had a striking clock.

Scotland was reputedly a poor country, though Glasgow was seldom described as a poor city and certainly not around Maister Adam's time. No one liked the climate and how the priest's velvet boots fared in Glasgow's winters is not recorded. "The sky is foul with frequent rain and clouds," wrote Tacitus around AD80, chronicling the life of his father-in-law Julius Agricola, governor of Britain. "The length of their days is beyond the measure of our world . . . If clouds do not hinder they say the sun's brightness is seen all night, and nor sets nor rises but passes across the sky".[1] When the French soldiers came over in 1385 to march against the English, they asked, "What could have brought us hither? We have never known till now what was meant by poverty and hard living". They told a joke and repeated it till the 19th century; when the Devil led Christ to the highest mountain, showing him all the glories of the world, "he keepit his meikle thoomb on Scotland". In the 19th century the joke was adapted to Russia.

So why did they come here? Money, power, land, dreams; the same reasons anyone goes anywhere. And work. Glasgow's first immigrant workers were the stonemasons and craftsmen who came

THE GLASGOW STYLE

The name of Charles Rennie Mackintosh is now internationally renowned. He did not work in a vacuum, however. Numerous other designers, craftworkers, teachers and architects contributed to the upsurge of progressive artistic activity in Glasgow in the early years of this century. Many of them deserve more widespread recognition, such as George Walton, Talwin Morris, Jessie Newbery, Ernest Taylor, Jessie King, John Ednie, George Logan or Ann Macbeth.

What bound those involved together was some form of training or contact with the Glasgow School of Art and its energetic leader, Francis Newbery. In the 1890s a distinctive Glasgow Style was forged – co-ordinated interiors and a wide range of decorative arts characterised by simple elongated forms, sleek surfaces, neutral or muted colours (particularly mauves, pinks and greens), and highly stylised motifs derived from plant life and emaciated human forms. It represented an idiosyncratic synthesis of Scottish elements with touches of continental *Art Nouveau*, symbolistic feeling and the English Arts and Crafts movement.

The experimental work of the 1890s had been produced for a small network of intimates. Before long, however, large furnishing stores such as Wylie & Lochead were promoting a tamer version of such designs to a much broader, middle class clientele. The Glasgow Style proved to be an important and socially acceptable vehicle for the talents of many middle class women, who worked as teachers or set up small craft studios in the city which lasted well into the 1930s.

Juliet Kinchin

1. Quoted by Agnes Mure Mackenzie in **Scottish Pageant**, 1946, from Tacitus' **Life of Julius Agricola**.

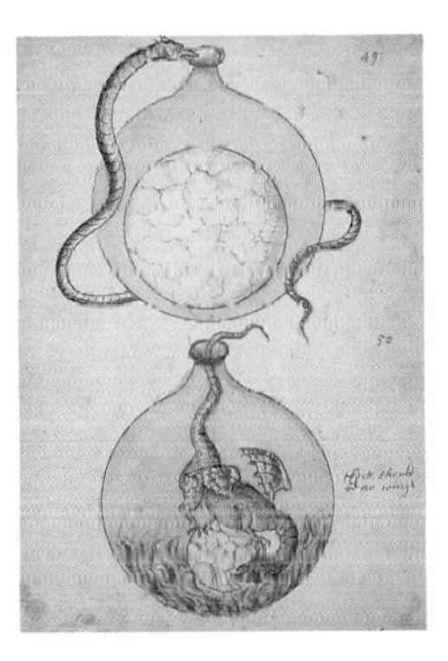

Evolution through Alchemy. The woman becomes a dragon and Christ emerges from the fire, from the 17th century *Emblemata, seu Hieroglyphica*.

to work on the Cathedral. Moving round the country, stone masons evolved their own identifiable signs and rituals, symbols which made them recognisable to each other and excluded the cowans, or non-skilled workers.

Medieval masons were responsible for some of the greatest, most visible achievements of the civilisation, the great cathedrals, castles and churches that must have dominated their landscapes. The 19th and 20th centuries have shrunk Glasgow Cathedral, but its location, scale and proportions must previously have made heroes of the men who built it.

From the late 17th century onwards, the masonic order was augmented by speculative, or non-working, members. They were quite often gentlemen interested in deistic ideas, who used the order as a shield, finding its older mythologies compatible with Enlightenment ideologies.

Freemasonry fitted snugly into the main ideal of the Enlightenment, the quest towards a more liberal culture where aristocrats, middle class thinkers and artists could meet on an egalitarian level, discussing the great topics of the time. This was what appealed to Robert Burns, to Wolfgang Amadeus Mozart, and the Venetian soldier, spy, gambler, poet, raconteur and prolific autobiographer Giacomo Casanova, who belonged to the Grande Lodge Ecossaise.[1]

In fact, the freemason's liberalism was so strong and posed such a threat, that in the years following 1789, propagandists of the old order put it about that masons were responsible for the French Revolution.

The spread and appeal of freemasonry meant it became the inevitable society for the professions and higher administrative posts. As architects became more involved with the bureaucratic planning of cities, masonic influence grew. Stone laying ceremonies in Glasgow around this time hint at the effect freemasonry had on public works.

The Broomielaw Bridge had been built in 1768, but the Town Council discovered that better facilities generated more traffic, so the Bridge Trustees removed the old structure and erected a new, cased in Aberdeen granite, 560 feet long, 60 feet wide with seven arches across the Clyde, all costing £34,000 with an extra £4,000 for additional ground. It was one of the widest river bridges in the country.

The foundation stone was laid by James Ewing, Glasgow's Lord Provost, on September 3, 1833, with full masonic honours. A contemporary document describes the event. "At the site of the

EARLY GLASGOW PAINTERS

The earliest painters we know of in Glasgow were not practising "fine art" but, like the 16th century James Scott, Painter-Burgess of the city, painted coats of arms or, like John Scougall and his son George in the next century, were employed to copy portraits by foreign artists, at 20 shillings a face, by Glasgow University and the Patrons of Hutchesons' Hospital.

Glasgow, however, can boast the first seriously organised school of art in Britain, set up by the brothers Foulis in 1753. But, maybe because the Academy paid its students apprentice wages and subsidised study visits to Italy for the most gifted, it failed to survive more than 20 years. Its alumni included James Tassie and the painter David Allan.

Alexander Nasmyth, the pioneer Scottish landscape painter in the Claudian manner, had a slight connection with Glasgow, having painted an act scene of the Clyde at Dumbarton for the original Theatre Royal. Nasmyth, in his turn was the teacher, so it is said, of John Knox whose reputation largely depends on the panoramic views in Glasgow's municipal collection.

To the studio of Knox J, Teacher of Drawing, at 40 Dunlop Street, came Daniel McNee and Horatio McCulloch, as students. Of these McNee would become one of the leading portrait painters in Scotland (his advice led the young William McTaggart to a career in art) while McCulloch grew to be the dominating figure in mid-19th century Scottish landscape painting with his grand views of loch and mountain scenery. Another popular landscape artist was Sam Bough who began his career painting theatrical scenery.

Cordelia Oliver

1. John Masters, Casanova, 1969.

Bridge a spacious platform and gallery were fitted up to contain 3,000 persons. The floor of a large enclosure on the platform, surrounding the Foundation Stone, was carpeted, and the parapets were covered with crimson cloth . . . The Grand Treasurer deposited a Glass Bottle hermetically sealed, containing Specimens of all the current Gold, Silver, and Copper Coins of the present Reign . . . The Grand Secretary deposited another Glass Bottle hermetically sealed, containing Records, &c".[1]

These Records must be the fullest account of what life was like in Glasgow, how the city was growing and how they saw themselves. The Act of Parliament for erecting the Bridge is there with a Glasgow Post Office Directory and ten Glasgow newspapers. There is a detailed population list, including a comparison with 1768, when the original bridge was built, and a note of the progressive population increase from 1560. The number of births, marriages, burials, families and the percentage of the population they comprise is recorded: "The population consists of 163,600 Scotch, 35,554 Irish, 2,919 English and 353 Foreigners; of whom 104,162 persons are of the Established Church, 71,299 are Seceders, Dissenters, or Episcopalians, and 26,965 Roman Catholics".

And Glasgow had 5,006 Paupers: "The sum expended for their maintenance or relief, £17,281 18s. ½d, shows the cost of each Pauper to be £3 9s. ½d. If this sum for the relief of Paupers were paid equally by the whole non-recipient population, the proportion to each would be rather more than 1s.9d. The sum of £17,281 18s. ½d includes the entire expenditure of the out and in-door Paupers, Surgeon's salaries, medicines, clothing, and educating children, maintaining Lunatics, Funeral charges &c". Finally, "there are about 32,000 Hand Loom Weavers working for Glasgow manufacturers. The number of Hand Looms was ascertained in August, 1819, during a period of distress among the working population".

What the depository does not tell us is equally interesting. This highly selective view of the city misses, amongst many other things, the fact that in 1832 Glasgow lost 1.4 per cent of its population, more than 4,000 people, in a cholera and typhus epidemic that lingered and returned with a vengeance in 1834.[2]

At the site of the present Albert Bridge, built in 1870, the Clyde was once spanned by Hutcheson's Bridge. Its foundation stone too was laid, in 1829, with mystic ceremonial. At the dinner which followed, one speaker referred to "mystic rites on the Clyde", which he squared with Christianity, and discussed egalitarian principles.[1] Meanwhile Glasgow's squalor and poverty was being internationally

TYPHUS

Of the great 19th century infections to hit Glasgow, the greatest killer was typhus fever. Transmitted by the body louse, and exacerbated by overcrowding and poor hygiene, typhus first visited the city in 1818, "following on stagnation of trade in 1816–17". Further epidemics regularly afflicted Glasgow until the 1870s, reaching a peak in 1847 when more than 4,340 Glaswegians fell victim. That year, the Royal Infirmary launched a public appeal to build a new fever hospital, spearheaded by its "indefatigable Treasurer", James Lumsden. As the founder some ten years earlier of the Clydesdale Bank, Lumsden knew about fund raising.

While typhus is now associated in the minds of 20th century observers with squalor and poverty, it took a particularly heavy toll of doctors and nurses during the last century. Dr Roget, of *Thesaurus* fame, was one of the lucky ones to survive an attack, during his medical student days in Edinburgh Royal Infirmary. Possibly the most poignant case was that of Dr James Armour, who died in 1831 while serving as Secretary of the Glasgow Medical Society. Touched by the plight of his mother, widow and family, the members of the Society voted to contribute £20 – almost half its total assets – to help in their hour of need.

Perhaps spurred by this tragedy, one of Armour's fellow members, Dr Robert Perry, intensified his study of typhus fever, becoming one of the first clinicians to distinguish typhus from typhoid, the latter being a water-borne disease with similar symptoms but a totally different mode of transmission.

Derek A Dow

No. 1.
CHOLERA MIXTURE.
A table-spoonful, with 60 drops of laudanum, in half a wine-glassful of cold water. If this fail to relieve, repeat two tea-spoonfuls, with 30 drops of laudanum every half hour.
Half these doses of mixture and laudanum for children of 14. One-fourth for children of 7.
Do not exceed the doses prescribed; and stop when the vomiting and cramps cease, unless you have medical advice.

No. 3.
CHOLERA PILLS.
To be used if the mixture No. 1 be vomited. Two pills at first, and then one every half hour if the first fail to relieve. Half these doses for children of 14; one-fourth for children of 7.
Do not exceed the doses prescribed; and stop when the vomiting and cramps cease, unless you have medical advice.

No. 4.
CHOLERA CLYSTERS.
Inject three tea-spoonfuls in a wine-glassful of thin warm gruel; and retain as long as possible by pressure below with a warm cloth. If not retained, repeat immediately, but otherwise not.
Half the dose for children of 14; one-fourth for children of 7.

No. 5.
MUSTARD FOR POULTICES.
A fourth part is enough for one person. Dust it thickly over porridge poultices, of which apply a large one on the belly, and others on the soles and calves. Remove when the patient complains much of the smarting.

"Cures" for cholera were desperately sought.

Bishop Rae's Bridge at the foot of Stockwell Street around 1845.

1. An Account of the Grand Masonic Procession and Laying the Foundation Stone of the Broomielaw Bridge, 1833.
2. Sir Alexander McGregor, Public Health in Glasgow, 1905–1946, 1967.

THE GEORGIAN CITY – ABBOTSFORD PLACE

The one district of Glasgow which is known worldwide is the Gorbals. Development started on the south side of the River Clyde in the 1790s, and in 1801 James Laurie, a city merchant, feued the central area to form a high-class residential suburb. With typical modesty he named it Laurieston, and commissioned the eminent London architect Peter Nicholson to lay it out and design the earliest buildings. These took the form of a riverside terrace called Carlton Place, still standing and forming the most attractive part of a much underrated amenity.

The development was characterised by wide streets flanked by four storey tenements in variation of the Italian palazzo style. The main north-south thoroughfare was 80 foot wide, and named Portland Street, while other streets were similarly called after members of the English aristocracy. Laurie Street was the name reserved for that in the very heart of the development. However, when building began in 1831 the name was inexplicably changed to Abbotsford Place.

The dignified unified frontage of nos. one to 47 was the finest part of the whole scheme. It was punctuated by projecting Ionic and Corinthian porches, while the end and centre pavilions were crowned by balustrades. The houses were large, averaging seven apartments, with only one on each upper landing, and were very popular with the new and increasingly prosperous mercantile class. The back elevation with its range of 14 circular brick stair towers formed one of the most impressive architectural features in the city. They were demolished in 1972.

Frank Worsdall

recognised. Such references still occur, for, as we have said before, mythology runs deep. "So well were the old masons masters of their jobs", writes a well known and honoured Glasgow historian[2] praising the building of the first stone bridge across the Clyde at the foot of Stockwell Street.

Despite their craftsmanship, great Glasgow landmarks have often proved ephemeral. Of the Bishop's Castle, only the name Castle Street survives; and nothing remains of the first Royal Infirmary building, completed in 1792 and designed by Robert Adam. By the beginning of this century that building was too small and work began on the new hospital in 1904. Parts were demolished and rebuilt, a few extensions were added and the hospital's most famous ward was removed altogether.

Today, a plaque in the High Street indicates the site where Sir[3] Joseph Lister revolutionised the medical world of the 1860s with his demonstrations of antiseptic surgery, which "saved a number of lives that has been calculated to be greater than all the wars of the 19th century had sacrificed".[4]

The preservation and conservation of important buildings came later to Glasgow and the demolition of the Lister Ward was simply an extension of the city's official vandalism. Protests from all over the world were ignored, but a single brick from the ward is on show in New York's Rochester University and a replica of the ward, built from the Glasgow scrap heap, stands as a permanent memorial to Lister in the Wellcome Medical Museum in London.

The same improvers thought it would enhance the Cathedral's appearance to remove the two medieval square towers from the western end of the building. Impressive though the Cathedral is today, drawings and etchings commissioned before 1840 leave one in no doubt that its importance as a place of worship and ecclesiastical centre were clearer in the past.

When they scraped the grime from Glasgow's buildings, some were found to be worth preserving. Glasgow has been viewed as a perfect deconstructionist landscape and it's easy to see why; another way of looking at it would be to say that the city is constantly renewing itself, but the fine buildings that disappeared made way for motorways, link roads, high rise flats, shopping centres and office blocks. Planners have done more to deconstruct our city than the Luftwaffe and it took a long time for the course to be reversed. The irony is that this belated preservation has helped change the city's image from a declining wasteland to the most magnificent Victorian city in Europe.

The Cathedral ground has supposedly been sacred for 1600 years.

Demolishing the Old Bridge in 1850.

Building the King George V Bridge at the foot of Oswald Street in 1925.

1. An Account of the Grand Masonic Procession and laying the Foundation Stone of the Hutchesons' Bridge, 1829. 2. C.A. Oakley, The Second City, 1946. 3. Though the foundations were recently revealed during an archaeological dig. 4. Nation, February 17, 1912.

MURDER BALLADS

It is very difficult to keep a good song within the bounds of the city where it originated; it is equally difficult to restrain a sensational story. So it is not surprising to find that Glaswegians sang of murderers from anywhere: Corder, Palmer, Buck Ruxton. And people elsewhere sang of Glasgow murderers; songs about Pritchard the poisoner, who was hanged in 1864, have been collected in oral tradition in Aberdeenshire and Orkney a 100 years later. Madeleine Smith was also featured in several broadside ballads, including a standard "Lament" in which the murderess is supposed to repent her misdeeds.

The strangest production of the flying stationers, however, was the "Sandyford Sensation", a *comic* medley on the Jessie McLachlan case. This was the "Glasgow Murder" which caused Norwegian writer A.O. Vinje to despair of the jury system, and deplore trial by the press. The song takes the popular view that Jessie was innocent and the villain was old Fleming:

Though old Fleming got clear of the law
From the public he has got many a claw,
For they swear that he got off by a hoax,
And they hunt him for a sly old fox.

The songsheets also preserve memories of less celebrated cases such as "the Gallowgate Murder", when Thomas Barr stabbed his wife and her mother, or "the Bishopbriggs Murder", when a domineering railway ganger was waylaid by some of his men.

Adam McNaughtan

St Ninian is said to have planted a cross and blessed the ground for Christian burial in 397. Though the Cathedral survives and the Royal Infirmary exists in name at least, most of the rest has gone.

In the same area, Glasgow children of indeterminate age will remember singing:

> There is a happy land down in the Duke Street Jail,
> Where all the convicts stand tied tae a rail;
> Ham and eggs they never see
> Dirty watter for their tea
> There they live in misery
> God save the Queen.

And Morris Blythman, who was sometimes known as Thurso Berwick, added a verse, so perfect that it is now inseperable from the original which inspired it.

> But noo the Corporation's cam wi a great big plan
> Tae build multi-storeyed tenements on the happy land
> There's 17 murderers buried there
> So watch it missus going up the stair
> Or a haun'll come oot and grab ye by the hair.
> God save the Queen.[1]

The happy land of Duke Street Jail faced the Infirmary across Cathedral Square. The prison entrance used to be in Duke Street, though it was later transferred to Cathedral Square after an incident which caused Duke Street Jail to feature in another song, an Irish Republican piece called "The Smashing of the Van".

In 1921 a number of Sinn Feiners were sprung from a Black Maria going up the High Street. A detective was killed in the process and there are still bullet holes in what's left of the Duke Street Prison Wall.

The second verse of the Duke Street Jail song celebrates the smashing of the prison and the construction of what is now known as Ladywell housing estate. Children play on the steps the hangman took to the gallows and the tree, which was the only view of the outside world to be seen from the condemned cell window, is still growing. The location of unmarked graves of the murderers who were hanged in the prison is supposed to be a secret, though I have met a couple of folk who have pointed out different sites. There are sets of initials carved into the wall behind High Street.

Facing Cathedral Square is a little miracle of survival known as Provand's Lordship. This is the oldest house in Glasgow and

The eastern wall of Duke Street prison by Muirhead Bone.

1. **Rebels Ceilidh Songbook**, undated.

GLASGOW'S VISITORS

"Glasgow is a city of business; here is the face of trade," wrote Daniel Defoe in 1726, and the result of its trade and growing wealth was that it was "a very fine city". Seventy years earlier, Cromwell's commissioner, Thomas Tucker, sent to report on the economic state of the city, spoke of the "mercantile genius of the people" and foresaw great growth if only they could dredge the shallow Clyde – which of course they did.

When the Quaker evangelist George Fox came to preach in Glasgow in 1657, "none of the town's people came". Were they too busy making money? Fox was used to persecution, but not to indifference. What a strange city!

Glasgow did turn out in force to hear Lajos Kossuth, the Hungarian national hero who visited Britain to drum up support after his defeat in 1849; before he came to address a packed City Hall, the police had rounded up local radicals whose enthusiasm for the republican cause might prove infectious.

It was another very Glaswegian moment when Queen Victoria came to visit the Cathedral, and the University Principal who was her guide paused at the gates to draw her attention not to the Cathedral facade but to Tennant's Stalk, the huge chimney of the chemical works at Sighthill, which was, as the Queen noted with awe in her Journal, "the highest I believe in existence".

Edwin Morgan

the city's second oldest building after the Cathedral. Provand's Lordship was built some 20 years after Glasgow University was founded, in, or around 1471, by Bishop Andrew Muirhead whose armorial bearings, three acorns on a bend, can still be traced on the lowest corbie stone of the south gable.

Originally attached to the Hospital of St Nicholas, patron saint of the sick, founded by the bishop to support twelve old and poor men, it was renamed Provand's Lordship when it became the town house of the Canon of Barlanark, whose rectory was known as the Lordship of Provan. Each canon had a prebendary, or an income from church lands, and with this title went 2,000 acres stretching from Cowlairs to Bishop Loch in Easterhouse.

When James IV was enrolled as a Prebend of Glasgow Cathedral, it was as Prebend of Barlanark. He was the first of our monarchs to stay at Provand's Lordship; his grand-daughter Mary, Queen of Scots, is said to have been the other. In 1562 Mary confirmed by charter that the church's lands now belonged to William Baillie and Provand's Lordship became his. It was during his time that the house's association with Mary and the notorious Casket Letters was fostered.

Mary came to Glasgow in 1567 to visit the ailing Darnley. Provand's Lordship was near to where Darnley was staying; Mary is reported to have visited her husband often during her short stay. Then she took him back with her to Edinburgh. Her concern for his welfare was suspected when he was blown up at Kirk o'Field and further questioned, when Mary married Bothwell three months later. When Mary was imprisoned in England, Elizabeth wanted to know why the Scots lords had rebelled against her cousin. The Lords produced the Casket Letters.

Their authenticity has always been in doubt, but if the surviving copies are genuine, they suggest that Mary not only had a liaison with Bothwell, but was party to a plot to kill her husband Darnley. If Mary did write the letters, the most incriminating pieces were composed in Provand's Lordship, assuming that was where she stayed. The letters supposedly exist in transcript and translation, but for more than 300 years, neither the letters nor the silver box which reputedly contained them has been seen.

After William Baillie's death, the house passed through a succession of owners until 1716, when the Town Council took it over. For a while in the 17th century it belonged to a wealthy tailor, William Brysone, who added an extension to the west side. He marked the renovation with a stone marked 1670 and for years this was thought to be the original date of the property.

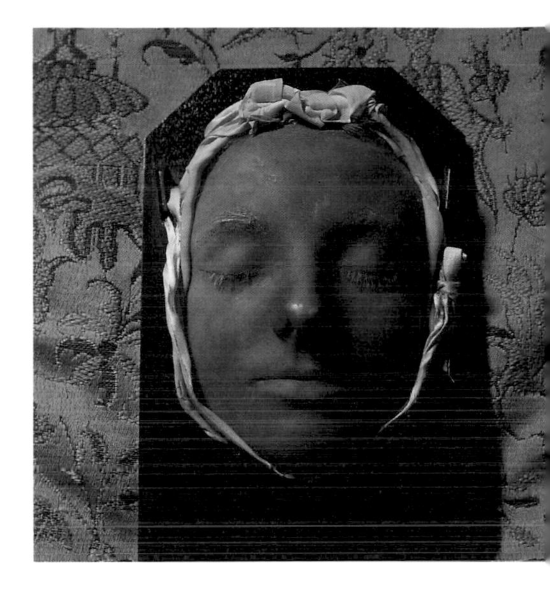

Mary's death mask. Following her death, at the age of 44, her admirers turned her into the saintly figure she had never been in life.

The Earl of Bothwell's remains. He died in a prison in Dragsholm, Zeeland, having been jailed for abandoning a woman he married there in 1560. His remains are now a tourist attraction.

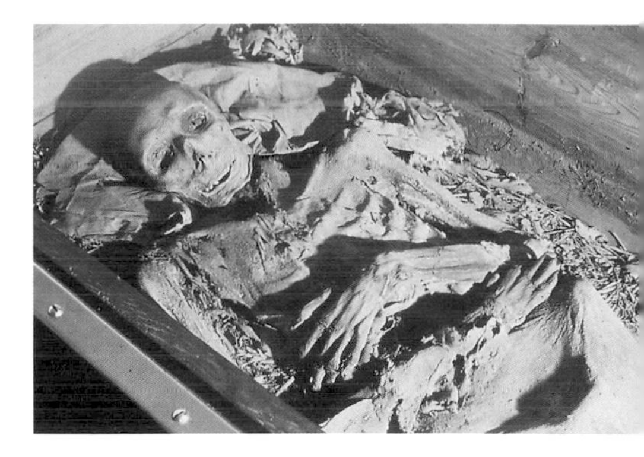

CRIMEAN SIMPSON (1823–99)

The first British war artist, familiarly known as Crimean Simpson, was a Glasgow man, the classic case of a poor boy with little official education, who rose to fame, if not to fortune, through his own efforts.

William Simpson's training in illustration was gained with a Glasgow firm of lithographers, Allan and Fergusson, which he joined as a boy of 14 and later in London where he made scenic impressions of the Great Exhibition for the firm of Day and Son. By October 1854 he was well enough known to be commissioned by Colnaghi's to make an on-the-spot visual report of the Crimean war in a series of drawings later published in two volumes of lithographs with the title, *The Seat of War in the East*.

Simpson held that war must not be romanticised. The range of his painstaking work mirrored the range of his observations, from the grand drama of burning buildings and lurid, smoke-filled skies, to the intimate details of human misery and occasional triumphs.

Much of Simpson's later life was spent as a roving reporter for the *Illustrated London News*, recording such different events as the Paris Commune and the Wedding of the Chinese Emperor (both in 1877). A major project, on which he spent many years, was the making of a visual record of mid-19th century India. The publishers, Day and Son, went bankrupt, but a volume of sorts was produced, and many of the original paintings and drawings remain as evidence of a remarkable, adventurous, colourful career.

Cordelia Oliver

In the 18th century, a lean-to was tagged on to the corner and this was where the town executioner stayed. Watty was the best known hangman of this time, or at any rate the busiest. Executions were carried out in what is now Cathedral Square, so the place was handy for the man's work, as well as being up the road from the Tolbooth Jail.

Things went from bad to worse and early in the nineteenth century Provand's Lordship became a public house. A drawing by William "Crimean" Simpson,[1] from 1843, shows Provand's Lordship as a dilapidated pub.

The Royal Infirmary extensions of 1904 threatened Provand's Lordship and when the place was offered for sale, a few citizens formed the Provand's Lordship Society. They bought the building, demolished Watty's lean-to and set about a renovation. It is thanks to their efforts and perseverance that the place is intact today.

By this time it was three shops – a sweetie shop, a greengrocer and a barber. Mrs Innes kept her sweetie shop till 1920 and the greengrocer and barber went eight years later. The last tenant was Isaac Morton who ran an aerated water factory.

Glasgow's other associations with Mary Queen of Scots are much less tenuous and are to be found on the south side of the city. The night before she fought at Langside in May, 1568, she stayed at Castlemilk House, where she is supposed to have planted a tree, demolished along with the building in 1969. Mary watched the battle from the Court Knowe of Cathcart Castle, which is now part of Linn Park. Her forces were stationed at Clincart Hill, where Langside College now stands, and the opposing army, led by her half brother,the Earl of Moray, Regent of Scotland, stood on a higher hill with better coverage, where now we find the granite steps of Queen's Park (named after Victoria).

The battle began at nine in the morning and was over by a quarter to ten. Mary's forces were commanded by the fifth Earl of Argyll whose military skills were hampered both by epilepsy and a sympathy for his brother in law, the Earl of Moray.

The Langside memorial was built in May 1887, before the district became part of Glasgow. It was designed by Alexander Skirving who lived in the village and worked in Glasgow as Alexander "Greek" Thomson's chief draughtsman. So, too, was the Langside Free Church, which decays beside the memorial.

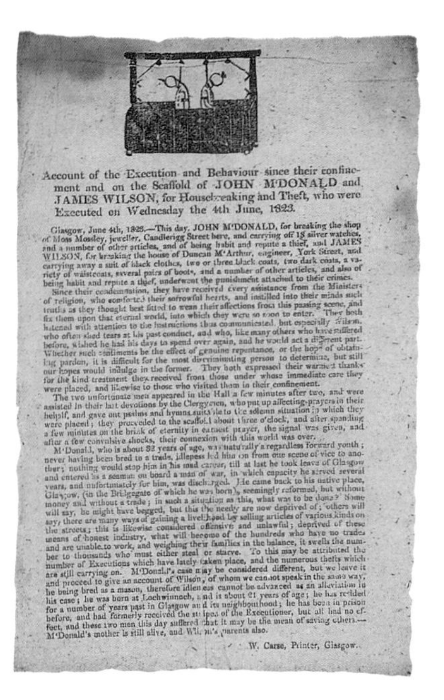

Account of the Execution and Behaviour since their confinement and on the Scaffold of JOHN M'DONALD and JAMES WILSON, for Housebreaking and Theft, who were Executed on Wednesday the 4th June, 1823.

Glasgow, June 4th, 1823.—This day, JOHN M'DONALD, for breaking the shop of Moss Mosdey, jeweller, Candleriggs Street here, and carrying off 18 silver watches, and a number of other articles, and of being habit and repute a thief, and JAMES WILSON, for breaking the house of Duncan M'Arthur, engineer, York Street, and carrying away a suit of black clothes, two or three black coats, two dark coats, a variety of waistcoats, several pairs of boots, and a number of other articles, and also of being habit and repute a thief, underwent the punishment attached to their crimes.

Since their condemnation, they have received every assistance from the Ministers of religion, who comforted their sorrowful hearts, and instilled into their minds such truths as they thought best fitted to wean their affections from this passing scene, and fix them upon that eternal world, into which they were so soon to enter. They both listened with attention to the instructions thus communicated, but especially Wilson, who often shed tears at his past conduct, and who, like many others who have suffered before, wished he had his days to spend over again, and he would act a different part. Whether such sentiments be the effect of genuine repentance, or the hope of obtaining pardon, it is difficult for the most discriminating person to determine, but still our hopes would indulge in the former. They both expressed their warmest thanks for the kind treatment they received from those under whose immediate care they were placed, and likewise to those who visited them in their confinement.

The two unfortunate men appeared in the Hall a few minutes after two, and were assisted in their last devotions by the Clergymen, who put up affecting prayers in their behalf, and gave out psalms and hymns suitable to the solemn situation in which they were placed; they proceeded to the scaffold about three o'clock, and after spending a few minutes on the brink of eternity in earnest prayer, the signal was given, and after a few convulsive shocks, their connexion with this world was over.

M'Donald, who is about 32 years of age, was naturally a regardless forward youth; never having been bred to a trade, idleness led him on from one scene of vice to another; nothing would stop him in his mad career, till at last he took leave of Glasgow and entered as a seaman on board a man of war, in which capacity he served several years, and unfortunately for him, was discharged. He came back to his native place, Glasgow, (in the Bridgegate of which he was born), seemingly reformed, but without money and without a trade; in such a situation as this, what was to be done? Some will say, he might have begged, but this the needy are now deprived of; others will say, there are many ways of gaining a livelihood by selling articles of various kinds on the streets; this is likewise considered offensive and unlawful; deprived of these means of honest industry, what will become of the hundreds who have no trades and are unable to work, and weighing their families in the balance, it swells the number to thousands who must either steal or starve. To this may be attributed the number of Executions which have lately taken place, and the numerous thefts which are still carrying on. M'Donald's case may be considered different, but we leave it and proceed to give an account of Wilson, of whom we cannot speak in the same way, he being bred as a mason, therefore idleness cannot be advanced as an alleviation in his case; he was born at Lochwinnoch, and is about 21 years of age; he has resided for a number of years past in Glasgow and its neighbourhood; he has been in prison before, and had formerly received the stripes of the Executioner, but all had no effect, and these two men this day suffered that it may be the mean of saving others.—M'Donald's mother is still alive, and Wilson's parents also.

W. Carse, Printer, Glasgow.

Before mounting the gallows McDonald and Wilson, executed publicly on June 4, 1823, "expressed their warmest thanks for the kind treatment they received".

1. Simpson earned his nickname as the first war artist.

Chapter Six

ARTS AND CRAFTS

"The Execution of Mary Queen of Scots" by Robert Herdman, painted in 1867.

"Port Glasgow Cemetery" by Sir Stanley Spencer. It was to inspire his "Resurrection" paintings.

Chapter Seven
CITY OF THE DEAD

John Knox glowers over Glasgow from the City of the Dead.

The Necropolis was the city's first planned cemetery and the Glasgow Victorians' finest monument to themselves. Prince Albert was very impressed and thought it a delightful sight; it was L.S. Lowry's favourite city haunt.

The model was Père Lachaise, which itself was adapted from a Parisian Jesuit's garden, and a garden was what Glasgow's planners had in mind. It was intended to enhance the Cathedral and "afford a much wanted accommodation to the higher classes [and] convert an unproductive property into a general and lucrative source of profit".[1]

In 1804, the Scots firs in the Fir Park were dying, almost certainly from industrial pollution. The Merchants' House, who owned the park, replaced them with bowers of elm and willow, turning Fir Park into a kind of Victorian pleasure garden. In 1825, they laid the foundation stone of the John Knox statue.

John Knox's statue in the Necropolis

It scowls at the city, 225 feet above the Clyde, from what was said to be the best view of the area. Even now it is impressive, despite the high rise flats, the motorways and the parallel lines of the Royal Infirmary extension.

Work began to convert the Fir Park into a cemetery in 1832, and in that September, the Necropolis had its first customer, Joseph Levi, a Jewish quill merchant who died of cholera.

By the beginning of the 1830s, Glasgow's population had almost trebled since the turn of the century. Irish and Highlanders flooded into the city, many with little more than the clothes they stood in, and housed themselves in areas which could not support them. They had no choice but to live in appalling conditions. Five thousand people a year died in the cholera, fever and typhus epidemics and most of them were buried in the already overcrowded churchyards, a practice which was considered "revolting to human nature" and "destructive to the health of the living".[2]

1. John Strang, **Necropolis Glasguensis** or **Thoughts on Death and Moral Stimulus**, 1831. **2.** Quoted in **The Glasgow Necropolis Heritage Trail Guide**, 1985.

Earlier, Robert Graham, the Lord Provost of Glasgow, had warned against burying anyone who had died in the Royal Infirmary in the Cathedral's new burying ground. The pit there was covered by a few planks "and the stench emitted in hot weather was insufferable". Previously, burial outside a churchyard had been reserved for the unbaptised, the murderers and the lunatics of the parish. The new middle classes however, wanted to protect themselves from the dangers of epidemic and infection in a place where visitors would be inspired with "a laudable ambition to imitate and emulate" the lives of those buried in the bosky dells which became the Necropolis.

Many interesting people are grandly remembered here, though we sometimes have to read between the lines on their tombstones to find what made them notable, apart, of course, from their money. The tombstones do tell, with stunning accuracy, what their occupants expected to find on the other side.

John Henry Alexander's tomb is a sculpted stage, with footlights and curtains. Alexander was actor and owner manager of the Theatre Royal in Dunlop Street where 65 people were trampled or suffocated to death in 1849 when a false fire alarm was raised. Alexander and his company tried to prevent the carnage, but he never recovered from the experience and died three years later. He is credited with inventing the Great Gun Trick, where a member of the audience fires a loaded rifle at the conjurer's head and the conjurer catches the marked bullet between his teeth.[1]

Vandalism and weather have almost ruined William Motherwell's memorial, erected by his friends 16 years after his death and occasionally remembered by a friend who on the anniversary of the poet's death, marked the spot with a card on which was written a quotation from his verse.[2]

Another Glasgow poet is remembered in the Necropolis, though his body lies in Tollcross Cemetery. Everyone knows William Miller's work, though they have never heard of him. His memorial refers to the Laureate of the Nursery. Miller wrote "Wee Willie Winkie" and everybody can recite the first verse.

The City of the Dead was intended to be non-denominational. In fact, the Merchants' House went out of its way to make this aspect as appealing as possible. Catholics could sleep "in a spot associated with the name of the Holy Virgin", said their promotional material. Jews could "slumber in a cave . . . Lutherans could lie among nature . . . Quakers could lie in sequestered nooks and strict Presbyterians could obtain graves around the column which proclaims the pure and unswerving principles of John Knox".[3]

CHOLERA

Watching the slow march of cholera from India, where the first epidemic to come to the attention of the Western World occurred in 1817, the inhabitants of Glasgow remained complacent until the scourge reached their very doorstep – Kirkintilloch – in January 1832. Despite belated attempts to restrict movement between the two communities along the Forth and Clyde Canal, the cholera arrived in Glasgow on February 9. Within eight months more than 3,000 inhabitants had died of this new disease which terrified the public and left medical men baffled.

Convinced that susceptibility to cholera was a sign of Divine judgement, many doctors and others were only too ready to blame this on the loose living of the lower classes; where it did strike the middle classes an explanation was frequently sought in the intemperance, alleged or real, of the victim. This, it was recorded of one merchant that "dram drinking" was his downfall, the cholera brought on by his "tippling during the first four days of last week".

Lacking knowledge, the profession was forced to rely upon traditional treatments, so that one unfortunate "previous to admission was bled to a broth plate full, had two opium pills and some dovers powders". Meanwhile the numerous quacks had a lucrative field day.

Further cholera outbreaks struck the city in 1848–49, 1853–54 and 1866. Although the second epidemic actually caused more fatalities than there had been in 1832, the public response was altogether calmer, with none of the near-riots and attacks on doctors which had marked the initial onslaught. As with AIDS in the modern era, familiarity had engendered a certain degree of complacency.

Derek A Dow

OLD GLASGOW THEATRES

Mention the Alhambra or the Metropole or the Empire or the Britannia to older Glaswegians and the floodgates of memory and anecdote will open. They will probably tell you of the barrow of rotten fruit that used to do a roaring trade on amateur nights outside the Britannia in Argyle Street or the long shepherd's crook which the management of that same theatre used to haul off performers who were so bad that they were in danger of their lives or of summer trips to the Five Past Eight Shows in the green marbled splendour of the Alhambra; and they will always have a memory of a pantomime be it posh and polished at the Empire, good clean Scottish fun at the Royal Princess's or good dirty Scottish fun at the Queens in Watson Street.

The old theatres of Glasgow have always fallen into two camps; the respectable, built to enhance civic prestige, like the Theatre Royal, Queen Street (1806–29), the facade of which still stands beside Stirling's Library, and the popular commercial theatres like the Metropole in Stockwell Street, never utterly respectable but still frequented by most Glaswegians. Until well into the century the theatre was the most popular form of entertainment in Glasgow with at least 15 theatres of all descriptions in the city centre alone.

These buildings, offering an irresistible escape from dreadful living conditions into a world of fantasy and, at the very least, creature comforts, like heat and light, are remembered with affection and their inexorable demolition is mourned. Only the Britannia remains, sad and neglected. Nostalgia alone won't save it.

Alasdair Cameron

1. Jack House, **The Heart of Glasgow**, 1965. **2.** Motherwell's bust was enshrined beneath a Tudor canopy, decorated with fleur-de-lis. **3.** Laurence Hill, **A Companion to the Necropolis**, 1836.

Cardinal David Beaton, James Beaton's uncle, who was murdered at St Andrews Castle in 1546 as an act of vengeance for his death sentence on the Protestant preacher, George Wishart.

Twenty-two years before Knox's pure and unswerving principles reached their apotheosis, the church became alarmed by the rapid spread of reformed doctrine throughout the country.

Jerome Russell was a Minorite friar at the monastery in the High Street. He came from Dumfries, but had spent most of his life with the Glasgow Franciscans until he decided he could no longer accept what was being taught and denounced his superiors as "perverts of the Christian faith".[1]

He supposedly had sympathisers, though most of them kept their feelings to themselves. John Kennedy, a 17 year old student from Ayr, had a brilliant scholastic reputation; he is also said to have been a fair poet, though none of his work has survived. When he met Russell, he produced a series of satires, "ten times more effective than the sober eloquence of the older man".[2]

The dissidents' fate was decided long before the charges were read. They were allowed no defence counsel and the prosecution produced a series of witnesses who testified to the heresy. The inevitable sentence was passed. Russell and Kennedy were handed over to the civic authority to be disposed of as heretics. They would be burned at the stake. They died at the forecourt of Glasgow Cathedral, near the Necropolis entrance in 1538.

James Beaton was Glasgow's last Catholic Archbishop. There are some minor discrepancies regarding his early life, but he was born in 1525 into a highly influential family of clerics and enough references are available to establish that he was reared close to his uncle, Cardinal David Beaton, Archbishop of St Andrews. James Beaton made a swift clerical ascent. Before he was old enough to be in Orders, he had been given the Rectory of Campsie.

In the larger scheme of national and continental changes, Scotland was without effective leadership. The country was torn by political, religious and material tensions. These stemmed from internal divisions as well as the conflicting pressure from England, France and Rome and ominous rumblings from Calvinists in Geneva.

Knox returned from the Continent in 1556. In the following year, heresy charges were dropped when he and a weighty retinue of supporters turned up at Edinburgh's Blackfriars Church. He then left Scotland for Geneva, where he stayed for three years, having sown the seeds of the new doctrine. Glasgow became a centre of Reform after the first Covenant, binding protestant noblemen together, was drafted in 1557.

John Knox returned to Edinburgh after the Beggar's Symmonds of New Year's Day, 1559, had breathed a spirit of resolution into the Reformers. While they began their campaign of change, Mary,

The Necropolis mausoleum for Major Douglas Monteath of the East India Company.

FROM SUNDAY SCHOOL TO BOYS' BRIGADE

It was a constant pre-occupation in Victorian Glasgow to bring the working population to church. Parents who did not themselves attend often sent their children to Sunday School. There their boys became increasingly noisy and troublesome with the passing years.

In the period after the Crimean War the British, alarmed by the aggressive war-like noises of the French Emperor, Louis Napoleon, began to organise themselves into Volunteer Regiments by which military training was given to men in the evenings and at weekends. This became a popular – and recreational – movement.

William Alexander Smith (1854–1914), a strong evangelical in Glasgow, conceived the notion of using the Volunteer principle of military drill to entertain and discipline the unruly Sunday School boys. This led to the establishment in October 1883 of the Boys' Brigade which aimed at "The Advancement of Christ's Kingdom among Boys and the Promotion of habits of Reverence, Discipline, Self Respect and all that tends towards a true Christian manliness".

In this way hundreds and thousands of boys in Scotland, England and overseas – the BB was always inter-denominational – were recruited for Christ. Enjoyment came through the parade ground; this military idiom aroused hostility from many, including the Peace Society.

But the Boys' Brigade and later the Boy Scouts (f.1908) did bring a sense of purpose to the lives of many. The summers were particularly exciting, for drill was then outdoors and boys, who had never been out of Glasgow, travelled on excursions and learnt how to live under canvas and enjoy the freedom of rural space.

Olive Checkland

1. George MacGregor, **History of Glasgow**, 1881. **2.** ibid.

John Knox lays down the law to the new queen in Samuel Sidley's (1829-96) painting. When Mary came back to Scotland in 1561, Knox was the Kirk's unquestioned leader.

Dowager Queen of Scotland, enjoyed the comforts and protection of the Bishop's Palace, offered by her mentor, James Beaton II. He had been one of her closest advisers and their correspondence reveals a strong and mutually supportive friendship.

Within days of Knox's return, the Reformers had sacked Perth. Beaton was sent with the Regent's army to "stay the audacity of the rebels".[1] A month later, in the June of 1559, he and his sympathetic nobles were forced to defend Glasgow Cathedral.

On October 12, while Beaton and the Regent were absent, his congregation visited Glasgow Castle and ransacked the place, but "there was no money to be found in the Bishop of Glasgow's coffers".[2] This is a local incident, but if that could happen to such a powerful man, consider what was happening elsewhere in the country.

The Archbishop's imminent departure was no doubt hastened by Mary of Guise's death. She passed away on June 10, 1560 and on July 18, Archbishop Beaton, Lord Seaton and others left Leith on the French transport vessel *Mynyon*. He arrived in Paris on August 3 and never again set foot in Scotland. By the close of 1560 he was referred to as "one of the principal doers about the Scottish Queen for the affairs of Scotland".[3] Fourteen years later he was top of the outlawed list of Catholic prelates.

His connections with Glasgow continued. He was appointed ambassador to the court of France, a position confirmed in 1561, and he continued to enjoy the temporalities of the See until 1570. Then in 1588, James VI formally and fully restored his rights to the income of the Regality of Glasgow, "notwithstanding, he never acknowledged the religion practiced within this realm".[4]

The long association the Archbishop had enjoyed with the House of Guise not only aided his sudden emigration, but also helped him maintain the dignity of his position. Mary Queen of Scots nominated him as the "chief manager and disposer" of her worldly possessions.

Beaton gave £4,000 to the Scots College in Paris and when the tensions had settled, he encouraged priests to return to Scotland. He continued his clerical roles and his personal revenues were increased with other ecclesiastical incomes. He continued his diplomatic work for the Catholic cause across Europe, negotiating with, and on behalf of, many Popes, the Duke of Guise and Philip of Spain. Coincidence allowed him to perform the last rites on the Earl of Lennox and he communicated by cipher with Queen Mary and the London Jesuits. He died on April 25, 1603 and is buried in the Church of St Jean de Lateran in Rome.

IMPERIAL GLASGOW

For me Glasgow, an endlessly suggestive place, is above all a city of imperial allusion. Today it is European City of Culture, once it vied with Calcutta for the title of the British Empire's Second City. The very idea of Empire is discredited now, and the functions of Glasgow have been transformed, yet there are moments when I can sense the old dynamic still.

Sometimes on a brilliant spring day, for instance, when the City Hall stands resplendent there, the University seems a very talisman of universal learning, and the fluttering flags make Glasgow feel more than ever like a City-State, I recall how the Victorian municipal ideal that here reached so monumental a climax reached out across all the Queen's dominions, implanting reminders of Glasgow, echoes of Glasgow, wherever a tropic Mayoralty was created or a civic sewage works established on the other side of the world.

Or sometimes on a winter evening, when the city's glow is diffused on the misty night, down by the river I can hear still (for nowhere feeds the romantic imagination more richly than Glasgow does) the beat of all the myriad ships that sailed out from here along the sea-routes of the Empire.

Most movingly of all, the unmistakeable voices, faces and manners of Glasgow remind me that for a brief period of human history some essence of this city was disseminated over half the world – the very same essence, in fact, that is now re-invigorating itself in such different kinds back home on the Clyde.

Jan Morris

1. **Calendar State Papers**, 67. **2.** Archbishop Eyre, **Memoirs of Beaton**, 1891. **3.** ibid. **4.** ibid.

Clever and powerful as Beaton was and important though his role in national and European affairs of the time may have been, his principle interest lies not in what he gave, but what he took. This city's historians have dubbed him as the man who removed our history and certainly many of the papers he took to Paris are of considerable value and interest. Since then they have passed through a variety of fingers, some sticky, others slippy.

We do have two volumes from Beaton's library; with heraldic arms stamped in gold: a bulky folio by Professor John Diedro dated 1552 and a copy of the Bible published in Paris by Robert Stephen in 1545, bearing the autograph of Andrew Melville. There are also 72 original letters from Mary Queen of Scots, addressed mainly to Beaton.

Scotland's only Catholic martyr died in Glasgow. Hanged in 1615, beatified in 1927, and canonised on October 17, 1976, Saint John Ogilvie was apprehended here in October 1614, having been found in possession of a number of Roman Catholic books, a lock of the hair of St Ignatius and some other relics.

Ogilvie was a Jesuit, which at the time was sufficient grounds for suspicion in this town. Judges sent from Edinburgh to try him were told he had come to save souls. They believed he was part of a revolutionary movement and tried to have him confess as much, keeping him awake for three days and nights until they had their confession. Ogilvie retracted it after a night's sleep.

When his trial was resumed, he proclaimed the superiority of the pope over the king and when asked to take the oath of allegiance said, "It is a damnable oath and treason against God to swear it,"[1] going as far as to call the king "a runagate from God". He was, of course, found guilty of treason and sentenced to a public hanging. On February 22, 1615, he wrote to a Jesuit on the Continent that he had been bribed and offered the favour of the king if he accepted another religion, which he refused to do, preferring to sleep under a two hundred weight load of irons. He had been kept awake for eight days and nine nights at the time of writing and expected two other tortures before death.

He was hanged on March 10, 34 years old. Ogilvie has always been a controversial figure, seen variously as a simpleton, a martyr or even a prophet. His presence in Glasgow of all places at that time has raised issues which have never been satisfactorily answered. "I have long been ready," he said when Provost James Hamilton asked if he was prepared to die on the morning of his execution.[2]

Bloodshed in the cause of religion did not end with Ogilvie. You can walk in almost any direction from Glasgow and quickly find

ALONG THE QUAYS OF GLASGOW

Born in Glasgow (South Side), raised on the Firth of Clyde, I think I know the city fairly well, Off and on, up and down, I lived in it twelve full years. I studied at Adam Smith's university, where the theology department (which I didn't frequent) was existentialist. I later gave lectures there – on Baudelaire, Rimbaud, Apollinaire. I also started up (early Sixties) a group devoted, if you please, to "cultural revolution".

But mostly I was an inveterate walker, an obsessive stravaiger. I'd wander through the streets and along the quays of Glasgow with bits of phrases in my head: "So many beauties in hell", "swarming city, city full of dreams, where ghosts clutch at the passer-by". I'm remembering those ghosts: my grandfather (worked at Dixon's Blazes), who tried to write music between two bottles of whisky; my father, who was part of the Bowler Brigade in the Gorbals (dandy dancers all); and John, railway clerk I used to meet in a café in Buchanan Street, reading Omar Khayam – in Persian (later jumped off the Larne boat in mid-Channel, well loaded with stones).

Glasgow dreams, so many beauties in hell. Now that Glasgow's miles better, I wouldn't want these and such as these to smile bitter. Let not Glasgow turn into a no-ideas-but-in-bankcards condominium, let the ghosts also have a place to walk. They tell me GOD's coming to Glasgow ("Glasgow Oriental Development"). Great. I just hope he comes with a touch of zen. Glasgow tao, right? After long riding of universal waves, and through the murky mists of history, the return, with a difference, of Kentigern. Here's tae us.

Kenneth White

Princes Dock and Mavisbank Quay, c.1900.

1. George MacGregor, op. cit. 1881. **2. Des Hickey and Gus Smith,** Miracle, 1978.

"Covenanters Communion" by George Harvey.

places associated in myth or reality with the Covenanters. Apart from the signing in an Edinburgh churchyard, where many of the names were written in blood, it is possible to construct a history of the National Covenant and covenanting times without even leaving Glasgow.

There is of course more fiction than truth in the story of rich and poor crowding into Greyfriars Kirkyard to sign the document on a flat gravestone. Nevertheless, the Covenant of 1638 was more than a declaration of faith; it was a political manifesto from a people who used it to declare their opposition to any change not approved by their Assembly and Parliament. Guileless Stuart ineptitude and political conceit were at the root of the trouble.

Of Charles I's several intrusions into religious affairs, the imposition of a new Prayer Book was especially unpopular and stories abound of ministers being chased for opening it; prelates who approved it were certainly pursued. During the summer of 1638, while Charles mustered his northern forces, Covenanters raised money to buy arms, trained and drilled their volunteers in the hills and appealed to Scottish mercenaries working abroad to come home to the cause. Charles tried compromise, but it was hedged in such confusion that when he invited subscriptions to his own Covenant, it was generally described as a trick, or as atheism and perjury.

A free General Assembly met in Glasgow on November 21. They declared their intentions immediately by electing Alexander Henderson of Leuchars, a product of Andrew Melville's reformed St Andrews University, and co-author of the Greyfriars covenant, as Moderator.

So began a struggle which would continue in one form or another till the Stuarts were finally defeated on Drumossie Moor in 1746 and the man in whose cause the Scottish Highlanders needlessly fought passed into legend. The struggle was religious, but became a battle for the throne itself.

Following the Covenanters defeat at the Battle of Kilsyth, the Glasgow magistrates, fearing the town was next, opened their doors and, excusing themselves for not contacting Montrose sooner, offered him their congratulations and hospitality. James Graham, Marquis of Montrose, stayed for two days with his army and left after borrowing £50,000 Scots, which he forgot to repay.

The strength of popular feeling around the Covenanting cause, responding to a policy always seen as the thin end of an English wedge, makes it the only war whose ordinary victims are remembered with individual memorials. Not until the Great War

Rev Alexander "Jupiter" Carlyle by Archibald Skirving. Carlyle's memoirs provide a colourful account of the Enlightenment.

DR ALEXANDER "JUPITER" CARLYLE (1722–1805)

From about the middle of the 18th century Church of Scotland ministers were divided into two mutually antagonistic groups. On one side were the "High Flyers", strict, unyielding, and of the most rigid orthodoxy. On the other were the "Moderates", who believed that a minister could be a Christian and a gentleman, that a tincture of secular learning, civil manners and a place in society were no bar to the pulpit.

Of these latter Alexander Carlyle was the epitome. He was educated at Glasgow University and ordained minister to the rural parish of Inveresk in 1740, despite, as he said, being convicted of having "danced frequently in a manner prohibited by the laws of the Church and having worn his hat agee"!

Following his attendance at the Edinburgh performance of his minister friend John Home's controversial play *Douglas* in 1755 he was libelled by his presbytery but was absolved by the General Assembly in an unusual fit of common sense.

His superb physique and upright carriage earned him the nick name of "Jupiter" Carlyle. He lived a long and active life and enjoyed the company of many of the leading figures of the day, from Adam Smith to David Hume, from the Duke of Argyle to David Garrick. His best memorial is without a doubt his *Autobiography* which he began in his 75th year. First published in 1860, its fascinating anecdotes and conversational style bring to vivid life the stirring times of the Scottish Enlightenment.

Joseph Fisher

of 1914-18 did small communities again erect memorials to their folk who died.

There used to be a Covenanters' memorial at the top of the High Street. In 1818 it was renewed by the owners of the Monkland Canal, again by the citizens in 1862. It was later mounted on the wall of a Castle Street cinema.

The cinema, canal and most of Castle Street are demolished, but a memorial of sorts remains. A carved replica, near enough to where the original stood, has been mounted into an arch of the motorway, for all to see.

Here lye Martyrs three,
of Memory,
Who for the Covenants did die;
And witness is,
'Gainst all these nations perjury.
Against the Covenanted cause
Of Christ, their Royal King;
The British rulers made such laws,
Declar'd twas Satan's reign.
As Britain lyes in guilt you see,
'Tis ask'd, o reader! art thou free? [1]

EARLY WORKERS' COMBINATIONS

It was in the early 18th century that journeymen craftsmen began to set up trade societies. These were first to provide mutual aid funds for widows and orphans and the aged, but soon they were used for trade purposes to try to shorten hours and to keep up earnings and to prevent too many unskilled new workers coming into the craft.

Tailors, hammermen, blacksmiths, butchers were all organised in journeymen's societies by the 1740s. As textiles became of increasing importance, tensions appeared there. The first Glasgow weavers' society was formed in 1767, but the biggest changes came from the 1780s with the expansion of the cotton industry. Workers were pulled into it from all sources. Establishment weavers tried to keep out the less skilled and to maintain their earnings and this led to more frequent conflict between the handloom weavers and the merchant manufacturers. In 1787 troops opened fire on demonstrating Calton weavers leaving eight killed and several wounded.

Under Scottish law, workers' combinations were legal as long as they were used only to petition employers and magistrates. But the pressures of developing capitalism were against legal regulation of industrial relations. In 1812 when Lanarkshire weavers looked to the courts to lay down minimum rates they found their leaders arrested and sent to prison. With the coming of the factory system in cotton spinning these workers too organised and, between 1809 and 1838, the Glasgow Cotton Spinners' Association developed into one of the most powerful of early unions. Colliers, printers, shoemakers were all organising in the years after the end of the Napoleonic Wars, seizing the opportunities of moments of good trade to make gains. It proved more difficult to sustain such gains when the economy was depressed.

W Hamish Fraser

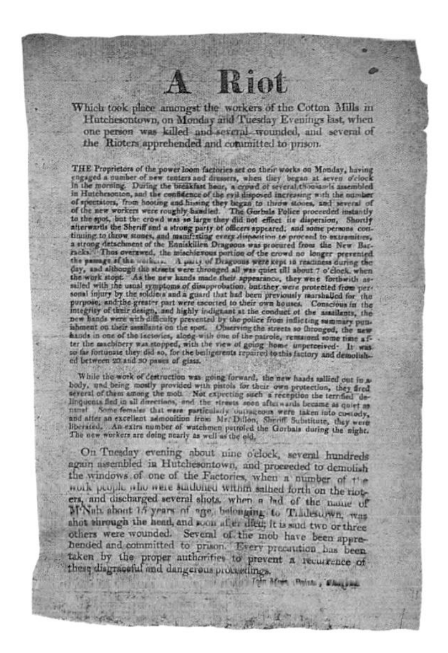

A Riot

Which took place amongst the workers of the Cotton Mills in Hutchesontown, on Monday and Tuesday Evenings last, when one person was killed and several wounded, and several of the Rioters apprehended and committed to prison.

THE Proprietors of the power loom factories set on their works on Monday, having engaged a number of new tenters and dressers, when they began at seven o'clock in the morning. During the breakfast hour, a crowd of several thousands assembled in Hutchesonton, and the confidence of the evil disposed increasing with the number of spectators, from hooting and hissing they began to throw stones, and several of of the new workers were roughly handled. The Gorbals Police proceeded instantly to the spot, but the crowd was so large they did not effect its dispersion, Shortly afterwards the Sheriff and a strong party of officers appeared, and some persons continuing to throw stones, and manifesting every disposition to proceed to extremities, a strong detachment of the Enniskillen Dragoons was procured from the New Barracks. Thus overawed, the mischievous portion of the crowd no longer prevented the passage of the workers. A party of Dragoons were kept in readiness during the day, and although the streets were thronged all was quiet till about 7 o'clock when the work stopt. As the new hands made their appearance, they were forthwith assailed with the usual symptoms of disapprobation, but they were protected from personal injury by the soldiers and a guard that had been previously marshalled for the purpose, and the greater part were escorted to their own houses. Conscious in the integrity of their design, and highly indignant at the conduct of the assailants, the new hands were with difficulty prevented by the police from inflicting summary punishment on their assailants on the spot. Observing the streets so thronged, the new hands in one of the factories, along with one of the patrole, remained some time after the machinery was stopped, with the view of going home unperceived. It was so far fortunate they did so, for the belligerents repaired to this factory and demolished between 20 and 30 panes of glass.

While the work of destruction was going forward, the new hands sallied out in a body, and being mostly provided with pistols for their own protection, they fired several of them among the mob. Not expecting such a reception the terrified delinquents fled in all directions, and the streets soon afterwards became as quiet as usual. Some females that were particularly outrageous were taken into custody, and after an excellent admonition from Mr. Dillon, Sheriff Substitute, they were liberated. An extra number of watchmen patroled the Gorbals during the night. The new workers are doing nearly as well as the old.

On Tuesday evening about nine o'clock, several hundreds again assembled in Hutchesontown, and proceeded to demolish the windows of one of the Factories, when a number of the work people who were stationed within sallied forth on the rioters, and discharged several shots, when a lad of the name of M'Nab about 15 years of age, belonging to Tradestown, was shot through the head, and soon after died; it is said two or three others were wounded. Several of the mob have been apprehended and committed to prison. Every precaution has been taken by the proper authorities to prevent a recurrence of these disgraceful and dangerous proceedings.

Early media account of a riot.

1. Thomas M Weir, **A History of the Martyrs' Monument, Castle Street, Glasgow and some notes on the District**, 1925.

AN EXTRACT FROM

AN ACT FOR AN UNION OF THE TWO KINGDOMS OF ENGLAND AND SCOTLAND

ARTICLE I

That the two Kingdoms of England and Scotland shall upon the first day of May which shall be in the Year one thousand seven hundred and seven, and for ever after, be united into one Kingdom by the Name of Great Britain; and that the Ensigns Armorial of the said united Kingdom be such as her Majesty shall appoint, and the Crosses of St. George and St. Andrew be conjoined in such Manner as her Majesty shall think fit, and used in all Flags, Banners, Standards and Ensigns, both at Sea and Land.

ARTICLE II

That the Succession of the Monarchy to the united Kingdom of Great Britain, and of the Dominions thereto belonging, after her most sacred Majesty, and in Default of Issue of her Majesty, be, remain, and continue to the most Excellent Princess Sophia, Electoress and Duchess Dowager of Hanover, and the Heirs of her Body being Protestants, upon whom the Crown of England is settled by an Act of Parliament made in England in the twelfth Year of the Reign of his late Majesty King WILLIAM the Third, intituled, An Act for the further Limitation of the Crown, and better securing the Rights and Liberties of the Subject.

ARTICLE III

That the united Kingdom of Great Britain be represented by one and the same Parliament, to be stiled, The Parliament of Great Britain.

ARTICLE IV

That all the Subjects of the united Kingdom of Great Britain shall, from and after the Union, have full Freedom and Intercourse of Trade and Navigation to and from any Port or Place within the said united Kingdom, and the Dominions and Plantations thereunto belonging; . . .

ARTICLE V

That all Ships or Vessels belonging to her Majesty's Subjects of Scotland, at the Time of ratifying the Treaty of Union of the two Kingdoms in the Parliament of Scotland, though foreign built, be deemed, and pass as Ships of the Built of Great Britain; . . .

ARTICLE VI

That all Parts of the united Kingdom for ever, from and after the Union, shall have the same Allowances, Encouragements, and Drawbacks, and be under the same Prohibitions, Restrictions and Regulations of Trade, and liable to the same Customs and Duties on Import and Export; and that the Allowances, Encouragements, and Drawbacks, Prohibitions, Restrictions and Regulations of Trade, and the Customs and Duties on Import and Export, settled in England when the Union commences, shall, from and after the Union, take Place throughout the whole united Kingdom; . . .

ARTICLE VII

That all Parts of the united Kingdom be for ever, from and after the Union, liable to the same Excises upon all exciseable Liquors, . . .

ARTICLE VIII

That from and after the Union, all foreign Salt which shall be imported into Scotland, shall be charged at the Importation there, with the same Duties as the like Salt is now charged with being imported into England, and to be levied and secured in the same Manner: . . . And for establishing an Equality in Trade, that all Flesh exported from Scotland to England, and put on Board in Scotland to be exported to Parts beyond the Seas, and Provisions for Ships in Scotland, and for foreign Voyages, may be salted with Scots Salt, paying the same Duty for what Salt is so employed as the like Quantity of Such Salt pays in England, and under the same Penalties, Forfeitures, and Provisions for preventing of Frauds as are mentioned in the Laws of England; . . .

ARTICLE IX

That whensoever the Sum of one million nine hundred ninety-seven thousand seven hundred and sixty-three Pounds eight Shillings and four Pence Halfpenny, shall be enacted by the Parliament of Great Britain to be raised in that Part of the united Kingdom now called England, on Land and other Things usually charged in Acts of Parliament there, for granting an Aid to the Crown by a Land Tax; that Part of the united Kingdom now called Scotland, shall be charged by the same Act, with a further Sum of forty-eight thousand Pounds, free of all Charges, as the Quota of Scotland, to such Tax, and so proportionably for any greater or lesser Sum raised in England by any Tax on Land, and other Things usually charged together with the Land; . . .

ARTICLE X

That during the Continuance of the respective Duties on stampt Paper, Vellum, and Parchment; by the several Acts now in Force in England, Scotland shall not be charged with the same respective Duties.

ARTICLE XI

That during the Continuance of the Duties payable in England on Windows and Lights, which determine on the first Day of August one thousand seven hundred and ten, Scotland shall not be charged with the same Duties.

ARTICLE XII

That during the Continuance of the Duties payable in England on Coals, Culm, and Cynders, which determine the thirtieth Day of September one thousand seven hundred and ten, Scotland shall not be charged therewith for Coals, Culm, and Cynders not consumed in Scotland.

ARTICLE XIII

That during the Continuance of the Duty payable in England upon Malt, which determines the twenty-fourth Day of June one thousand seven hundred and seven, Scotland shall not be charged with that Duty.

ARTICLE XIV

That the Kingdom of Scotland be not charged with any other Duties laid on by the Parliament of England before the Union, except these consented to in this Treaty; . . .

ARTICLE XV

That whereas by the Terms of this Treaty, the Subjects of Scotland, for preserving an Equality of Trade throughout the united Kingdom, will be liable to several Customs and Excises now payable in England, which will be applicable towards Payment of the Debts of England, contracted before the Union; it is agreed, that Scotland shall have an Equivalent for what the Subjects thereof shall be so charged towards Payment of the said Debts of England, in all Particulars whatsoever, in Manner following, viz.

ARTICLE XVI

That from and after the Union, the Coin shall be of the same Standard and Value throughout the united Kingdom, as now in England, and a Mint shall be continued in Scotland, under the same Rules as the Mint in England, and the present Officers of the Mint continued, subject to such Regulations and Alterations as her Majesty, her Heirs or Successors, or the Parliament of Great Britain shall think fit.

ARTICLE XVII

That from and after the Union, the same Weights and Measures shall be used throughout the united Kingdom, . . .

ARTICLE XVIII

That the Laws concerning Regulation of Trade, Customs, and such Excises to which Scotland is, by virtue of this Treaty, to be liable, be the same in Scotland, from and after the Union, as in England; . . .

ARTICLE XIX

That the Court of Session, or College of Justice, do after the Union, and notwithstanding thereof, remain in all Time coming within Scotland, as it is now constituted by the Laws of that Kingdom, and with the same Authority and Privileges as before the Union, subject nevertheless to such Regulations for the better Administration of Justice, as shall be made by the Parliament of Great Britain; . . .

ARTICLE XX

That all heretable Offices, Superiorities, heretable Jurisdictions, Offices for Life, and Jurisdictions for Life, be reserved to the Owners thereof, as Rights of Property, in the same Manner as they are now enjoyed by the Laws of Scotland, notwithstanding this Treaty.

ARTICLE XXI

That the Rights and Privileges of the Royal Burghs in Scotland, as they now are, do remain entire after the Union, and notwithstanding thereof.

ARTICLE XXII

That by virtue of this Treaty, of the Peers of Scotland, at the Time of the Union, sixteen shall be the Number to sit and vote in the House of Lords, and forty-five the Number of the Representatives of Scotland in the House of Commons of the Parliament of Great Britain; . . .

ARTICLE XXIII

That the aforesaid sixteen Peers of Scotland mentioned in the last preceding Article, to sit in the House of Lords of the Parliament of Great Britain, shall have all Privileges of Parliament, which the Peers of England now have, . . .

ARTICLE XXIV

That from and after the Union, there be one Great Seal for the united Kingdom of Great Britain, which shall be different from the Great Seal now used in either Kingdom . . .

ARTICLE XXV

That all Laws and Statutes in either Kingdom, so far as they are contrary to, or inconsistent with the Terms of the Articles, or any of them, shall, from and after the Union, cease and become void, and shall be so declared to be, by the respective Parliaments of the said Kingdoms.

The Act of Union of 1707, including Glasgow's seal.

SIR WALTER SCOTT AND GLASGOW

Scott was frequently in Glasgow on legal business, attending the old Court House in Jail Square. He liked to stay at "a quaint hostelry in King Street", the Institution, where "the Sheriff" met, ate a chop and drank wine with the prototypes of Bailie Nicol Jarvie, MacVittie and MacFinn, later to feature in *Rob Roy.*

Researching *The Lady of the Lake* in 1809, Scott passed through Glasgow on his way to Ross Priory, on Loch Lomondside, the home of his legal friend Hector Macdonald Buchanan, an excursion which later became almost an annual visit. In July 1817, John Smith, the Glasgow bookseller, refreshed Scott's recollections of "the noble cathedral, and other localities of the birthplace of Bailie Jarvie", Lockhart records. "Mr Smith took care also to show the tourist the most remarkable novelties in the great manufacturing establishments of his flourishing city". Scott expressed delight on seeing "the process of *singeing muslim*"; drawing a red-hot iron over it to banish impurities. "The man who invented that", said Scott, "was the Shakespeare of wabsters". Scott embarked from the Broomielaw in July 1825 on a steamer for Belfast, drinking punch with "a worthy old Bailie of Glasgow". In September 1827, Scott had dinner at the Buck's Head with Mrs Maclean Clephane and her daughter, had a pleasant evening "paid for by a restless night", and next day, "went down by steam to Colonel Campbell's Blythswood House."

After Scott's death, £1,200 was raised by subscription for David Rhind's huge classical pillar in George Square, carrying Handyside Ritchie's statue of Scott in his Border plaid.

Maurice Lindsay

"A View of Glasgow from the South-East".

Chapter Eight

INTO THE LIGHT

The Scottish Enlightenment is as hard to date as it is to define. Some say it stretched from the Union of 1707 to the death of Sir Walter Scott in 1832, but there is such a diversity of activity within these dates that it is impossible to locate a single cultural movement.

History does not occur in recognisable segments and the Scottish Enlightenment ought to be assessed in terms of its personalities and their diverse achievements. It is also important to recognise the climate and intellectual environment which created the Enlightenment.

There had been an increased interest in education following the Reformation. More importantly, the 1696 Education Act compelled landholders in every Scottish parish to provide a commodious schoolhouse and a small salary for a schoolmaster. The people were no longer obliged to concentrate solely on survival, but were encouraged to expect more from life.

As an inextricable part of the society which supported it, the Enlightenment is sometimes difficult to distinguish from simple Improvement. Everyday changes in farming methods, such as the introduction of marling, or the use of lime generally to regenerate the soil, and attempts at selective breeding to raise livestock standards, encouraged and allowed farmers to leave what had virtually been a subsistence economy and start producing for the ready markets which were developing in the towns. It is an over-simplification to suggest that such Improvement led to the Enlightenment, but there are many examples of their interaction; perhaps the most obvious is Adam Smith's development of Political Economy as a specialisation within his wider subject of Moral Philosophy.

Why the Enlightenment should have existed principally as an urban phenomenon has never been properly explained. The simple answer involves the three props of Scottish urban existence: the universities, the church establishment and the legal profession. They

"Queen Anne Receiving the Articles of Union 1707" by Sir Walter Monnington.

The Old College in 1672, where two large, interlinked courts are joined by a pend, above which the Dutch tower rises.

These flag designs, approved by the Earl of Nottingham, marry the crosses of St Andrew and St George into one flag. They date from around 1604.

THE ANDERSONIAN INSTITUTE'S DEVELOPMENT

John Anderson, Professor of Natural Philosophy in Glasgow University, was a man of vision. He would forsake the cloistered walls of the College in High Street and wander through the workshops of Glasgow talking with the men and learning something of their manufacturing skills and, in return, inviting them to come in their working clothes to his special "anti-toga" classes. "These are the men who need a knowledge of Natural Philosophy for their daily work. Why should it not be placed within their reach for a full University course?"

Artisans and mechanics came into Glasgow University and were, for the first time in their lives, instructed in the ways of Science. Anderson was harnessing the spirit of the future and by his initiative laying the foundations for Scotland's (and Britain's) future greatness as an industrial power. Ladies were also invited to attend classes. This was indeed revolutionary!

Anderson was not popular with his fellow professors. For his part, he did not like them either. When he died in 1796 he left instructions for the setting up of a new university which would not be run by the professors, "who are drones or drunkards in certain other Colleges", but should be managed by laymen. Within a year of his death his trustees had established the Andersonian Institute.

It went through a series of metamorphoses – Anderson's University (1828–77), Anderson's College (1877–87), Glasgow & West of Scotland Technical College (1887–1912), The Royal Technical College (1912–56) and the Royal College of Science & Technology (1956–64). Following integration with the Scottish College of Commerce, it emerged in 1964 as the University of Strathclyde.

Bill Fletcher

help account for Edinburgh's prime role in the Enlightenment, especially in relation to Glasgow, which also had a successful university, but lacked the capital's added pull as the seat of the law courts, and the established venue of the General Assembly of the Church of Scotland. Like most capitals, Edinburgh, especially after the '45 rebellion, was in the money. The university towns which contributed most to the Enlightenment also had histories of foreign trade which put them in a position to encounter and be receptive to new ideas.

The varying attitudes to social and economic changes produced in different parts of the country can be illustrated in the Jacobite Risings of 1715 and 1745. It is generally true that the Lowlander, especially the Glaswegian Lowlander, wished to make use of the Union and continue with Improvement and did his best to ignore and even circumvent the Stuart cause. There was a new and growing preference for English manners and speech amongst many Lowland Scots. David Hume sent his texts south to have them weeded of "Scotticisms".

The novels of Sir Walter Scott helped crush the language of a man he admired, Robert Burns; though even Burns believed English was the proper medium for serious thought and wrote his worst poems in it. Scott's works appealed for and found England's respect and though some of his best passages are written in Scots, he effectively ruined native speech as a literary medium. The issue is especially relevant in Glasgow, whose argot the *Scottish National Dictionary* described as "hopelessly corrupt".[1] Glaswegian writers have since disagreed with this contention and are currently enjoying considerable success, having imaginatively turned this apparent weakness into strength.[2]

In the Age of Enlightenment, Scotland had four universities. St Andrews, Glasgow, Aberdeen and Edinburgh were all founded before the Union of the Crowns in 1603. It may have been the scepticism of youth which led Edinburgh to abolish the traditional regenting system of teaching in 1747. Regenting had effectively discouraged specialisation; under its guidance tutors were expected to teach a variety of subjects to the same students for the duration of their university education. Glasgow was the workshop of the Enlightenment, but it wasn't the capital; that immutable fact and the university's love of its old regenting ways meant the Enlightenment was generated elsewhere.

By the middle of the 15th century, Glasgow was a neat little township with a few main streets and a Cathedral. Imagine a straggle of wooden houses gathered round the church, reaching down the brae to the settlements on the banks of the Clyde. Four streets met

NEW GLASGOW POETRY

The city's poetry owes an immense debt to Edwin Morgan, the first Glasgow writer to step outside self-examination and introspective "Glasgowness" and "Scottishness", to become aware of world poetry from modern Russian to concrete experimental, and to absorb these influences and combine them with a Glasgow voice, confident and assured, in volumes like *The Second Life* (1968) and *Themes on A Variation* (1988), which contains his wonderful sequence on the theme of Scotland (visited by time/space travellers) from prehistory to the present, *Sonnets from Scotland* (1984).

Morgan gave other Glasgow poets confidence in themselves. Two names stand out: Liz Lochhead and Tom Leonard. Lochhead uses a particularly highly developed sense of beat and rhythm to capture the voices of her modern lovers, rivals, solitaries in collections like *Memo for Spring* and *Dreaming Frankenstein*. Beneath the comic and virtuoso punning symbolism of her poems lies an ironic wryness about dreams, love, pretensions, which in typical Glasgow idiom reduces ideals and romance to world-weary common sense – and yet falls for the romance next time round.

Intimate Voices (1984) revealed how Tom Leonard's work over 20 years, whether in brief dramatic monologue or surrealist sketch, added up to a sustained exposure of authoritarian, narrow-minded and sadistic attitudes at every level of Glasgow *and* British society. One poem imagines the Six O'Clock news read in broad Glaswegian, as though the dialect of the exploited had in some alternative historical development become Britain's language of power. Such revealing changes of perspective are hallmarks of this new and still developing Glasgow group.

Douglas Gifford

1. William Grant, Introduction, Volume 1, **Scottish National Dictionary**. 2. See Page 243.

Thomas Annan's photograph of the High Street and Old College.

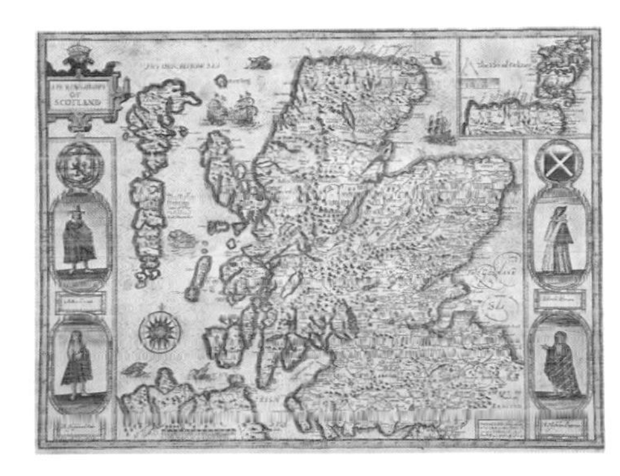

John Speed decorated his 17th century map of Scotland with figures emphasising the differences in dress and appearance between Highlander and Lowlander.

"Portrait of Erasmus" by Holbein.

at the Wyndheid: the present High Street, Castle Street, Drygate and Rottenrow.

On June 20, 1451, it must have been mobbed with worthy citizens, fat merchants and magistrates, their wives, the yeomanry and their retinue, some monks, the Black Friars, a few priests and, this being Glasgow, weans and dogs as well. We can imagine everybody would have been delighted with the great honour recently come from Rome. There was to be a sale at the Cathedral; sins would be forgiven at bargain prices.

Glasgow was given this special honour because she had just been granted a centre of learning. The Scottish clergy had no university till St Andrews was established in 1410. Bishop William Turnbull believed his town to be in need of academic distinction and set about lobbying support. Pope Nicholas V satisfied himself that Glasgow was a suitable place and issued a Papal Bull authorising Bishop Turnbull to establish a university.

The Pope requested Glasgow's new university be modelled on Bologna, though there also seems to have been a strong influence from the University of Cologne, which was very popular with Scottish students in the Middle Ages.[1]

The university's early lectures were held in the Chapter House and Lower Church of the Cathedral and the foundation was popular by the standards of the times, when education was by no means either open to all or freely available. More than 200 students enrolled in the first two years.

After a spell in the Auld Pedagogy, Rottenrow, the new establishment moved to the High Street in 1460, to the site which later became the College Goods Station. At first the collegians lived within the buildings, whose gates were shut at nine o'clock of a winter's night and at ten o'clock in the summer. Regents ensured their students were in bed. As numbers increased, many were forced to find lodgings in the town, eventually at fixed rents supervised by Bishop Turnbull.

By the middle of the 19th century the university was surrounded by the worst slums in Glasgow. When Lord Kelvin's brother died of typhus, Kelvin maintained he had been infected by the Havannah and New Vennel, running east from the High Street and reckoned to be the filthiest closes in the city. Kelvin was one of many who wanted the University elsewhere and in 1870 it moved to Gilmorehill. There was no public competition; instead, the London architect Sir George Gilbert Scott was chosen to design the new buildings.

Part of the old college was incorporated into the fresher airs of Gilmorehill. The Lion and Unicorn Staircase was saved from

WILLIAM THOMSON, LORD KELVIN (1824–1907)

William Thomson helped lay the foundations of the science of physics. Born in Belfast in 1824, Thomson's family moved to Glasgow in 1832. He was only eleven when he became a Glasgow student, attending lectures for six years at the University before being admitted to read mathematics at Cambridge. A period of study in France followed, and then in 1846, aged only 22, he was appointed to the Chair of Natural Philosophy at Glasgow, a post held until 1899.

Within a few years, Thomson created in Glasgow the first real physics laboratory. In addition to his mastery of the abstruse depths of mathematical physics – Thomson's synthesis helped create the science of thermodynamics – he also had a firm grip on physical reality, and tried to illustrate even the most complex mathematical notion with a physical model.

Thomson's scientific insight and skill in instrument design were the vital ingredient in the 1866 success of the project to lay a submarine telegraph cable across the Atlantic. Thomson's intimate relationship with the Glasgow instrument-making firm of James White was vital to such achievements. Indeed, in declining the prestigious chair of Experimental Physics at Cambridge in 1870, Thomson cited "the convenience of Glasgow for getting mechanical work done".

Thomson's redesign of the mariner's compass, manufactured by White of Glasgow, became standard issue. His sounding machine subsequently led a P & O Captain to call Thomson, "the greatest friend of the sailor who ever lived".

In addition to his titles, recognition came when the scientific community agreed that the scale of absolute temperature should be measured in degrees Kelvin.

D.J. Bryden

1. The route had been established through trade with the Low Countries and Germany.

The Foulis Academy of the Fine Arts, from a David Allan drawing, 1760.

"Agrippina With the Ashes of Germanicus" by Gavin Hamilton, who studied at the Foulis Academy.

James Tassie, born in Glasgow, the celebrated medallion maker and portraitist.

demolition and now forms part of Professors' Square. Govan shipbuilder Sir William Pearce paid for the old college entrance to be dismantled and re-erected on University Avenue, where it was renamed the Pearce Lodge.

In 1951 Glasgow University ceremoniously unveiled a set of gates on University Avenue to commemorate their 500th birthday celebrations. The Memorial Gates are inscribed with the names of 28 men who brought honour and recognition to the University. Twenty-eight names may not seem like a big return for 500 years of graduations, but some, like James Watt and Lord Lister, are very well known.[1] The main qualification seems to be academic recognition and this probably explains why some of the University's best known graduates, who distinguished themselves in other ways, are missing. John Knox studied at Glasgow, but his name does not appear on the gates. Neither do those of James Boswell or Tobias Smollett, both Glasgow graduates whose work has lasted better than the gates' sole literary representative, Thomas Campbell. Widely popular in his day, Campbell is now faintly remembered though he has a statue in George Square.

Campbell lived near the site of the old Grammar School, which also began in the Cathedral. The school, now known as Glasgow High, predates the University and is one of the oldest in Britain. It once stood near the junction of High Street and Ingram Street.

In Ingram Street itself, on the pavement outside St David's Ramshorn Kirk, is a slab inscribed with a cross and the initials RF and AF. The kirkyard used to extend across the street and the slab marks the grave of the Foulis Brothers, who are also on the Memorial Gates.

They have been credited with founding the first Glasgow industry to have significance outside the city. For most of their lives – Robert was born in the year of the Union, Andrew in 1712 – the Foulises were at the centre of Glasgow's intellectual life. Robert had been apprenticed to a barber when he met Dr Francis Hutcheson, then Professor of Moral Philosophy at the University. It was Hutcheson who suggested he become a bookseller and printer. Andrew was intended for the ministry. At first their literary stock was imported from France, but they began to print their own works in 1741 and by 1743 had been designated University Printer. They belonged to Glasgow's first literary and philosophical society, formed around 1747. This society met every Friday evening throughout the winter, from the first Friday in November till the second Friday of May, at half past five. Hutcheson was a member, as were Adam Smith, Thomas Reid and Joseph Black, the discoverer of latent heat.

JOSEPH LISTER (1827–1912)

Lister, the son of a London wine merchant, was educated at Quaker schools, then studied Medicine at London University. A year after graduation, he arrived in Edinburgh with a letter of recommendation to the leading surgeon, Syme. Lister married his chief's daughter in 1856 and soon afterwards was made Assistant Surgeon at the Edinburgh Royal Infirmary. His interest was roused by gangrene and he published his first classic paper the following year "The Early Stages of Inflammation".

Lister was appointed to the Chair of surgery at Glasgow Royal Infirmary in 1860 and continued his work on inflammation. At that time, 45 per cent of amputation cases died but Lister noticed that the ones that survived were free from putrefaction. His attention was drawn to the work of Pasteur on fermentation and he came to the conclusion that there were organisms in the air that must be destroyed before they entered the wound. But, how?

His first experiment was made in 1865 on a compound fracture. He applied carbolic acid undiluted to the wound. This was a success but unsuited for general surgery. He concentrated now on refining the idea but moved back to Edinburgh to his father-in-law's Chair of Clinical Surgery. Here he invented the carbolic spray. This was to provide an atmosphere free from germs around a wound which would not harm the body's tissues.

It was Lister who discovered that the surgeons of the time and all those that have followed must operate in a sterile atmosphere. This discovery of antiseptics opened the door to modern surgery.

Hugh W Simpson

1. Others, like Bute, Bradley, Poole and Stair, may not be so immediately identifiable.

INTO THE LIGHT

GLASGOW UNIVERSITY

Glasgow University's 1864 decision to appoint Sir George Gilbert Scott as architect for their new Gothic West End building provoked considerable resentment in a city which had almost always excluded outsiders from major commissions. Yet, he had more experience than any architect alive of large buildings with varied demands.

Money and time were short, problems with the latter being compounded by a lengthy builders' strike, but by 1870 five sevenths of the main building, together with professor's square, was completed and the University moved in.

The second phase of the University's construction made it Scott's final masterpiece. A bequest and a donation allowed Scott to expand greatly his ideas for the central cross range (Bute and Randolph Halls and the Hunterian Stair). He threw himself into the work, signing the drawings only days before his death in March 1878. The Bute Hall was raised over an open-vaulted chamber and made immensely light and spacious, featuring richly detailed Early Geometrical windows. Both halls are rich in recently restored Victorian decorative art, glowing in colour and stencilled pattern. The wrought iron rail of the magnificent Hunterian stair is Victorian metal work of the very highest class.

Appreciation of the University has always been clouded by the loss of the Old College and the Glasgow architectural profession's resentment at not being employed. Appreciation of Scott has grown, however, and the University is one of his best buildings, ranking close to the London Law Courts and Manchester Town Hall among the select few major monuments of High Victorian Gothic public building.

David M Walker

James Tassie was a student at the Foulis Academy of Art, working as a stonemason by day and drawing at night. His portrait medallions provide us with a gallery of the leading faces of the day. Tassie's artifice extended to the making of paste gems which looked so real others would sell them as authentic.

Scotland's universities faced serious difficulties at the turn of the 17th century; political and religious changes and the ensuing poverty had left them disordered. Yet they embarked on a programme of development and expansion, opening new fields of study and approaches to learning.

In the beginning, the sections of the Scottish community who had engineered the Union, got their immediate and promised, short term benefits; there was a new market, increased trade and, compared to the previous five hundred years, a kind of political stability. This climate, in truth more of a hope than a reality, was essential to the process of expansion, which was led by Glasgow and Edinburgh Universities, with Aberdeen and St Andrews following some way behind. Another important element was the forceful influence of the Cathcart-born William Carstares, who was Edinburgh University's Principal from 1703 to 1715. Carstares not only generated reforms. He encouraged the universities to give jobs to the Enlightenment writers, who, with himself, were an important link with the landed classes.

The life of the mind was not confined to universities, but overflowed into the city. Glasgow's Hodge-Podge Club was founded in 1750 as a serious intellectual concern, ending as a drinking club; of the 31 members admitted from 1752 to 1783, 20 were merchants. The Glasgow Literary Society had a majority of University Members, though the Political Economy Club, which existed from around 1743 to sometime after 1762, was more successful in uniting the interests of the merchants and academic economists. It stimulated the reprinting of some economic classics and included Adam Smith amongst its members, as well as the lesser known economist Sir James Steuart.

Of course, not all Glasgow clubs pretended to be anything other than what they were. The favourite tipple was Glasgow Punch. John McDowall not only gives the recipe published by the West India Club in 1780 but goes a step further by telling us what to expect: "on reaching the open air the effect was instantaneous".[1]

In an age when people had to take their meals in the bedroom, the warmest place, friends could not be invited round for the evening. Clubs proliferated. They sometimes met to discuss the important topics of the day, or, better still, play cards and sing. Card playing

Sir George Gilbert Scott's drawing of the interior of the Great Hall of Glasgow University.

Tassie Cabinet

1. John McDowall, The People's History of Glasgow, 1899.

Alexander Nasmyth - Portrait of Robert Burns.

clubs were popular and, according to the Glasgow chronicler Senex, one man supposedly made 300 pounds a year.[1] However noble their original intentions, the clubs became an excuse for a good drink and nothing was allowed to interfere with the serious business of the evening, which was to make sure no-one left the place sober.

The Anderston Club met in John Sharpe's Tavern every Saturday at two o'clock. The club had been founded by the University's Professor of Mathematics, Robert Simson, who left the College at 1 pm precisely and walked to Anderston with slow and measured step. No-one tells us how he left Anderston, far less how he got back to Glasgow. The Anderston Club had an immense tureen of Glasgow Punch which the professor divided equally amongst the members, who included Robert Foulis and Adam Smith.

When Robert Burns came to Glasgow in the spring of 1786 with his poems in his pocket, he carried a letter of introduction to the resident poet of the Partick Duck Club, William Reid,[2] an employee of Dunlop and Wilson, Booksellers, Publishers and Printers, Trongate.

A silver mounted snuff box made by Milne and Campbell of Glasgow in 1780.

Reid told Burns to take his poems to Edinburgh, but the poet, famously, went first to Kilmarnock. Dunlop and Wilson were not interested in publishing poetry. Their output was mainly psalms and sermons, editions of the Bible and Scripture commentaries. The services of Glasgow's most famous publishers were no longer available.

The Foulis Brothers were out of business, though in 1764 they had brought out an edition of Thomas Gray's work which had pleased the author so much he said his London edition was "far inferior to that of Glasgow".

Burns' connections with the city would be better known, but when the Clyde burst its banks in February 1831, William Reid's house was flooded and his Burns letters destroyed. Many attempts have been made to link Burns with Glasgow, and most parts of Scotland, offering the obvious paths through his friends and acquaintances, who may have lived here or there. His eldest son studied at Glasgow University, a daughter lived in Pollokshaws[3] and Burns himself supposedly first heard the tune "Duncan Gray" being whistled by a Glasgow carter.

William Simpson's painting of the High Street and University in the 1830s. The Professors' lodgings are on the right, the Tolbooth steeple in the distance.

Following the Edinburgh edition of Burns' poems in 1787, the Glasgow bookseller John Smith was asked to distribute the book. Smith took only five per cent commission and Burns remarked that Glasgow booksellers seemed decent people, compared to their Edinburgh counterparts.

In Part One of his *Analysis of the Statistical Account for Scotland*,

SOCIAL DRINKING IN 18TH CENTURY GLASGOW

Sugar from the West Indies had become a major Glasgow import before the middle of the 18th century, the union of 1707 having opened up West Indian sugar imports to the city just as it had opened up tobacco imports from Virginia. Rum (made from sugar) thus became the characteristic Glasgow spirit of that century. Bankers, merchants, doctors and lawyers regularly took a "meridian" or noon drink in a tavern or coffee house, often meeting their clients or customers there and giving and receiving advice or conducting business deals over a glass of rum and hot water ("three-waters" rum or "five-waters" rum according to strength). Sometimes they drank claret, and the less prosperous would indulge in a chopine (half-pint) of two-penny ale. But rum was the greater Glasgow drink.

"Glasgow punch" was a favourite beverage on social occasions: it consisted of rum mixed with lemon-juice and sugar ("sherbet"). Punch was often served after dinner parties, when the toast "The trade of Glasgow and the outward bound" was the signal for the ladies to retire. Ladies drank tea, wives of the Tobacco Lords often entertaining their female guests in the bedroom at the "four hours". They competed in the display of their delicate china cups.

Clubs proliferated in 18th century Glasgow. John Strang's classic work on *Glasgow and its Clubs* (1856) lists 27 founded in that century. The Meridian Club was one of the best known: it specialised in providing alcoholic refreshment for employees of the Ship Bank between the hours of one and two in the afternoon, when the bank was closed.

David Daiches

1. Glasgow, Past and Present, 1851. **2.** As such he "hit off the worthy convener, who was a carnivorous gourmand . . . 'The ducks at Partick quake for fear, / Crying, "Lord preserve us! there's McTear!" '." **3.** Where she was visited and eulogised by Hugh Macdonald.

published in Edinburgh in 1826, more than 20 years after the last volume of evidence, John Sinclair stressed that, in Scotland, literature was an industry and therefore part of the material wealth, whose products were as important as those of any other branch of industry. In 1795 Scotland's population was around 1,500,000; of which 20,000 people or 5,000 Scottish families, were dependent on literature for their subsistence, while 3,500 families, or 10,500 people, were dependent on teaching. He does not say why he allows four per family for those dependent on literature, while teachers merely have three.[1]

Only woollens, linen and hemp, iron and liquors employed more people than the paper industry. In Part Two, Sinclair notes that reports from 30 parishes indicate that even the poor were so eager for education, that they saved their money to pay for it and sold clothes to buy books. In some parishes all children over twelve could read and write.

In the "Glasgow Account" we are told printers and compositors[2] earned an equivalent of between 52 and 90 pence a week, pressmen between 50 and 60 pence and bookbinders were paid from 35 to 52 pence, which compares favourably with carpenters who earned between 40 and 60 pence while weavers received between 60 and 70 pence. Printing and publishing were obviously thriving and from the beginning of the 18th century Glasgow's education was supposedly cheap enough to make it accessible to even the poorest families.

The flourishing of intellect, invention and industry, which became known as the Scottish Enlightenment, was all the more remarkable coming from a small, peripheral country at the knuckle end of Europe. It paved the way for Imperial Britain, nourished it with talent and blood and made an immediate return to Scots independence impossible by laying the foundations of the future firmly within a United Kingdom. Crofters transformed themselves into competitive farmers fuelled by a peasantry who had no romantic yearnings for their immediate past. The expanding middle classes debated power, profit, social control and moral responsibility while they simultaneously learned to dominate trade, expand industry, and, for the first time ever, court success in the arts and sciences. Industry was creating a working class who, realising they had more in common with each other than their fellow countrymen, abjured national boundaries in a way the architects of the Treaty of Union could never have dreamed. They later gave the British Labour movement the fire in its guts and the gleam in its eye.

Scotland was in every sense a divided country and geography propelled visitors like Dr Johnson to ascribe national distinctions.

THE LINEN TRADE AND ITS IMPORTANCE TO GLASGOW

As early as 1686 the first Parliament of James VII passed an "Act for Burying in Scots Linen to encourage the manufacture thereof and discourage imports". Despite such measures the trade languished.

By 1700, there were three joint-stock companies formed to weave wool and linen cloth in Glasgow, but it required the attentions of the Board of Trustees for Improving Fisheries and Manufactures in Scotland, set up in 1727 at the suggestion of the Convention of Royal Burghs, to bring real expansion. The Board stimulated the activities of yard merchants in towns, and assisted in the setting up of bleachfields, as at Gray's Green in Glasgow, and printfields at Pollokshaws in 1742, and Dalsholm on the Kelvin in 1753. During the 1720s the manufacture of white linens was begun in the city, followed in the 1730s by printed linens and inkles, or tapes, while the British Linen Company was issuing notes from 1752, though not officially recognised as a bank until 1849.

Colonial markets stimulated massive expansion during the second half of the 18th century, with linen "forming for a long period the staple industry of the city", providing nearly 3,000 looms in Barony parish alone in 1780. By 1771, Glasgow was recognised as the principal town in Britain for the linen trade, importing Irish and Baltic linen and flax to supplement its own manufactures. Twenty years later, cotton had almost entirely superseded flax, and weavers were mainly occupied in making muslins.

Andrew Gibb

"A Weaver's Workshop" by Cornelis Decker, painted in 1659. Skilled Dutch weavers were brought to Glasgow in the early stages of the textile industry.

The Bookbinders assembled to the number of 70, and marched with the letterpress printers. They were distinguished by a trade flag, and carried models of bookbinders' laying press, with plough standing press filled with books, and imitations of business books. A model of a paper-ruling machine was also borne by one of the men. A little working model of a man hammering vigorously at a book was accompanied with the motto "We beat all the authors that ever we saw".

Anon. Foundation Stone Ceremony for City Chambers, *1883.*

1. Anand Chitnis, The Scottish Enlightenment: A Social History, 1976. 2. ibid.

GLASGOW AND HER BARRACKS

The first barracks in the city was on the Gallowgate and was built in the late 1790s on the site of The Butts, the old target place for the citizen archers. As a result of army reforms after the Crimean War it was deemed that Gallowgate Barracks was too small to hold a full battalion of infantry; its garrison was reduced to a detachment of infantry from whichever battalion was stationed in Paisley.

These changes did not please the Lord Provost or Corporation of Glasgow. Their desire for resident troops is easily explained. In 1866, Mr A Turner, the Town Clerk, wrote to a Colonel Erskine, saying that "The fact that 100,000 Irish (many of them Fenians) are now in Glasgow . . . ought to call for the early attention of the Government".

The War Office agreed that a new infantry barracks was necessary. Finally in 1869 a site was bought on part of the Garrioch Estate at Maryhill and Maryhill Barracks was completed in 1877. Although extended to provide room for one squadron of cavalry the customary denizens were usually just the infantry and artillery. Various regiments were stationed there in succession over the years. Then in 1920 the Depot of the HLI moved there from Hamilton on what was intended to be a temporary arrangement.

The HLI Depot left for Ayr in October 1958, just prior to amalgamation. Maryhill Barracks was demolished in 1961, giving way to the Wyndford housing estate. The perimeter wall, the main gate and the guardroom survive as a memento.

Donald Mack

[1] The Highlanders' support for the Stuarts in 1715 and 1745, albeit partial, was seen as general and not exactly welcomed south of the Tay where a new breed of Scots man and woman was enjoying the fruits of the Union. They were embarrassed by the behaviour of countrymen who did not know what was good for them. Highlanders had neither the means nor the faith to enter into any agreement with Edinburgh; the Golden Age of the Scottish Enlightenment was not a jolly time for anyone living in the Scottish Highlands.

On July 5, 1745, Charles Edward Stuart disguised himself as a divinity student, boarded the *Du Teillay* and against his father's wishes sailed from Nantes on the 18 day journey to Scotland. On the fifth day his small convoy was attacked by a British man-of-war while leaving the English Channel. The skirmish forced the Prince's boat to carry on alone through rough seas and mists till they were piloted to a safe harbour at Eriskay.

Nearly four weeks later the red and white silken standard of the House of Stuart was raised in the vale of Glenfinnan at the head of Loch Shiel. Charles' father was proclaimed King with the Prince as Regent. A month later Charles' troops commanded Edinburgh.

Glasgow's merchants had done well under the Hanoverians and were upset when the Prince wrote from the capital demanding £15,000, any arrears to taxes due to the Government and all the arms in the city. The magistrates delayed payment, hoping Sir John Cope's Government army would solve their problem. But when Cope was routed at Prestonpans, Charles sent his quartermaster John Hay, an Edinburgh lawyer, and a contingent of the Clan MacGregor to Glasgow. The magistrates were persuaded it was in their and the town's best interests to offer a donation towards the Prince's expenses. Hay accepted £5,000 in cash and £500 pounds worth of goods as an interim payment.

On Boxing Day that year, when Charles led his ragged army into Glasgow on the march from Derby, the magistrates must have been worried men. Not only was the remainder of the debt now due, but the town had raised 1,200 men against him. In the week before Christmas, the university's principal received a letter from the Marquis of Tweeddale, Secretary of State, saying George II was pleased to hear "the University of Glasgow had unanimously engaged to raise and maintain a company of 50 men to be employed wherever His Majesty's service should require".[2]

The Highlanders gathered round the Market Cross and Charles was again proclaimed Regent of Scotland. He set up headquarters in Shawfield House at the foot of Glassford Street, later named

Lord Prestongrange who helped support the restoration of Glasgow's losses which resulted from the Jacobite Rebellion.

A pair of duelling pistols carried by Prince Charles Stuart in Scotland.

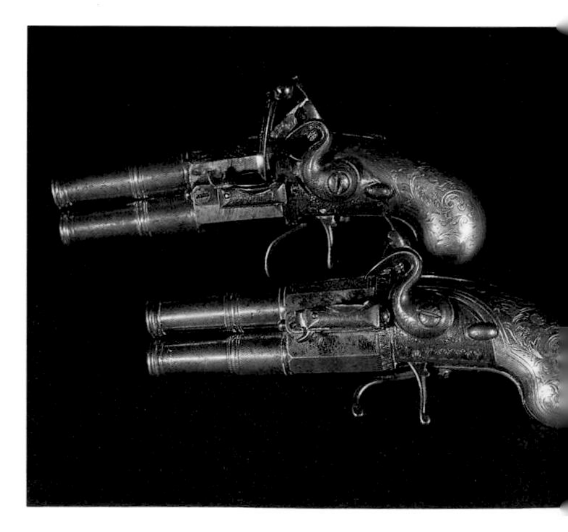

1. Oats and the highroad to England notwithstanding, Boswell also quotes Johnson as saying, "Much may be made of a Scotchman if he is caught young." **Life of Johnson**, 1791.

2. Letter in University of Glasgow Special Collections.

GLASGOW'S MERCHANT CITY

The Merchant City inhabits streets west of the High Street and north of the Trongate built as Glasgow's New Town in the late 18th century. It was produced by a series of private speculations within an area already dotted with houses, a church, factories, Tobacco Lord villas, and ancient cattle tracks.

Existing buildings determined the street pattern: Ingram Street was focussed upon the Tobacco Lord mansion to the west (now Royal Exchange) and Candleriggs upon the Ramshorn Kirk. Glassford Street was closed by the Star Inn, Hutcheson Street by Hutcheson's Hall, and Garth Street by the Trades' Hall at one end and the Merchant's Hall at the other. Ingram and Wilson Streets were originally spacious plazas graced with important buildings.

Fashionable architects Robert and James Adam were imported to design a number of projects including entire street blocks in George Square and Ingram Street, the Tron Kirk and a Corn Exchange in Shuttle Street; but only the Trades' House, part of Stirling's Square and the Professors' Lodgings were ever built. Glaswegians left grand architectural gestures to Edinburgh.

In the early 19th century the New Town, like London's Covent Garden, became occupied by markets and traders. It largely survived the redevelopment boom of the 1960s by sheer good fortune.

The Merchant City's current re-occupation as a primary residential location for the 1980s overturns some 150 years of established wisdom that *nice* people would not wish to live in the city centre. Its buzz is more redolent of Paris' South Bank than Calvinist Scotland.

Charles McKean

after John Glassford of Dougalston, the house's owner, and set about putting on a display of confidence. He dressed in a tartan silk coat and crimson breeches and went to Christmas parties, balls and functions. Glasgow women did not flock around him, as they had in Edinburgh, though he did meet Clementina Walkinshaw.

Charles celebrated New Year in Glasgow and left on January 3, 1746: Nowhere, he said, had he found so few friends. He left with 6,000 coats, 12,000 linen shirts, 6,000 pairs of hose and shoes and 6,000 blue bonnets. With his men in their new clothes, the Prince held a review on Flesher's Haugh, but that did not impress the town. Some shopkeepers closed their doors to show their contempt. Charles considered sacking the town, but was persuaded against it by Cameron of Lochiel. He also tried to discover who had subscribed to the Glasgow Regiment, but Provost Andrew Cochrane refused to tell and was fined £500. Cochrane later tried to retrieve the £14,000 the Jacobite stay had cost the town and in 1749 Parliament granted them £10,000. According to Provost Cochrane, the only recruit the Prince found in Glasgow was "ane drunken shoemaker".

Whoever he may have been, we do know Dougal Graham joined the Jacobites; he wrote a doggerel history of the rebellion, returning to take up a career as pedlar, broadside writer and town bellman. Five months after Culloden, his rhymed *History of the Rebellion*[1] appeared and had run to eight editions by 1809. He was a survivor and an early Glasgow character, dispensing broadsheets, advice and ready wit to passers by. Most descriptions emphasise his physical appearance; John Strang's is typical: "Only fancy a little man scarcely five feet in height, with a Punch-like nose, with a hump on his back, a protuberance on his breast, and a halt in his gait, donned in a long scarlet coat nearly reaching the ground, blue breeches, white stockings, shoes with large buckles, and a cocked hat perched on his head, you have before you the comic author, the witty bellman, the Rabelais of Scottish ploughmen, herds, and handicraftsmen!".

By all accounts, he only had to ring his bell and his unusual looks would draw crowds of staring children. His song "The Turnimspike" was admired by Burns. Scott said it was enough to "entitle its author to immortality". Graham adopts the pose of the ingenuous Highlander innocently abroad, poking fun through his wonderment at the marvels of the big city, relating a story of how his lack of worldly wisdom got him through; like "The Turnimspike", phonetically told and spelled, "John Highlandman's Remarks on the City of Glasgow"[2] paints a curious picture of the 18th century town.

Charles Edward Stuart, wearing the order of the Garter, painted by Antonio David.

A wee bird cam' to our ha' door,
He warbled sweet and clearly,
And aye the o'ercome o' his sang
Was "Wae's me for Prince Charlie!"

Oh! when I heard the bonnie soun'
The tears cam' happin' rarely;
I took my bannet aff my head,
For weel I lo'ed Prince Charlie!

From William Glen, "Wae's Me For Prince Charlie".

1. Issued as a chapbook. No copies of the first two editions have survived, the earliest known copy being the 1774 third edition. See **The Collected Writings of Dougal Graham**, ed. George MacGregor, 1883.
2. **The Glasgow Courant** advertisement for the first edition of **History of the Rebellion**, September 29, 1746, claims of Graham's poetry, "The like has not been seen since the days of Sir David Lindsay."

DALE AND OWEN

David Dale was born in Stewarton in 1739 and after a time in Paisley, Hamilton and Cambuslang, moved to Glasgow in 1763. Within six years or so he had a thriving business in imported yarns. He later became the first Glasgow agent of the Royal Bank, helped found the Glasgow Chamber of Commerce and established the mills at New Lanark, Katrine, Blantyre, Spinningdale and Oban. He was also a Director of the Town's Hospital ("Poor House") and was known as the "Benevolent Magistrate" in Glasgow. His charity work and Christian commitment were recognised and the humane and progressive conditions at New Lanark drew visitors from around the world. Glasgow people lined the streets at his funeral in 1806.

Robert Owen, born in Wales, was 28 when he bought New Lanark in 1799, the same year in which he married Dale's daughter. The village became the testing ground for Owen's theories on education and social reform. His reforms went rather too far for some of his partners, however, and Owen left for America in 1824 to try again with the community of New Harmony, Indiana. After four years and a great deal of money, the community virtually disintegrated and Owen returned to live in London. He became a leading figure in the Co-operative and Trades Union movements. During the latter stage of his life, he travelled and lectured through Europe, still believing in his "new moral world" and eventually returned to Newport, the town of his birth, where he died in 1858.

David McLaren

Glasgow's principal casualty of the Stuart cause was Clementina Walkinshaw. Her story is enough to start and maintain a feminist movement all on its own. Charles' treatment of her after his escape from Scotland in 1746 was despicable. Nonetheless, she outlived both the prince and their daughter and the last years of her life were surprisingly the hardest. She also survived the French Revolution and outlived another Glaswegian who was in Paris at that time, Thomas Muir. Her state was so desperate that a plea was made to the British Government on her behalf. It was refused. She died in Paris in 1802 of what seems like malnutrition. She always spoke with affection and respect of the man who did not know the meaning of the word gratitude. To the end, she longed for Scotland.

She would hardly have recognised Glasgow and Glasgow would certainly not have recognised her. Thomas Muir died in 1799, the year Charles Tennant successfully manufactured bleaching powder at St Rollox, serfdom in the mines was abolished, Robert Owen took over the New Lanark mills, famine was widespread, Joseph Black and James Tassie died and Thomas Campbell published "The Pleasure of Hope". David Mushet discovered black band ironstone, previously disregarded as "wild coal" in 1800, the year Robert Adam's posthumous masterpiece of Charlotte Square, Edinburgh was completed. In 1801 a programme of free vaccination against the smallpox was instituted for poor children in Glasgow. Sir Walter Scott issued the two volumes of his *Minstrelsy of the Scottish Border* in 1802, Watt and Boulton established factory gas lighting and an Act was passed safeguarding the Health and Morals of apprentices.

Portrait of Robert Owen by Mary Ann Knight.

Chapter Eight

INTO THE LIGHT

New Lanark villagers in 1890.

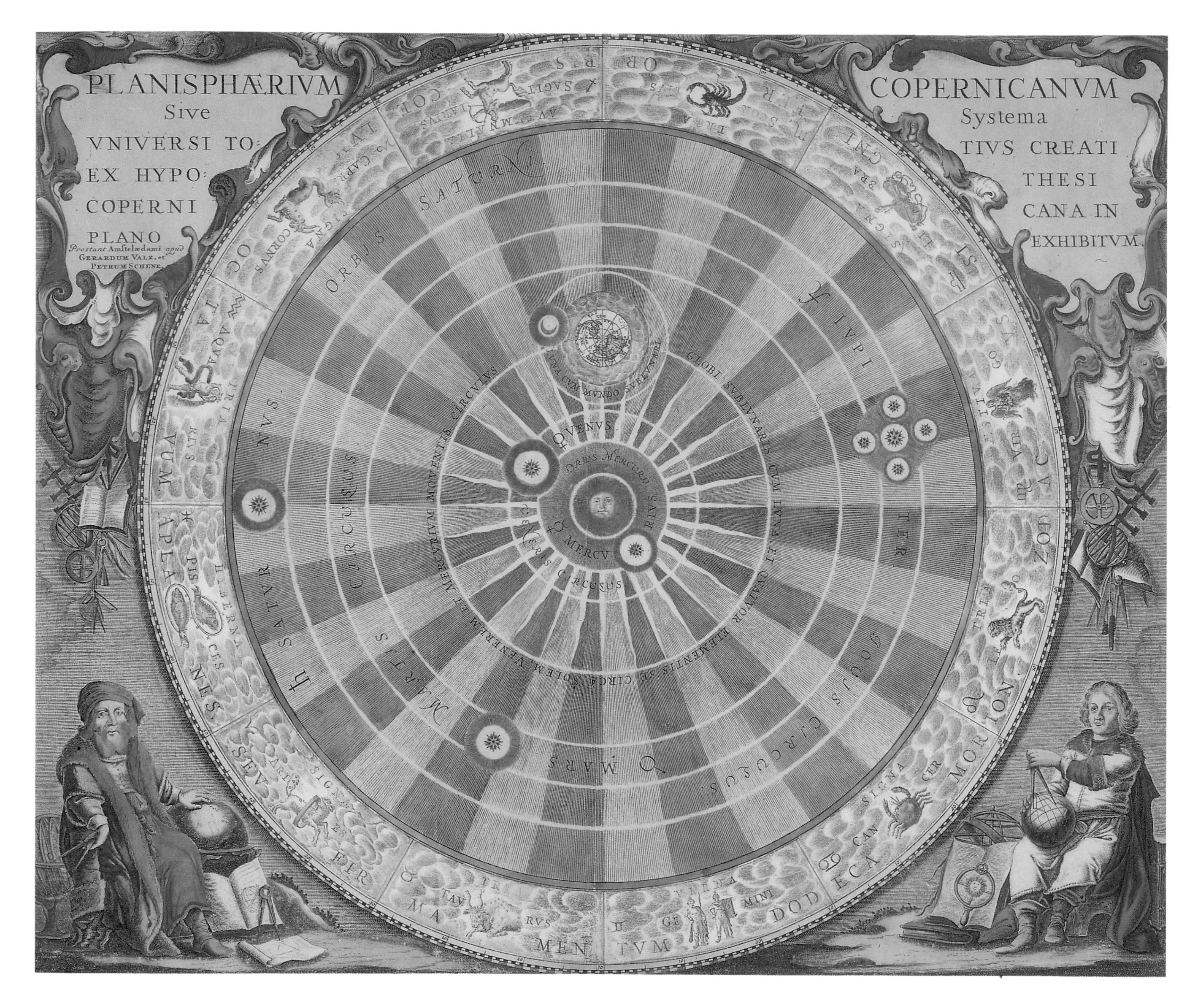

"Planisphaerium Copernicanum Sive Systema Universi Totius Creati Ex Hypothesi Copernicana" by Peter Shenk and Gerard Volk, 1706. The Copernican theory placed the Sun at the centre but the Earth is still the most beautifully drawn object. A telling artefact for the Enlightenment.

Chapter Nine

WEALTH OF MINDS

In June 1746, scarcely a month after the Battle of Culloden, Glasgow University "unanimously and with the greatest cheerfulness" conferred an honorary Doctor of Laws upon William Augustus, Duke of Cumberland, still known in Scotland as The Butcher. George Frederick Handel composed "See the Conquering Hero Comes" for his thanksgiving services in St Paul's Cathedral.

A public exhibition of paintings at Glasgow University in 1761, attended by gentry and tradesmen in their aprons. The smoke comes from a bonfire to celebrate the first anniversary of George III's Coronation and fireworks explode in the air.

Nearly a hundred years later in 1842, when Queen Victoria was staying at Taymouth Castle, John Wilson, a Scotch singer, submitted a proposed list of songs for Her Majesty's approval. She amended it, asking him to sing "Wae's Me For Prince Charlie", her favourite song. This was the first indication that Jacobite sentiments were welcomed in court.

The song was the work of a Glasgow writer, William Glen, who was born in Queen Street in 1789, the year after Bonnie Prince Charlie died. No Jacobite he, Glen saw an opening for another piece of lachrymose mythology and wrote the most enduringly popular Jacobite song.

Glen was the second son "of a considerable West Indian merchant, and descended from a family which had some pride in its past".[1] When the Glasgow Sharpshooters were raised in 1803, to allay the citizens' fear of a French invasion, Glen joined as a lieutenant and later transferred to the Renfrewshire Yeomanry. A fire in Trinidad decimated the family fortune, but Glen went to the West Indies, returning to Glasgow as a colonial manufacturer and trader who was elected manager of the Merchants' House and became a director of the Chamber of Commerce. He was a member of the Coul Club and bard of the Anderston Social Club, a patriotic gathering which liquidated itself in 1815, following the Battle of Waterloo. In the same year the steamship *Britannia* was launched on the Clyde. There was severe unemployment. Men were discharged from the army into a different world. No jobs were available. An economic

1. George Eyre-Todd, **The Glasgow Poets**, 1903.

19th CENTURY MUSIC HALL SONGS

The forms of the music hall song were developed before the halls themselves evolved from the free-and-easies of the Saltmarket. In the legitimate theatre it was not uncommon for Mr Mackay, Mr Lloyd or Mr Cowell to fill the space between the tragedy and the farce with a song in character; the quickly-written topical or local song with a punchline or catch-phrase ending each verse was an established favourite in saloons like the The Shakespeare, The Jupiter and Mrs Dupain's Waverley before The Britannia Music Hall opened in 1860.

The song writers were often themselves performers. James Livingstone wrote and sang songs like "The Humours of Glasgow Fair" in the 1820s. James Curran, who died in 1900, wrote over 1,000 songs for other performers before he made his debut at the Scotia in 1890. He specialised in parody and eccentric comedy, but several of his songs, such as "Fitba Crazy" and "The Chap frae Dalry" are to be found in oral tradition today. The 19th century's most famous singer-songwriter was Harry Linn, a beanpole of a comic who was the author of "The Stoutest Man in the Forty-Twa" and "Jim the Carter Lad".

The sentimental heather-and-homeland songs were also well established in Glasgow's halls before Harry Lauder came along to take the blame. Significantly, two of the greatest successes, "Mary of Argyle" and "The Rose of Allandale" were produced in London by Charles Jeffrey.

Adam McNaughtan

recession followed the war, workers demanded universal suffrage, the right to join a union and the right to strike. They called for the repeal of the Corn Laws and cheaper bread. There was a trade depression and William Glen like many another Glasgow businessman was ruined, though he published his first collection of *Poems Chiefly Lyrical* and from then till his death lived by his verse, helped by his father's allowance and an uncle in Russia. "In his latter days", says Dr Strang, "he took severely to the bottle".

Hutcheson, Smith and Adam Ferguson were sympathetic to the needs of the poor at a time when hardly a page of English writing mentions their plight. Owning land for the accumulation of wealth, and the south's sacred totem, property, were strongly criticised in Scotland. The Union had, for the first time, brought economic liberty and Scots advocated a relaxation of the mercantilist system.

Francis Hutcheson was Adam Smith's teacher and one of the most important influences in 18th century Scotland. He based his politics on his philosophical assumptions. Liberty would be balanced by man's natural moral sense, which would harmonise his own and the general good. This common interest, rather than what he called the exaltation of a few, should be the aim of political association, so that privilege would be based upon merit. Hutcheson also disapproved of inherited offices, believing no-one had the right to power, or to inflict misery upon others, unless it was in the public interest. Government ought to be constructed to prevent mischief should it fall into bad hands. Rotating duties would safeguard against evil men, would prevent corruption and bring new talent forward; it would also mean the people would select better representatives.

Hutcheson was a strong advocate of parliamentary reform, as was his pupil Richard Barton, a Yorkshireman who was attracted to Glasgow by Hutcheson's reputation and who must have attended classes with David Hume and Adam Smith. Barton was one of the 18th century's most radical dissenters. He saw no difference between the Stuarts and Hanoverians, and despised titles, courts and haughtiness whether it came from William Augustus, Duke of Cumberland, or the Earl of Chatham (William Pitt), whom Barton called the "scrounge of impious ministers, their tools and sycophants".[1]

Francis Hutcheson was born in Armagh in 1694, though his family had earlier emigrated from Ayrshire. His father and grandfather were Presbyterian ministers, which excluded him from Irish or English universities, so like many another, he enrolled in Glasgow University around 1710 and studied in the High Street for six years.

JOHN MILLAR (1735–1801)

John Millar entered Glasgow University at the age of eleven and remained there for the next six years. During this time he took classes taught by Adam Smith and in fact left to us (through Dugald Stewart) one of the fullest accounts of Smith's style and of the content of his teaching.

He was called to the Bar and translated to the Chair of Civil Law in the University in 1760 with the active support of Adam Smith and of Henry Home, Lord Kames. Millar was to prove an enormously effective lecturer who transformed the curriculum by choosing to follow the example of Smith's lectures on jurisprudence; lectures which were remarkable for their emphasis on sociological, economic and historical factors.

The first fruit of Millar's development of Smithian themes, notably in the context of the deployment of the four distinct socio-economic stages which Smith had isolated, was the *Origin of the Distinction of Ranks* (1771). In 1787 he published another remarkable work, *The Historical view of the English Government from the Settlement of the Saxons to the Accession of the House of Stewart* (2nd edition, 1803).

This work (significantly dedicated to Charles James Fox) is felt by many to be the clearest statement made by Scottish historical writing in the 18th century. It is certainly notable for the claim that it was the advent of the modern exchange economy which had freed mankind from the bonds of feudal dependence. The work is also remarkable for its celebration of the dominant influence of the House of Commons.

Andrew Skinner

1. Caroline Robbins, The Eighteenth Century Commonwealthman 1961.

Marble Bust of Adam Smith, Francis Hutcheson's most famous pupil.

He tutored the fourth Earl of Kilmarnock before being licensed as a probationer in his father's church. Rather than accept the Magherally congregation's invitation to be their pastor, he set up his own academy in Dublin, married Mary Wilson in 1724 and lived above his college at the corner of Dominick Street and Dorset Street until 1729, when he was elected to a professorship at Glasgow University. With his wife and son Francis, he moved to Glasgow the following year and stayed until his death in 1746. He died suddenly on a visit to Dublin and is buried there in St Mary's Churchyard.

His influence was felt in many areas, not least in the number of Irish students he brought to Glasgow. A page from *The Matriculation Albums of the University of Glasgow (1728 -1858)* dealing[1] with 1730 lists six of the 35 students as coming from Antrim, Cork, Derry and Co Down. There is ample evidence to suggest his influence in his own century, but his message survived as an inspiration to parliamentary reformers, anti-slavery propagandists, colonialists and early utilitarians. The same could be claimed for his most famous pupil, Adam Smith.

Margaret Thatcher came to Scotland in the summer of 1988. She went to the Scottish Cup Final and ignored both the red cards being waved from the terracings and the new words being sung to the tune of "Auld Lang Syne". She attended the General Assembly and gave her "Sermon on the Mound", wearing a hat that made her look like a Greek Archbishop.

For more than 280 years successive political leaders have answered our complaints by telling us it's our own fault. This time, as you might expect, the message was put a little more subtly. This time we were directed to the Scottish Enlightenment for the spiritual roots of Thatcherism. The source of the policies we have yet to appreciate, was a Scot. "You know," she said on the teatime telly news, though in truth no-one had ever heard this line before, "the first Thatcherite was Adam Smith. Now he was a good Scot, wasn't he?". Rather than Adam Smith, she may have meant the Adam Smith Institute, though it's doubtful if Adam Smith would have approved of the right-wing think tank, far less have been a member.

If an institute of economics were to choose a figure-head, it could hardly do better than pick the father of its discipline, a man still renowned for his innovative thinking and prophetic insights into the future of the Industrial Revolution.

The Adam Smith Institute may be located in SW1, but its heart, it says, is in his birthplace, Kirkcaldy. The policies and views of the Institute are said to be identical to those of the great man and deeply

System of Moral Philosophy by Francis Hutcheson, published in 1755. One of the 18th century's influential books and seen by many as the basis of the Scottish Enlightenment.

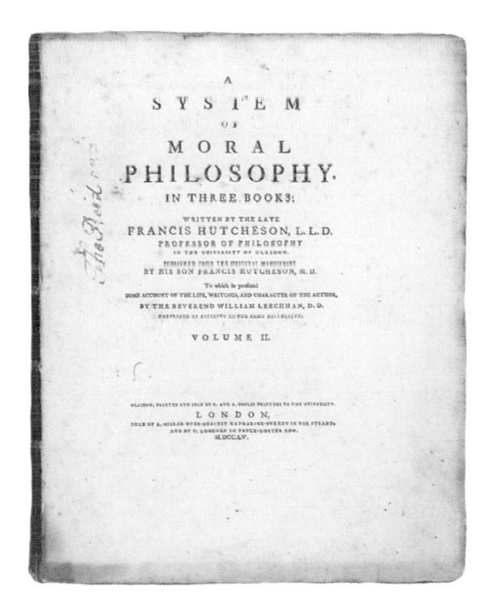

A
SYSTEM
OF
MORAL
PHILOSOPHY.
IN THREE BOOKS;
WRITTEN BY THE LATE
FRANCIS HUTCHESON, L.L.D.
PROFESSOR OF PHILOSOPHY
IN THE UNIVERSITY OF GLASGOW.
PUBLISHED FROM THE ORIGINAL MANUSCRIPT
BY HIS SON FRANCIS HUTCHESON, M. D.
To which is prefixed
SOME ACCOUNT OF THE LIFE, WRITINGS, AND CHARACTER OF THE AUTHOR,
BY THE REVEREND WILLIAM LEECHMAN, D. D.
VOLUME II.
LONDON,
M.DCC.LV.

ADAM SMITH (1723–90)

Adam Smith was born in Kirkcaldy and attended the Burgh School before going to Glasgow University (1737–40) where he studied under the "never-to-be-forgotten" Francis Hutcheson, one of the great moralists and lecturers of the age.

After completing his studies in Glasgow, Smith went to Oxford and stayed there for six years. He found it to be at a low ebb academically, but like Edward Gibbon after him benefited greatly from access to great libraries. The experience was to stand him in good stead when he received an invitation from Henry Home (later Lord Kames) to give lecturers of an extra-mural type in Edinburgh (1748–51).

In 1751 Smith was translated to the Chair of Logic in Glasgow, moving in the following year to Hutcheson's old chair of Moral Philosophy. It was from this chair that Smith delivered his major lectures on natural theology, ethics, historical jurisprudence and economics.

These lecturers were to form the basis of the *Theory of Moral Sentiments* (1759) and of his greatest work, the *Inquiry into the Nature and Causes of the Wealth of Nations* (1776). Smith's work provided the basis of Classical Political Economy and his defence of economic liberalism still commands respect. But he wished to be remembered as the author of a system of the moral sciences, embracing morals, the history of civil society and economics; an intention which he announced in the concluding pages of the *Theory of Moral Sentiments* (1759) and which he repeated in the advertisement to the sixth and last edition of 1790, immediately prior to his death.

Andrew Skinner

1. Edited by W Innes Addison, 1913.

CANALS AND THEIR IMPORTANCE IN GLASGOW

For five decades before the River Clyde assumed its dominant role, Glasgow's canals provided a transportation system for products and people, crucial to the textile industry. Three canals, the Forth and Clyde, the Monkland, and the Paisley (originally planned as the Ardrossan), served the city.

The first sod of the Forth and Clyde canal was cut at Grangemouth in 1768. By 1790, the western terminus at Bowling had been opened, and further large basins had been excavated at Hundred Acre Hill, where a new village, to be called Port Dundas, developed rapidly. By the same date, the Monklands canal, driven into the city from the coal and iron fields of Lanarkshire, had joined with the Forth and Clyde spur to make Port Dundas the most important inland canal port in Britain, a centre for industrial production of all types.

Less successful was the Paisley canal, which reached its terminal basin at Port Eglinton in Glasgow by 1811. The canal's principal function was as a heavily-used passenger line, with over 423,000 people carried in its peak year of 1836. Railway competition then eroded its status. By 1869 the canal was almost derelict, and, after purchase by the Glasgow and South-Western Railway, was infilled, becoming a railway line between 1881 and 1885.

Railway competition also signalled the downturn in fortunes of the other two canals though they survived longer. The raw material and processing needs of the Port Dundas industrial zone kept the Forth and Clyde in operation, but gradual decline brought closure in 1962.

Andrew Gibb

rooted in the soul of every Scot. Left wing activity on the Clyde would then be no more than an aberration and similarly most of last century's political activity an unfortunate mistake.

Smith believed in a *laissez faire* economy, which means a minimum amount of Government intervention and a free and vigorous exercise of market forces. In *The Wealth of Nations* he speaks of individual self-interest leading to the creation of general as well as individual wealth. Taxation, he reckoned, should be low with rewards for society's innovators. The resultant increase in the wealth of the country would lead to an increase in the affluence of its workers. Social mobility and the entrepreneurial spirit are preferable to the accumulation of wealth by landed families. The unimpeded flow of cheap foreign imports would leave the nation's capital free to be invested in the products it could economically produce.

The Adam Smith we see today is something of a changed man. A brief abduction by gypsies at the age of three was only the first instance of Smith being kidnapped to serve the ends of others.

He was not so innocent as to believe that an uncontrolled market would prevent the formation of cartels against the public interest. "People of the same trade seldom gather together even for merriment and diversion but the conversation ends in conspiracy against the public or in some contrivance to raise prices," he said. He therefore proposed government intervention to protect the general good. He went further, advocating that in areas where poverty and unemployment were rife, government aid was necessary for the increased health and welfare of society.

Smith was a great believer in upward mobility, for all classes. He was trying to break the medieval stranglehold the landed gentry had on the country's wealth and to encourage industrial growth and experiment. He also recommends training for all workers and assents that the value of the product lies in the labour which makes it.

The Wealth of Nations is refreshingly free of dogmas, written at a time when people were looking for explanations. Smith had nothing but suspicion and scorn for the politician: an "insidious and crafty animal", he said. The book covers diverse and difficult subjects. Its basic framework is a history of human society.

Smith saw Glasgow flourish in the 1750s; trade was active, the university a vital, questing place. These two energies fused perfectly and worked upon each other. The town was an unending subject of examination. He watched Glasgow developing into an international port, refused to be taken in by this superficiality and, identified a contentious reason for the Glasgow phenomenon. Their merchants

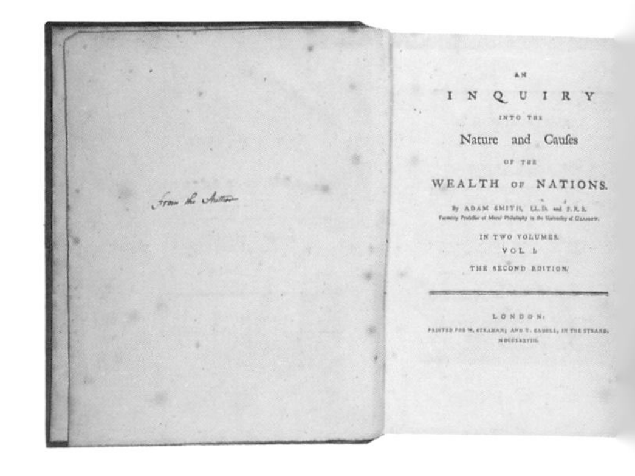
AN
INQUIRY
INTO THE
Nature and Causes
OF THE
WEALTH OF NATIONS.
By ADAM SMITH, LL.D. and F.R.S.
Formerly Professor of Moral Philosophy in the University of Glasgow.
IN TWO VOLUMES.
VOL. I.
THE SECOND EDITION.
LONDON:
PRINTED FOR W. STRAHAN; AND T. CADELL, IN THE STRAND.
MDCCLXXVIII.

Title page of *The Wealth of Nations*. The first edition sold out in six months and within a few years the book had been translated into several European languages.

Boswell, whose personal confessions are of more interest today than his snobbishness and pushy admiration of the great.

ROBERT AND ANDREW FOULIS

No-one could have foreseen the day when Glasgow would rank with Venice, Antwerp and Leiden and the names of the brothers Robert and Andrew Foulis would be added to the litany of scholar-printers, after Aldus, Plantin and Elzevir.

The brothers' bibliomaniacal appetite was first indulged during their visits to Europe, returning to Glasgow to set themselves up as booksellers in 1741. Within a year Robert had expanded into publishing and printing, producing his first book in 1742 and the first Greek book to be published in Glasgow in 1743.

What distinguished the work of the Foulises from that of their predecessors and contemporaries was the elegant, well proportioned layout of their texts, only in part due to Alexander Wilson's fine types. Their exclusive employment of capital letters on the title page gave an appearance reminiscent of ancient classical lapidary inscriptions; and in the setting of Greek texts they insisted on a simplified, more legible character set, omitting most of the complex ligatures. They also showed an almost obsessional concern for textual accuracy, requiring some texts to be proof read six times. Edward Harwood, who dubbed their edition of Horace (1744) "immaculate", relates the story of how the printed sheets "were hung up in the college of Glasgow, and a reward was offered to those who should discover an inaccuracy".

From 1754 onwards Robert became increasingly absorbed with his Academy of Art, recently established within the College. Sadly, this ambitious venture,aimed at inculcating a taste for art amongst Glasgow society, drained his finances and eclipsed the work of the press.

David Weston

had special privileges, which manacled the Unseen Hand of the free market; the balance was lost, competition was not equal. Mercantile progress contrasted dramatically with the older forms of life within the burgh. This created the perfect climate for sociology and political economy to separate and for jurisprudence to develop from moral philosophy. Smith moved amongst his subjects with enviable skill and seeming ease, preparing the *Theory of Moral Sentiments* and teaching the principles he later embodied in *The Wealth of Nations.*

Glasgow University might also have acquired the services of the Enlightenment's other great philosopher, David Hume. At the same time Smith became Professor of Moral Philosophy, Hume aspired to the Chair of Logic. His religious beliefs, or their lack, here as elsewhere in Scotland, denied him an academic position.

When Boswell brought Samuel Johnson north for his rowdy trip amongst us, he is said to have arranged a meeting between Smith and Dr Johnson at the Saracen's Head Inn in the Gallowgate. The evening ended with two of the 18th century's greatest moralists swearing at each other. There are various second hand accounts of their meeting, though not from Boswell, and all agree Smith got the better of Johnson and the last word, calling him "the son of a bitch" and slamming the door. It is a pity we do not know more of the conversation that took place between these two great philosophers, but the meeting supposedly happened when, by most accounts, Adam Smith was in Kirkcaldy.

Boswell and Johnson arrived in Glasgow in 1773, on their way south. "Friday 29 October. The professor of the university being informed of our arrival, Dr Stevenson, Dr Reid and Mr Anderson breakfasted with us", wrote Boswell. "Mr Anderson accompanied us while Dr Johnson viewed this beautiful city. He told me that one day in London, when Dr Adam Smith was boasting of it, he turned to him and said, 'Pray, sir, have you ever seen Brentford?'"[1]

Of a visit by "Messieurs Foulis", Boswell wrote, "Though good and ingenious men, they had that unsettled speculative mode of conversation which is offensive to a man regularly taught at an English school and university. I found that, instead of listening to the dictates of the sage, they had teased him with questions and doubtful disputations. He came in a flutter to me and desired I might come back again, for he could not bear these men".

The Foulis brothers were fairly unusual Glaswegians, but they were typically unimpressed either by Johnson or his reputation and refused to be taken in by his supercilious manner and need to pontificate on whatever came up his humph. They chose to do what

David Hume, painted by Ramsay. Hume's mother is supposed to have said her son was good natured but "uncommon weak minded".

1. James Boswell, **Journal of a Tour to the Hebrides with Samuel Johnson**, ed. Frederick Pottle and Charles Bennett, 1936.

TEMPERANCE

The Scottish Temperance Society was founded in Glasgow in 1830 supported by William Collins, a publisher in the city, and John Dunlop, a Greenock lawyer. Their views, advocating temperate use, were opposed by the total abstainers who believed in the complete renunciation of all alcoholic drinks. The temperance and teetotal movements gathered force as the century progressed, joining with other campaigns to improve the lot of the working classes, particularly savings societies such as the Good Templars.

The advocates of abstinence were quick to recognize that it was essential to convert the young. Band of Hope youth clubs, which originated in England, were established throughout Scotland from the 1850s. With their soirées and social activities they became very popular with children.

The Temperance movement succeeded in securing reduction in opening times of public houses in the mid-1850s and, 40 years later, in persuading Glasgow Corporation not to grant any further licences until the 1960s. It reached the height of its political power under the Liberal Government immediately before the First World War, which passed the Temperance (Scotland) Act in 1913.

Under the terms of this legislation veto polls to prohibit the sale of alcohol were taken in 1920. The results were disappointing for the prohibitionist with only 76 of the 584 districts voting for limitation or removal of all licenced premises. More significant in cutting consumption was the high level of duty imposed during the war.

Michael S Moss

any self respecting Glaswegian would do in the circumstances, they took a len o' him. Johnson left for Ayrshire the following day.

The Saracen's Head was Glasgow's first hotel. There is still a pub of the same name in the Gallowgate, but the original inn was demolished in 1905 and replaced with the red standstone Saracen's Head Buildings.

The Inn was built by Robert Tennent, who founded the brewing firm which still makes the lager. In 1754, Glasgow's magistrates and council made him a gift of St Mungo's Kirk, its graveyard and its ground. This was where Mungo is supposed to have met Glasgow's first Christian converts when he returned from Wales, where he reputedly met St Columba and a little well in the ground refreshed the saints. The well supplied water for the Saracen's Head Inn, gravestones from the churchyard lined the ovens and the Inn itself was built with stones from the old Bishop's Castle in the High Street.

Tennent called his hotel after the famous Saracen's Head Inn in London and when it opened in 1755, he advertised there was no need to go outdoors to reach the 36 separate bedchambers which all had fires and whose beds were "very good, clean and free from bugs". It had a ballroom which could take a hundred dancers, its stables held 60 horses and carriages, which were washed with water from St Mungo's Well. All the stagecoaches stopped at the Saracen's Head and one of the sights of the city was the two tall porters who carried in the luggage. They and the waiters wore embroidered coats, red plush breeches, white stockings and powdered wigs.

Scotland's Judges, the Lords of the Court of Session, stayed there when their circuit duties brought them from Edinburgh. They walked in grand procession down the Gallowgate to the Court Hall at Glasgow Cross where they sent pickpockets and sheep stealers to the plantations or the gallows. At night they entertained the bailies and councillors to a shoulder of mutton and gallons of claret, with two town officers standing guard on the Saracen's Head staircase wearing scarlet red robes and carrying halberds. Their lordships mingled with the elite of Glasgow as well as officers from the Gallowgate garrison, whose only other excitement was the regular Saturday night battles with the rabble who objected to their presence, which one historian suggests "proved such valuable practice for sterner conflicts in foreign fields".[1]

The original cellars still exist and so does the Saracen's Head punch bowl, now in the People's Palace and a relic from the days when excessive drinking was considered normal. The bowl is made of blue and white china from the local Delftfield Pottery.

The back of the Saracen's Head Inn in 1904, photographed by William Graham.

Saracen's Head Inn in 1884, painted by David Small. The building had been converted to shops and houses in 1791.

1. ibid.

The bottom is decorated with the tree, the bell and the fish, with "Success to the Town of Glasgow" inscribed round the top, beneath a floral border. This bowl could hold five gallons of booze and the outside is decorated with scenes of Bacchanalian revelry.

Visitors as diverse as Robert Burns and John Wesley stayed at the Saracen's Head and in the summer of 1803 William and Dorothy Wordsworth arrived. Dorothy's observations were as sharp and practical as ever.

"The shops at Glasgow are large, and like London shops, and we passed by the largest coffee-room I ever saw. You look across the piazza of the exchange, and see to the end of the coffee-room, where there is a circular window, the width of the room. Perhaps there might be 30 gentlemen sitting on the circular bench of the window, each reading a newspaper. They had the appearance of figures in a fantoccine, or men seen in the extremity of the opera-house, diminished into puppets".[1]

Earlier, on a cold, wet morning, they had walked on the Green, where Dorothy described the washing and bleaching as well as the particulars: "'so much' is to be paid for each tub of water, 'so much' for a tub, and the privilege of washing for a day, and, 'so much' to the general overlookers of the linen, when it is left to be bleached. An old man and woman have this office, who were walking about, two melancholy figures."

She was sorry not to have seen the High Church, bad weather again, and "at about three o'clock, in a heavy rain" they left Glasgow. "Every person as we went along stayed his steps to look at us; indeed, we had the pleasure of spreading smiles from one end of Glasgow to the other – for we travelled the whole length of the town". A party of schoolboys followed their coach and were rewarded with a hurl when the passengers got out to let the coach climb a hill near the end of town: "I would have walked two miles willingly, to have had the pleasure of seeing them so happy".

William Simpson's watercolour of Glasgow Cross, looking east from Candleriggs, paintied in 1849.

The Garrick Temperance Hotel in Stockwell Street, photographed by William Graham. This was Glasgow's last 17th century building, demolished in the Sixties to make way for a car park entrance.

ALEXANDER SMITH (1829–67)

Almost single-handedly Smith pioneered the use of urban and industrialised landscape in poetry, demonstrated new directions for the literary essay after Lamb and Hazlitt, and in *A Summer in Skye* (1865) dealt sympathetically yet magically with the lore and lifestyle of the West Highlands.

One of those worker-poets who were almost entirely self-educated, for nine years he laboured as a pattern-designer in Glasgow muslin warehouses (a plaque now marks the location of one in Queen Street). As an apprentice he read the English classics voraciously as well as romantic poets such as Keats, Byron and Shelley. Furtively writing his own early verses on pattern paper, he slipped them into his pocket and took them back to the family's attic flat in Charlotte Street.

In 1854, after the great success of *Poems* (containing principally the long and uneven "A Life Drama") he was offered the post of Secretary to Edinburgh College. Shortly afterwards his extravagant poetic style was parodied and he was labelled the leader of the Spasmodic school of poets. *City Poems* (1857), containing a haunting picture of Glasgow, marks his high point. Unjustly accused of plagiarism Smith then turned to periodical journalism.

Every year Smith went with his wife Flora Macdonald and their growing brood to the Sleat peninsula in Skye. The result of these annual visits was Smith's most popular book, rarely out of print since 1865.

He had far from robust health and overwork contributed to his early death by typhoid at his home at Wardie on the Firth of Forth.

A sacredness of love and death
Dwells in thy noise and smoky breath.
("Glasgow" 1854)

Simon Berry

1. Dorothy Wordsworth, **Recollections of a Tour Made in Scotland AD 1803**, ed. J.C. Shairp, 1874.

"Glasgow Cross" by William "Crimea" Simpson. Mid - 19th century.

Chapter Nine
WEALTH OF MINDS

One of Glasgow's most notorious medical figures, the poisoner Dr Edward William Pritchard. After murdering his wife and mother-in-law he was hanged in 1865.

"The Physician as God", attributed to Werner Van Der Valckert. Late 17th century.

Chapter Ten

SCALPEL AND PALETTE KNIFE

Some Glasgow Boys photographed at Cockburnspath. They are (left to right) E.A. Walton, Joseph Crawhall, George Walton, James Guthrie and J Whitelaw Hamilton.

The Whole Course of *Chirurgerie* by Peter Lowe, who is buried in the grounds of Glasgow Cathedral.

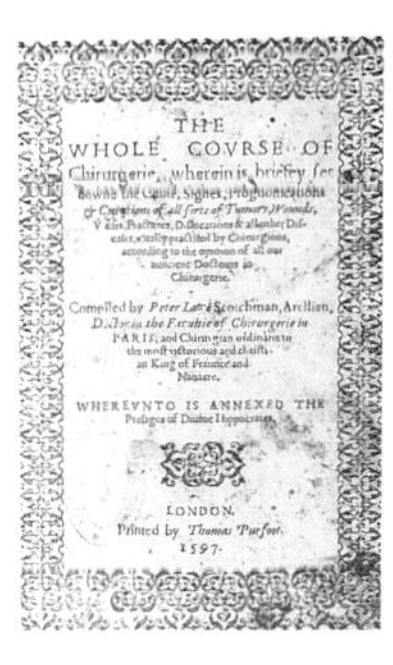

THE
WHOLE COVRSE OF
Chirurgerie, wherein is briefly set
downe the Causes, Signes, Prognostications
& Curations of all sorts of Tumors, Wounds,
Vlcers, Fractures, Dislocations & all other Dis-
eases, usually practised by Chirurgions,
according to the opinion of all our
auncient Doctours in
Chirurgerie.

Compiled by *Peter Lowe* Scotchman, Arellian,
Doctor in the Facultie of Chirurgerie in
PARIS, and Chirurgian ordinarie to
the most victorious and christi-
an King of Fraunce and
Nauarre.

WHEREVNTO IS ANNEXED THE
Presages of Diuine Hippocrates.

LONDON.
Printed by *Thomas Purfoot.*
1597.

The plague gave Glasgow a start in medicine. In 1597 a Glasgow surgeon Peter Lowe published the first edition of *Chirurgerie*, believed to be the first surgical text book written in English. Two years later he created the Faculty of Physicians and Surgeons, based on the principles of state medicine he had learned in Paris. The Faculty, which later became the Glasgow Medical School, included both physicians and surgeons in the original charter, diminishing rivalry in a highly competitive field.

The Faculty of Physicians and Surgeons further strengthened its monopoly between 1719 and 1722 when it separated surgeons and barbers and admitted as physicians only those with an MD degree and, as surgeons, only those whom it had examined. Tobias Smollett, born in 1721, was apprenticed to the Glasgow faculty, and when he was 27 published *Roderick Random*, which illustrates both the gap and bad feeling between the old breed of surgeon apothecaries who had been apprenticed to their trade, learning their rough skills by practical experience, and the rising breed of doctor who attended classes and read text books.

In 1733, Glasgow built its first hospice on Clyde Street, near the present Roman Catholic cathedral. The Faculty of Physicians and Surgeons appointed themselves as medical and surgical superintendents over what was a mixture of workhouse, hospital, lunatic asylum and poorhouse. The hospital subscribers came from the Town Council, the Merchants' House, Trades' House and the Kirk Sessions. Faculty members gave their services free and clinical teaching was instituted as early as 1741, though by 1766, the year Joseph Black left Glasgow for a Chair in Edinburgh, the Infirmary had only 20 beds. Sunday worship was obligatory and the patients were encouraged to attend weekday sermons as well. This was Glasgow's main hospital until the Royal Infirmary was built in 1792.

Black teaching in Glasgow. His discovery of carbon dioxide led to the identification of many other gases.

Joseph Black, an inspired teacher and chemist and a meticulous analyst and measurer.

PUBLIC HEALTH

Professor W.T. Gairdner, the city's first Medical Officer of Health, told a British Medical Association meeting in Dublin in the late 1860s that he would back Glasgow against the world respecting the horrors of its fever dens.

Measures to combat the combined evils of rampant infection, inadequate cleansing and poor housing were slow to be implemented, especially in the face of repeated opposition from rate-payers who grudged the expenditure. Concerted efforts to limit infection began with free vaccination against smallpox, introduced by the Faculty of Physicians and Surgeons of Glasgow in 1801, continued with compulsory vaccination in the 1860s, and reached its bureaucratic peak with the passage of the Infectious Disease (Notification) Act of 1889.

With regard to sanitation, perhaps the most significant advance was the opening of the Loch Katrine water scheme in 1859, 25 years after the Town Council had first contemplated a publicly-funded water supply; one consequence of this project was a more widespread adoption of the water closet, the installation of public toilets and the growth of sanitary engineers such as Walter Macfarlane's Saracen Foundry in Possilpark and Shanks of Barrhead.

Reporting to the Handloom Weavers' Enquiry in 1838, Dr Symons described the wynds and closes of Glasgow as an area where "Numberless entrances lead into small square courts, each with a dunghill reeking in the centre". The City Improvement Trust found itself financially hamstrung for nearly 30 years and it was not until the 1890s that any real progress was made in removing the worst of the city's slums; half a century later the process would be repeated in a fresh programme of slum clearance.

Derek A Dow

William Cullen is credited with founding Glasgow's Medical School in 1744. In 1747 he became Glasgow's chemistry professor; an early student was Joseph Black. Black chose to study medicine at Glasgow's fledgling school, which had nothing like the academic importance or international reputation of Edinburgh, because of its staff. William Cullen was one of the century's best teachers of medicine and Black became his assistant in the chemistry laboratory, eventually taking the great road east to continue his studies in 1752.

For most of the 18th century, Edinburgh was reckoned to be the best medical school in Europe and by the latter decades, when things in Scotland had quietened down, for one class at any rate, students came from all over Europe, Russia and North America to study with such inspired teachers as Cullen and Black. Both men earned their reputations in Glasgow and went to wealthier Edinburgh in much the same way as the high road south later attracted James Watt and has proved consistently enticing ever since. Scotland's greatest and best export has always been its people.

William Hunter was a medical pioneer, a scholar and philanthropist. By any standards he was a remarkable man, whose achievements came without connections. Like most Enlightenment figures, Hunter saw Scotland's hopes collapse at Culloden and he similarly became a model of a new breed of emigrant Scot – talented, ambitious, opportunistic and, above all, a survivor.

Following his triumphs in London, William Hunter returned to Glasgow in 1750, the year Glasgow's first bank was founded. He renewed his acquaintance with Dr Cullen and Robert Foulis. The University gave him the complete output of the Foulis Press, which can still be seen in the extraordinarily varied Hunterian Collection he left to Glasgow University.

Hunter's own purchases occupy an impressive place amongst the paintings in the Collection. There are works by his contemporaries Stubbs and Reynolds as well as Rembrandt and Rubens. In 1891 the Hunterian became the first gallery anywhere to buy a painting by James MacNeill Whistler, which prompted his heiress Rosalind Birnie to leave several hundred examples of his work to the gallery. The pieces were in Whistler's studio when he died. Some are unfinished; there is a range of work in many media, as well as furniture, letters and personal mementoes, making the Hunterian Whistler Collection the finest in the world. This is not a dead archive; the Hunterian's acquisitions continue, from Picasso and the Surrealists to the contemporary Glasgow Gang.

Part of the Hunterian Gallery is a reconstruction of Charles

WILLIAM AND JOHN HUNTER

William Hunter (1718–83) and his brother John (1728–93) were born in Long Calderwood in East Kilbride to John and Agnes Hunter. At the age of 14, William went to Glasgow University where he studied for five years. Although at first intended for the ministry, he was persuaded by William Cullen to turn to medicine. He was Cullen's resident pupil between 1737–40, and then undertook more formal studies at the Edinburgh medical school in the 1740–41 session.

He proceeded to London in 1741 and entered St George's Hospital as a pupil. In 1748 he undertook further studies in Leyden and Paris.

On returning to London Hunter began to lecture on anatomy and commenced practice as an obstetrician. In the latter capacity he attained a considerable reputation. He was appointed physician-extraordinary to the Queen in 1764. Drawing on his researches in this field, Hunter in 1774 produced a magnificent folio volume on the anatomy of the gravid uterus.

Unlike his brother, John had little formal education. In 1748, however, while visiting William in London, John showed great dexterity as a dissector and remained to assist his brother. After studying surgery, he was appointed house-surgeon at St George's Hospital in 1756, rising to full surgeon in 1767.

His principal publications were a *Treatise on the Venereal Disease* (1786) and a work on *Blood, Inflammation and Gun-Shot Wounds*, published posthumously.

He died from a heart attack induced by a rowdy meeting with his colleagues at St George's. His zoological and pathological museum passed to the College of Surgeons of London, where it can still be seen.

Stephen Jacyna

William Hunter teaching, by Johann Zoffany. Hunter's anatomy lectures were attended by members of fashionable London society as well as medical students.

Two 18th century Acid Jars from the Andersonian Institute.

Bust Bronze of Muirhead Bone by Sir Jacob Epstein. Bone was war artist during the First World War.

Rennie Mackintosh and his wife Margaret's Glasgow home at 78 Southpark Avenue, where they lived from 1906 to 1913 and which the university demolished 50 years later. Their exterior doorway is now half way up an outside wall, a design feature not normally associated with Mackintosh's work, but when the new wing of the Hunterian Gallery was opened in 1981, the principal interiors were reconstructed around the existing furniture and fittings with the addition of the Derngate guest bedroom. It's an interesting piece of architectural photofit, which gives a glimpse of how Mackintosh designed to please himself.

The similarity between Charles Rennie Mackintosh and the Glasgow Boys is remarkable. Like him, they were ignored or treated with contempt and therefore forced to depend on a small number of patrons in the early years. They were castigated by the Glasgow press and public and many of their important works have disappeared.

Unlike Mackintosh, some of the Glasgow Boys found fame and fortune in their later years, though a final similarity is that all their work, and Mackintosh's, commands phenomenal prices in today's art markets.

Glasgow and the wider Scottish arts were not untouched by the Boys. They helped set the tone for the International Exhibition of 1888, with its genuine Venetian gondoliers on the Kelvin, and it is doubtful whether the profits from the enterprise would have gone to build the Kelvingrove Art Galleries and Museum if the Glasgow Boys and their activities had not shown the city's facilities for displaying work to be sadly inadequate. Without their persuasion Glasgow would not have bought Whistler's portrait of Carlyle, and the painter James Guthrie's weight behind the move to award an honorary doctorate to Whistler helped forge the link between Whistler and the city. The Glasgow Boys' influence on the later Scottish Colourists is clear and it was their work which led directly to J. D. Fergusson, S. J. Peploe, Leslie Hunter, Francis Cadell and many others taking up careers as painters.

The climate they formed was certainly felt by Glasgow artists who followed, such as Kate and Sir David Cameron, Muirhead Bone, whose etchings were said to be the finest since Rembrandt, and the Glasgow optician John Quinton Pringle. They also influenced Joan Eardley who in turn is seen by many of the present Glasgow Gang as a source of inspiration and power.

A hundred years after the Boys, Glasgow art is again enjoying an international reputation with the emergence of the Glasgow Gang or Glasgow Pups. Again it would be easy to see them as

ALEXANDER REID AND THE SCOTTISH COLOURISTS

Alexander Reid (1854–1928), the son of a framemaker and art dealer, was sent to Paris to gain experience and a wider outlook. There Alex met Vincent Van Gogh, who painted his portrait, but he also made contact with the dealers who were supporting the Impressionists.

By the First World War, Reid had become not only the leading dealer in Glasgow, but also one of the most enterprising in Britain. Just before 1914 he realised that the work of a group of young Scottish painters had much in common with the latest work to appear in Paris and he offered to show their work in his Glasgow gallery. These four painters are now known as the Scottish Colourists – Peploe, Cadell, Fergusson and Hunter.

Reid had cultivated a group of collectors who were regularly buying Renoir, Monet and Degas from him. He introduced them to the Colourists, and persuaded them to support these young artists by regular purchases from his exhibitions. Leslie Hunter, in particular, held a number of one man exhibitions at Reid's.

In London, Reid persuaded other galleries to show the Colourists and organised several exhibitions in Bond Street in the 1920s. His French contacts allowed him to arrange more exhibitions in Paris, where "Les Peintres Ecossais" were well-received.

His death signified the end of serious collecting in Glasgow for over half a century, but Reid's legacy to the city, and to Scotland, was the quality of the paintings in the collections of Burrell, McInnes, the Cargill brothers and many more.

Roger Billcliffe

JOHN QUINTON PRINGLE
(1864–1925)

As most customers in his shop at 90 Saltmarket, saw him, John Quinton Pringle, in 1902, was just a craftsman, "OPTICIAN AND ELECTRICIAN", who was devoted to his work and was mildly eccentric, like many folk. To visitors at the XV Secessionist Exhibition in Vienna that year, he must have seemed an interesting *petit maitre*, painting miniature portraits on ivory. But today one hails, above both the other Pringles, the artist who depicted Glasgow in its industrial heyday with unequalled luminosity.

Initially self-taught – he left school at twelve – Pringle went for several years to evening classes at Glasgow College of Art. Fellow students who respected his talents highly included Charles Rennie Mackintosh, who may have been responsible for Pringle's showing in Vienna.

There is, however, a mystery about Pringle's evolving technique. How did he come by later methods reminiscent of French Neo-Impressionism? Could he have seen paintings by Seurat? Or did he just work it out for himself?

No matter. Look at his painting (in Edinburgh City Art Centre, of all places) of "Muslin Street, Bridgeton" in 1895, red-roofed buildings glowing under an overcast sky and the smoke from their own fires and tall industrial chimneys. Or his 1908 version of "Tollcross", colours dissolving in light, which is in the Hunterian Gallery. In both, Glasgow ceases to be the heavy black and white city of old photographs and becomes as effervescent and evanescent as Paris.

He painted what he happened to see before him, with, as he once wrote, "no longing, no desire to sell."

Angus Calder

a phenomenon rising from nowhere, rather than a continuation of the previous generation of Glasgow artists and teachers, though they too have also had to leave the city for recognition.

Architects, designers and engineers, loosely grouped as the New Glasgow Stylists, no longer have to leave the city to develop their talents. Glasgow is now recognised as an emerging international design centre. These are early days and there is a long way to go. The problem is one of belief, and their future seems to lie beyond 1992, when Europe becomes a complete internal market.

Nonetheless, the suggestion we've been hearing from certain, easily recognisable quarters, that institutional assistance to the arts is unnecessary in a country rich in disposable income, simply is not true. For proof we need look no further than the effect Francis Newbery's influence and his new Glasgow School of Art had at the turn of the century, when something like 70 talented young artists came together in the 30 years leading up to 1920 and created what has become known as The Glasgow Style.

Newbery was in no doubt. If quality is not cultivated and maintained, people will buy whatever rubbish is available, most attractively packaged and marketed. He and his group set about establishing quality design and workmanship, which the general public are now discovering and which almost a century after it was made, still has an appealing freshness and remains the only style Glasgow ever had or can identify with.

Had his influence lasted, it might have changed the face of both artistic design and industry. Unfortunately the financial pressures and conservatism of the time meant that the benefits of the Glasgow Style were reaped only by those who could afford them and it is only now that T-shirts, posters and the advent of new technology can make the Style available to a wider public. The Style was marketed by companies like the furnishers Wylie and Lochhead and the Greenock Cabinetmaking Company in something of a package deal. Furniture, glass, tiling, fabrics, carpets, light fittings, ornaments and houses were all produced by various members of the loose association of Glasgow Style designers, so the package wasn't too hard to put together.

Complete rooms were frequently assembled in showrooms and exhibitions such as the Vienna Secession Exhibition in 1900, the Glasgow Exhibition of 1901 and the Turin International Exhibition in 1903. European and British art and design magazines also carried lavish illustrations of the Style's latest works. Interestingly enough, the present reproductions of Mackintosh chairs and tables are still displayed in time honoured fashion, as part

Ebonised Wood Cabinet by Charles Rennie Mackintosh and Margaret MacDonald.

"The Queen Otomis", a pen and ink drawing by Jessie M King, a former student of Glasgow Art School. Now chiefly remembered for her book illustrations, she was also a varied designer.

of a total interior, even if their prices have taken an impressive hike.

By far the best known Glasgow Style exponent, of course, is Mackintosh who allowed himself to range through every aspect of design from the shape of the windows or the pitch of the roof to the size and shape of the fireside cushions for his cats, and even the colour of the cats themselves.[1]

"Charles Rennie Mackintosh (1868-1928)" by Francis Henry Newbery.

FRANCIS HENRY NEWBERY (1853–1946)

Francis Newbery was appointed Headmaster of the Glasgow School of Art in 1885. It was then housed in the McLellan Galleries, in a corner of the block which later became Trerons store. Like many schools throughout the country it had its beginnings as a Mechanics Institute but Newbery revitalised both its design and fine art courses. Metalwork and embroidery were two classes in which Glasgow had no equal before 1914 and his students – led in embroidery by his wife Jessie – won prizes throughout Europe for their work. He also brought in as visiting lecturers and assessors the young Glasgow painters (the Glasgow Boys) who were beginning to make a reputation abroad.

In 1902, Newbery was asked to supervise the Scottish section of the International Exhibition of Decorative Arts at Turin. He cheated, somewhat, by selecting only students from his own School, but the impact of work by Jessie King, George Logan, Ann MacBeth, Annie French, John Ednie, E. A. Taylor, Mackintosh, Herbert MacNair and Frances and Margaret Macdonald more than justified his natural bias.

Newbery was forced to spend much of his time raising the money for the School's relocation in the new building in Renfrew Street. He also secured for Charles Rennie Mackintosh the commission to design it. When the £14,000 he first raised was shown to be sufficient for only half the building he threw himself into fund raising through exhibitions, concerts, masques and plays, all performed by the students of the School. By 1910 the new building was completed but Newbery's health was severely damaged and he retired in 1918.

Roger Billcliffe

1. **Charles Rennie Mackintosh**, Richard Drew Publications, 1987.

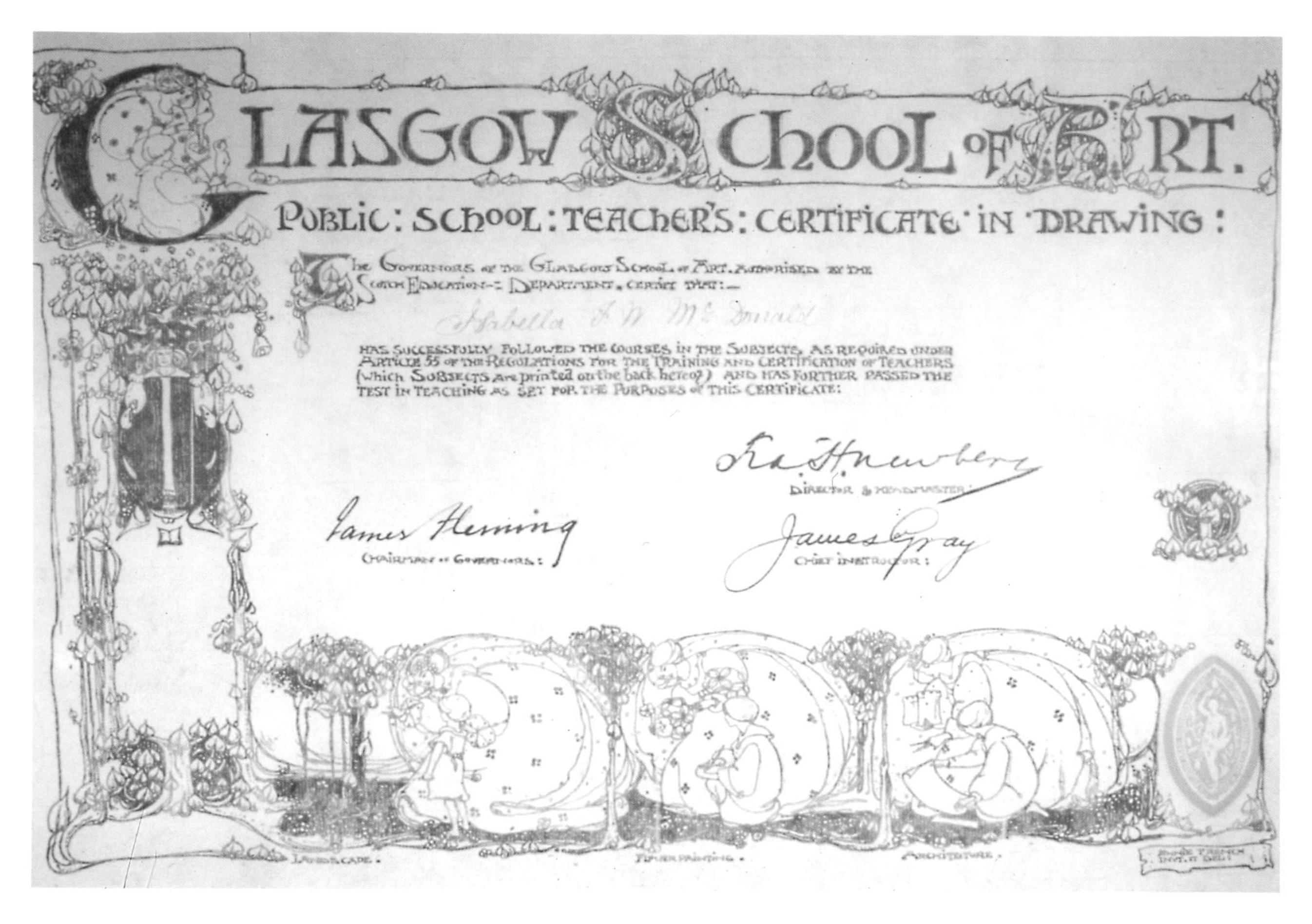

Certificate embroidered by Jessie M King.

NEWBERY'S "GLASGOW GIRLS"

The names of the "Glasgow Girls" – and how the strongest among them would have abhorred this patronising title – make a surprisingly long list. But, in truth, not all were exceptionally gifted: most were simply middle class young women seizing their chance of the new freedom in a welcoming environment of the Glasgow School of Art under Newbery, and really no more creative than their 18th or early 19th century counterparts, whiling away the leisure hours with fancy needlework and watercolours.

Among the exceptions were the Macdonald sisters, Margaret and Frances, who, in a married team with Charles Rennie Mackintosh and Herbert McNair, gained fame and notoriety, as the "Spook School", for their languorous, attenuated figurative designs. Ann Macbeth, known for strong and stylish *appliqué* work, succeeded Jessie Newbery (wife of the Headmaster) in 1908 as Lecturer in Needlework at GSA and became a force in craft education.

Most interesting of all were Annie French and Jessie M King, the former a designer with a highly decorative style that, at her best and in a far more intimate, slighter fashion, echoes that of Gustav Klimt in Vienna. Jessie King's was an altogether more robust talent. She was an all-rounder, turning her able hands and rich imagination to everything from book illustration, stained glass design and watercolour to the designing of jewellery and fabrics for Liberty, and vellum covers for luxury volumes published by Maclehose of Glasgow. It was she who, living in pre-war Paris, learned the craft of *batik* and introduced it to Scotland. Bessie McNicol, another gifted student, became a painter.

Cordelia Oliver

Women working in Lyle's sugar refinery,
Greenock, Second World War.

"Muslin Street, Bridgeton" by John Quinton Pringle.

Chapter Eleven

SWEET TOOTH AND TOBACCO BREATH

Robert Perry (1738-1848). Perry was president of the Royal College of Physicians and Surgeons of Glasgow from 1843-45. The unsigned portrait is by Sir Daniel McNee.

Glasgow children being exposed to light treatment.

Writing in 1736, Glasgow's first historian John McUre said the town was "surrounded with corn fields, kitchen and flower gardens and beautiful orchards, abounding with fruits of all sorts, which by reason of the open and large streets send forth a pleasant and odoriferous smell."[1]

There were other smells. Stinking middens lined the streets and folk threw all manner of unmentionable things from their windows, despite the fact that the council told them not to do so. McUre says there are "sweet water wells in several closes . . . besides sixteen public wells." Glasgow's population would be less than 20,000. Seventy years later, when it was more than 70,000 there were 30 public wells.

The prevalence of disease ensured that medicine would be one of Glasgow's perennial interests. Joseph, later Sir, still later Lord, Lister could be said to have made, in this city, the most important medical discovery of all. While working as a house surgeon in the University College Hospital, London, Lister became convinced that gangrene began with local infections. Young's chloroform had removed the operating theatre's agony, but most people were unwilling to submit to surgery because they knew the chances of their wounds healing were slight. When Lister was appointed to the Chair of Surgery in Glasgow, the Royal Infirmary was notorious for the amount of surgical deaths.

Working at the Royal, Lister concluded that infection was air-borne. Accordingly he developed and introduced antiseptic methods, such as the carbolic spray, devised in 1865, which revolutionised surgery.[2] Lister was one of the many remarkable people associated with the Royal. This was where Robert Perry first distinguished typhoid from typhus, where Sir William MacEwen pioneered brain surgery; it was the first British hospital to use X-rays for diagnosis, and inaugurated the systematic education of nurses.[3]

Glasgow's health is a continuing problem. We are still the

"The Glasgow Royal Infirmary" engraved by J.C. Nattes, 1801.

Robert Adam drawing for the Royal Infirmary he designed

1. John McUre, **History of Glasgow**, 1736. 2. See **Lister and the Lister Ward, a Centenary Contribution**, 1927.
3. **Scottish Firsts,** Scottish Development Agency, 1985.

TUBERCULOSIS

Many Glaswegians will recollect the stern warnings about the penalties for spitting displayed on all modes of public transport but few now remember the association this had with tuberculosis.

"Consumption", "phthisis" and the "white scourge" were only three of the names used to describe this wasting disease which could affect the lungs, bones, joints, abdomen, skin or lymph glands. Originally believed to be hereditary, tuberculosis was recognised as infectious only after Robert Koch's discovery of the tubercle bacillus in 1882.

In 1891 the Medico-Chirurgical Society of Glasgow, led by Professor William Tennant Gairdner, former Medical Officer of Health for the city, launched a campaign to persuade the Town Council to make proper provision for those suffering from the disease. 1898 saw the formation of a National Association for the Prevention of Tuberculosis; this was followed in 1899 by the foundation of a Glasgow Branch of the new body.

The crusade against TB produced sanatoria or "colonies" such as those at Bridge of Weir and Bellefield, and TB wards at hospitals such as Ruchill, Knightswood and Robroyston. Meanskirk Hospital, dedicated solely to TB patients, was opened in 1930.

With no effective therapy, all of these units catered for long-stay patients, many of them children whose schooling continued in hospital classrooms. The introduction in the late 1940s of streptomycin as the first successful drug treatment was followed by the adoption of BCG vaccination, with the anti-TB campaign culminating in the great mass X-Ray campaign of 1957, when more than 750,000 Glaswegians were examined in less than six weeks.

Derek A Dow

unhealthiest city in Britain. Glasgow 2000 follows Good Hearted Glasgow and Look After Yourself Glasgow as a city based health initiative. A leaflet explains, "To help bring about major improvements in its citizens' health and social well-being, Glasgow has joined the World Health Organisation's Healthy Cities Project.[1]

"The Project aims by the year 2000 to reduce death rates, infant mortality and accidents, virtually eliminate infectious diseases and promote healthier life-styles."

The same leaflet does not underestimate the problem. Glasgow's health rate compares badly with the rest of Scotland and Scotland's is among the worst in the developed world. "Almost 1,000 fewer people would die each year in Glasgow if death rates among people under 65 were cut even to the current Scottish average.

"The city's death rates from lung cancer and heart disease are among the highest in the world. And people living in Glasgow's most deprived areas are two-and-a-half times more likely to die before the age of 65 than people living in the most affluent areas . . . Glasgow has the highest levels of social deprivation of any city in the UK. These are increasing, and becoming concentrated in areas of public sector housing . . . research shows that unemployed people die earlier and suffer worse physical and mental health records than those in work. Average unemployment in Glasgow stands at 18.2 per cent with the rate in some wards as high as 37 per cent . . . levels of dampness, disrepair, overcrowding and lack of adequate heating are high, contributing significantly to ill-health . . . theft, vandalism and crime increase stress and anxiety . . . lead piping in the water supply is still a hazard."

The picture is not entirely bleak. Death rates are falling and the infant mortality rate was reduced from 22.5 per 1,000 of population in 1974 to nine per 1,000 in 1987. Life expectancy for women has increased from 73.1 years in 1974 to 75.1 in 1985 and for men from 66.2 in 1974 to 68.6 in 1985.

Of the 11,000 deaths in Glasgow each year, 4,200 are the result of heart disease and strokes. Over one third of the population of the United Kingdom have heart disease; the figure for Glasgow is almost two thirds. Smoking, alcohol and diet are to blame.[2]

Sweet tooth and tobacco breath were acquired long ago. Glasgow's public and private money, from individuals, town and university, had been squandered on the Darien Scheme. When the parliaments were united in 1707 and the Anti-Union riots had died down, Glasgow's merchants seized the new opportunities which came with the ending of the Navigation Acts. The sugar and tobacco trades began. In 1771, while work on the deepening of the Clyde continued, Glasgow's

SMOKING IN GLASGOW

From the financial point of view, Glasgow owes a lot to tobacco. It brought prosperity, paid for many impressive buildings and, even today, employs some 1,200 people in the the city. The benefits, however, have been far outweighed by the toll in ill health and death borne by the inhabitants of the city.

Lung cancer, ischaemic heart disease, bronchitis and emphysema are the main illnesses associated with smoking and the number of people dying from these illnesses is staggering. It is estimated that every year in Greater Glasgow around 2,214 residents die because they smoked (948 from lung cancer, 833 from ischaemic heart disease, 433 from bronchitis and emphysema). In addition, 4,427 residents were admitted to hospital with smoking-related diseases. The above figures mean that in an average month 185 persons in Greater Glasgow will die because they smoked and every day 180 residents will be in-patients in hospital because of smoking induced disease. The cost of this to the Scottish Health Service is at least £5,043,000 per year.

It is small wonder that Glasgow has been labelled as the "lung cancer capital of the world" but the future is not without hope. Projects such as Glasgow 2000 which is designed to reduce smoking related diseases by the year 2000, have been set up. Surveys have shown that two thirds of Glasgow smokers would like to stop smoking and are looking for help. The challenge is to provide this help and to convince the remaining third that it makes overwhelming sense to give up tobacco in order to avoid so many preventable yet potentially deadly risks.

Daniel Reid

1. Glasgow 2000, Healthy Cities Project, Position Statement, 1989, and Strathclyde Social Trends No. 2, October 1989. 2. ibid.

Sweetie makers at Agnews Confectionery Works, Well Street, Calton.

A Mass X-Ray Campaign Unit outside Ibrox Park, 1964.

The X-Ray Campaign's advertisement in George Square.

tobacco lords imported more than 46 million pounds of the weed. Three million stayed in this country and most of the rest was sent to France. The sugar trade was almost as extensive and in the course of a lifetime the increase in Glasgow's wealth was stupendous.

Sugar and rum came from the West Indies, tobacco from America and following the War of Independence, a new breed of Glasgow entrepreneur developed. Patrick Colquhoun founded Britain's first Chamber of Commerce and Manufacture in Glasgow in 1783, a year of riot and famine in a decade of business depression for Glasgow, when the population multiplied to more than 67,000. Many of Colquhoun's supporters were men like David Dale, manufacturers rather than merchants.

By the middle of the 18th century we were the greatest tobacco trading town in Europe, in spite of our location as a small, out of the way place with no port. All this in the face of fierce competition from London and Bristol. Tobacco changed Glasgow forever, providing the financial springboard and the business certainty which transformed us from a provincial backwater to the Empire's Second City.

After the Union, Scots were allowed to trade with Virginia, which until then had been an English colony, and Glasgow's merchants weren't slow in establishing a connection. They won contracts to supply tobacco to the Farmers-General of France, who had bought a tobacco monopoly from the King of France. The tobacco lords contracted to supply the huge quantities needed, cheaper and more frequently. From the beginning of the 18th century, England had been almost continually at war with France. Privateers packed the English Channel waiting to pick off single ships, so the merchants had to form a convoy, making their journeys less frequent and more expensive. Glasgow's merchants avoided the danger by taking the north-west route to Virginia. They also established trading links with other Scots towns, dealing in for example, linen, serge and muslin from Stirling, Aberdeen and Edinburgh as well as goods from as far south as Birmingham.

By the middle of the century, tobacco lords imported around 30 million pounds of tobacco to Port Glasgow where it was warehoused before being shipped to the continent. Needless to say, London and Bristol were displeased. They firstly accused Glasgow merchants of smuggling and even though English officials took over the Customs House and established a Court of Inquiry, the charge was never proven.

In 1724 Daniel Campbell, MP for the Glasgow burghs (Glasgow, Rutherglen, Renfrew, Dumbarton), was accused of supporting the

HENRY BELL (1767–1830)

"It is only the beginning of the uses that steam engines will be put to in the way o' conveying passengers, if ye leeve lang ye'll see them fleein' an' bizzen about on land wi' croods o' passengers at their tail, lively as a spittle loupin' along a tailor's het goose," said Henry Bell.

His first attempt at a steamboat was tried in 1800. After its failure he instituted a long running campaign calling on the Government to help his idea to fruition. The result, despite Nelson's support, was ridicule from James Watt and the Duke of Wellington, who suggested he had rather attempt to "bottle off these great national waters".

For a while he laid his steamer to rest and moved to Helensburgh. He became the town's first provost but his many townsfolk "couldnae be fashed". As proprietor of the Baths Hotel, however, he had a keen sense of how to attract custom.

Successful trials on a manual paddle system in 1811 resulted in the *Comet*, built to Bell's own design. The maiden voyage to Helensburgh was watched by many expecting certain disaster, but they were disappointed and the commercial steamship was born.

The *Comet* was a success though the creditors of Bell, "a child in the matter of money", including David Napier who supplied the boiler, remained unpaid. This however should not detract from appreciation of his depth of vision and perseverance. A fitting tribute came from I.K. Brunel: "His scheming ended in Britain's steaming".

Martin Bellamy

THE GLASGOW MALT TAX RIOTS

In June 1725, the Government imposed a tax of threepence a bushel on malt. This was half of the English rate but was still regarded as a breach of the Union of 1707.

When the revenue officers went to assess the Glasgow maltsters, "a parcell of loose disorderly people" barred the way, effectively preventing the imposition of the tax in the short term. On June 24, the Glasgow crowd attacked and more or less razed the house of Daniel Campbell MP who had supposedly supported the malt tax in Parliament.

The Provost then refused to deploy troops sent in to deal with disturbances. After a time, the military were attacked by the rioters and the soldiers opened fire on the crowd. As many as eight civilians in the crowd were killed and the Provost quickly ordered the troops to withdraw, which they did only with difficulty. The magistrates then spent much more time investigating the tragic deaths of the unarmed but rioting civilians than in trying to catch those responsible for attacking Campbell's house.

Duncan Forbes, Lord Advocate and effectively chief Government minister in Scotland, went to Glasgow in some alarm, arrested the magistrates and carted them off to Edinburgh. After an unsuccessful attempt at prosecution for neglecting their duties in quelling riot, they returned to an enthusiastic reception from the Glasgow crowd. Eventually, however, several rioters were apprehended and sentenced to transportation, while Campbell of Shawfield received compensation from the proceeds of a fine on the Royal Burgh of Glasgow.

Ken Logue

new malt tax and a mob attacked his Shawfield Mansion with hammers and crowbars. The little sympathy the merchants had for Campbell, already suspected of betraying tobacco secrets, evaporated completely when General Wade occupied the town and the Government had Glasgow's provost and magistrates jailed in Edinburgh.

The most serious attempt to ruin Glasgow's tobacco trade came in 1751, when the government demanded a deposit of three farthings per pound on tobacco lying in bond. The attempt failed because the tobacco lords set up their own banks and used its investments to build up enough credit to cover the new demands.

The tobacco lords were a law unto themselves. They formed their own aristocracy, dressed in black satin suits and scarlet cloaks. They wore a powdered wig and a three-cornered hat, black shoes with jewelled buckles and carried a gold topped ebony cane. The Trongate was the first street in Glasgow to be fully paved. The pavement was known as the Plainstanes and covered the front of the Town Chambers and the Tontine Coffee House. Any ordinary citizen who encroached on the Plainstanes got a swipe from the ebony cane.

Folk said tobacco would cure deafness if it was blown into your ear; it was used as a compress for boils and ulcers and doctors claimed it was good for the lungs. It was also thought to purify the air and at one time the boys at Eton were made to smoke their pipes before going into the classroom to reduce the dangers of infection.

Tobacco lords owned vast plantations in Virginia, which cost them dear during and after the War of Independence in 1775-83. William Cunningham, wilier than most, made a second fortune by buying up what stock he could lay his hands on, storing it and reselling it later at a greatly increased profit. He completed what was then Glasgow's most imposing mansion in 1778 and it still stands today, having survived a demolition attempt. The building was recased and enlarged between 1827 and 1832, thereby evolving into the Royal Exchange, and in 1880 Corinthian pillars were added to the front. It enjoys a third lease of life as Stirling's Library.

While a mechanised society was being established in the Lowlands of Scotland, a tribal system was being dismembered in the north and these two simultaneous processes were used as the basis for sociological studies. The first, and best remembered, was by Adam Smith; the other was by Glasgow University's Professor of Law, John Millar. Son of a Hamilton minister, Millar was heir to a small estate at Millheugh, Kirk o'Shotts. He was born in 1735

"County of Peebles" by Frank Mason. The Clyde built the first four masted iron ship.

An early American tobacco label.

Steam-driven sugar mills made by Fletcher and Stewart of Glasgow.

WILLIAM CULLEN (1710–90)

William Cullen was born in Hamilton, Lanarkshire; his father was a factor to the Duke of Hamilton. Cullen studied at Glasgow University before becoming the pupil of a medical practitioner in Paisley.

He visited London in 1729 and became surgeon on a merchant vessel. In this capacity he spent some time in the West Indies. He returned to Scotland in 1731 and commenced practice at Auchinlee. In 1734–36 he resumed his studies, this time at Edinburgh University. he then settled for some years as a practitioner in Hamilton. In 1740 he obtained an MD from Glasgow University.

In 1744 Cullen moved to Glasgow and began a career as a teacher, giving lectures on medicine and chemistry in the University. In 1751 Cullen was appointed Professor of Medicine in Glasgow. He was, however, disappointed with the slow growth of the medical school and of his private practice; and in 1755 moved to Edinburgh as Professor of Chemistry. He subsequently occupied the Chairs of the Institutes of Medicine (1766) and the Practice of Medicine (1773) in Edinburgh University.

But Cullen's greatest fame derived from the clinical lectures he delivered at the Edinburgh Royal Infirmary from 1757. These were considered as models of their kind; and Cullen attracted students from all over the world. His fame as a clinical lecturer is attested by the numerous sets of notes taken by his students that still survive. Cullen retired from teaching in 1789.

Stephen Jacyna

and as a student at Glasgow University, attended Adam Smith's lectures.

Millar has been described as a "giant among political thinkers" and "of far greater importance (but sadly much less influence) than Karl Marx". His work has also been viewed as a natural bridge between Smith and Marx.[1]

Just as Smith tutored the young Duke of Buccleuch, so Millar spent two years in Lord Kames' household, teaching his son. Kames was, of course, the leading advocate of his day and in 1760, the year Kames published his *Principles of Equity*, John Millar was admitted to the bar and was elected to the Chair of Civil Law in Glasgow a year later.

Smith and Millar were born into an age when it was natural for Scotsmen to study history. They watched their country change. Glasgow grew fat on tobacco and absorbed the displaced Highlanders. The Clearances turned clansmen into labourers, at home and overseas. Both Smith and Millar knew Adam Ferguson, who is widely regarded as the first sociologist because of his investigative work into the history of civil society, which influenced Marx and John Stuart Mill. Millar raised the Glasgow Chair from obscurity to international fame. Smith was the first economic sociologist and Millar the first political sociologist. One is immortal, the other virtually forgotten.[2]

John Millar died in 1801. That same year the Charlotte Dundas steamed on the Forth and Clyde Canal, which was meant to bypass Glasgow. Parliament had approved a scheme to take the canal west of Maryhill, but effective lobbying by interested Glaswegians brought it nearer the city to Port Dundas. The 35 mile stretch of water was finished in 1790 when the company chairman poured a hogshead of Forth water into the Clyde at Bowling. During the first 50 years of its existence, the Forth and Clyde Canal carried 3,000 ships a year and as late as 1837 the company were paying shareholders a 30 per cent dividend per annum. James Watt inadvertently established himself as a canal engineer when he went into partnership with Robert Mackell to survey the proposed route. In the process, he invented several new surveying instruments. He went on to build the Monkland Canal and surveyed the route of the Caledonian Canal 35 years before Thomas Telford built it.

In Glasgow, Watt was a prominent member of the Anderston Club, with Adam Smith, Joseph Black and William Cullen. In Birmingham, their influence and the dynamic effect of Watt's arrival, helped create the Lunar Society. Its members included Joseph Priestley, who shared Watt's fascination with the constituents of

"James Watt Devising a Major Improvement for the Newcomen Engine" by James E Lauder.

1. Neil McCallum, **A Small Country**, 1983. 2. ibid.

water, and William Murdoch, who first saw the potential of gas lighting, developed it on a wide scale and lit his home in Redruth, Cornwall, in 1792. "Indeed," wrote a contemporary source, "there was not an individual, institution or industry with pretensions of contact with advancing technology throughout the length and breadth of the land, but some member of the Lunar Society group had connections with it".[1]

Murdoch had walked the 300 miles from his home in Auchinleck, Ayrshire, to Birmingham to ask Watt and Boulton for a job. While visiting Boulton, Murdoch put his hat on the floor. When asked why it clattered, Boulton was told the hat was made of wood, Murdoch having turned it himself on an oval lathe he had invented. Another of Murdoch's creations, a steam engine, ran away and left him one night in the parish of Redruth. Running behind it, he heard distant cries of despair and discovered a terrified pastor who had been going into town on business when he met the engine and believed himself to be "face to face with that Evil One of whom he was accustomed to make such uncomplimentary remarks in the pulpit".[2]

After Watt's death in 1819, Samuel Smiles visited his last house at Heathfield and in the undisturbed workshop found evidence of experiments in optics, his proposed calculating machine and the remnants of his sculpting machine, along with a withered bunch of grapes and his son's old school books.

By Watt's time, Glasgow's city centre ground plan was much as we see it today. Streets ran north and south between the Trongate and Ingram Street and though the lay out is regular, it does not seem to have been determined by a general plan.

By 1768 when the first Jamaica Bridge opened, the city extended as far as Buchanan Street and Jamaica Street, though there were obvious gaps for the town houses and mansions of the prosperous. Most people still lived in the older parts of the town, by the Saltmarket and eastwards along the Gallowgate. The streets did not have the continuous facades we see today, but were broken up by cottages and gardens.

A modest house from this time survives. The two storeys at 42 Miller Street were built in 1775 by John Craig. The Dreghorn Mansion, built in 1752 was an undistinguished Clyde Street warehouse until it was recently destroyed. The most imposing 18th century house in Glasgow was said to be the Shawfield Mansion, where Charles Stuart stayed and where Daniel Campbell hid from the mob. It was demolished in 1795. Another striking building of the time, the Tontine Hotel, was originally built as part of the Town Hall and worked upon by Mungo Naismith, bought by the Tontine Society

A LOCOMOTIVE BUILDER'S DAY IN 1869

The locomotive builder worked a 58 hour week, including seven and a half hours on Saturday. The day varied according to which trade the worker had. The élite were the moulders, turners and boilermakers, who in 1869, were paid 27 shillings (£1.35) a week. The turners in the machine shop honed the 5,000 individual metal parts which went to make up a locomotive so that they fitted together. Next in the hierarchy, on 26 shillings (£1.30) a week, were the smiths and erectors. In the Smithy, iron was forged by hand or by using steam hammers.

The engine was assembled on the frame by erectors, a separate trade in itself. Machine attendants and tradesmens' assistants received 18 or 20 shillings a week (90p or £1). The works made its own rivets and bolts, the latter being given their screws at machines attended by boys. One, described in 1869 by David Bremner, was a "little fellow about twelve years of age who is so expert that he makes ten or eleven shillings a week". Bremner does not record the wages of unskilled labourers.

These operations required great strength as well as skill. The machines and the workshops themselves were dangerous; the more so when long hours brought exhaustion. Elderly people continued to work to keep themselves when they were unfit for the job. The workers week was reduced to 48 hours after the First World War and health and safety measures were introduced after 1945. By then Glasgow locomotive building was in decline. Locomotives may be romantic but building them wasn't.

Mark O'Neill

"William Murdock" by John James Gilbert. Murdoch changed the spelling of his name as an aid to English pronunciation.

June 30, 1779
Birmingham
Hallelujah! Hallelujee!
We have concluded with Hawkesbury,
217l. per annum from Lady-day last;
275l.5s for time past; 157l. on account.
We make them a present of 100 guineas –
Peace and good-fellowship on earth –
Perris and Evans to be dismissed –
3 more engines wanted in Cornwall –
Dudley repentant and amendant –
Yours rejoicing,
James Watt

Letter to Matthew Boulton, in Samuel Smiles, Lives of Boulton and Watt, *1865.*

1. Robert E Schofield, **The Lunar Society of Birmingham**, 1963. 2. William Buckle, quoted in J.P. Muirhead, **Origin and Progress of the Mechanical Inventions of James Watt**, 1854.

in 1781 and transformed by David Hamilton into the Tontine Coffee Room, which so impressed Dorothy Wordsworth.

The Trongate bears little of its former elegance, but Candleriggs preserves something of the commercial heart of the city at that time and with Ingram Street, Cochrane Street, Virginia Street and Wilson Street, forms what property developers now call the Merchant City. Numbers 31-35 Virginia Street is known as the Tobacco or Sugar Exchange, a court and timbered galleries complete with the window where the auctioneer sat.

Around this time, Glasgow made early attempts at formal design. Its first square was laid out in 1768 and built around St Andrews Church. Most of the buildings have gone and the square is rather dingy. The other two city squares of that time have hardly fared any better. St Enoch's square was planned to bring Buchanan Street to a formal end, sweeping down to the river. It is now unrecognisable and even the plan is confused by later buildings. George Square began to be laid down in 1786 and though it has been knocked about a bit, it is still possible to see what it could have been like. All that remains is the Copthorne Hotel, which used to be called the North British in keeping with the railway line. An additional storey has been stuck on top and the bigger buildings around it seem to suit the scale of the square.

Glasgow is indifferent to such matters. Despite two wars, European squares are still intact, even if they have had to be reconstructed brick by brick. History for Glaswegians is an open issue and rather than taking pride in preservation, our cultural mores appear to permit change bordering on recklessness. Indeed, survival often seems to be by default.

Robert and James Adam built in Glasgow, though little of their work remains. The Assembly Rooms in Ingram Street stood to the back of the present Post Office. They are long since demolished, though the centre-piece survives, reconstructed as the McLellan Arch on Glasgow Green. The Adam Brothers built the Infirmary beside the Cathedral in the ruins of the Bishop's Castle. Work began in 1792 and the building lasted till the present Royal Infirmary was built at the turn of this century. The house Robert Adam designed for David Dale has long been demolished, as have James Adam's University houses on High Street, though the middle of the building at 60 Wilson Street is thought to have been done by[1] the brothers. The mansard roof is modern and the ground floor originally had an open arcade. The only Adam building which is reasonably intact is the Trades House at Glassford Street. Pollok House, a building of ingenious invention, was designed by the

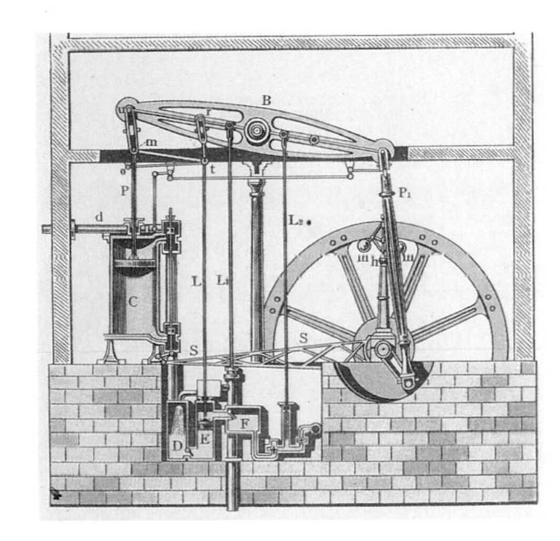

A patent drawing for James Watt's steam engine.

Portrait of Robert Adam.

GLASGOW'S UNIQUE ARCHITECTURE

Glasgow ploughed an architectural furrow distinctly separate from mainstream Scottish architecture.

The arcaded terraces with which the central four streets were rebuilt after the dreadful 1652 fire were different in kind from those in Edinburgh, Aberdeen or Elgin. A few decades later, the lavish two-storeyed Netherlandish houses which merchants erected for themselves, principal rooms on the first floor signalled by serried ranks of dormer windows, similarly had no parallels elsewhere in Scotland.

Nor was the concentration and vigour with which Glasgow rebuilt its downtown grid-iron streets toward the end of the 19th century with tall, steel framed offices in rippling red sandstone – creating a virtual "Chicago-upon-Clyde" – matched anywhere else within the country.

Yet Glasgow's unique contributions to Scottish architectural history originate from the 18th century: the Tobacco Lord Mansion and the Glasgow Square. Miller, Buchanan, Jamaica, Argyle, and Virginia Streets were developed as suburban streets of tall self-indulgent Palladian villas of a type particular to western Scotland, with high roofs, pediments and urns. Each was linked to its neighbour by a pavilion or coachhouse. The suburban plan of linked villas, in contrast to the terraces of houses then prevalent, is found nowhere else.

Glasgow also rejected the typical 18th century square of houses enclosing a large and usually private garden. Instead, terraces of houses or mercantile chambers were built around existing buildings like St Andrew's Church, St Enoch's and St George's Tron.

The glory of them all is Royal Exchange Square. In place of Edinburgh's elegant suburbanism, it offers the sensation of being at the hub of a great city.

Charles McKean

1. Andor Gomme and David Walker, **Architecture of Glasgow**, 1968.

father, William Adam, started around 1737 and finished by his son John in 1752.

Daniel Defoe came in 1715. Glasgow, he said, was "one of the cleanliest, most beautiful and best built cities in Britain". The many visitors who followed have not always concurred.[1]

Major James Wolfe arrived with Lord George Sackville's regiment in 1749. He stayed at Camlachie and when 150 Gorbals families were made homeless by fire, *The Glasgow Courant* recalls, "Many of the soldiers exerted themselves in quenching the flames and saving people's lives," and Lord George's 50 pounds subscription headed the relief fund.[2] In a letter to his mother, Wolfe says of another disturbance that he "Expected a great tumult and some mischief at the punishment of the two men concerned in the mob: but they have prevented all that by escaping from prison".[3] The riot was caused by a corpse being raised by a party of resurrectionists. Wolfe also witnessed the start of a Glasgow to Edinburgh coach service, which began on April 24, 1749. The journey took two days, passengers were allowed a stone of luggage and coaches left from either town twice a week. "If I say I'm thinner", he wrote, complaining of his Glasgow hardships, "you'll imagine me a shadow or a skeleton in motion. In short I'm everything but what the surgeons call a subject for anatomy".[4]

In 1819, Coleridge's neighbour, the Poet Laureate Robert Southey came to Glasgow with Thomas Telford on their way back from the Trossachs and the Highlands. He found rowan berries on sale for sore throats and "apples and pears are sold in Scotland by the pound". The Lion and Unicorn staircase featured "the most comical Lion I ever beheld; more like a Toad, sitting erect in a grave attitude, than anything else".[5]

THE GLASGOW HERALD

The Glasgow Herald is the city's longest running newspaper. From its modest beginnings as the *Glasgow Advertiser* (it became *The Glasgow Herald* in 1805), hand-printed weekly at the rate of 100 copies per hour, it soon established itself among the other Glasgow newspapers as reliable and comprehensive in its coverage of local and international affairs and of special service to commerce. Its circulation by 1815 was 1,100. With the introduction of the steam press in the 1840s mass production became possible (1,500 copies per hour) and the railway system offered overnight distribution throughout Scotland. At one time there was even a separate Edinburgh edition.

The *Herald* usually kept to a middle course politically, perhaps leaning more to the right than the left, which enabled it to reach a wide readership. It successfully competed with any opposition, though it was closely rivalled in the second half of the 19th century by the *North British Daily Mail*. The *Herald* itself went daily in 1859. Over the years many distinguished men have occupied the editorial chair, among them Samuel Hunter, George Outram, James Pagan and Sir Robert Bruce. It was a shrewd Edinburgh man, John Mennons, who founded the *Glasgow Advertiser* and set it on its prosperous way. His requirements are still being met by today's *Glasgow Herald*: "advertisements, commissions and articles of intelligence".

Hamish Whyte

The interior of the Tobacco Auction Rooms in Virginia Street, photographed by William Graham.

Pollok House, whose surrounding land contains three golf courses and the Burrell Collection.

"Glasgow Stagecoach leaving Edinburgh" by William Allan. The first regular service began in 1749 and took twelve hours.

1. Daniel Defoe, **A Tour Through the Whole Island of Great Britain**, 1726. **2. Glasgow Courant**, June 6, 1749. **3.** R Wright, **Major General James Wolfe, a Biography**, 1864 **4.** ibid. **5.** Robert Southey, **Journal of a Tour in Scotland in 1819**, 1929.

Chapter Eleven

SWEET TOOTH AND TOBACCO BREATH

BONNYMUIR, *by* Dominic Regan.

Boys playing beside the Molendinar, by Thomas Annan.

"COUNTER ACTIVITIES" AND THE TEMPERANCE MOVEMENT

In recent years the Temperance Movement, strong in 19th century Glasgow as elsewhere, has received a bad press. Emphasis on the restrictive and repressive elements of the movement have predominated. This is less than fair.

The "counteractivities" organised by Temperance societies offered to many, opportunities for leisure and pleasure hitherto unknown. In winter temperance societies organised soirées with singing, recitations and lantern slides for large numbers of appreciative members. It is true that such occasions gave ample opportunity for the moral homily but in general the warmth and the welcome were valued, especially perhaps by the women and children. In summer it was even more exciting as excursion trains and charabancs whisked their passengers off for country and seaside adventures. Glasgow was particularly fortunate, for the steamboats allowed hundred and thousands to escape and travel "doon the watter", to the sea-coast on the river Clyde.

The energy and initiative of temperance organisations in providing counter-attractions was important. Their activities provided new interests for working class families, occupying the leisure time of people never before catered for. The use of free time by pleasurable temperance occasions was an educational experience opening new horizons to people living drab and dull lives. Many had much for which to thank the Temperance Movement.

Olive Checkland

Chapter Twelve

POVERTY AND REFRESHMENT

Man lying on the steps of a church, photographed on June 5, 1911.

Sarah Murray published her *Guide to the Beauties of Scotland* in 1799. Glasgow gets eight lines. Her attitude is not untypical.[1] By this time, with the population increasing daily, the housing stock was overloaded. Anyone who wandered off the streets and up what are sometimes represented as picturesque wynds and closes found unbelievable poverty and disease.

Glasgow's population almost trebled, from 77,000 to 202,000, between 1801 and 1831.[2] The Irish and Highlanders were flooding into the city, finding housing in areas which could not support them, where sanitation was often non-existent.

The 1832 cholera epidemic killed more than 4,000 people including a couple of demented souls immortalised as Glasgow Characters and known as Major and Mary. Major sang in the streets, accompanying himself on two sticks which he played like a fiddle. Mary was his dancing partner. She reputedly never washed her face, which Peter Mackenzie described as resembling "a plateful of coldish porridge through which some stray hen had sauntered."[3] Mackenzie was not an unfeeling man. He helped publicise the Reform Movement in this city and often courted official displeasure. He argued that excessive anxiety over other people's souls could make their lives miserable, occasionally expediting their passage from this world into the next. His most famous example concerns an Irish family who, on a Sabbath January evening in 1847 when "a bitter, scowling east wind was mingled at intervals with gusts of sleet and rain" and snow lay on the ground, were found outside a so-called House of Refuge. There were seven children, all under ten, their mother, who was in the last stages of consumption, and father. All were taken to a police station where the woman died. The youngest child was already dead. The police said their deaths had been caused by starvation; soup kitchens were not allowed to open on the Sabbath. Yet in Mary's case, Mackenzie seems unable to make the connection; perhaps she had no water with which to wash her face.

"Bridgegate Winter" by Patrick Downie. 1891. The outdoor pulpit on the right allowed the minister to preach to the public.

Derelicts at Phoenix Park, Cowcaddens.

1. Between Chapters 7 and 8 in Part Five. **2.** J Cunnison and J.B.S. Gilfillan (eds.), **Glasgow, The Third Statistical Account of Scotland**, 1958.
3. Peter Mackenzie, **Old Reminiscences and Remarkable Characters of Glasgow**, 1875.

RUM AND SUGAR IN GLASGOW

Between 1667 and 1700, four sugar houses were built in the town, and because of the fire hazard were located in then peripheral situations in Candleriggs, King Street, Gallowgate and Stockwell Street. Waste molasses from sugar boiling was used for distilling rum, while the loaf and powder sugar, candy and some molasses were marketed mainly in the Glasgow area. Dutch expertise in sugar refining provided strong competition for Glasgow, so the city hired a Dutchman as master boiler, and imported copper vats, iron drip-pots and clay moulds from the Low Countries. Profits must have been considerable since while quantities refined were never great, the first major fortunes in Glasgow were made on sugar.

The 18th century saw further expansion of the trade with exports to Ireland and, after 1800, development of a large market in Edinburgh. After the end of the American war in 1783, sugar became one of a range of commodities replacing tobacco in European and Russian markets. By the middle of the 19th century there were new large-scale works in Washington Street, Alston Street and Port Dundas. All three were short-lived.

Competition from nearby Greenock as well as from Liverpool and the Continent, contributed to their decline, but a legacy of a large confectionery and jam industry continued the links with sugar. Very rapid expansion from the 1880s brought the names of Wotherspoon, Buchanan and Birrell into prominence, while with a fine geographical irony, the firm of Hay Brothers sent a large proportion of their chocolate production to markets in the West Indies.

Andrew Gibb

In 1839 Lord Shaftesbury visited Glasgow, walking "through the 'dreadful' parts of this amazing city". He reckons nine tenths of the crime and nine tenths of the disease must come from such conditions. "Health would be impossible in such a climate," he says. "The air is tainted by exhalation from the most stinking and stagnant sources, a pavement never dry, in lanes not broad enough to admit a wheelbarrow."[1]

Three years later another report on the *Sanitary Conditions of the Labouring Population*[2] said Glasgow was so shocking it had to be seen to be believed; the sanitary conditions were unquestionably the worst in the country, the courts off Argyle Street had neither privvies nor drains. Hawkers often shared rooms with their horses and families lived with the pigs and litters.

In 1800, every twelfth house in Glasgow was a drink shop. When John Keats arrived in July 1818, the first person he met was a drunk man, who told him he had seen many strange and foreign visitors, but never one like Keats.[3]

There are various theories regarding the origin of Glasgow's association with alcohol. Some say it had to do with population, that when so many people gather in the one place at the one time, the law of average dictates a good few will be drunks; but that does nothing to explain why the problem has increased over the last few years as the population has diminished. Other theories are that Glasgow's population is largely made up of a volatile combination of Irish and Highlanders, with neither group distinguished by their love of temperance. The city's notoriously poor social and living conditions have been blamed and one genius even concluded that the reason we have such a drinking problem in Glasgow is that a lot of people who live here like a good bucket. For a while it was thought the trouble started when the tax on spirits was lowered in 1822, but by then the country's massive drinking habits were well established.

The People's Palace on Glasgow Green mounted an exhibition, Scotland Sober and Free, in 1979 to commemorate the 150th Anniversary of the foundation of the Temperance Movement. The accompanying booklet[4] is a clear introduction to the subject and the way a drinking attitude has permeated the Scottish psyche. For example, when an apprentice became a journeyman, he celebrated. Many trades drank to the completion of a job. A workman's neglect of some practice, late arrival in the morning or any one of a series of petty offences, brought fines in drink. Booze was drawn into family life. Even today, the idea of a teetotal wedding or funeral is virtually unthinkable and many a father still wets the baby's head.

The Boundary Bar was removed in the Sixties' cancellation of Springburn.

A sketch from William Simpson's notebook, showing Provand's Lordship as a pub.

Broadside warning on the evils of drink.

ONE GLASS MORE.

Stay, mortal stay! nor heedless thus
Thy sure destruction seal:
Within that cup there lurks a curse,
Which all who drink shall feel.

Disease and Death, for ever nigh,
Stand ready at the door,
And eager wait, to hear the cry,
Of "Give me one glass more."

Stay, mortal, stay! repent: return!
Reflect upon thy fate!
The poisonous draught indignant spurn
Spurn! spurn it, ere too late.

Fly! fly the horrid ale-house din,
Nor linger at the door;
Lest thou, perchance mayest sip again
The treacherous "One glass more."

Behold that wretched female form,
An outcast from her home,
Bleach'd in affliction's blighting storm,
And doom'd in want to roam.

Behold her! ask that prattler dear
Why mother is so poor?
She'll whisper in thy startled ear,
"'Twas father's "One glass more."

PRINTED BY ROBERT HARRISTON, 29 JAMAICA STREET, GLASGOW.

1. The Journal of Lord Shaftesbury, 1888.
2. Edwin Chadwick, Poor Law Commissioners Report, 1842.
3. In a letter to Thomas Keats, July 10–14, 1818.
4. As well as to the continuing temperance attempts to stem the flow.

Chapter Twelve

POVERTY AND REFRESHMENT

The Forbes Mackenzie Act of 1853 shut pubs at eleven o'clock and all day Sunday. Glasgow had a population of 350,000 and a public house for every 130 people. The main effect of the Act was an increase in the number of city shebeens. The temperance cause has left a substantial number of descriptive writings which tell what the places and their customers were like. They are entirely as one would imagine. One of the better accounts is *The Doings of a Notorious Glasgow Shebeener or How He Made His Drink* published in 1892:[1]

"My first acquaintance with doctored drink was in a shebeen in my native Saltmarket, kept by a man of the name of Johnny Crichton." The shebeen doubled as a dance hall and the dancers cooled themselves with "a mixture of Johnny's own invention" – five gallons of water and one gallon of raw grain whisky, sixpence worth of meths and "about a pint of raspberry vinegar to colour." This "half and half" sold at sixpence a gill. A gallon of raw grain whisky cost six shillings and sixpence, the vinegar and meths cost less than one and six, "so friend Johnny sold his mixture at a nice profit."

Our Shebeener emulated friend Johnny's example and opened an independent club which never closed, employing 13 waiters who worked in shifts around the clock, with the boss on from eleven at night till seven in the morning, except for Saturdays, when he stayed till two in the afternoon. From eleven on the Saturday till two on the Sunday, the takings were never less than £5 an hour and the weekly take was around £80. The entry fee was a shilling, which the Shebeener kept for himself, so he "was in clover", making between £12 and £13 a week.

In December, 1870, the *North British Daily Mail*, which had been the city's first penny daily, published a series of articles exposing "The Dark Side of Glasgow".[2] At that time the *North British Daily Mail* (which became the *Daily Record* in 1901) was one of three daily newspapers in Glasgow.

Using a technique which began with Daniel Defoe, now its known as investigative journalism, the reporter spoke to policemen and criminals, to the prostitutes and their clients, to the shebeeners and their customers, took part in police raids and did undercover work on his own to build up a picture of the degradation and low life which was commonplace in the wynds and closes around the Gallowgate, often in buildings which had been taken over by the City Improvement Trust.

The articles are packed with the sort of information not usually found in history books and though a lot is repetitive, they do what

GLASGOW'S OTHER CLUBS

"A heart made in a foondry", specified a Clyde stalwart when asked which qualities were required of a supporter. The same could be said for all of Glasgow's other clubs, lacking the sectarian-induced revenue of the city's twin behemoths.

It was not so at first. Queen's Park are Scotland's oldest club (1867) and virtual patent-holders for the game in this country, so effectively did they popularise it. They won the Scottish Cup ten times in the 19th century but abdicated by retaining their amateur status when professionalism was introduced in 1893. With a last throw of the dice, Queen's Park secured imperishable fame by building the modern Hampden Park (1903) – then the greatest stadium in the world and still the epicentre of Scottish football.

Partick Thistle (1876), avowed favourites of vast numbers never seen at their matches, have even-handedly claimed two major trophies. In 1921 they stubbornly beat Rangers in the Scottish Cup Final. Fifty years later it was Celtic's turn; Thistle improbably lashing them 4–1 in the League Cup Final.

These days Thistle share their ground in Maryhill with Clyde (1878), a club who have known periods of real strength (especially the Fifties – when two of their three Scottish Cups were won).

Glasgow's other clubs are durable; Thistle currently plan to rebuild their stadium. Yet, they have been infuriatingly patronised. Boardroom chicanery saw Third Lanark go bust in 1967 but a fraction of the vim shown since in mourning them would have saved the club then.

Kevin McCarra

SHADOW

It is difficult to read *Midnight Scenes and Social Photographs* by "Shadow" (1858) and remain unmoved. It is a book every Glaswegian should read. The descriptions of poverty, degradation and drunkenness in the square mile round Glasgow Cross are heartbreaking, but the impression is given that were it not for Victorian propriety the author would have been even more explicit.

"Shadow" was Alexander Brown, of the printers Miller and Brown, 108 Argyle Street. He was probably a Liberal in politics and a Christian, though not of the do-gooding kind. Wishing to explore for himself the human jungle, he spent a week of nights in different districts and tried to describe impartially what he saw. In 142 telling pages he shows in graphic detail how the other half lived. This is the word of photographer Thomas Annan's *Old Closes and Streets* brought to life. Here is one exchange, between Brown and a ragged match boy:

"How many of you live together?" –
"Five; we a' live thegither."
"How many rooms or apartments have you?" – "One."
"Does the Protestant minister ever call upon you?" – "No."
"Never?" – "Yes, ten months ago."
"What did he do when he called?" –
"He left us tickets."
"Tickets for coals, or for soup?" –
"Tickets to read."
"Tracts, you mean?" – "Yes, tracts."
"What were the tracts about?" – "We didna ken; nane o' us could read them."

Cries of pity and disgust keep breaking through Brown's account – he had no use for those who blamed the people and built more churches. He proposed razing the slums before saving souls. "Either these neglected people are our fellow creatures, or they are not."

Hamish Whyte

1. I am grateful to Professor T.C. Smout for sending me a copy of the pamphlet.
2. The subject has been returned to many times by newspapers published inside and outside the city.

GLASGOW'S INTERNATIONAL EXHIBITIONS OF 1888 AND 1901

When Glasgow staged its first International Exhibition in 1888 it was entering the image business, out to prove to a disdainful world the cultural and industrial strength of the Second City of Empire. It was imperative to upstage the recent exhibitions of Edinburgh and particularly Manchester. With zealous season-ticket men pushing up the admissions to 5.75 million, "Bagdad by Kelvinside" pulled it off.

Galleries full of art, a canvas castle crammed with historical exhibits, displays of manufactured goods and thundering "Machinery in Motion" were undeniably impressive, and trading connections had roped in a strong Indian section. The imperial ethos of the show can be judged from its only significant survivor, the Doulton Fountain, now on Glasgow Green: the Empress Victoria, supported by British servicemen, crowns the derelict remains of Canada, Australia, South Africa and India.

Altogether this great show "where the sun shines all day and the electric all night" went to the heads of the local population, who adored the switchback, and gondolas on the albeit smelly Kelvin. Its profits were put towards the construction of the Kelvingrove Art Gallery and Museum.

How better to open that new civic jewel than with another exhibition? So Kelvingrove Park became once more a wonderland. The 1901 exhibition was similar to 1888's though more sophisticated – and of course bigger, with admissions doubled to 11.5 million. Genuine foreigners took trouble to exhibit too, most notably the Russians, who invested extravagantly in a "village" of astonishing pavilions.

So, with characteristic panache, Glasgow celebrated its past strength, and launched itself confidently upon the treacherous new century.

Perilla Kinchin

the writer intended and let us see how some of our population were forced to live. They have a familiar ring to them: "The effect of the shebeens is to keep the streets in their neighbourhood in a continual turmoil; drouthy and disreputable characters and thieves turn night into day, prowl about till four or five in the morning, every now and then refreshing themselves at the shebeens until they become drunk and disorderly and are carried off to the Police Office, making night hideous with their yells and imprecations.

"On these occasions the Cross of Glasgow is a veritable Pandemonium, and the rogues and vagabonds, when they have no innocents to fleece, wrangle and quarrel amongst themselves like a pack of hungry curs. At these times it is dangerous for any respectable citizen to pass through the streets in the Central District, as they stand a good chance of being plundered and maltreated."[1]

Central District was "King Street, Goosedubs, Bridgegate, Princes Street, Saltmarket, Gallowgate, High Street and that portion of Trongate lying between King Street and Saltmarket." The area had "200 houses of ill fame and 150 shebeens". It was an area where "numerous convictions have been recorded".[2]

The houses of ill fame conform to other descriptions of Victorian brothels and bear a remarkable similarity to the massage parlours of today, though, if contemporary reports are true, we have supplemented alcohol with amphetamines and heroin.

The Shebeens fell into two main categories, Respectable and Disreputable. The latter appear to have offered attractions other than drink. The former looked decorous only in comparison. One Respectable Shebeener told the reporter he would sell drink "to Satan himself if he had the money to pay for it." The larger establishments could take between 30 and 40 people, with a smaller room for select customers. The overflow went to the kitchen. It seems they were often crowded, especially when the pubs were shut. "It has often puzzled us what pleasure can possibly be found in sitting for hours amidst a conglomeration of fish-bones and fragments of sodden pastry, in crowded low-roofed rooms, filled with clouds of bad tobacco smoke, and reeking with the tainted breaths and perspiration of a most unprepossessing company, not to speak of the danger incurred of an arrest."[3]

The Rev James Hall, later chaplain to the Earl of Caithness, who came to Glasgow in 1803, the same year as William and Dorothy Wordsworth, saw some different sights, "it being a Sunday when I landed."[4]

He is greatly impressed by Glasgow's number of praying societies, their activities and dress and also records astonishing prosperity

The Glasgow Spy;
OR, THE
Works of Darkness laid open.

The following is published as a guide to the drunkard, and as a lesson to the thoughtless, to caution them against the numerous artifices which are practised in the age in which we live, by groups of unprincipled men and women; the former of whom appear to set law at defiance, and the latter, to have cast away all sense of decency. These two classes combined, may be considered as the bane of every evil with which the city of Glasgow is now visited, and which will gradually increase, unless some remedy be applied to seize these victims of delusion, and prevent them from falling into a deeper and wider circle of crime.

The shocking account which we are about to relate, will in some measure verify the truth of the above observations, which is given, not with a desire of exposing the persons engaged in it, but to prevent others from running in the same mad career.

Broadsheet complaint of the effects of drink.

Back Court of a High Street tenement at the turn of the century, photographed by William Graham.

1. **North British Daily Mail**, December 27, 1870. 2. ibid. 3. ibid. 4. James Hall, **Travels in Scotland**, 1807.

in some quarters; but so abandoned are the lower orders that on the Green on a Sunday for a Scotch pint of gin, "one of the inhabitants, with an abandoned woman, that had agreed to it, while his companions, and those forming the ring, continued to shout and applaud him, did what even cats, elephants and many other of the inferior animals avoid in public."[1]

"A View of Glasgow" showing the Green from beyond the Humane Society House.

GLASGOW ROCK (1975–90)

Still courting notions of American glamour, Frankie Miller sounded as though he gargled New Orleans moonshine. Dundee-Glasgow hybrid the Average White Band sounded a better-than-average black band, exporting funky coals to Newcastle (and everywhere else, especially to funk's American homeland). Simple Minds at least looked elsewhere, to London punk, to Genesis, and to Europe, before eventually falling prey to American stadium rock convention. The consciously fey and artfully be-fringed jingle-jangle boys and girls of the Postcard label, run from a shoebox off Byres Road, took their inspiration from New York's laconic Velvet Underground and their attitudes from Bearsden and the Barras: they were ramshackle and pretty, an original rejoinder to Glasgow macho bluster. But times got serious: unable under the iron heel of the Thatcherite junta to obtain the shipyard apprenticeships that their parents wanted for them, Glasgow youth turned the forming of bands into an industry. They did not wish to be electricians anyway; as they had as much chance of getting on Top of the Pops as attaining such "proper jobs", they opted to aim for the charts. Most saw themselves as funky Statesiders rather than raucous Southsiders: Hipsway, Texas, Deacon Blue, Love and Money, Gun, Slide. Alone, The Blue Nile explored the universe of the emotions. The future? Newcomers such as the Wild River Apples still set their sights on American waters that from this distance look "wilder" and more alluring than the Clyde or Kelvin. Shame.

David Belcher

1. ibid.

(8)

A COMPLETE LIST OF ALL THE

SPORTING LADIES

Who are to be in Glasgow during the Fair, with their Names, Characters, and where they are to be found; together with an account of their different Prices.

IT is a tale that has been told,
Amongst the people, young and old,
That in all ages have been plenty,
Of sporting girls, all fu' dainty.

To Glasgow Fair, I understand,
Lately there has arrived to hand,
Sporting Ladies of every age,
In Venus' wars for to engage.

There's Miss M'Nab from Edinburgh town,
To Glasgow come to play the loon;
She charges high, but yet she's willing,
Before she wants—to take a shilling.

There's sporting Meg from Aberdeen,
The like of her was never seen;
Her price is only half-a-crown,
And when she's paid, she quick lies down.

There's Jean from Perth, both clean & neat,
And Ann from Crieff, who is not blate,
And Kate M'Kay from Inverness,
A bonny sporting Highland lass.

In the Candleriggs they all dwell,
In the *holy land*, which is known well,
You'll find them there at any hour,
To welcome strangers to their door.

From Inverary in the west,
Comes Miss M'Nair that's neatly drest,
She is without crack or flaw,
The best that e'er came here awa.

From Hamilton, there's lately too,
Arrived Nan, Sweet Bett, and Sue,
In the High Street, without blotch or stains,
You'll find them all in Lucky M——s.

From England too, of the best kind,
There has arrived, as I do find,
Some sporting ladies, frank and free,
That wont refuse to sport a-wee.

There price is only half-a-crown,
Excepting one, they call Miss B——n,
And half-a-guinea she must hae,
In M'K——s they all do stay.

There's Bet, Jean, Kate, and pretty Poll,
Who ne'er thought shame to blaw the coal,
For to increase the lewd desire
Of men, and then their buttocks fire.

Their price is low, if that's your mind;
They swear they're not a jot behind
The rest; although their price is scant,
They'll take a gill before they want.

From Greenock, all for sporting drest,
A large assortment of the best;
And if the hire you cannot pay,
They'll trust you to another day.

About the gloamin', neat and clean,
In the Goosedubs there's to be seen,
Numbers whose price are sma',
Just twopence or ane gang awa.

Each one is justly advertised,
To serve all ranks, if they are pleased;
Thir habitations, price, and name,
And how they're dress'd and whence they came

Now to conclude, from what's laid down,
From priest unto the country clown,
I pray each one for to take care,
And don't be caught into their snare.

Printed for the Flying Stationers.

A list of one of the Glasgow Fair's other attractions.

Chapter Twelve

POVERTY AND REFRESHMENT

The Glasgow Fair of 1825, drawn from the Courthouse roof, showing penny geggies, circus and side shows.

"Gorbals Steeple" by William Simpson.

JAMES CLELAND (1770–1840)

Born in 1770, James Cleland worked with his father in the building trade. He was involved in a series of large speculations, including the purchase of the old jail and buildings at Glasgow Cross for some £8,000, where he built a block of tenements and shops.

In 1814, having established himself as a builder of considerable talent and public spirit, not least through his unpaid supervision of the construction of St George's Church, and his plans for the city's new High School, (built in 1807) he was appointed Master of Works and Superintendent of Statute Labour for the city. He held the appointment until 1834. His service to the city was marked by a public subscription which raised in excess of £4,500, and the presentation of the building in Buchanan Street known as "Cleland's Testimonial".

During the years of trade depression he had supervised (between 1819 and 1820) the substantial works on Glasgow Green, to improve the area's amenity and provide work for unemployed weavers. He also undertook the standardisation of the various weights and measures used by traders in the city, and introduced live cattle markets.

His most notable publications are the statistics of Glasgow, published in 1820, 1832 and in compendium form in 1837, and his *Annals of Glasgow*, published in 1816 as a fundraising project for the city's Royal Infirmary. But these were accompanied by numerous pamphlets. All of them as invaluable to the historian of Glasgow today, as his practical works were to the city's inhabitants of the 1820s.

Nicholas Morgan

Chapter Thirteen

THE GREEN AND THE GREY

Hugh Macdonald's *Rambles Round Glasgow*, first published in 1854, notes folk from the Gallowgate, "unfortunate females" and "owlish-looking knaves", on Glasgow Green. Their children are "hungry looking, with precocious lines of care on their old-mannish features."[1]

The Green was used for drying clothes, and Macdonald advises bachelors to look at the washing rather than the women. A well-scrubbed washing will tell you more about a girl's character than the way she looks, says Macdonald, adding that the "smart-handed and strapping maiden may well glance with pride at the dazzling results of her morning's toil."[2]

Sixty species of wildflower grew on Glasgow Green; and on April 30, girls from Bridgeton and the Calton gathered bunches of yarrow to put beneath their pillows so they could dream of their future husbands on a May Day morning.[3]

For more than 800 years Glasgow Green has served the city as a source of income, a sports ground, a religious and political meeting place, a park, Glasgow's first golf course and the place where Rangers Football Club was formed.

The Green is thought to be the oldest public park in Britain. Many began as royal or private parks, but James II granted Glasgow Green to Bishop William Turnbull in 1450 and it has belonged to the city ever since, continuously used as a common grazing ground till the end of the last century. Glaswegians regard the Green as their own and have fought to protect it against a variety of speculators, including Glasgow Corporation.

The first proposal to turn the Green into a coal mine was made in 1822 when James Cleland, Glasgow's Superintendent of Public Works who had drawn up the plans for Glasgow Green, commissioned extensive borings and estimated there was enough coal to bring out 15,000 tons a year for a hundred years. The idea was not taken seriously until 1858 when the town council

A Gymnasium For Adults on Glasgow Green.

"Washing House, Glasgow Green" by Thomas Fairbairn, near where the idea of a separate condenser occurred to James Watt.

On Tuesday last, as an old Man was lying in the Green reading a book, he was attack'd by the Town Bull, who tore two of his Ribs from the Back Bone, and broke his Back bone. His life is dispair'd of.

Glasgow Journal, *June 21, 1742.*

The Amusements of the average Glasgow man are now of a simple character. For eights months of the year he follows football – as a spectator.

D. MacLeod Malloch, The Book of Glasgow Anecdote, *1912.*

1. Macdonald is careful his reader should not confuse "these parties with what are called the lower orders of our city". **2.** Hugh Macdonald, **Rambles Round Glasgow**, 1854.
3. Macdonald also found shamrocks, "which the Irish Catholics of our city gather on Saint Patrick's Day".

FOOTBALL IN GLASGOW

"Week's wastit", complained the man discovering his team's game was cancelled. Football is Glasgow's heartbeat.

The city's whole life is to be seen in its stadiums. In 1909 Celtic and Rangers fans united to riot at Hampden, smashing down the goal posts and setting fire to pay-boxes. Ostensibly they were peeved by the lack of extra-time in the drawn Cup Final replay. Consciously or not, they were also expressing a mood of popular turmoil and belligerence. This was the period when mechanisation was seeing skilled men in the Clydeside yards thrown out of work. Three years before Glasgow had elected its first ILP member, six years on would come the Rent Strike.

The intensity of the football obsession created records. The first ever international, against England, was played at Hamilton Crescent Cricket Ground in the West End in 1872. On consecutive Saturdays in 1937 crowds nearing 150,000 on each occasion watched the "England game" and the Scottish Cup Final – still European attendance records for an international and a domestic fixture. Tragically, the pulsating crowds have not always been accommodated safely. In disasters at Ibrox 26 people died in 1902 and 66 in 1971.

Knowledgeable Glaswegians provided a perfect, idolatrous setting for the greatest football match of all time – Real Madrid's 7–3 defeat of Eintracht in the 1960 European Cup Final at Hampden.

Teeming casualty departments after Old Firm matches show another aspect. Not all Glasgow's footballing passions are benign.

Kevin McCarra

got themselves into £100,000 worth of debt by buying Kelvingrove and Victoria Parks and the site for the McLellan Galleries. When they were presented with a scheme to clear the debt by leasing the Green for coal mining, the majority of the councillors approved, even though mine refuse and subsidence would turn the Green into a rubbish tip. Protest meetings were organised and the plan was dropped, but it was resurrected twice more in the next 30 years.

The Glasgow Monkland and Airdrie Railway Company wanted to build a viaduct across the Green in 1847 and that proposal was defeated in Parliament, but more recently, proposals to bring the east flank of the inner ring road through the Green dragged on for eight years until the Secretary of State for Scotland deferred the plans in 1981. Glasgow's continuing love for the internal combustion engine has recently put similar plans back on the agenda.

The Green was always the city's favourite meeting place. John Wesley preached there and the great evangelical rallies of the last century were held on the Green. Though Moody and Sankey, the first American evangelists to visit Britain, preached from a tent near Nelson's Monument, the Green is best known as a political meeting place. The Calton Weavers and Chartists gathered here; as did all the great demonstrations which preceded the 1832 Reform Bill. The Red Clydeside rallies continued the tradition and the May Day marches ended there until the 1950s when they were moved to Queen's Park. Before flower beds decorated the front entrance, speakers attracted huge crowds. The Green was Glasgow's Hyde Park Corner. Every weekend the orators would place their boxes or platforms between the High Court and Nelson's Monument. Harry McShane reckons that many Glasgow MPs and councillors in the early part of this century were graduates of "Glasgow Green University".[1]

Glasgow's early theatres, mostly open air affairs, but sometimes held in tents, were sited here. Over the years there have been many attempts by theatre and circus owners to maintain permanent or semi-permanent buildings on the Green. Shows that came with the Glasgow Fair tended to linger: from the foot of the Saltmarket down to the Clyde were circuses, shows, stalls, theatre, geggies, performing bears and cock-fights. Benny Lynch first fought here and though the Fair diminished over the years, especially when it was moved to the football pitches, the Green was still the natural venue for travelling shows.

The last of its circuses performed in 1981. It's sad to think that this spectacle on the Green has gone for good, especially since it saw the fulfillment of one of seer Alexander Peden's more terrifying

ARROL – JOHNSTON

Between 1900 and 1901 the Mo-Car Syndicate Ltd built Arrol-Johnston dogcarts at Camlachie, in Glasgow. It had been registered in December 1898, with a capital of £40,000, and until 1905 made dogcarts, conventional cars and financial losses.

Johnston – the most creative of the early Glasgow motor engineers – had been developing his dogcarts since 1895. They concealed an odd mix of innovative and conventional technical ideas behind a distinctive but archaic exterior that was no help to sales. It was really their great reputation for reliability that sold them, especially to Scottish doctors.

The factory had been edged out of Glasgow in 1901 by a fire and had taken up residence in Paisley; there he had been eased out by John Napier, who gradually replaced the dogcarts with conventional vehicles. William Beardmore (later Lord Invernairn) took over in 1905 and created The New Arrol-Johnston Co, with a capital of £100,000; although lorries and buses were added to car making, losses went on until T.C. Pullinger was imported from Humber, in 1909.

His experience was wide, firstly in the French motor industry, then with Sunbeam and Humber, in England. His new Renault-like 15.9 hp model, along with an 11.0 and a 23.9, soon put the firm into profit, demand growing to such an extent that Underwood had to be abandoned for a fine new factory at Heathhall, near Dumfries in 1913.

After it the Company was gradually pulled down, along with the rest of the Beardmore industrial empire – not fit reward for what had been Pullinger's finest achievement.

George Oliver

1. Harry McShane, **No Mean Fighter**, 1978.

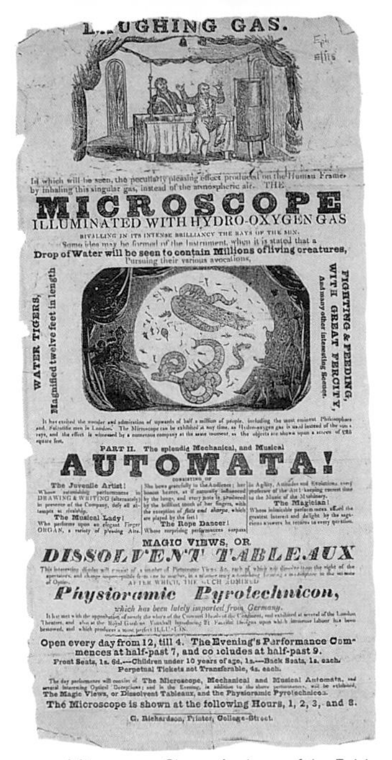

Microscope Show. And one of the Fair's attractions.

A cartoon from *The Dailie*, December 15, 1897, showing Glasgow men what to expect when the People's Palace opens.

Undated picture of a Glasgow single-end.

prophesies – that the day would come when lions would be whelped on Glasgow Green.

The People's Palace was opened on January 22, 1898, having taken more than 30 years to build. The wonder is not that it took so long to be completed, but rather that it was finished at all. In Glasgow's *annus mirabilis*, 1866, the Corporation got more than [1] £2,500 from the sale of the old Bridgeton bleaching green. The money was deposited with the Clydesdale Bank and the interest used to help pay for the building that became the People's Palace. The Corporation had other things to worry about, but 1866 was the year of the City Improvement Act and the People's Palace was part of Glasgow's municipal provision.

The case was argued by Councillor Robert Crawford, who was chairman of both the Health Committee and the Committee for Galleries and Museums. He did not separate the functions, the physical well-being of the city being as important as its cultural welfare.

London's People's Palace included an art gallery, a library and reading room, swimming baths and a gymnasium, winter gardens a play room and a concert hall. It was also tied in with active education, was more than three times over-subscribed and had been built by teams of labourers working non-stop, 24 hours a day, seven days a week. Glasgow's Palace was constructed with the London model in mind – a cultural museum and winter garden for the working class. Edinburgh's People's Palace in the Grassmarket was and still is a doss-house.

The building on the Green was recognition of a Glasgow blight. Rev Thomas Chalmers, the great Disruptionist and a future Moderator of the Free Church Assembly, had St John's as his charge. In 1823 he gave a full and complete *Statement in Regard to the Pauperism*, [2] following an investigation into urban industrialised problems conducted in the parish between 1819 and 1822. Chalmers inadvertently laid the foundations for most Victorian social work, with its large element of piety. The very same attitudes later gave rise to the Young Men's Christian Association and the Boys' Brigade.

Visitors saw what they wanted to see: poverty then as now, in Glasgow as in the world, could be invisible. Even William Cobbett missed the squalor when, on October 19, 1832, he wrote from Glasgow for his *Weekly Political Register*. [3]

Those who lived here paint the truest picture. Robert Graham was Professor of Botany at the University and a Physician at the Royal Infirmary and in 1818 he published a pamphlet, *Practical Observations on Continued Fever*. Continued fever was typhus,

THE MITCHELL LIBRARY

"A cemetery of books" Lord Rosebery called The Mitchell Library when he opened the North Street building in 1911. In fact, the library has always been alive to the needs of its readers; it has provided the citizens of Glasgow with their own open university for over 100 years. It is named after Stephen Mitchell, a tobacco manufacturer in Glasgow ("Prize Crop"), who left £67,000 "for the establishment of a large public library in Glasgow, with all the modern accessories connected therewith".

Since its opening in Ingram Street in 1877, "The Mitchell" has outgrown three buildings. Originally it was a closed-access library, books being issued through a central point. This gradually changed towards the establishment of specialised subject departments with a basic stock on the open shelves. The additional space offered by building on the site of the St Andrew's Halls accelerated this trend, so that there are now ten departments – from Rare Books to Business Users Service – accommodated in the extended library (opened 1981). The Mitchell's reputation as a source of information is worldwide; with the extension and stock of 1.5 million volumes it also enjoys the distinction of being the biggest public reference library in Europe.

While the library has often attracted prestigious donations (such as the Jeffrey Library with its Audubon's *Birds of America*) two important collections were projected from the start: the Glasgow Collection ("all papers which illustrate the city's growth and life") and Scottish Poetry (including the Robert Burns Collection, the largest in existence). And the basic principle of the library, laid down by Mitchell, that books on all subjects "not immoral" are to be freely available, continues to this day.

Hamish Whyte

1. As well as the City Improvement Act, the Glasgow Armorial Insignia was approved by the Lord Lyon. **2.** See Olive Checkland, **Philanthropy in Victorian Scotland**, 1980. **3.** Cobbett came in the wake of the Reform Bill and considered "the conduct of the Scotch" concerning reform to be "exemplary beyond description".

LOCOMOTIVE BUILDING IN GLASGOW

The Private Companies
The Scottish Railway boom in the 1830s and Forties created a huge demand for steam locomotives. Scottish general engineering firms like Johnston & McNab, Murdoch and Aitken, the St Rollox Foundry Co, and Mitchell & Neilson were soon grabbing a share in the market. Walter Montgomerie Neilson established the Hyde Park works in Springburn in 1860–62. He was then bought out but, believing himself cheated, returned to set up the Clyde Locomotive works in the same area in 1884. Four years on it was sold and renamed the Atlas works. In 1903, Hyde Park, Atlas, and the south side-based Queen's Park amalgamated to form the North British Locomotive Company, the largest firm of its kind in Europe, employing upwards of 8,000 men. The collapse of the international market for locomotives, foreign competition, and failure to innovate led to the closure of NBL in 1962. By that date NBL and its predecessors had built over 28,000 locomotives, about 75 per cent of them for export.

The Railway Companies
The early railway companies found that they needed workshops to keep their engines in repair. In 1842 The Edinburgh and Glasgow Railway Company set up the Cowlairs Works in 1842, the first in Britain which built locomotives, carriages and wagons in one complex. By the 1850s, the Caledonian Railways's works at Greenock was overcrowded, and they moved to St Rollox, south of Springburn, in 1854–56. By 1927 St Rollox and Cowlairs had been demoted to repair workshops. They had built about 800 locomotives each.

Mark O'Neill

which had been part of Glasgow life since soldiers brought it back from the Low Countries in the 1740s. Seven people in every thousand of the whole population died in the first epidemic of 1818, though the death rate was obviously much higher in the wynds, closes and vennels, where Graham suggested the disease could be contained by fumigating victims' houses. He also proposed an isolated fever hospital for Glasgow.[1]

"In a lodging-house," he wrote, "consisting of two rooms separated by boards, the first 13 feet by eleven, the other 15 by eight, 23 of the lowest class of Irish were lately lodged. Today there are 14, of whom two are confirmed with fever, three are convalescent, and one only has hitherto escaped. There are only three beds in this house (denominated, with that facetiousness which enables an Irishman to joke with his own misery, Flea Barracks), one of them in a press half-way up the wall, the others wooden frames, on which are laid some shavings of wood, scantily covered with rags. Most of the patients were lying on the floor."

Glasgow's expansion can be simply told, though the cost in human misery is a complicated story, packed with individual suffering and dignity. According to the 1842 *Topographical, Statistical and Historical Gazetteer of Scotland*, "In 1831 there were 19,200 inhabited houses; in 1841, 22,751 . . . This striking fact indicates a sensible falling-off in the domestic comfort of the great mass of the population." In a period when Glasgow's population increased by more than 50,000 only slightly over 3,500 extra houses were built.

The landscape was transformed; firstly by the cotton mills, factories, bleachfields, printworks and the tenements built to house the workers; and secondly by the increased traffic on the recently deepened river, the new canals and the railways. Goods and people used the new arteries and the town began the steady move towards industrialisation.

The first public passenger railway in Scotland, from Glasgow to Garnkirk, was opened in 1831. The company placed their first orders for the English-made Planet-type engines, designed by George Stephenson. The first was called the St Rollox. It arrived on June 28, 1831 and its trials on the line on July 2 were accompanied by cheering crowds, despite the fact that on June 1 Goldsworthy Gurney's steam road coach, a highly popular attraction which was visiting Glasgow, had blown up in the Cavalry Barracks Square.[2] The effects of the explosion were more or less horrific, depending on whether the press reports or the steam lobby's disclaimers were to be believed. The Glasgow public's casual attitude to steam transport later caused

David Octavius Hill's engraving of the Glasgow – Garnkirk railway opening.

"The Falls of Clyde" by Jacob More, painted in 1771.

George Stephenson *en famille*. His son Robert engineered the Berwick viaducts and station.

1. Building of a fever hospital began in 1828, and Lister's surgical ward was later built on the burial ground.

2. See **The Glasgow Courier**, June 4, 1831.

NEW LANARK

The mills at New Lanark began spinning in 1786 and within 13 years the "model community" had become famous for its cotton and for its enlightened social conditions. Dale ensured that his pauper apprentice children were well clothed and fed and that they attended a proper evening school. The social and educational provision for these children was far ahead of anything else on offer in Britain.

In the post-tobacco era, cotton spinning flourished and New Lanark was employing 1,300 people. Its reputation drew Robert Owen north from his employment in the cotton trade in Manchester and in 1799 he bought the mills.

Owen, inspired by his vision of a kind of utopian socialist community, was to bring New Lanark into the industrial age. He believed a man's character was formed by his environment, so workers' committees were formed, streets cleaned, houses converted and fines imposed on those who broke the rules. In 1816, the New Institution for the Formation of Character was opened as a focus for the village. Here children were taught by progressive methods (singing, dancing and even animals in the classroom) and, in the evening, adults used it for educational and social purposes.

Owen's utopian community became world famous but by 1824 he had left to further the cause in America. The village continued to produce cotton but the crusading energy of Owen was gone. Production ceased in 1968. The village has since been almost completely restored and is now a World Heritage site.

David McLaren

many fatalities and serious accidents, whether from leaping on and off moving locomotives, or wandering onto the track.[1]

According to Sinclair's 1793 *Statistical Account of Scotland*, Glasgow's "spirit for manufactures" became prevalent between 1725 and 1750. "The variety of manufactures now carried on in Glasgow . . . are very great; but that which seems, for some years past, to have excited the most general attention is the manufacture of cotton cloths of various kinds . . . For this purpose cotton mills, bleachfields and printfields have been erected on almost all the streams in the neighbourhood." Production was low until steam revolutionised the industry, but by 1831, Glasgow had 41 mills with over 1,000 spinners.

In 1780 James Monteith had discovered a way of weaving an imitation Indian muslin from cotton and so started the scramble. His six sons all became cotton manufacturers. Henry Monteith caused an early industrial dispute by reducing weavers' wages and twice became Provost of Glasgow. His brother James is said to be the father of the Glasgow cotton industry. He set up an auction room in London in 1793 when trade had slumped badly and with David Dale, invited Joseph Arkwright to Glasgow to demonstrate his new invention, the cotton spinning frame.

Arkwright redefined a waterfall. Dale took his visitor to a local beauty spot, the Falls of Clyde, which Arkwright saw as a source of power and the township of New Lanark was born.

The Monteiths inspire respect from Glasgow historians; David Dale inspires affection. His silhouette shows him as a wee, fat man wearing buckle shoes, hose, breeches, a frock coat and Napoleon hat, carrying a gold-topped cane. Contemporaries believed Sir Walter Scott used him as the model for Bailie Nicol Jarvie in *Rob Roy*.[2]

Religious convictions led Dale to believe in sharing at a time when huge fortunes were being made in a man-mind-thyself economy. His social conscience never left him. He encouraged others to treat their employees as he did and the fact they thought him foolish hardly seems to have mattered. He believed in treating people as he would like to have been treated himself.

Textile production was revolutionised by developments in the chemical industry. While analysing gas works refuse, Charles Mackintosh dissolved india rubber, joined two sheets of fabric together and produced the first piece of waterproofed cloth. He and George Hancock developed the idea and founded a waterproofing business in Glasgow in 1824 (later transferred to Manchester) overcoming obvious distrust then outright opposition from tailors. Inadvertently he gave his name to an item of clothing which still keeps us dry.

New Lanark dancing lessons as observed by G Hunt in 1825.

They were generally indolent, and much addicted to theft, drunkenness, and falsehood, with all their concomitant vices, and strongly experiencing the misery which these ever produce. But by means so gradually introduced, as to be almost imperceptible to them, they have been surrounded with those circumstances which were calculated, first to check, and then to remove their inducements to retain these inclinations; and they are now become conspicuously honest, industrious, sober, and orderly; so that an idle individual, one in liquor, or a thief, is scarcely to be seen from the beginning to the end of the year; and they are become almost a new people, and quite ready to receive any fixed character which may be deemed the most advantageous for them to possess.

From Robert Owen, A Statement regarding The New Lanark Establishment, *1812.*

1. Contemporary newspaper accounts of such events must be balanced against the Glasgow–Garnkirk Railway Letter Books which have a number of complaints from the public concerning "the reckless driving of which your omnibus coachman is guilty". **2.** Though the gossipy John Strang makes no mention of it.

CHARLES TENNANT (1768–1838)

Charles Tennant was a bleacher in a Renfrewshire bleachworks when he became aware of the remarkable power of chlorine-based compounds as bleaching agents. The bleaching liquors of the time were unstable and therefore had to be made at the point of use.

Charles Macintosh devised in 1799 a dry "bleaching powder", produced by passing chlorine gas through a bed of moist lime. The powder could be transported in kegs and made up into a bleaching liquor as required. The process was patented by Charles Tennant, and was first exploited by a partnership Tennant, Knox & Co, which established the St Rollox chemical Works in 1798. This works was conveniently situated at the junction between the Monkland and Forth & Clyde Canals, and grew to become the largest chemical works in Europe by the 1830s.

Charles Tennant was quick to exploit new processes associated with bleaching powder manufacture, and introduced soda making by the Leblanc process in 1818. He was also acutely conscious of the problems caused by atmospheric pollution, and commissioned the construction of what was in its day the tallest chimney in the world, 450 feet high, to remove noxious fumes from the plant.

To secure reliable deliveries of coal he became involved with railway developments including, as a link with the Coatbridge pits, the Garnkirk & Glasgow Railway, a locomotive-worked line. He also promoted the first, unsuccessful scheme to build a railway from Glasgow to Edinburgh.

Interestingly, Tennant's firm, Charles Tennant & Co Ltd, still survives in the business of chemical merchants.

John R Hume

Charles Tennant's chemical works at St Rollox, the largest in Europe, were established to make the bleaching powder their owner invented. St Rollox briefly had the tallest chimney in Europe, known as Tennant's Stalk, and caused one of the city's worst eyesores by dumping chemical waste, locally referred to as the Stinking Ocean. It was cleared in the Sixties and is now occupied by Sighthill housing estate.

St. Rollox Workers, to the number of no fewer than 800, marched in the procession. They were preceded by the 5th Lanark Brass Band and their pipers. One banner and 14 trade flags were exhibited, and at intervals in the procession were lorries, to the number of half a dozen, laden with the products of Messrs. Charles Tennant & Co's extensive works, and numerous models and specimens of machinery in motion. One lorry was laden with beautifully-crystallised blocks of washing soda, and on another was a model of the lofty St. Rollox chimney-stalk.

Anon. Foundation Stone Ceremony for City Chambers, *1883*

Charles Tennant as seen by *The Bailie*, with the Stalk behind him.

Chapter Thirteen

THE GREEN AND THE GREY

CALTON WEAVERS' STRIKE, *by* Tony O'Donnell.

Railway poster advertising long distance Pullman trains.

Chapter Fourteen

CHARACTERS AND CHANGES

By the end of the 19th century, Glasgow dominated the world in engineering and industry. The term Clydebuilt was a hallmark of engineering excellence. The reasons are many and varied, but they all stem from the privileged position Great Britain held in the vanguard of the Industrial Revolution, a position which owed much to geography.

Britain was blessed with plentiful reserves of coal and iron ore and a coastline and river system which enabled their relatively simple extraction and distribution. Her position in Europe and the Atlantic is also important, but perhaps ought not to be exaggerated. In England and Wales, and by implication Scotland, during the 1820s, manufactured goods provided 80 per cent of the export trade, though only one third of the country's industrial output was exported. The domestic market appears to have provided the basis for industrial growth in the early years.

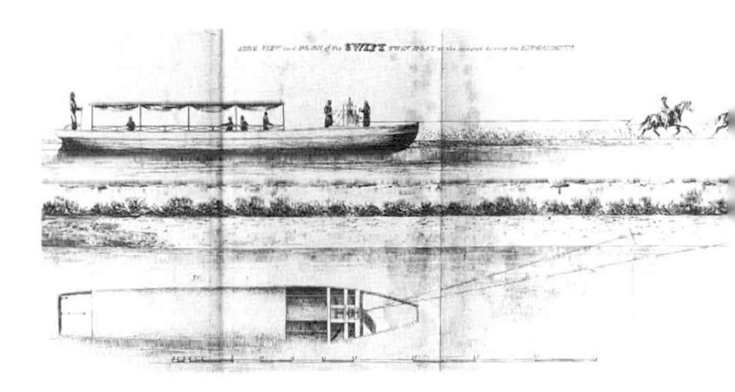

Elevation and Plan of a horse-drawn canal boat.

The Industrial Revolution is generally considered to have started in the 1760s, but some sources place it as early as 1740 and others much later. It has even been dated January 1, 1760, when the Carron Ironworks lit their first furnaces.[1]

Industrial evolution, a better concept than revolution, means the date is hard to place. Mechanical ingenuity was not a new phenomenon. It is evident in the numerous intricate mechanisms for clocks and orreries, some of which were made as early as the Renaissance. The real innovation lay in the scale of the new machines.

'The Glasgow Stock Exchange', a pencil drawing by A. P. Thomson

Capital requirements were very low. In 1792, when the average wage in the cotton mills was a shilling a day, a 40 line spinning jenny cost £6. It was therefore relatively easy to start up in business.[2] The capital usually came from entrepreneurs whose private wealth had been built in other ventures. Banks also increased the available capital, but usually only on short terms loans, which made partnerships particularly useful and common. Family connections were also a way of finding capital. Some have tried to establish the

Neilson locomotive and works' managers from around 1857.

1. James Watt's revelation on Glasgow Green has also been frequently cited as the start of the Industrial Revolution.
2. Thomas Johnston, **The History of the Working Classes in Scotland**, 1920.

link between entrepreneurs and religion, claiming that Protestant non-conformists with capitalist ideals were barred from university and therefore tried to attain social stature by other avenues.[1]

The technical changes may have been evolutionary, but the social changes were definitely revolutionary. The move from an agrarian and cottage based industry, where daily tasks and decisions were influenced largely by nature, into the factory system, was abrupt, though agrarianism wasn't much fun either. In the old paternalist relationship between employer and worker, the logic and reasoning behind their actions could be seen and discussed. The new and emerging working class were now thrown into a situation where machines dictated the rate of work and the working day was an arbitrary fixture.

Workers were isolated from their employers when the factories moved to town. The workers and their masters lived entirely separate lives, which led to segregation within society. Living conditions reduced the workers to an almost sub-human level and they began to be regarded as a separate species. Women and children were considered better suited to work in the textile factories, which degraded the father's position since his children were disciplined, often harshly, by factory overseers.

The Carron Iron Company was set up in 1759 but it was Neilson's hot blast process, introduced in 1828, which was responsible for the massive growth of the foundries in the west of Scotland, enabling the exploitation of Lanarkshire's abundant black band iron stone. This iron was extremely cheap and consequently a high proportion was exported. The iron founders concentrated on the primary production of smelting pig iron and not processing malleable iron. The increase in the local use of iron to meet the demands of engineering led to forges being set up in the city at Lancefield and Parkhead in 1837. However, iron was not suitable for all purposes. Cast iron was very brittle and wrought iron could not be moulded. The natural progression was to steel.

The Crimean War's heavy demands led to the invention of the Bessemer converter and the advent of cheap steel. Steel first replaced iron in the railways, then shipbuilding and civil engineering began to adopt it.

Transport changes also provided a catalyst for industrial change. Railways were usually built in competition with canals, though their main income came from passengers. Their first major effect was to reduce canal rates and because they were lucrative financial propositions, they helped accumulate enough capital to lead indirectly to Glasgow establishing a Stock Exchange in 1844.

CLYDEBUILT QUALITY

"Clydebuilt" stood for quality in construction and performance. That reputation was hard earned by the shipbuilders and engineers between the 1840s and the First World War. Partly it was a reward for risk-taking and innovation, the prize for pioneering so many of the developments that transformed shipbuilding from a craft in wood and sail, to a complex engineering and assembly industry in metal and steam. Partly, the reputation reflected the high standard of builders and the long life of Clyde built vessels and machinery.

It is a feature of Clyde yards that for much of the 19th century quality took precedence over cost. This was certainly the philosophy expounded by Scotts of Greenock who were so sure of their skills in design, construction and engineering, that they offered a free analysis of engineers' log books to the customers to monitor and improve performance. Similarly the Dennys allied theory and experimentation in establishing at Dumbarton the first commercial test-tank in the world in 1881. Other Clyde builders followed with more modest facilities but all contributed to a fine reputation for leadership in design, performance efficiency and economy.

To a considerable extent this was promoted through the very active forum of the Institute of Engineers and Shipbuilders in Scotland and the regular publication of their "proceeding" which kept the whole industry alert to advances in theory and practice. To a very real extent "Clydebuilt" reflected a successful marriage of practical experience, technical skill, and constant enquiry in the theory of design and thermodynamics.

Anthony Slaven

THE HOT BLAST PROCESS

In the 18th century French scientist Jacques Charles discovered that when gases were heated they expanded in a fixed proportion. Among the earliest practical users of the gas laws were the managers of the first gas lighting companies. These included James Beaumont Neilson, who attended lectures on science at the Andersonian Institute. Neilson also found time to act as a consultant, and did so for the Muirkirk Iron Company, with works in Ayrshire. They found that there was not enough air pressure in one of their blast furnaces for melting iron. Neilson tried heating the air, to discover that it noticeably improved the output and quality of the iron. As Muirkirk was then (1826) a long journey from Glasgow, Neilson continued his experiments at the Clyde Ironworks, on the eastern outskirts of the city.

There he learned that increasing the temperature of the air entering the furnace not only made more and "richer" iron, which fetched a higher price, but also reduced the input of fuel by up to a third. He also found that with a hot blast, raw coal could be used as a fuel instead of coke, further cutting costs. The apparatus needed was simple; the effect dramatic. As Scottish ironstone and coal were particularly suited to the process its introduction gave the Scottish ironsmelting industry a relative advantage. Its rapid rise coincided with and encouraged the growth of railway engineering, iron shipbuilding and other iron-using trades in the West of Scotland.

Hot blast, employing much higher temperatures, is still used today.

John R Hume

1. See Rory Fitzpatrick, **God's Frontiersmen, The Scots-Irish Epic**, 1989.

CHARACTERS AND CHANGES

Glasgow Smoke over Motherwell.

Cowlairs Works Main Erecting Shop in Springburn, 1921, with a new class of engine being built.

A Hydepark engine arrives in India around 1908.

Because of her pioneering role in railway development, Britain played a large part in setting up foreign railways, providing finance, engineers and hardware. The invested funds returned later to procure more locomotives and rolling stock.

Glasgow was in an excellent position to take advantage and became known for locomotive building. The firm of Murdoch and Aitken was established as early as 1831 although it was not until the 1860s that Springburn became the centre for locomotive building, with Neilson and Company, Glasgow Locomotive Works and Clyde Locomotive Works establishing themselves there, followed by the Atlas Works and the North British Locomotive Company.

Directly and indirectly, the railways increased the demand for coal. Improved engine designs meant they were not great coal consumers themselves and used only two per cent of the country's output. However, the vast quantities of iron required for both the permanent way and the rolling stock boosted mining.

Glasgow iron wasn't only used for heavy industry. Walter Macfarlane's Saracen Ironworks turned it into the Victorian equivalent of plastic, producing a wide range of household and industrial products. Buildings, such as Gardner's warehouse in Jamaica Street, were also made of iron.

Coastal shipping is often overlooked when analysing internal trade. The advent of the steamship increased its importance and a century later this combination gave Scottish fiction one of its more delightful fancies, a crew of eccentrics who never seem to land a cargo, puffing the *Vital Spark* under Captain Para Handy through Neil Munro's tales.[1]

The Clyde estuary was the ideal slipway for steam navigation. Clydeside was not a great builder of wooden sailing ships, the *Cutty Sark* being a fine exception. Our reputation lay in iron steamships. The Napier cousins Robert and David were responsible for the development of the Clyde as a shipbuilding centre. David Napier built the boiler for Henry Bell's *Comet* and also adapted hull forms to be compatible with steam power. He moved his engineering business from Camlachie to Lancefield in 1821 where he also established a shipyard. Robert Napier took over his cousin's forge at Camlachie and later took charge of the Lancefield works where he was said to be the best engineer on the Clyde. The Napier yard had such a high reputation, it became the equivalent of an industrial university, where great engineers learned their trade. From this yard came such men as Tod and McGregor, Elder and Denny.

Tod and McGregor set up their own shipyard in 1836, the first in the world to be designed for the exclusive production of iron

THE NEILSON FAMILY

The Neilson family were among the most inventive and entrepreneurially active of all the Glasgow dynasties in the early and mid-19th century. James Beaumont Neilson was the first to rise to prominence.

He was appointed manager of the Glasgow Gas Light Company when it was established in 1818. This was a most influential post leading to his employment as a consultant and ultimately to the invention of the hot blast process (patented in 1828) which in the 1830s and Forties made him a considerable fortune and which gave the West of Scotland iron industry an advantage which it retained into the 1860s and Seventies.

James Beaumont Neilson's brother John set up business in the early 19th century as an ironfounder and engineer at the Oakbank Foundry, off Garscube Road. Like many of his contemporaries he combined ironfounding with the making of complete machines. His great claim to fame is his construction, in 1831, of the little iron steamboat *Fairy Queen*, the first sea-going iron steamer built on the Clyde. John Neilson founded the Summerlee Iron Company, at Coatbridge, in 1836 and his firm built in 1841 a wrought-iron works at Mossend which became one of the largest in Scotland.

The last notable member of the family was Walter Montgomerie Neilson, who as a partner in the firm of Mitchell & Neilson (1837), later Neilson & Co, was the most successful private locomotive builder in Scotland. Neilson & Co was the progenitor of all the three works that became in 1903 the North British Locomotive Company Ltd, the largest locomotive builders in Europe.

John R Hume

1. Hugh Foulis (Neil Munro), **Para Handy**, 1911.

JOHN SCOTT RUSSELL (1808–82)

John Scott Russell is the great engineer who is revered in typical Glasgow fashion, not for his achievements but as the man who put Brunel in an early grave.

His life's work lay in naval architecture. Russell's researches into hydrodynamics included following a wave along a canal for many miles on horseback. Identifying the Solitary Wave led to his fundamental theory that ship resistance is composed of two independent elements, frictional and wave making. The ramifications of this are still under continual scrutiny.

After moving to London he organised small trade exhibitions and in 1849 announced the idea of the Great Exhibition. His involvement led to work on other international exhibitions including plans to roof the Colosseum with cast iron.

Meanwhile he embarked on his ruinous project with Brunel to build the massive *Great Eastern*. Despite incorporating Russell's other revolutionary concept in shipbuilding, longitudinal stiffening, it was a disaster. Brunel was enraged by its means of construction – it took five years to build and three months to launch. One letter from Brunel ended, "If you were my obedient servant I should begin with a little flogging".

The vicious smear campaign by Brunel's supporters in the Institute of Civil Engineers left Russell's reputation and finances in tatters. Their hostility was due in part to resentment at his founding a rival and highly successful Institution of Naval Architects. From its inception in 1860 till his death in 1882 he contributed many valuable papers to the Institution in which his genius was unquestioned.

Martin Bellamy

ships, a further impetus for the iron industry. In the light of such activities, it is hardly surprising that Glaswegians like James Young and Lord Kelvin led the 19th century's scientific revolution.

The experiments Kelvin started into diffusion are still continuing at Glasgow University today. Diffusion is the process whereby a still liquid mixes with another liquid. The molecules of each liquid have their own energy and will move, mix and integrate as completely as if stirred; the best illustration happens when you put milk in your tea. Kelvin wanted to examine this further and initiated a long term experiment by setting up two large volumes of liquid and leaving them motionless in sealed containers. They are fulfilling Lord Kelvin's intentions at Glasgow University to this day. He also shot at things, but was considered so ham fisted that no-one liked to be around for these experiments. He destroyed an observer's hat during another piece of research. His science seems like play.

The iron steamship *Great Eastern* laid Lord Kelvin's Atlantic Cables and popular imagination has captured the building of the *Great Eastern* as one of the mightiest engineering feats of the century. It was one of John Scott Russell's many claims to greatness, ship design transformed into naval architecture.

Scotland's first Nobel Prize Winner was one of Kelvin's pupils, a Glaswegian who had attended his physics classes. Sir William Ramsay received the Nobel Prize for Chemistry, for his discovery of the noble gases, from King Oscar II of Sweden in Stockholm on December 10, 1904. His main discovery was to show the relationship between alkaloids which led him to study the properties of liquids and vapours, work he continued when he was appointed Professor of Chemistry at Bristol University in December 1879. An early interest in glassblowing came in handy; Bristol University's continuing financial problems forced Ramsay to make his own apparatus.

He was knighted in 1902 and in 1903 his work on the noble gas Radon led to his study of radioactivity. His work laid routes which others, especially the physicist William Rutherford, would follow. [1] Ramsay died of cancer in 1916.

Sir Alexander Robertus Todd, now Lord Todd of Trumpington, the Glasgow born former Chancellor of Strathclyde University, completes the line. He defined and elucidated the structure of thiamine (Vitamin B) and as Professor of Chemistry at Cambridge studied the nucleic acids DNA and RNA. His work cleared the way for Crick and Watson to discover the structure of DNA. He was awarded the Nobel Prize for Chemistry in 1957.

The story of Glasgow's industrial development is not all success, invention and discovery; these things did not happen in isolation,

John Scott Russell.

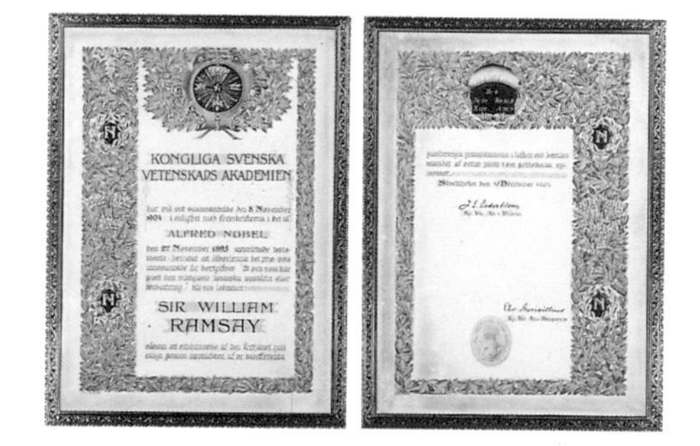

Sir William Ramsay's Nobel certificate.

Lord Kelvin by Frank McKelvey.

1. There are others: Alexander Anderson (1794–1871) first advocated cotton wool being used for burns in an article in the **Glasgow Medical Journal** of 1828, Alick Isaacs (1921–1967), who discovered interferon, was born in Glasgow and Ian Donald (1910–) developed body scanning in general and pregnancy scanning in particular in Glasgow.

CHARACTERS AND CHANGES

PETER MACKENZIE (1799–1875)

Peter Mackenzie's abilities as an investigative journalist, a fair knowledge of the law and a fervent belief in the necessity for Parliamentary reform made him an eminent early Glasgow radical and by the middle of the century the best known man in the city.

He began his career in the legal profession but becoming security in 1827 for a gentleman who went bankrupt was himself sequestrated. He then left conveyancing and set up as professional advocate of Reform. One of his first publications, *Exposure of the Spy System*, 1833, revealed how in 1816 Kirkman Finlay, Glasgow MP, had by means of an *agent provocateur* inveigled some Calton weavers into signing a "Treasonable Oath". When they were charged with high treason they escaped sentencing only by the surprising confession of a prosecution witness that he had been suborned by the Crown. The publication for which he is best known is his *The Reformers' Gazette*, a long series of pamphlets denouncing the Government, the Tories, the Whigs and almost every other political party in a slapdash, slipshod, conversational style. Typical of its snook cocking aptitude was this entry: "Arbuthnot, Harriet, pension 1823 . . . £930. The Duke of Wellington is aware of this lady's services". Harriet was, in fact, the Duke's mistress.

Towards the end of his life he brought out his *Old Reminiscences of Glasgow* – the first two volumes giving a history of the Reform movement in Glasgow and gossipy accounts of local scandalous law cases while the third supplied vivid descriptions of famous Glasgow characters.

Joseph Fisher

but in this period, as in all others, vast areas of life go unrecorded.

Goods and chattels have never written histories and for the mass of the common people of Scotland who were bought, sold and mated like livestock throughout the feudal centuries, the weight of hereditary slavery has ensured silence. All we learn of them in this pre-industrial area comes from the laws their masters used to control them and the punishments inflicted for the smallest transgression.

It is not perhaps until the 19th century that telling accounts of Glasgow life begin to emerge. In his writings on what he termed "Characters of Glasgow" Peter Mackenzie gathered a group of individuals who lived off their wits, beating the system by staying well outside it. [1]

Both Jamie Blue and the Auld Hawkie certainly took advantage of phenomenal wits, dispensing wisdom to passers by, along with songs, prophesies and other more tangible items. Jamie, dishonourably discharged from the army, and Hawkie, crippled by an early accident at work, were famous rivals who gained not only dignity, but a degree of immortality in their struggle to make ends meet.

Glasgow has always appreciated a good talker, and took the "Reverend" John Aitken to its heart. He was the son of a comfortable family who unilaterally declared himself a divine and preached hell-fire sermons near Glasgow Green for pennies.

The various pronouncements of Bell Geordie, at one time the city's town crier, were equally appreciated, but as a civic employee, Geordie fell foul of the powers that be when he chose to compare himself with the powerful Glasgow bailies. His quick tongue lost him his job.

It wasn't only verbal skills that won on the busy streets. Old Malabar, whose juggling balls are on show in the People's Palace, was a traditional street entertainer who would not appear out of place in a shopping precinct or park today. Penny a Yard, a strolling chain-maker and amateur mathematician, would have no difficulty attracting attention, nor would Rab Ha', the Glesca Glutton, who ate anything except oysters served with sugar and cream. In the early years of our own century, the Clincher, journalist and controversialist, claimed to have a silver brain cell for clinching arguments and a certificate which declared him the only sane man in the city. [2]

The skilled and quick witted could have survived anywhere, but it was a hard life for those who were too backward or disturbed to work. Bewildered souls like The Major survived by exhibiting himself as a freak. Wee Jamie Wallace led a more mysterious existence. He took it upon himself to guard the fruit stalls at

Peter Mackenzie with *The Reformers' Gazette*, from *The Bailie*.

Edward Holt's watercolour of Old Malabar.

FOUND, a BLACK SHEEP, at 251 Duke Street. If not claimed in Three Days, will be Sold to defray expenses.
Apply at Mrs Paul's, at the above address.

Glasgow Herald, *May 29, 1865.*

1. Peter Mackenzie, **Old Reminiscences and Remarkable Characters of Glasgow**, 1875.
2. Joe Fisher, Notes to **Auld Hawkie and other Glasgow Characters**, 1988.

ROBERT DREGHORN (DIED 1806)

Most of the Glasgow "Characters" came from the lowest levels of society. One, however, came from the other end of the social spectrum. Robert Dreghorn was tall, thin and gaunt. Small pox had scarred his face with pock-pits as big as threepenny pieces and left him only one eye, while his large nose turned awkwardly to one side. Not surprisingly, he was regarded as the ugliest man in the city and naughty bairns were warned that "Bob Dragon" would get them!

The foible which attracted most attention and which gave the unmarried Dreghorn the undeserved reputation of a *debauche* was his habit of following close behind any good-looking maid-servant or factory girl, particularly if they wore no shoes or stockings! He never molested them in any way and indeed it was a matter of some pride to claim to have been followed by him. Boys who came into his way received his cane across their shoulders, but little children, meeting his strange innocence with theirs, delighted to chat and joke with him.

His wealth, inherited from his father, and increased by astute trading and a miserly and grasping nature, apparently brought him little comfort, for in 1806 he took his own life, and his vast fortune was divided among his four sisters. His town house in Clyde Street just west of the site of the Roman Catholic Cathedral lay empty for years after his death and common repute had it that his ghost stalked its rooms carrying a plate and begging for money.

Joseph Fisher

Kent Street Market. From time to time he vanished and no-one has been able to discover where he went.

Women had their place in this tenuous underworld and their accomplishments tell us a good deal about the hard times. The equality of poverty made Coal Mary carry sacks of the stuff up the tenement stairs before she took to beggary along with The Major.

Hirstlin' Kate dragged herself around the south-east of Glasgow on a little cart, singing songs to children in exchange for pins. Big Rachel was over six feet tall. She smoked a pipe and was a baton wielding Special Constable during the Partick Riots in the 1870s. She also had a remarkable succession of jobs, including foreman navvy and farmhand.

Mackenzie's stories are filled with the resilience of humanity, with a bitter centre of death, disease, loneliness and abject poverty never far away. Whether beggars and vagrants, the homeless souls of 1990 will have such a fine memorial a century from now remains to be seen. We appear to be producing a different class of character these days, and those we remember as Old Glasgow Characters are lovable because they are safely remote.

One of Mackenzie's characters who has to some extent been overshadowed by contemporaries, in death as he was in life, was Feea, The Poor Glasgow Idiot Boy. "Poor Feea!" wrote Mackenzie. "Poor, dear Feea! We can never think of him without emotion."[1]

Feea was born "in the lower part of the Stockwell, of the poorest but most honest and virtuous parents in that locality." He lost both his father and mother "ere he was four or five years of age" which sent him crazy and, living on the streets, "he was suffered to grow up in this city like a wild Arabian colt in all the frivolities of nature."

Feea slept wherever he could, in closes, hay lofts and on tables, though where his clothes came from was difficult to tell. At 15 "he was one of the most nimble and best-shaped youths in the city", a happy boy with a mild and docile temperament, popular with other boys of his own age and different station – until it rained.

During the heaviest showers, "the loudest peals of thunder and the most vivid flashes of lightning", Feea clapped his hands and danced with joy. On his hands and knees in the pouring rain he gathered the worms and swallowed as many as he could, whole and alive.

He could jump from one side of Glassford Street to the other, could run the length of Argyle Street, then just over half a mile, in less than two minutes, and when the Nelson Monument on Glasgow

Bob Dragon, "a batchelor on the pursuit".

Contrarie Paddy.

Contrarie Paddy.

This is one of the many rare old songs which can only be found in the Poet's Box, 130 Gallowgate Street, Glasgow. To any one whose fancy for the muse is at all bent, the Poet's Box is the place to repair thither. The Poet there makes you all welcome to give him a call; and if he has nothing to satisfy you in the way of songs, he is determined to satisfy you with other nic-nacks, which he exposes for sale—such as his prime Glittering Paste Blacking, which he sells to all and sundry for one halfpenny a packet, which he has neatly put up in packets after the Hanoverian style; Laces also he gives away for one penny a dozen; and Beautiful Toilet Soap he puts out for a penny a cake, richly perfumed, after the French style. And as for his Lucifer Matches all Glasgow, Ayr, and miles round, can tell they are to be got only at the price in the Poet's Box.

AIR—*Christmas Day.*

Come all you good people, pray listen,
I would have you draw near, but stand off;
A story I'm now going to mention,
I would have you to smile, but don't laugh,
Concerning a maid that was frantic,
She was merry, but very bad crack;
At night she goes out in the morning,
Comes in with a full empty sack.
Singing fal de dal la de dal la da laddie.

My street I through down upon twopence,
I being in a terrible haste,
Until that the weight of my pocket
Drew me on the back of the face;
And there in the streets I lay sprawling,
The stones with my head they were cut,
The nose from my blood it was running,
As thick as the stobl of a fit.
Singing, &c.

The broth ate came down with my girl,
She emptied them into a jug,
But when it began to flow over,
To stop it she pulled out the plug.
She seldom appears in the diamond
To Monday the last of the week,
And there in the streets she sits trembling,
Her heart like the flax of a strick.
Singing, &c.

As I went down, down Derry Street,
Thinking to be the last first,
I met with an old brown beggar,
Just newly knocked out of the dust;
I being in a terrible passion,
I called him a long legged ghost,
I hit him a thump on the back,
With a thing like the gate of a post.
Singing, &c.

When I heard that Donald was listed,
I thought it was only a joke;
I got up on the top of the house,
And my shoulders I threw round my cloak;
Then into the city I hastened,
By this it was late in the night,
The first man I met on the street,
Was Surgeon M'Gonnagal's wife.
Singing, &c.

Letters and Petitions written in the Poet's Box on the most reasonable terms. Saturday, Oct. 26, 1850.

1. Peter Mackenzie, **Old Reminiscences**, op. cit.

Green was decapitated by lightning, Feea threw a hand ball over the top and caught it on the other side.

He was friendly with the Reverend John Lockhart, father of Sir Walter Scott's son-in-law, who often gave Feea sermons and cake at his home in Charlotte Street. Feea was also given a fine suit of clothes to wear for the wedding of one of Dr Lockhart's neighbours. Another neighbour was James Mitchell, a commissioner of police who later became chief of police, the man who stopped body snatching in Glasgow. His men referred to him as The Adjutant. He caught Feea raking his midden and gave him such a beating the boy shouted, "No kill Feea!" Mackenzie refuses to name Mitchell, though he draws heavy hints and names Feea's saviour, who wanted to prosecute on the boy's behalf, but found there were no grounds.

No one knows how Feea died. One rumour has it he froze to death in a Goosedubs cellar. Another says he fell to the Clyde from the old wooden bridge at the foot of the Saltmarket. It is most likely he was murdered by the Resurrectionists.

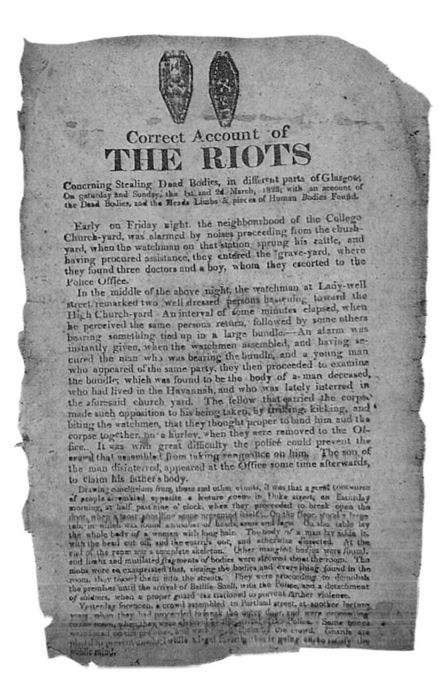

Correct Account of
THE RIOTS
Concerning Stealing Dead Bodies, in different parts of Glasgow, On Saturday and Sunday, the 1st and 2d March, 1823; with an account of the Dead Bodies, and the Heads Limbs & pieces of Human Bodies Found.

Early on Friday night, the neighbourhood of the College Church-yard, was alarmed by noises proceeding from the church-yard, when the watchman on that station sprung his rattle, and having procured assistance, they entered the grave-yard, where they found three doctors and a boy, whom they escorted to the Police Office.

In the middle of the above night, the watchman at Lady-well street, remarked two well dressed persons hastening toward the High Church-yard. An interval of some minutes elapsed, when he perceived the same persons return, followed by some others bearing something tied up in a large bundle.—An alarm was instantly given, when the watchmen assembled, and having secured the man who was bearing the bundle, and a young man who appeared of the same party, they then proceeded to examine the bundle, which was found to be the body of a man deceased, who had lived in the Havannah, and who was lately interred in the aforesaid church yard. The fellow that carried the corpse made such opposition to his being taken, by striking, kicking, and biting the watchmen, that they thought proper to bind him and the corpse together on a hurley, when they were removed to the Office. It was with great difficulty the police could prevent the crowd that assembled from taking vengeance on him. The son of the man disinterred, appeared at the Office some time afterwards, to claim his father's body.

Drawing conclusions from these and other events, it was that a great concourse of people assembled opposite a lecture room in Duke street, on Saturday morning, at half past nine o' clock, when they proceeded to break open the door, when a most appalling scene presented itself.—On the floor stood a large tub, in which was found a number of heads, arms and legs. On the table lay the whole body of a woman with long hair. The body of a man lay aside it, with the head cut off, and the entrails out, and otherwise dissected. At the end of the room was a complete skeleton. Other mangled bodies were found, and limbs and mutilated fragments of bodies were strewed about the room. The mobs were so exasperated that, seizing the bodies and every thing found in the room, they threw them into the streets. They were proceeding to demolish the premises until the arrival of Baillie Snell, with the Police, and a detachment of soldiers, when a proper guard was stationed to prevent further violence.

Yesterday forenoon, a crowd assembled in Portland street, at another lecture room, when they had proceeded to break the outer door, and were proceeding to the room, when they were [illegible] of the Police. Some bones were found on the premises, and were [illegible] by the crowd. Guards are placed to prevent [illegible] while a legal [illegible] is going on, to satisfy the public mind.

"Correct Account of the Riots" – Anti-Resurrectionist literature.

GRANVILLE SHARP PATTISON
(1791–1851)

At the beginning of the 19th century the growing appetite of the dissecting table for "subjects" and the inexorable law of supply and demand led to many a rifled grave in many a Scottish burying ground; in 1814 Granville Sharp Pattison, anatomist, surgeon and teacher at the College Street Medical School, Glasgow went on trial at the High Court in Edinburgh for having "violated the Sepulchres of the Dead".

In December 1813, Mrs McAllaster, the deceased wife of a Glasgow wool merchant, had been interred in St David's Ramshorn churchyard and the Lord Advocate set out to prove to the satisfaction of the jury and the Lords of Justiciary that the poor woman had been "resurrected" from there and had ended up in parts in the dissecting room of the Medical School through the direct action of Pattison. Forensic medical history was made during the trial, for the teeth of the corpse were positively identified as Mrs McAllaster's by her dentist. Fortunately for Pattison he was able to establish a secure alibi for the time of the crime, and the peculiar Scottish verdict of "Not Proven" allowed him to walk from the court a free man.

Strange to say, despite the extremely unsavoury nature of the case, he remained in Glasgow for another two years before leaving for America where his role in founding Baltimore Infirmary, the country's first teaching hospital, was an important contribution to medical education in the United States.

Joseph Fisher

Mary and the Major. Two of Mackenzie's "characters".

Chapter Fourteen

CHARACTERS AND CHANGES

Vagrants at a brazier, early this century.

John Maclean, middle of front row, with other Glasgow socialists.

"The Loom" by John Quinton Pringle.

Chapter Fifteen

A COMMON CAUSE

The Reformation promised much for the common people of Scotland; individual ministers were supported by their flocks as they preached a new theocracy and an end to noble privilege. The realities of the Reformation were very different as the Court and landed interests divided the newly liberated church properties between them and proceeded to reinforce their feudal stranglehold with a holy terror. It would be centuries before popular campaigning brought even a partial fulfilment of that promise.

The dissolution of the Church's property meant that much of the little provision there had been for the poor also came to an end. Clerics had been lining their pockets for centuries, but although bishops had their palaces and prisons, they also provided relief, treatment and short term accommodation for the destitute. Between 1693 and 1699, feudal exploitation of land and peasant labour, which left good land uncultivated or underworked, brought another spasm of famine with the Seven Ill Years. This and the removal of church relief left vast numbers destitute. By the close of the century, a great many vagrants were wandering aimlessly around Scotland.

In the 17th century however, slave labour in manufacturing was fading fast, as workers increasingly chose to sabotage or desert, risking death or starvation with the vagrant army rather than work in unbearable conditions. Wages began to enter the equation and the cost of paying a tied labour force, as well as supporting what was a dependent body of men, women and children, became completely uncommercial. A notable exception was the case of the miners, legally serfs, living in company houses of an appallingly low standard and often fined more than they were paid each week.[1] The Lanarkshire coal fields were to breed generations of militant miners, including Bob Smillie, John Wheatley and Keir Hardie.

Accidents of history also meant that Glasgow, unlike Edinburgh, did not have strong ties of custom and loyalty with England. While the Select Society in Edinburgh invited tutors in southern manners,

A miner underground, early 20th century.

1. John Hannan, **The Life of John Wheatley**, 1988.

THE GLASGOW TEA ROOMS

Glaswegians of mature years remember the city's tea rooms with strong affection, and rightly, for they are one of Glasgow's great inventions. The first was opened in 1875 at 2 Queen Street by Stuart Cranston, a tea dealer. He was closely followed by his sister Kate, the redoubtable Miss Cranston, who founded her separate empire in 1878.

They had many imitators, including one J Lyons. By 1901 Glasgow could be dubbed "a very Tokyo for tea rooms", and the "movement" had spread to other British cities and then throughout the world. Through her bold taste for the design of Charles Rennie Mackintosh, Miss Cranston made the "artistic" Glasgow tea room an object of international admiration.

The tea rooms flourished along with the Temperance movement, catering for business men who could lunch lightly and fraternise in the all-male smoking rooms; and for women of leisure who now at last had a respectable meeting place in town. Prices were modest, and quality of service, food and decor far outstripped those of such places elsewhere.

The tradition of excellence persisted after the First World War when the scene was dominated by the great family bakers, chief among them James Craig and the City Bakeries with its Ca'd'Oro. But smaller businesses too – Miss Rombach's, Miss Buick's, Wendy's, Fuller's – all had their loyal devotees.

Like so much that was fine about Glasgow, the tea rooms perished in the Sixties and Seventies, victims of rising overheads and changes in fashion and social habits. Now they are virtually extinct. Perch on a replica Mackintosh chair in Miss Cranston's "Willow", partly restored to its original use, and contemplate a sad loss.

Perilla Kinchin

customs and the correct pronunciation of the King's English to the capital, no such provision was being made for 18th century Glasgow. In the vital 50 years which straddled the beginning of that century and saw the shaping of the Scottish middle classes, Glasgow, never the seat of parliament or kings, was a city whose working people were concerned with other matters, principally the revolutionary examples of both America and France.

In Glasgow's first recorded strike, six weavers were shot by the military. There ensued in Edinburgh the country's first trial for union membership and one of the strikers was whipped through the streets and banished from Scotland for seven years. Glasgow's historians ignored the strike and its consequences until Harry McShane did enough detective work to publish an excellent pamphlet[1] outlining the events. The bicentenary of the Calton weavers' massacre was honourably marked in 1987 when the People's Palace commissioned commemorative murals from Ken Currie.

In 1787, Calton was on the outskirts of Glasgow. On June 30 an estimated 7,000 weavers from all over the city marched to Glasgow Green protesting against the second wage cut in eight months.

The lair where the murdered weavers were buried, in Calton Graveyard, lies neglected and the memorials are barely legible. There was a campaign to have the Sighthill Martyrs' Memorial restored as a public monument, but no-one is sufficiently interested in taking up the weavers' cause.

As France celebrated the bicentenary of its revolution and uncovered a sizeable minority of ardent royalists, it became increasingly obvious that the tensions of the 1789 uprising are still to be reckoned with. The explosive effects of the French Revolution as it took place were, of course, even more formidable and when the seeds of change fell to earth, they flourished far beyond the Bastille; when the Bourbons toppled, the shock waves rocked the whole of Europe and Scotland was no exception.

Merchants and their men brought more than goods from France and French began to creep into the language: *douce* or *menage* means the same in Partick as in Paris. By the 18th century, French ideas were impressing themselves on the Scottish psyche. Along with illegally imported copies of Tom Paine's *The Rights of Man*, the works of Voltaire, Rousseau and Diderot were receiving keen attention from Scottish students and intellectuals alike.

Scotland's response to the French Revolution has been largely ignored, along with many of its leading figures. Thomas Muir of Huntershill, has been inadequately remembered. In 1794 he was transported to Botany Bay on board the *Surprise*. Peter Mackenzie,

THOMAS MUIR (1765–99)

Thomas Muir of Huntershill, was a young advocate with an already radical turn of mind when in 1792 he began to talk about reforming the corrupt political system of the time.

He helped found the Friends of the People in Glasgow while he also addressed the working people there and in the surrounding villages on the dangerous subject of reform and encouraged them to set up branches of the organisation.

He was a prime target for a repressive and fearful Government and in December 1792 he gave them their chance when he read out a potentially seditious "Address from the United Irishmen to the Convention of Friends of the People". The Government swooped and Muir was charged with sedition.

While on bail he crossed to France ostensibly – and, given his tendency to self-importance, possibly genuinely – to intercede for the life of the French King. He did not succeed but Britain and France then went to war and Muir had difficulty getting back.

When he did return, his trial was an overtly political affair. "If the real cause of my standing as a pannel at your bar is for actively engaging in the cause of parliamentary reform then I plead guilty". He was standing trial for stirring up the ignorant country people and "manufacturers" who had no place in governement.

The jury found him guilty and he was sentenced to 14 years' transportation to Botany Bay. This champion of democracy eventually escaped to die, alone, in France before any of his ideals could be realised in his own country.

Ken Logue

1. Harry McShane, **Calton Weavers' Memorial**, published by Glasgow Trades Council, undated.

A linen scarf commemorating Thomas Muir's exile.

Thomas Muir of Huntershill.

An Australian invitation to domestic bliss.

called him "one of the most amiable reformers that ever breathed".[1] Indeed, his activities for political change seem so moderate, so constitutional, that the ferocity of the Establishment's action against him is all the more senseless. Thomas Muir's story reads like a Hollywood script and were it not so firmly rooted in the appalling flood of persecutions and repression that swept Scotland in the 1790s, it would almost appear fanciful.

The verdict on Muir at his trial for sedition was a foregone conclusion, but his speech from the dock is still considered a[2] classic and to this day is studied by American law students.

Huntershill House is now part of a sports complex. A tiny museum, opened in the old servants' quarter in the attic and now to be found in Bishopbriggs Library has never been developed. In the late 18th century, illegal copies of the French *Declaration of the Rights of Man* were circulated and as the middle class support for reform waned, either crushed by the force of legislature or reeling from the later excesses of the revolution, the cause of republicanism flourished and grew amongst the working masses.

It would not be long before Scotland would take part in its own abortive rising in 1820 and Peter Mackenzie would champion the cause of other radicals, sent to Australia for crimes against the state and their part in the Battle of Bonnymuir, whose name is now rich in painful irony.

Revolution and a knowledge of libertarian philosophy were not, of course, confined to the middle classes in Glasgow, a city of confirmed autodidacts. There was a long history of riots motivated as much by a positive political fervour as by hunger and discontent. As early as 1582 burgh elections were attended by popular riots. The vast mass of the membership of the Society of the Friends of the People was working class, their moves towards self determination always linked with education, particularly in the case of the weavers. Glasgow's Society of United Scotsmen, founded in 1793, combined literary activities with peaceful agitation for reform, but there were other more radical thinkers and organisations, despite the savage suppression of the authorities which continually creamed off their leaders. Former Friend of the People the Reverend Neil Douglas was arrested for preaching against the regency from the pulpit of Anderston church and Gilbert McLeod, editor of the Glasgow-based *Spirit of the Union*, a radical broadsheet, was eventually sentenced to five years transportation.[3]

McLeod was to die in exile, but in 1820, the year of his arrest, became forever linked with the most remarkable repression of Scots radical and national feeling since the days of Wallace and Bruce.

THE CONVENTIONS OF THE SOCIETIES OF FRIENDS OF THE PEOPLE

When the First Convention met in Edinburgh on December 11–13, 1792, 160 delegates attended representing 80 societies in 35 towns and villages, including nine different parts of Glasgow. Their declared object was to achieve an equal representation of the people in Parliament and the frequent opportunity to exercise their right of election by the proper, legal and constitutional method of petitioning Parliament.

The Second and Third Scottish Conventions, the latter incensed by Thomas Muir's trial in August 1793, were more radical and more representative of the working classes. Shortly after the Third, in October 1793, the 160 delegates were recalled to attend the First British Convention when a number of English delgates arrived. There, secret plans were made to oppose certain specified measures restrictive of liberty, should Parliament decide to introduce them. For the first time the reformers – who were now looking a bit like revolutionaries – seemed to accept that they had to take some sort of initiative and that the British Establishment was not going to crumble under the weight of popular opinion.

The Government decided to act: the Convention was broken up and, as the Sheriff's men approached on the final evening to break up the Convention, English delegate Joseph Gerrald called out, "Behold the funeral torches of liberty!" Apart from a few spurts, the flame of democracy was dimmed for many years thereafter.

Ken Logue

1. Peter Mackenzie, **Reminiscences of Glasgow and the West of Scotland**, Vol. 1, 1866. **2.** Mackenzie quotes sizeable chunks, ending with the best known portion, "the time will come when men must stand or fall by their actions; when all human pageantry shall cease; when the hearts of all shall be laid open," ending, "I am careless and indifferent to my fate." Mackenzie also tells us, "He then sat down on his seat much exhausted, haven spoken for nearly three hours; commencing his address at ten at night and finishing about one in the morning." **3.** Thomas Johnston, **The History of the Working Classes in Scotland**, 1920.

GLASGOW AND THE REFORM BILL

There was great excitement in Glasgow in 1831–32 over the prospects for the Reform Bill. Before it became law in July 1832, following the passing of the (English) Reform Bill in June, Glasgow sent no member of the House of Commons but joined with the three royal burghs of Rutherglen, Renfrew and Dumbarton in electing a Member of Parliament for the Clyde burghs. Thus, four delegates, appointed by the magistrates and councillors of each burgh, decided, "by the mere puffs of their own mouths", as Mackenzie put it, who should be the single representative of Glasgow and the other Clyde burghs in Parliament.

As Glasgow grew in population and prosperity the demand for the vote by its merchant and professional classes grew more and more urgent. The working classes joined in the cry for reform, though it was the middle classes and not they who would benefit from it when it came.

There was near frenzy in the city when the Lords twice rejected the Bill. When it was finally passed Glasgow was illuminated and riotous celebrations took place. The franchise was now conferred on householders occupying premises with an annual rental value of £10 and Glasgow was given two seats. 7,024 Glasgow electors registered, and in the General Election of December 1832 the two Whig candidates topped the poll with over 6,000 votes between them. The Tories were routed (as they were in all the Scottish burghs) and a new era in Glasgow political life began.

David Daiches

Indirectly, however, Bonnymuir would also provide hope for those who dreamed of a free society.

Surviving correspondence from some of the transported tells of their grief at being separated from loved ones and native land, but it also bears witness to the massively increased liberty and opportunity experienced in Australia.[1] Many believed they had been transported to a land of freedom at Government expense. Thomas White is thought to have returned to Scotland and Andrew White, bookbinder, died in Glasgow and was buried at Sighthill, near Hardie and Baird. None of the other 19 made any attempt to return home, and their exemplary lives go some way towards proving the debilitating effects of Scotland's government and the desperation it induced in well-read and normally law abiding men. Given Australia's liberal climate, they took no further part in politics.

Some prisoners were joined by their wives; others, like Andrew Hart, who was scarred for life by his Bonnymuir injuries, married in Australia. All set about making a new life. John Anderson became precentor at the first Presbyterian Church in Australia and was also a teacher, as was Robert Gray. Alexander Johnston, another staunch Presbyterian, became an innkeeper and was later referred to as a pillar of society.

In Scotland, the remaining middle class reformers attached themselves to the cause of the Reform Bill and for a while the working classes demonstrated in its support. Their potential strength was formidable. In 1831, 100,000 marched on Glasgow Green and, beyond the moderate demands of the intellectuals and trade combinations, called for the abolition of the House of Lords and the mustering of an army of the people.

After the massive anti-climax when the Reform Bill became law, the Whigs, having made use of union support, expressed their intention to dissolve political unions. Chartism rose up as a protest. In November, 1834, 20,000 paraded on the Green for "Liberty or Death" and at the 1835 elections, 200,000 heard Daniel O'Connell. In December that year, Glasgow masons and the United Iron Moulders came out in favour of political action and the National Radical Association flourished under Dr John Taylor. The provost's son, George Mills, stood as a Radical candidate in 1835 but was defeated by his father's appointee Lord William Bentinck. A year later and again on Glasgow Green 200,000 demonstrated in favour of Chartism, including 70 trade unions.

In 1848 the harvest failed and the potato blight bit. The Government proposed to raise taxes and news was reaching the Scottish

Australia offering the physical and economic freedom which was always its chief asset.

Army drum, reputedly used in the 1848 Bread Riot.

1. Various contributors, **That Land of Exiles: Scots in Australia**, 1988.

radicals of the Paris commune. Demands for bread brought riots in Edinburgh and Glasgow. In February that year, a crowd assembled on the Green and, influenced by Chartist ideals, called for work and a two shillings a day minimum wage. The magistrates offered soup tickets. Later in the day the crowd tore down the railings on Monteith Row and sacked the shops for food and arms. That night, police, specials and cavalry were gathered against the rioters. There were cavalry charges along the High Street and Saltmarket and 150 arrests. The next day soldiers at Bridgeton were attacked and factories were hit as more troops were brought from Edinburgh. The crowd again began to gather on the Green, but were scattered by cavalry with the sheriff at their head. A barricade built across the Gallowgate was broken down and two ringleaders, Smith and Crosson, were arrested and given ten and 18 year sentences respectively. A 14 year old boy, arrested at the time, was jailed for a year.

The emphasis switched to union combination and agitation. In 1861, the United Trades of Glasgow had 35 unions in favour of franchise reform, but Reform Bills were repeatedly talked out of Parliament. By 1864 the Trades Political Union had lost patience and said it would no longer support any candidate who did not espouse manhood suffrage. The very presence of such a threat shows the growing power of the unions and the organised Left in this city.

Gladstone's Great Reform Bill of 1866 proved to be a disaster which ousted the Liberal Government and as Ernest Jones was telling 200,000 people on the Green that the voice of the people was the voice of God, it was becoming obvious that reform and political representation for the working classes lay outside the existing political parties.

In 1868, with minimal franchise reform passed in Scotland, the Working Men's Association and others set about raising funds for candidates. In that year's elections, there was only one genuine working class candidate, Alexander MacDonald, a radical Lanarkshire miner. Fellow miners raised money with a shilling a head levy. He stood at Kilmarnock, but withdrew from the contest as gifts of free whisky and bribes in support of the Whigs and Tories made it obvious the fight would be unfair.

The Ballot Act of 1872, which introduced secret voting, made the fielding of minority candidates a more realistic propositition and a year later Glasgow Trades Council, the oldest in Britain, was seriously debating the possibility of putting forward Labour candidates. They fielded three workers and a university professor

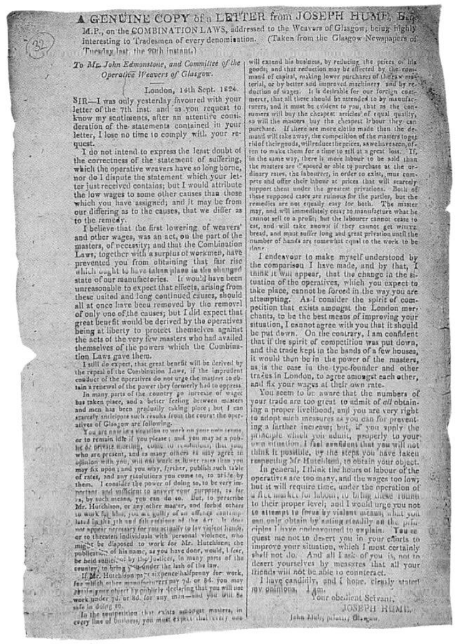

GLASGOW CHARTISM

A number of radicals kept alive a tradition of political reform in Scotland from the 1790s. The arrival of the flamboyant Dr John Taylor as editor of the *Liberator* newspaper in 1836 and the formation of the Scottish Radical Association revitalised the movement. It linked up with the spreading political associations of the North of England demanding the six points of the People's Charter.

The tensions created by industrial discontents brought increasing working class support for political change. Very quickly a debate emerged on the most effective way to bring about such change. Taylor tended to favour threats of violence, but other leading Glasgow activists like the pirnmaker, Abram Duncan, the tea merchant, James Moir and the engineer, William Pattison emphasised what was called "moral suasion", convincing the middle class that the working class was "worthy" to exercise the franchise. Commitment to total abstinence, education and co-operation was seen as one way to show such moral worth.

In 1839, the Glasgow Universal Suffrage Association published the *Scottish Patriot* and successfully linked middle class and working class radicals. But such unity did not last long and by the 1840s the leadership was hopelessly divided on the issue of tactics. Some favoured collaboration with the middle class Anti-Corn Law League, while others favoured working class exclusivism. Many working class activists turned to temperance work and to the Chartist Churches which offered a sympathetic environment away from clerical control.

After 1842 the movement was fairly dormant and even in 1848 when it revived elsewhere the response in Glasgow was muted and never succeeded in regaining the fervour of the early years.

W Hamish Fraser

An attempt to pacify the Glasgow weavers.

Spy's caricature of Cunninghame Graham from *Vanity Fair* of 1888.

Cunninghame Graham by Epstein.

in the School Board elections of 1873, but all were defeated; the 1874 General Election saw no Scottish Labour candidates, but Alexander MacDonald became Scotland's first Labour export when he was returned successfully for an English constituency.

Gladstone's further electoral reforms in 1884 gave the vote to rural tenants, separating them from their Tory lairds and adding 200,000 voters to Scotland's roll. Many Working Men's Parliamentary Associations were founded and the Glasgow Trades Council asked 20,000 trade unionists to give a shilling levy for parliamentary candidates. The following year there were votes polled for Labour candidates across Scotland from Aberdeen to Argyllshire. In the Blackfriars constituency of Glasgow, Mr Shaw Maxwell, the Socialist, received a significant 1,156 votes. Crofter candidates in Argyllshire, Inverness-shire and Caithness-shire were returned.

In 1886, Gladstone was defeated over Home Rule for Ireland, a topic which remained close to the hearts of many Irish Glaswegian [1] voters for decades. Robert Bontine Cunninghame Graham, author, former gaucho and "The Miners' Justiceman" became a Liberal candidate for North West Lanarkshire and Angus Sutherland, a crofter's son, was elected as a Liberal member for Sutherlandshire. They represented the tip of the Labour movement, which would soon abandon the Liberal Party to build the ILP. Both Cunninghame Graham and Sutherland supported Labour.

During this period, the radical George Henry toured Scotland, preaching the message of Labour and he greatly impressed a young Lanarkshire miner, Keir Hardie. In 1887, Hardie was publishing [2] *The Miner*, in which he demanded direct Labour representation in Parliament, independent of Liberals or Tories. The following year, he was invited to stand for Mid-Lanark by the Larkhall miners. He sat as a Liberal initially, then went it alone as a Labour candidate with the support of the Glasgow Trades Council and other activists like Cunninghame Graham, Ramsay MacDonald and the Scottish Home Rule Association.

Hardie, of course, went on to lead the Independent Labour Party and to shape the radical socialist organisation which would find a golden age in Clydeside and an enduring Scottish support; a support whose potency was destroyed by Ramsay MacDonald and the English vote.

SCHOOL BOARDS (1872–1918)

The Education (Scotland) Act of 1872 required all children between the ages of five and 13 to attend school.

School Boards were elected to assess the accommodation requirements of their district with a view to taking over existing schools or building new ones for which they could levy a local rate. They also appointed teachers, fixed their salaries and decided on fees, for education though compulsory was not yet free.

Many parents could ill afford to lose their children's earnings or help at home, let alone pay school fees, and as a result truancy was a major problem. To combat this a system of part time education was introduced for children over ten years of age. This unsatisfactory solution was phased out by 1900. Fees themselves were abolished by 1891.

To satisfy the immediate demand for extra teachers extensive use was made of pupil teachers who studied for Queen's Scholarships to enable them to enter teacher training colleges for a further two years of study. Once married a woman could no longer teach.

Many city children were unused to discipline so the first task of the teacher was to instil order and obedience. The typical classroom had ranks of desks facing the teacher who dominated the room from a high desk. Most teachers had a tawse or leather belt with which to punish an offender. One method of teaching discipline especially to boys, was drill. Pupils lined up in the playground and marched military style in response to commands.

Jemima Fraser

1. Thomas Johnston, op.cit. **2.** Thomas Johnston, op. cit.

Chapter Fifteen

A COMMON CAUSE

THOMAS MUIR, A GLASGOW TRAINED LAWYER, HAD HIS DEMOCRATIC CONVICTIONS MOULDED BY THE PHILOSOPHY OF JOHN MILLAR. HIS ADVOCACY AND POPULARISING OF THE DEMANDS FOR POLITICAL REFORM ENRAGED THE AUTHORITIES. AS THE SOCIETY OF THE FRIENDS OF THE PEOPLE PROSPERED, HIS FATE WAS SEALED.

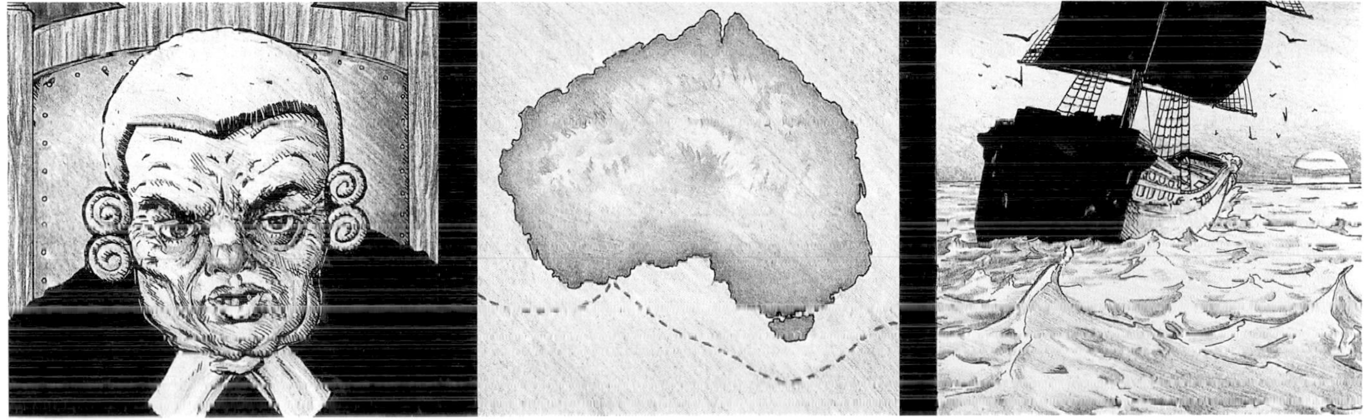

HE WAS TRIED AND TRANSPORTED TO AUSTRALIA. HE ESCAPED AND EN ROUTE TO SPAIN LOST AN EYE IN A SEA BATTLE. HE WAS LATER WELCOMED IN FRANCE WHERE HIS SUPPORT FOR THE REVOLUTION WAS WELL-KNOWN. THOMAS MUIR DIED AT CHANTILLY, SUDDENLY AND ALONE, IN 1799, 33 YEARS OLD.

THOMAS MUIR, *by* Andrew Hope.

Selection of Labour Press cuttings.

MATERNAL AND CHILD WELFARE

Because the health problems of "Mothers and Babies" reflected the low standard of housing, feeding and education in Glasgow it required a major effort to keep mothers healthy and babies alive. Much of the credit for this must go the health visitors, the "Green ladies" whose homely presence was supportive and re-assuring. As one such remarked (in 1930 after 25 years experience), "It took a few visits to establish a friendship . . . you must be interested not only in the family but in other household affairs. Health visiting cannot be done in a hurry".

Earlier women had operated voluntarily and pragmatically, organising many new ventures including Schools for Mothers, Infant Welfare Centres, Dinners for expectant and nursing mothers, Fresh Air Fortnights, Holiday Homes, Milk for babies, Day Nurseries, Crèches and Nursery Schools.

The services later set up by the corporation were of undoubted value to mothers and babies. None the less infant mortality rates in Glasgow remained high and some felt that of all sections of the community, wives and mothers were least cared for.

When the second war came in 1939 there was still much to be done. The war proved a blessing in one way for positive discrimination was practised. The Ministry of Food, taking overall responsibility for feeding the nation, singled out pregnant women, babies and young children for special issues not only of free concentrated orange juice and cod liver oil but also for priority supplies of other foods. After the war, when the conscience of the nation demanded a National Health Service, it was possible for large resources to be channelled into the care of mothers and their babies.

Olive Checkland

Chapter Sixteen

FORWARD

Childron in straight lines with straight backs and hands by their sides outside school.

Undesirable work is the lot of the immigrant. Irish agricultural labourers, forced off their land by famine, made up most of the Lanarkshire collieries' increasing workforce. As early as 1848, a quarter of the Lanarkshire miners were Irish. The area produced huge physical and financial support for early Labour candidates and the seeds of the movements which would win the important Irish vote for the ILP.

In 1843, a British Miners' Conference was held in Glasgow, after a series of spring strikes throughout Scotland, to discuss a Parliamentary Bill which was being prepared; had the Bill become law it would have meant a "disobedient servant" could be imprisoned on the word of a Justice of the Peace. The Glasgow miners' meeting voted against national action, but three months later, Lanarkshire miners were on strike and other colliers around Scotland were adopting the "wee darg", still used today and called the go slow.

Scottish miners united into the Scottish Miners' Federation in 1894. Robert Smillie, a mild faced man with a drooping moustache, was at its head. For decades they would form the central pillar of Labour's support, until the disastrous strike of 1926 led what had become the National Union of Scottish Mineworkers into the decline which culminated in the 1984 strike and the MacGregor cuts.

Not only the miners were combining. The Glasgow Cottonspinners' Union, founded in 1806, struck in 1837 and '38 so successfully that their leaders were put on trial.

In 1858, Glasgow established a Council of Trades Delegates and others followed in Edinburgh, Aberdeen, Dundee and Greenock. The exclusion of these bodies from the TUC finally decided Scottish representatives to found the STUC, an independent organisation, to deal directly with the issues of Scottish labour and maintain strong links with the Trades Councils.

In 1888, a major step forward came when the Scottish Labour

Eastfield Colliery in the mid-1890s.

THE CLASSROOM (1872–1918)

Lessons reflected the traditions of Scottish education – reading, writing, arithmetic and religion. Religious instruction was provided within the board schools but parents could withdraw their children. Since the Government grant to the schools was directly related to the degree of success shown by the pupils at the annual inspection of the HMI, children were driven by a combination of rote-learning, drilling and corporal punishment to achieve the prescribed standards – the so called "payment by results" system. Though subsequent Acts abolished this system, rote learning and strict discipline dominated all aspects of the curriculum.

In city schools classes were segregated from the age of seven and after the Qualifying Examination (introduced in 1903) at the age of twelve, additional subjects taught to those pupils who remained at elementary schools were vocational; needlework, housewifery, laundry and cookery for girls and metalwork, woodwork and drill for the boys.

The Qualifying Exam allowed for pupils with ability to go on to secondary education, but many pupils could not afford to pay the fees or for books and so continued at elementary schools.

Children's social welfare was not neglected during the period of the School Boards. Though legislation of 1908 introduced a school meals service and medical inspection into schools, many of these reforms had already been pioneered with local School Boards. Clothing from charitable organisations was distributed through the schools and free or cheap dinners reached children through day/industrial schools. The 1918 Education Act replaced School Boards with larger Education Authorities.

Jemima Fraser

Party was founded under Keir Hardie and Cunninghame Graham. The SLP was not a socialist party, rather it was an effort to give independent representation to working people. In 1892 the Trades Councils formed their Scottish United Trades Councils Independent Labour Party under R Chisholm Robertson, the Stirling miners' leader whom Cunninghame Graham would describe as "Robespierre". Both parties had the same broad aims: payment for Members of Parliament, nationalism of major industries and an eight hour day. The original purpose of the SUTCILP was to maintain a connection between Parliamentary Labour and the Unions, something which Hardie himself saw as vital. The general election of 1892 was not a success for either of the independent Labour Parties. They won no seats and there were accusations from the Edinburgh Trades Council, some of whose number were opposed to independent labour action, that the Tories had paid the SUTCILP £1,000, or even £3,000, to stand against Liberal candidates and split the left wing vote. In January 1893, Keir Hardie had established the Independent Labour Party in Bradford and though the SUTCILP had a last gasp of popularity. Serious Labour supporters soon switched to the ILP, looking for a coherent and unified approach, free of the personality clashes between Hardie and Chisholm Robertson. The SLP and the ILP under Hardie now had control of the Labour movement in Britain and the Socialist Labour Party, formed in 1903 as a break from the Marxist Social Democratic Federation, also maintained a steady but low support. By the outbreak of the First World War, they had only two MPs at Westminster to show for their massive support and efforts.

For Glasgow, the ILP and British politics as a whole, the 1914-18 War was a testing ground. The West of Scotland, as usual, contributed heavily to the toll of on average 20,000 fatalities a week on the Allied side by 1917. In 1915, Glasgow witnessed a massive rent strike and a major confrontation. The years which followed would forever paint the Clyde red in popular imagination.

Despite the war and the remoteness of the event, Russia's February Revolution brought 100,000 on to the Glasgow streets in 1917; John Maclean, appointed Soviet Consul for Scotland by the Bolshevik Government, would reach the peak of his popularity and be martyred by the authorities;[1] and John Wheatley would perfect the welfare policy which still shapes the public perception of the Labour Party to this day.[2]

On Saturday, October 13, 1906, the first issue of *Forward* appeared in Glasgow. This weekly independent Labour paper, founded and edited by Tom Johnston,[3] carried contributions from the leading

"GREAT JOHN MACLEAN" (1879–1923)

Man or myth? Was Glasgow socialist teacher John Maclean an isolated, somewhat paranoid sectarian or the creator of a uniquely Scottish marxism? Maclean, embraced the "scientific" materialism which replaced ethical socialism as the driving force of working-class ideology at this period, and drew huge crowds of workmen to his Sunday evening "classes", particularly as real wages declined in the years of depression after 1906.

The combination of unrest among craftsmen and this heady marxist brew contributed to the Red Clyde and made Maclean a marked man. He spent many months in prison but was rewarded for his intransigence by being made first Soviet Russian consul in Scotland after the revolution of November 1917. Government persecution continued, but had the effect of isolating him both from the developing ILP and from the Moscow-oriented Communist Party of Great Britain.

Maclean's response was a combination of revolutionary socialism and Scottish nationalism which he, and a small but talented following, continued to preach until, in 1923, he simply wore himself out. Despite the onset of severe economic depression, Maclean's revolutionary tradition vanished from Scotland, but from the 1930s on his memory came to be venerated by socialists and left-wing nationalists, until in 1948 Hamish Henderson's justly famous "Freedom Come All Ye" – the alternative Scottish national anthem – could end with the words:

When Maclean meets wi' freends in Springburn,
A' the roses an' geans will turn to bloom,
An' the black boy frae yont Nyanga
Dings the fell gallows o' the burgers doon.

Christopher Harvie

1. "Maclean died in poverty: he had given all he had to others." Dr William Knox, **Scottish Labour Leaders 1918–1939**, 1984. 2. "Wheatley left over £16,000, a substantial house overlooking Sandyhills golf course, and a controlling interest in Hoxton and Walsh". Dr William Knox, ibid. 3. Ian MacDougall, **Labour in Scotland, A Pictorial History**, 1985.

Family portrait of John Maclean.

Chapter Sixteen
FORWARD

Labour figures of the day and became the unofficial voice of the ILP. James Connolly wrote a weekly column for many years; John Maclean, a leading figure in the Marxist SDF and still a school teacher, also appeared regularly, as did John Wheatley, whose pamphlet *Mines, Miners and Misery or How The Miners Were Robbed* was serialised in its pages. Special editions were produced[1] when necessary. Martin Haddow of the ILP wrote on education and Frank McCabe, a gravedigger at Lambhill Cemetery, wrote a regular piece aimed at Irish Catholics.

In the build up to 1914, *Forward* was among the voices speaking out against the, by then, almost inevitable conflict. John Maclean and James Maxton were very active in the anti-war cause, as was the Reverend James Barr, who gave renowned sermons against the slaughter. The International Socialist Bureau had produced a manifesto which came out strongly against a possible war and Keir Hardie was one of the British signatories. Initially, public opinion in Glasgow was also broadly pacifist, but the mood soon changed with the outbreak of hostilities. The jingoism of press and public announcements took hold as the list of deaths and atrocities to be revenged grew. Labour and trade union activists became a potentially seditious minority and would in some cases be prosecuted under the Defence of the Realm Act, but in another three years Glasgow, Scotland and Britain were not only tired of the killing fields abroad, but weary too of the erosion of wages and living standards at home.

Partick Rent Strike Demonstration in 1915, with appropriate warning.

During the first two years of the war, prices rose by 65 per cent, while interest rates rose from three and a half to five per cent by 1916. It wasn't until 1917, when 1911's sixpenny loaf cost a shilling, that bread was subsidised.

When Mrs McHugh of Shettleston was taken to court for non-payment of rent, the Soldiers' and Sailors' Families Association sided with her factor, saying that income of £1 8s 9d, with 3/6 for each son, was more than enough to keep body and soul together.

The reality of the situation in 1915 saw Glasgow with less than one per cent of its houses unlet. Many dwellings were unfit for human habitation. The Government recognised they had to house their munitions workers and to a certain extent were aware of the widespread distress in industrial areas, but the rent strike of 1915 – one of the most remarkable in Glasgow's history – forced them into action.

Some of the women involved in the rent strike later agitated for peace, but they largely dropped from the political scene. The activities of other Labour activists like John Maclean, James MacDougall

Women leading the Rent Strike demonstration to George Square on October 8, 1915.

RENT STRIKE AND FORTY HOURS STRIKE

Perhaps the most famous, and misleading, image of the Red Clyde is that of the red flag being flown in George Square on February 1, 1919, at the climax of a strike which some of the leaders, and some of their opponents, saw as a revolutionary move. But the Forty Hours Strike, through which the Glasgow Trades Council, led by Emanuel Shinwell, demanded a reduced working week in order to provide jobs for returning ex-servicemen, was essentially peaceful, and made notorious only because of panic reactions by the police (who were themselves in a highly discontented mood) and the Scottish Secretary. After the *fracas* in George Square the unions and managements came to an agreement, and the ex-servicemen were rapidly integrated, avoiding trouble when, 18 months later, the bottom fell out of the post-war boom.

In the long term the rent strike of 1915 was much more successful, in the influence it had on subsequent housing policy. Following strikes by engineers, an agitation headed by ILP politicians, trade unionists and – unprecedentedly – women activists led to the mass withholding of rents. A song written by Jimmie Maxton ran:

To hell with the sheriff, to hell with his crew;
To hell with Lloyd George, and with Henderson too.
To hell with the factor, his rent I won't pay.
Three cheers for John Wheatley! I'm striking today!

As far as the munitions managers were concerned, the private landlords were fair game, and rent control was introduced, laying the basis for the public control of housing which lasted for most of the century.

Christopher Harvie

1. John Hannan, **The Life of John Wheatley**, 1988.

THE MYTH OF THE RED CLYDE

"He is gruff, intractable and independent, and his latent irritability takes fire when his rights are infringed. Of servility he has not a trace". Thus did James Hamilton Muir see the skilled Clydeside engineer before the First World War – not the easiest person to integrate into the mass-production of guns and shells. The Ministry of Munitions after the outbreak of hostilities, and its chief Clydeside organiser William Weir, didn't tackle the problem with much diplomacy. Craft pride, suspicion of women and the Irish, hostility (well-grounded) towards employers and concern over inflation – salted with a dash of left-wing polemic – led to an explosive situation in the engineering shops as the Government tried to gear them up for the great offensives expected in 1916.

"Dilution" was purchased with the carrot of higher wages for the unskilled and semi-skilled, canteens, welfare measures and rent control, and the stick of an assault on shop stewards, several of whom were arrested and imprisoned. Resistance was broken which could later have been dangerous when, during 1917, the casualty lists lengthened. The main phase of the Red Clyde was over by the time and the Forty Hours Strike of January 1919 was really a separate incident.

But by the end of the war a mass Labour movement, centred on the ILP, was coming into being. Labour swept forward, and in November 1922 returned ten out of the 15 Glasgow MPs. "We'll soon change all this", said Kirkwood to Maxton when they entered the House of Commons. But the red rebel of Beardmores ended his career on the red benches of the House of Lords.

Christopher Harvie

and the exiled Russian Peter Petrov, drew anti-war campaigners from all over the country to the one city where they would get a sympathetic hearing.

Members of the Clyde Workers' Committee were also strongly opposed to the war. In the six months after the rent strikes, the CWC organised a ten day strike where 10,000 men won a small, though significant, increase in wages. The unions fought a running battle against the erosion of pay and conditions, treading a tightrope with their Labour Withholding Committee between legality and arrest for sedition.

The Government had given employers greatly increased powers to alter conditions, control employees' rights to leave or strike and bring in unskilled labour. Clydeside employers wanted more. Christopher Addison, Parliamentary Under-Secretary at the Ministry of Munitions said of them, "They wanted all sorts of powers over workmen – a sort of martial law – which they themselves might administer, obviously an impossible demand. They gave us the immediate impression of being a poor lot."[1]

In December 1915, Lloyd George, then Minister for Munitions, came to Glasgow to see the Red Clydesiders for himself, confident of his powers of persuasion. He managed to offend union officials by changing the date for their meeting from December 23 to Christmas Day without consulting them and the Trades Council poured contempt on the whole enterprise. Lloyd George spent three days in Glasgow. His encounter with the Clyde Workers' Committee was frosty, as were most of his other meetings, but none could match the final debacle at the St Andrew's Halls when Lloyd George could hardly get a word out. The banning of *Forward* was, in part, an act of retribution by the authorities for such scenes.[2]

In March 1916, a strike broke out at the Parkhead Forge and when it threatened to spread, the Government saw its chance. The Conscription Act had already provoked demonstrations in Glasgow, and *The Worker*, the newspaper of the CWC, was also campaigning against it. In the fourth issue an article appeared under the headline, "Should The Workers Arm?" The piece actually decided that, on balance, they should not, but it was the perfect opportunity to break the power of the CWC and stop the strikes. The editors of *The Worker*, John Muir and Willie Gallacher, as well as printer Walter Bell, were jailed and the protest strike of 5,000 men was not reported in the press until almost a week after it had taken place. Kirkwood was obstructed in his union business at Beardmores. He resigned his convenorship and a sympathy strike broke out again. Kirkwood and several other CWC leaders were deported, initially to Edinburgh.

1932 General Election poster for Tom Anderson.

A copy of *Forward*.

FORWARD

A GLASGOW SCANDAL!
M'INNES SHAW; AND THE PLUNDER OF THE COMMON GOOD.
STOP THIEF!

1. Iain McLean, **The Legend of Red Clydeside**, 1983. **2.** ibid.

JAMES MAXTON (1885–1946)

On his death in 1946, thousands lined the route to the Maryhill Crematorium. The Orpheus Choir sang there in his memory. Gandhi sent a message of condolence. The House of Commons stood silent for a minute in a tribute almost unique for an MP who had never held high office.

Too lazy to go for it, detractors said, Too principled, supporters felt. Maxton had led the ILP out of the Labour Party in 1932 because the latter wasn't sufficiently Socialist. He was a pacifist in both World Wars. His most memorable parliamentary speech remained one made not long after his election for Bridgeton in 1922, when he was suspended for denouncing as "murderers" Tory MPs supporting a motion to cut health grants to local authorities.

But outside the House, his best lines, surely, were those once uttered at a Scottish ILP conference. He'd been told that he couldn't ride two horses. "My reply to that is, that if my friend cannot ride two horses – what's he doing in the bloody circus?" He was, after all, a pragmatic politician.

Pacifist, parliamentarian and revolutionary, middle-class graduate who became the soul of Bridgeton – the man of legend was a man of paradox. But the power of legend is such that even Communists forget today that Maxton was denounced as "pink" by the "Red Clyde" heroes Gallacher and Maclean.

That appealing visage beloved of cartoonists has come to symbolise Glasgow's Red tradition.

Angus Calder

Within days John Maclean, Jimmy Maxton and James MacDougall were all arrested for sedition. They had addressed meetings, spoken against conscription and accused the Government of entering the war to save its economic neck. Maxton and MacDougall got one year, Maclean got three. Public outcry led to their early release, but none of them would be safe from arrest until the war was over. Left wing opposition had, for the moment, been silenced by the muscle of Central Government in London.

After the Armistice, radicalism returned; *The Worker* and *Forward* were back in circulation and free of censorship. In January 1919, 1,800 trade union delegates, the wartime suppression behind them, made a decision to strike for a 40 hour week. A Joint Committee, with the ILP Councillor Emmanuel Shinwell as its chairman, was formed and they called a one day general strike for January 27. Their intention, with thousands of soldiers being demobilised, was to avoid unemployment by reducing the working week.

On Thursday, January 30, *The Strike Bulletin* called for workers to assemble in George Square the following day to hear the Lord Provost's response. Thousands packed the Square. Davie Kirkwood, Neil McLean and a small deputation went into the City Chambers while William Gallacher addressed the crowd. What happened next is not entirely clear.

It could have been that some disturbances broke out when trams, some of which were still running, tried to make their way through the densely packed crowd. Whatever the reason, the police, batons drawn, charged into the crowd and the crowd retaliated. What became known as Bloody Friday left many under arrest and many more injured. Davie Kirkwood was knocked unconscious and arrested with Shinwell, Gallacher and others. Shinwell was sentenced to five months, Gallacher and James Murray got three months and the rest were acquitted.

Lloyd George's coalition government, terrified that a Red Revolution was about to break out on the Clyde, could not rely on a local regiment, especially, he felt, the Highland Light Infantry, to control the situation. English troops were brought north to occupy the centre of the city, while the local troops were confined to Maryhill Barracks. The 40 hour week was not introduced until after the Second World War.

The Russian Revolution was not the only major socialist move abroad made in the shadow of the First World War; 1916 had seen the ill-fated Easter Rising in Dublin.

Glasgow and the industrial west of Scotland had always been

The red flag flies in George Square on Friday, January 31, 1919.

A leaflet from the Forty Hours Strike.

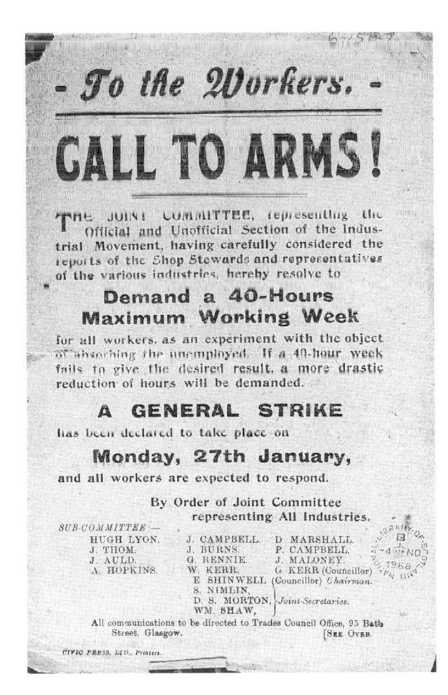

- To the Workers. -

CALL TO ARMS!

THE JOINT COMMITTEE, representing the Official and Unofficial Section of the Industrial Movement, having carefully considered the reports of the Shop Stewards and representatives of the various industries, hereby resolve to

Demand a 40-Hours Maximum Working Week

for all workers, as an experiment with the object of absorbing the unemployed. If a 40-hour week fails to give the desired result, a more drastic reduction of hours will be demanded.

A GENERAL STRIKE

has been declared to take place on

Monday, 27th January,

and all workers are expected to respond.

By Order of Joint Committee
representing All Industries.

SUB-COMMITTEE:—
HUGH LYON. J. CAMPBELL. D. MARSHALL.
J. THOM. J. BURNS. P. CAMPBELL.
J. AULD. G. RENNIE. J. MALONEY.
A. HOPKINS. W. KERR. G. KERR (Councillor)
E. SHINWELL (Councillor) *Chairman.*
S. NIMLIN, D. S. MORTON, WM. SHAW, *Joint-Secretaries.*

All communications to be directed to Trades Council Office, 95 Bath Street, Glasgow. [SEE OVER

CIVIC PRESS, LTD., Printers.

WOMEN'S LIFE AND LABOUR

Before 1914 no-one was more disadvantaged than working women in Scotland. As women they suffered low wages; as wives, too many pregnancies and poor health; as mothers, bad housing and poor food. The burdens of domestic work, of cleaning and washing, required long hours of hard physical labour. The challenge of feeding and clothing a family was never ending. Mothers served themselves last. Women's willingness to sacrifice their own interests made them docile employees. Employers preferred them; a preference not expressed in higher wages.

Even in factory or mill, economic imperatives forced complaisance from a female workforce. It is not suggested that informed women workers were incapable of forming a union or ignorant about the possible benefits of industrial action but that because there were no margins, no-one could afford to risk her earnings in a union cause. Choice was a luxury they did not have. Before 1914 it was left to women in easier circumstances, like Emma Paterson and Mary McArthur, to take up the cause of women's trade unionism.

By 1914 there was a range of trade union activities involving working women in Scotland. Despite the efforts, most working women remained unattached to any union although few can have remained ignorant of their work. Women were still considered to be more comfortable, and in their proper element, if employed exclusively in the home with the family. The war was to bring a radical – if temporary change – in women's work and expectations.

Olive Checkland

a magnet for the poor Irish leaving a starving island in search of work. In the build up to the First World War, a further 100,000 Irish workers came into the West of Scotland; 60,000 to Glasgow itself to work in munitions.

In the early years of the 20th century, the United Irish League was still a powerful force in Scotland and the struggle for land in Ireland and the Highlands of Scotland had further united the countries. Men like John Wheatley, the son of Irish immigrant parents, would see that the condition of Ireland would do little to affect the state of the poor Irish Catholics in Scotland and made moves to win the Catholic vote for Labour by converting them to the cause of socialism and a socialist future for Scotland. His half-way house, the Catholic Socialist Society, would be a phenomenal success. It was far from the sectarian organisation the name and some portrayals suggest. Wheatley made the transition, firstly to the ILP and then [1] to Parliament, but he linked Catholicism and Socialism, for some people irrevocably, before becoming the Member for Shettleston.

In the year before Dublin's Easter Rising, James Connolly was a familiar figure in Glasgow and may, as John Maclean believed, have seen his native Scotland in general and Glasgow in particular as European Socialism's best hope for revolution. The events of early 1916 and the Government's effective suppression of the Left seem to have changed his mind; which is certainly what John Maclean believed. He said Connolly resolved on the Easter Rising after seeing the succession of sentences the High Court in Edinburgh imposed on the strikers under the Defence of the Realm Act.

Confidence was shaken following the spring events of 1919. Even after the tanks left the Cattle Market, organised Labour turned away from any further serious commitment to revolutionary action. They had been defeated and knew it.

Labour concentrated on creating the Parliamentary road to Socialism, where the conflict between the Ramsay MacDonald camp's willingness to compromise and court public opinion and the fervent idealism of the Clydeside contingent, which provided so much of the drive and inspiration for the early Labour Governments, established the now familiar tradition of Labour Party civil war.

The ILP grew in strength throughout the 1920s and was particularly popular in Glasgow, where there were more than 200 branches. The party and its Clydeside contingent made their great leap forward in 1922, the year they supported Ramsay MacDonald as the party's new leader, and sent a total of ten out of 30 Labour MPs to Westminster.

The Independent Labour Party won ten of the eleven Glasgow

Girls from the Screening Plant, No. 1 Pit, Bothwellhaugh in 1925.

Tanks were brought into Glasgow on the night of January 31 and stationed in the Cattle Market.

1. Iain McLean, op. cit.

JOHN WHEATLEY (1869–1930) AND HIS INFLUENCE

Housing was the issue that changed the political face of Glasgow. It brought John Wheatley to Parliament and a post in the 1924 Labour Government.

His Housing Act, the one achievement of that Government, was an ambitious project designed to build houses at rents which workers could afford. It was the culmination of work which began almost 20 years earlier with his conversion to socialism.

As a Catholic of Irish origin Wheatley first entered politics throught the Irish Home Rule movement. He came to the realisation that Irish independence would do nothing to end the exploitation of the Irish living in Scotland and converted to socialism. He endeavoured to draw Clydeside's Catholic population into local Labour politics, incurring the wrath of his clergy.

It was his campaign in the Council (1912–22) for improved housing conditions which earned him broad working class support. A scheme he proposed for cottages was rejected by the Council and in a bid to mobilise support a Glasgow Housing Association was formed. This association spearheaded the fight against increased rents during the war years which forced the Government to bring in legislation to prohibit increases. In 1922, in an election orchestrated by Wheatley, housing and rents were the issues which resulted in Labour providing Glasgow with two thirds of its elected representatives at Westminster.

John Wheatley fought with vigour in the interests of the poor, and was not corrupted by office. His inspiring life offers many lessons.

John Hannan

seats they contested and the band of teetotal, solidly working class men attended a victory rally at the St Andrew's Halls, the site of Lloyd George's previous sherracking. To the 8,000 who had gathered to see them off, they pledged that they had resolved to dedicate themselves "to the reconciliation and unity of the nations of the world and the development and happiness of the people of these islands." They were escorted to Central Station and the night train to London by thousands singing "The Red Flag" and Psalm 127; no one at the time seems to have found the two a curious combination.[1]

In London, the Red Clydesiders were of novelty interest to the press and tales of social ineptitude abounded. Their penetrating, well argued speeches, particularly by Wheatley, went unsupported, despite the fact that praise for his abilities crossed the benches.

He and the other Clydesiders brought the social realities and consequences of Tory policies to Parliament for the first time. Here were a group of articulate, intelligent men who talked about disease, poverty and misery from experience and to a certain extent, they impressed the Tories and Liberals more than some of their painstakingly moderate colleagues.

Proposed amendments to the Rent Restrictions Act, which would decontrol rents, brought the marchers out again and focused the Parliamentary Labour Party's minds wonderfully. The Tories were once more on the brink of sanctioning a major cause of mass poverty and again Wheatley's housing experience served Labour well. The Housing Bill left him asking, "Why do you propose these boxes for the people, are they less useful to society than yourselves?"

At the end of 1923, another General Election was called and Glasgow's Red Ten returned to the Clyde with serious doubts about the Parliamentary Labour Party's commitment to Socialism with Ramsay MacDonald at its head.

If MacDonald had hoped the Glasgow voters would rap the extremists' knuckles, he was sadly mistaken. The ILP's percentage of the vote had risen from 44.6 per cent to 51.1 per cent. Liberalism was no longer a serious alternative for left wing voters.

Following a vote of no confidence, MacDonald was asked to form a Government and agreed to a coalition with the Liberals, much to the dismay of those who believed that socialism should try to keep itself free from compromise, an opinion firmly stated by Glasgow's Members. Wheatley was appointed Minister of Health, as a sop to the Clyde; if this was a move to keep him occupied, it certainly succeeded. It seems that many of Wheatley's colleagues lacked the scale of vision to govern effectively and in the autumn

John Maclean's funeral procession to Eastwood Cemetery. No film record is known to exist.

HIS FUNERAL – on the Monday following, to Eastwood New Cemetery, was a revelation to the bourgeois and the Labour fakirs of our city. At least 5,000 Comrades took part in the march from Eglinton Toll to the Cemetery, a distance of four miles: and double that number followed the funeral, which was led by the Clyde Workers' Silver Band. The march was known as The Silent March, *each comrade marching with his head uncovered and observing due silence.*

Comrade Tom, Comrade John MacLean, MA *1930.*

1. John Hannan, op. cit.

of 1924, the Government fell into an ugly scandal over MacDonald's manipulation of events surrounding the prosecution of John Ross Campbell, the editor of *Workers' Weekly*, who found himself accused of inciting men at the Aldershot Barracks to mutiny. Rather than face a Liberal-inspired committee of inquiry, MacDonald went to the country in October, 1924, the second General Election in nine months.

This was the General Election where the Tories first adopted the Union Jack as their emblem and the Liberals and Tories agreed not to oppose each other if there was a chance of Labour taking a seat.

The faked Zinoviev letter from the Communist International to British Communists, urging revolutionary action, shook the Labour vote. Emmanuel Shinwell and Tom Johnston lost their Glasgow seats and the ILP's majorities were reduced. A Tory Government was returned.

MacDonald's credibility was at a low ebb and for a time it seems as though Wheatley and what was described as the extreme Left, might come to power, but MacDonald held the TUC; he was always ahead of Wheatley in the politics of party organisation. Wheatley came out strongly in favour of the General Strike, but, as was the case in 1984, the Government was more than ready for the strikers.

John Wheatley died of a cerebral haemorrhage in 1930, having become a prophet of doom, surrounded by "the Bad Five", including Maxton, who were all that remained of his Clydeside support.[1] Maxton continued through the Second World War years, working till his death in 1946; his had become the ILP's sole remaining Parliamentary voice. He and his party separated from the Labour Party in 1932 following years of increasing friction between the two. Organised Labour denounced MacDonald as a traitor when he formed and led a Coalition Government with the Tories and Liberals following the 1929 Wall Street crash. The Labour Party suffered a humiliating defeat in the 1931 General Election, losing 30 of their 37 Scottish seats. David Kirkwood left the ILP to join the Labour Party in 1933.

The man for whom Sir William Beardmore bought "the best hat in Glasgow", in respect of their close relationship in organising production at Parkhead Forge during the First World War, was created First Baron Kirkwood of Bearsden in 1951. Campbell Stephen died in October 1947, four days after rejoining the Labour Party. George Buchanan[2] held his Gorbals seat till 1948 when he became first chairman of the National Assistance Board and Baron Shinwell

WALTER ELLIOT (1888–1959)

"That man talks too much," was Winston Churchill's verdict on one of Scotland's most talented politicians, which ended his career in 1940, after he had created the agriculture subsidy system and the modern Scottish Office. Walter Elliot, who sat for Kelvingrove between 1924 and his death, was a dangerously innovative figure, competent to deal with everything from pigs (his doctoral thesis) to the drama (his closest friend, from their riotous university days, was James Bridie).

A Tory, but never much of an ideologue – "Will stand, which party?" was the telegram which announced his *début* in 1918 – Elliot strove to combat the *malaise* of Scotland in the depression years, and pioneered the sort of consensual approach which between 1936 and 1938 created the Scottish Economic Committee, the Scottish Special Housing Association, and the Empire Exhibition in Bellahouston Park.

Our of office, he collaborated with Tom Johnston on the Scottish Council of State which between 1941 and 1945 produced the North of Scotland Hydro-Electric Board and blueprints for social reform after the war. In 1934, he married Katharine Tennant, of the great St Rollox chemical family, and a politician in her own right. After his death she became one of the first Life Peeresses, and remains active in the Lords. Her verdict on 25 years of marriage? "Never a dull moment, and never an angry word."

Christopher Harvie

Tom Johnston in plus-fours with fellow North of Scotland Hydro Board executives.

Men outside the Beardmores gate during a strike on March 28, 1937.

1. Iain Mclean, op. cit. 2. Iain McLean, op. cit.

outlived them all, dying in 1985, aged 101. Like Gallacher and Kirkwood, he was never as heroic as his autobiography suggests.

In 1970, the Rt Hon Arthur Woodburn, a former Secretary of State for Scotland, told an interviewer, "The most revolutionary thing that ever happened in Scotland at that time was when J. S. Clarke's wife made Davy Kirkwood wash the dishes – which he'd never done before."[1]

The Hungry Thirties found the working class bearing the brunt of Glasgow and the West of Scotland's singular inability to adapt their monolithic heavy industries. Unemployment was rampant. Hunger marchers were on the roads again, chalking messages to each other and the general public wherever they went. The Means Test, possibly the single most hated piece of British legislation, was introduced in 1931 by Ramsay MacDonald's "National" Government. For those who wish a key to Glasgow's resilience, the following song offers a clue:

> I'm no the factor nor the gasman,
> Napoleon nor Ronald Coleman;
> When you hear me tap-tap-tappin at your door
> Have your money in the bank, or money in the store.
> You'd better watch out or else I'll get ye,
> Just try and dodge me if you can;
> For I'm neither Santa Claus nor Douglas Fairbanks:
> I am the Means Test Man.[2]

The Second World War brought a temporary reprieve for the Clyde shipyards. They produced 400,000 tons of shipping every year between 1939 and 1945. A whole generation of women gained an unexpected independence and self respect through war work, just as their predecessors had in the century's first great conflict, though their tasks were generally menial and any lessons society may have learned were soon forgotten; sexual stereotyping in industry returned with the Armistice and general employment.

On March 14, 1941, German bombers, unencumbered by the radio interference which had jammed their signals over England, took advantage of a clear night to bomb Glasgow and the "Holy City" of Clydebank. The same pathfinder unit which had led the bombers to Coventry the previous year, now guided the Junkers and Heinkels towards industrial targets including the massive Singer factory, the many shipyards and their workers' homes. Singer's timber yard and a distillery at Yoker both went up and their fires could be seen by RAF planes flying into Dyce Airbase in Aberdeen.[3]

THE WORLD OF THE GLASGOW SOCIALISTS

For those who joined it, the socialist movement of the late 19th and early 20th century was less a party than an almost religious cause. The Independent Labour Party, in particular, set out to offer an alternative to the other life-styles available – whether "rough" (pubs, dance halls, betting) or "respectable" (temperance soirées, the churches, athletics). The model for this tended to be the German Social Democrats, who had been forced to create their own culture through Bismarck's persecution, and whose example was taught both by exiles and by the socialist press – Blatchford's *Clarion*, Keir Hardie's *Labour Leader*, and after 1906 Tom Johnston's immensely successful *Forward*, edited from Glasgow itself.

The movement started with the youngest, who could be christened in a Labour Church, and then go to a Socialist Sunday School. Then there were cycling clubs, often organised in conjunction with the *Clarion* as a means of distributing the paper, choirs – the famous Orpheus choir had its origins here – artists' guilds, and drama societies. The Co-op created its own organisations, which catered in particular for women.

These, and party meetings, could occupy practically every free hour in a week, but the more militant groups which developed in the 1900s argued that such activities were "bourgeois" and that what was needed was a "revolutionary consciousness" inculcated by "proletarian education". John Maclean was the greatest exponent of this approach, but it – and the ILP's "alternative world" – was weakened both by Government repression during the First World War and by the impact of radio and cinema in the 1920s. By the 1960s it had virtually ceased to exist.

Christopher Harvie

"Building Cargo Vessels" by Henry Rushberry.

Denny's apprentices on strike, April 9, 1937.

1. Iain McLean, op. cit. 2. Norman Buchan and Peter Hall (eds.), **The Scottish Folksinger**, 1973.
3. Various contributors, **The Glasgow Diary**, 1984.

Stanley Spencer sketching on the Clyde.

A SHIPYARD WORKER'S EXPERIENCE

The harsh metallic din which echoed across the Clyde before 1939 was the sound of manual rather than mechanised work. It was the sound of hard, dirty, dangerous work often done by men clambering all over the exposed skeleton of the ship under construction. In winter the boilermakers' summer outfit of oily moleskin trousers and sweat-absorbent flannel shirt was transformed by layers of patched cardigans and discarded jackets until they resembled "walking rag-bags".

The great "Clydebuilt" ships were "wrought" by sheer physical effort. Shipyard work was overwhelmingly skilled, based on manual dexterity, strength and, above all, experience. While dozens of different trades were employed on every ship it was the boilermakers – platers, riveters and caulkers – who fashioned the hulls and largely organised the construction process. In an industry beset by uncertainty, management hired and fired labour according to their short-term requirements. The shipyard worker belonged to a skilled squad, often based on his family, which was hired to perform a specific section of work. The gang was responsible for organising its efforts efficiently, generally with little or no management supervision.

The teeming throngs of men outside the yard gates during the inter-war depression were testimony to the human costs of a casual labour market. It was the chronic insecurity of shipyard employment which lay behind the Clydeside workers' fierce loyalty to their trade and their union, traditions which have persisted to the present day.

Anthony Slaven

The flames attracted more bombers to destroy the schools, churches, hospitals and houses. Another legend tells us only eight Clydebank houses were left untouched. In the following night of the Blitz, the bombers returned and bombed until morning. The recorded fatalities for both nights in Glasgow alone, were 647 people.

As late as the 1970s, hopes for the rebirth of Glasgow were still centred on the industries which had supported her almost two centuries previously. In July, 1971, the last chapter in Glasgow's love affair with her industrial past began in Clydebank when Jimmy Reid and the workers in John Brown's Shipyard closed the gates in the face of the Upper Clyde Shipbuilders' imminent liquidation. They called themselves Clyde Workers Unlimited and announced not a sit-in, but a work-in.

On June 29, 1981, a Victory Rally commemorated the 10th birthday of UCS as a great workers' victory. The facts are a little different.

As leaders Jimmy Airlie, Jimmy Reid and Sammy Barr made it very clear, the men laid off as part of the liquidation would work on in the yards while the liquidators would be decidedly unwelcome. In actual fact, the liquidators did gain access to the yards and did carry out the task of winding up the business, reducing the workforce by 18.5 per cent during the work-in. At the height of the movement's popularity, in August 1971, 69 per cent of those made redundant were still working, but by the end of the work-in the figure was only 14 per cent.

"Burners" by Stanley Spencer, one of his monumental studies of Clydeside wartime workers.

The leadership policy was that all four yards affected should be dealt with together, or not at all and any plans for rescue should take this into account. In the fourth week of the dispute, the leaders met with industrialist Archibald "Cash Down" Kelly at his holiday home in Islay. Some eyebrows were raised, given Kelly's exploitative history on the banks of the Liffey. The deal fell through when Kelly was asked to put up £10 million of his own money and take on all four yards.[1]

Glasgow businessman Hugh Stenhouse was chosen as the Government's negotiator for the discussions to end the work-in and find a mutually acceptable settlement for the yards' future. Negotiations at the North British Hotel in George Square led to a radical change in approach. Now all four yards would be "dealt with cumulatively".[2] This phrase became increasingly familiar and spelt the end of a united UCS future. The lame duck yard at Clydebank was left out in the cold when Govan Shipbuilders came to bid for the other three.

Meanwhile, the UCS assets were disappearing as first three, then one, then another two completed ships were released to their new

UCS meeting at Govan, August 9, 1971. The unseen speaker is Jimmy Airlie.

1. Stephen Johns, **Reformism on the Clyde: The Story of UCS**, 1973. **2.** ibid.

owners in climb down after climb down by union leaders who seemed more anxious to please negotiators than the workforce.

The press was filled with praise for plucky little UCS as the[1] bargaining with Govan Shipbuilders began. Clydebank remained steadfastly unappetising for potential British buyers and Danny McGarvey of the Boilermakers' Union eventually had to go to America to unearth Wayne Harbin and the Marathon Manufacturing Company who were willing to risk John Browns in Clydebank as a manufacturing base for their oil exploration work. By the end of the year, Govan Shipbuilders had agreed to take on Scotstoun as well as Linthouse and Govan and the cumulative package was complete.

Reid, Barr and Airlie were now facing a disillusioned workforce. They were predictably chosen for the final negotiating committee which signed away the workers' right to strike for four years and impose punitive bonus and productivity schemes redolent of the First World War Munitions Act. Reid told the press, "This is a very good agreement which in no way violates the principles or policies of trade unions."

At the end of the UCS saga in 1972, the labour force had been cut by 25 per cent, union rights had been eroded at every turn and the Heath Government, far from being toppled, had introduced the Industrial Relations Act.

SHIP ASSEMBLY AND ASSOCIATED INDUSTRIES

In the hey-day of shipbuilding up to one third of the output of the Scottish steel industry was destined for use on the Clyde. But while the hull is the most visible evidence of the construction of the ship, it is the provision of machinery, and the ultimate fitting out of the shell that creates the most diverse demands for products from other industries. The great engines were frequently supplied by specialist firms like David Rowan, Rankin & Blackmore or John Kincaid. Boilers too could be supplied by firms like Howden, while the whole complex of valves, pipes and pumps provided markets for specialist firms like Weirs of Cathcart.

The fitting-out process also called for painters, joiners, electricians, and upholsterers. In all of these trades there were specialist suppliers, and in fitting out the great staterooms of the liners, specialist furnishers like Rowan & Boden, turned steel shells into ornate floating hotels of the highest quality. Beyond that, the great liners also provided work for designers, sculptors and artists, producing original works on commission to grace the cabins and public rooms of the vessels.

Every ship, indeed, generated numerous demands from associated industries. When the *Queen Mary* was being built at Clydebank, employing 4–5,000 men, it is said that the orders for equipment spread work over 80 towns and cities in Britain and, at one time or another, involved 250,000 men and women in supplying them. While this was an exceptional spin-off, it typifies the nature of the shipbuilding process and the creation of work for associated trades.

Anthony Slaven

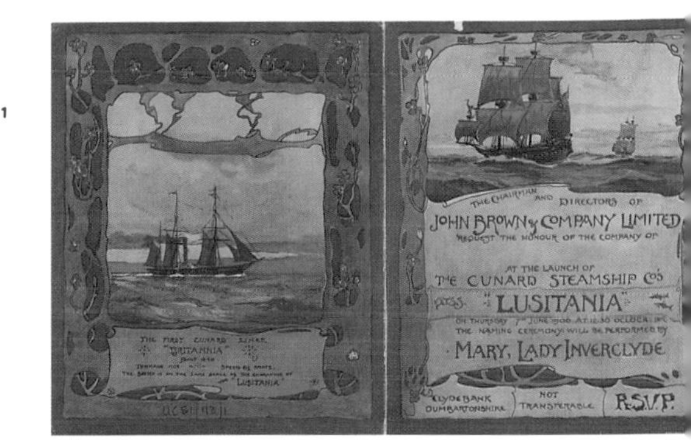

The Lusitania is launched on June 7, 1906, 15 months after the keel was laid.

UCS banner.

1. An obscure Backbencher, Nicholas Ridley, prepared a confidential report which concludes, "We could put in a Government 'butcher' to cut up UCS and sell (cheaply) to Lower Clyde, and others, the assets of UCS to minimise upheaval and dislocation." Ridley's other conclusions have a familiar ring.

SHIPBUILDING, *by* Danny Vallely.

Chapter Seventeen

A MODEL CORPORATION

"Glasgow close" by R Henderson Blyth.

Since the 16th century, Glasgow has had tenements and closes of one kind or another. There are still people alive who would measure a person's standing in terms of the colour of sandstone building they lived in, and whether their close was tiled, half-tiled or whitewashed.

Glasgow's image is changing and a proportion of the population are housed around elevator shafts rather than in tenements or wee houses; yet the influence of tenement living and morality still plays a surprisingly large part in Glasgow's idea of itself.

Up until the post war redevelopment, doctors, coalmen or members of the unemployed all lived in a tenement, albeit in different parts of the city. The enforced proximity and shared responsibility seem to have accentuated the Scottish idea of not getting above your station; sharing a lavatory with another family reduces the amount of airs and graces you can reasonably cultivate.

Glasgow Corporation property at 5 King Street, Calton, in 1916.

Sir J. M. Barrie, knight of the Kailyard, observed, "There are few more impressive sights in the world than a Scotsman on the make."[1] Social climbers have never been revered in Scotland and the Scots' almost unrivalled determination has brought them rewards in countries all over the globe, though rarely in the land of their birth. This trend has been magnified in the last ten years, when positions of influence in Scottish life have repeatedly been filled by candidates born outwith Scotland.[2]

A Glasgow steamie, photographed in the early Sixties.

The shapers of Victorian Glasgow were simply celebrating what they bought. Wealth has always bought ability and there were exceptional engineers and architects whose combined talents made Glasgow one of the world's finest 19th century cities. Clyde-built ships carried the city's name and goods around the world where they were drawn by Glasgow-made locomotives. Nowhere reflects Victorian Glasgow's pride in their achievements, confidence in themselves and the future more than the City Chambers. The

1. J.M. Barrie, **What Every Woman Knows**, Act II.
2. Various local media, such as the **Glasgow Herald** and Scottish Television have on a number of recent occasions highlighted this growing trend.

GLASGOW MUNICIPAL BUILDINGS (CITY CHAMBERS)

In 1878, the year of the City of Glasgow Bank collapse, Glasgow borrowed £400,000 to build its opulent City Chambers. The competition to design it was won by Paisley born William Young.

The assessor was the London architect Charles Barry, unior, who made the result a triumph of the Victorian Renaissance of the Fifties and Sixties over the more modern French *Beaux Arts* classicism. It was opened, complete except for the Banqueting Hall, on August 22, 1888. It is 250 feet square, 76 feet high to the parapet, and 216 feet to the top of the tower. It is built of 350,000 cu ft of Polmaise and Dunmore stone, chain-bonded all the way and cut and carved in the masons' yard far from the site. The bricks for the internal work came from the Corporation's own brickfields. Internally, Young tells us that the main hall with its ceramic mosaic floor and Pompeian mosaic vaults – actually these are from Venice – are based on a Roman Church: flanking it are two stairhalls, that on the south to the Council Chamber, the Provost's Room and the Committee Rooms rather like a very grand country house stair. Much more elaborate is that to the Banqueting Hall on the north. The marble is from Brescia, the granite from Aberdeen and Peterhead, the mosaic is Numidian. The reception rooms are reminiscent of Young's work at Chelsea House and Chevening, elements of 16th, 17th and 18th century decoration being fairly freely employed.

The Banqueting Hall was decorated by four Glasgow Boys: Alexander Roche, E.A. Walton, Sir John Lavery and George Henry under the supervision of William Leiper.

David M Walker

Corporation held their first meeting in the new building on October 10, 1889, and have been there ever since.[1]

By 1846 various new Acts had added to the council's burden. They were responsible for, amongst other things, police, statute labour, and lighting. The boundaries had been extended to include Anderston, Calton and the Barony of Gorbals. The city's water supply became their responsibility in 1855, parks and galleries between 1852 and 1859; the City Improvement Scheme was inaugurated in 1866, gas supplies were taken over in 1869 and in 1870 the Corporation tramway system was authorised.

By the turn of the century, Glasgow's municipal control was one of the wonders of the civilised world. Apart from the massive slum clearance and the provision of a fresh water supply the Corporation had built an infectious diseases hospital, set up a system for inspecting and controlling meat and milk production, established and maintained refuse disposal and sewage plants and provided baths and wash houses.

In 1869 when Glasgow Corporation decided to use gas to light the streets, they appropriated the private companies which had been operating in the city for more than 50 years. The scheme was so successful, that they did the same with electricity in 1890, when there were barely 300 consumers in the city. By the start of the First World War there were almost 28,000 customers. Glasgow had the first electric fire alarm system, the first station to be lit by electricity and the first electrically lit hotel. We had the world's first municipal tram system and the busiest tramway crossing in the world was the junction of Union Street, Argyle Street and Jamaica Street, an area known today as Yankee Corner as Pizza Hut, McDonalds and Dunkin' Donuts have moved in.[2]

The tram car was a bigger part of Glasgow than any other British city; and Glasgow kept their tramcars longer. Years after London, Birmingham, Liverpool, Manchester and Edinburgh had given them up, Glasgow still rattled to the sound of the shooglies.

In previous times the volume of horse-drawn omnibuses was so great, that magistrates were forced to draft what were amongst the world's first transport regulations in 1845, three years after the road traffic offence, committed by the Dumfriesshire blacksmith, Kirkpatrick MacMillan in the Gorbals in 1842.

MacMillan was a perfectly practical man, who saw his primitive bicycle invention as a means of personal transportation rather than a commercial proposition. He took an evening and part of a day to cycle the 70 miles to Glasgow and unintentionally knocked over a child who was amongst the crush of people gathered to

THE TRAMS

Although I do recall magnificent Clydesdales helping to pull motor lorries up West Nile Street, I have to deny that I travelled by horse tram. But even the electric cars of my young days had an immemorial feel about them.

They were ours and they were there. I assumed that yon lost Roman legion had been minced by a Green car thundering along the Gallowgate. We sometimes put halfpennies on the rails to be spread into pennies by the wheels. All we got were bent halfpennies, but hope sprang eternal.

I am back with the models that had a little five-seat compartment at each end of the upper deck, and in the front compartment I had many a chat with the driver below, who was glad of the company and didn't have to worry about a steering wheel while he blethered.

You could nearly flit on a tram. In our penny-pinching days my wife and I bought things like chests of drawers at Morrison McChlery's salerooms, and carried such a creature across Sauchiehall Street to load it on the driver's platform of the first blue car going west. He never failed to remember our stop, helped us off with the purchase and kept happy.

Then we modernised into buses and pollution. There hath passed away a glory from the earth.

Cliff Hanley

1. "When in 1889, a 10 day public preview was arranged, around 400,000 people took the chance to marvel at this latest display of Victorian confidence." **The City Chambers,** Glasgow District Council, 1988. **2.** Three have recently opened other branches and Boots have moved, though folk still meet on their corner.

"People on a Yellow Tram Going West" drawn by Bet Low around 1948.

The famous Auchenshuggle tram travelling east past the world's busiest tram junction.

Kirkpatrick MacMillan and his bicycle, known as the Dandy Horse.

see his strange contraption. He was fined five shillings at Gorbals Police Court. Around this time, his niece Mary Marchbank took to riding her uncle's machine, which makes her the world's first lady cyclist.

It seemed the trams would stay forever. When they celebrated their Golden Jubilee in 1922, the Tramways Committee boasted they had "carried out a good deal of work on behalf of the unemployed. The whole staff, including men taken on because of unemployment, numbers 9,084." Their entire debt had been paid and their revenue for the year 1921-22 was £2,354,294. "The tramways in Glasgow have always been successful financially," they said, "but never more than now and we see no reason why this should not continue."[1]

Trams were part of the Glasgow landscape. Two of our great unsung geniuses, neither of whom were Glaswegians, Bud Neill and Chic Murray, with many another music hall comedian, employed jokes about them. Any out of town comedian wishing to win a Glasgow audience started with, "I was coming in on the tram," and the story goes that one poor soul told a Friday evening Glasgow Empire second house about the old lady who asked the driver if she would be electrocuted if she put her foot on the rail, and the audience shouted the punchline back in unison: "Only if you get your other leg round that wire up there, Missus."

Trams were said to cause congestion. A week after the last of the Liverpool trams had gone, in September 1957, the *Weekly Scotsman* published photographs of a line of trams outside Central Station in the smoky rain; the copy concerned Glasgow's traffic: "Motorists are blamed for selfishly causing the congestion," it said, "and they in turn accuse Glasgow's famous tramcars for the hold-ups."[2]

In that year too, when there were 881 trams in the city, the Corporation began to undo their investment. Five years later the trams were gone. Glasgow was becoming another place where tramcars were no longer needed. The tram belonged to a smoky city with iron setts in cobbled roads, three or four-storeyed tenements and corner shops. The new Glasgow needed motorways, high rise flats, tarmaced roads and supermarkets. All that's left are the electric riggings, the iron rosettes that still cling to the buildings. It's easy to be nostalgic about the trams, uncomfortable and slow as they were, but, for many, they became a metaphor for something that didn't need to be changed. Everything went in deference to the motor car and it's not the trams folk miss so much as what they symbolise: their lost communities.

From 1900 to 1907, Glasgow Corporation maintained the city's telephone system. By 1910 when the basis for the Post Office to

THE ARGYLL

Alex Govan and Argyll were inseparable; he was the car and he was the company and the tragedy is that he did not live to see his great ambitions realised. This industrious and energetic Bridgeton man had much experience in the cycle trade and in general engineering before he joined W.A. Smith in Hozier Engineering in 1899. Clearly Govan had plans far advanced before he even moved to Smith's Bridgeton works for well within a year Argyll cars were in production there. Smaller, lighter and more up-to-date in looks than Albion and Arrol-Johnston dog-carts, their sales grew swiftly; by 1905 major expansion was long overdue.

With considerable commercial bravado Govan and his associates then launched Argyll Motors Ltd and spent almost half its capital of £500,000 on a lavish new plant at Alexandria, 20 miles west of Glasgow. After Govan's sudden death in 1907 his great Company lost momentum, lost heart, its prime mover gone.

A deficit of £360,000 compelled major fiscal surgery, and with reduced capital, a new Board and a new Managing Director, J.S. Matthew, Argyll Ltd was launched in 1909. Good new cars were introduced; four-wheel brakes were a feature of the 1911 12hp car and of the fine single-sleeve-valve cars that soon formed the major part of production. Claimed output for 1913 rose to 612 – but in June 1914 the unlucky concern was in liquidation with a deficit of £80,000, and this time there was no rescue operation.

A third company was registered in 1917 and between 1920 and 1928 built a few hundred Argylls, Their strongest selling factor, by then, may have been sentiment.

George Oliver

1. Jubilee of the Glasgow Tramways, 1872–1922. 2. Cedric Greenwood, Glasgow Trammerung, 1986.

take over the service was being agreed, *The Times* admitted the country was benefiting from an enlightened telephone policy in which "Glasgow has played no inconspicuous part".[1]

Alexander Graham Bell had gone to Canada in search of a cure for his tuberculosis. In 1873, he was Professor of Vocal Physiology at Boston University where he fell in love with a deaf pupil. This gave him a further impetus to mechanically reproduce sound. His idea was to change sound waves to a fluctuating current which would be reconverted back to sound waves at the end of the circuit; and the story goes that while experimenting with a device he had built to test his theory, he spilled battery acid on his trousers and, without thinking, he shouted to his assistant, "Watson, please come here. I want you."[2] Which seems quite restrained in the circumstances. Watson was at the other end of the circuit on another floor. He heard the command and the telephone was born.

In 1876 Bell patented his invention and put it on display at Philadelphia's Centennial Exhibition. Pedro the Second, Emperor of Brazil, was the first visitor to try it and the world's first royal conversation was duly recorded: "By God," said King Pedro, "it talks." The second visitor was Lord Kelvin, who brought the telephone to Glasgow and so introduced it to Britain.

The first telephone exchange in the country was opened in Douglas Street, Glasgow in 1879. It was exclusively used by Glasgow's doctors and led to legal, stockbroking and general commercial switchboards being set up in the city. Subscribers were charged £15.00 a year, which included a Post Office royalty, since phones were legally defined under the Telegraph Acts.

The Douglas Street Exchange was set up by David Graham, who established a second in St Vincent Street in 1881 when the Bell and Edison Telephone Companies also opened Glasgow exchanges. By 1884 there were over 800 exchanges and 300 private telephone lines in Glasgow. The telephone companies had amalgamated into the National Telephone Company whose offices were, naturally enough, in Exchange Square. Subscribers could have private wires between two or more points, or they were connected to the exchange, which obviously gave them access to other subscribers. Private subscriptions varied, depending on the distance between your house and the telephone exchange. Exchanges were opened day and night Sundays included, and there were ten call boxes in the city.

By 1900, Glasgow had 5,000 phones and the feeling was that the system should be run by the Government. A compromise was reached and municipal authorities were allowed to operate their own

Arnott Simpson's after the fire in 1951.

Glasgow Fire Brigade, around 1900.

Telephone Exchange.

THE SCOTTISH EXHIBITION OF 1911

Glasgow's third great exhibition in 1911 was very different in style from its cosmopolitan predecessors of 1888 and 1901. Proceeds from this "Exhibition of National History, Art and Industry" were earmarked for a chair in Scottish History and Literature at the University. Reflecting the spirit of the age it was both a serious expression of Nationalism and a lot of fun.

The scenic contours of Kelvingrove Park lent themselves perfectly to a temporary fantasia of Scots Baronial architecture, executed in board and plaster. History this time took precedence over Industry, and a building modelled on the Palace of Falkland housed a truly overwhelming collection of national treasures, designed to educate the populace, particularly the young, in their heritage.

Not surprisingly the public was more enthusiastic about the "living history" which was prominent at this exhibition; historical plays, pageants of ship models on the Kelvin, and best of all, an Edwardian Disneyland – a fake Auld Toon, evoking a romantic burghal past, complete with picturesque inhabitants and souvenir shops. There was also a Highland Clachan, a "village" of typically primitive dwellings staffed by genuine Gaels, who could be observed spinning, bagpiping, and singing in their unintelligible tongue.

There were other native peoples in the Amusements section – villages of Laplanders (plus reindeer), and West Africans – while the Baby Incubator Institute offered another human freak show. Complaints of insufficient entertainments at the 1901 exhibition had been registered: there were non-stop concerts and several thrill rides, including an "airship" flight on wires over the Kelvin. With lovely weather, and 9,369,375 visitors, Glasgow's great Scottish exhibition was indisputably a success.

Perilla Kinchin

1. F.G.C. Baldwin, **History of the Telephone in the United Kingdom**, undated. **2.** **Scottish Firsts**, Scottish Development Agency, 1985.

THE SUBWAY

"The A-Train" and "The Glasgow Underground" are the only two hymns dedicated to subways, and I wrote the latter for a Christmas show at the Citz, where it went down a bomb, a rattle and a lot of squeaks.

My first experience was on a damp bank holiday, when a schoolmate and I went into the deserted city and decided that the subway was the ideal place for us, our pieces and our bottles of ginger. On our penny tickets, we could travel around as long as we liked, so we spent the holiday submerged, even going to the South Side where, I had been warned, they ate their young. We survived, possibly because we were fairly stringy.

Later, I always expected romance down there. The seats ran along the sides, facing each other, so that if a beautiful girl, a White Russian countess or something, was sitting opposite, we couldn't avoid looking at each other, and one day something would click.

What clicked were my muscles. The seats were high, my legs were short, and rather than have my feet stupidly dang ling, I crossed my legs and forced the lower one down till its toes could touch the floor; and stood up to get out at Hillhead and crumpled from what felt like a tennis ball of cramp in the left thigh. Not the way to win a White Russian countess.

Never mind. I finally found the dream girl on the train from Shettleston to Queen Street, but the subway remains magic. We don't need a toy trainset for Christmas. We've got one.

Cliff Hanley

telephone systems. Glasgow's was by far the most successful. In 1906 the Corporation and Postmaster General agreed that the GPO should take over, but for four years a private operation continued in Glasgow, running alongside the national system. In 1907, when the Government version began in Glasgow, there were more than 40,000 private telephones in the city, more than Birmingham, Manchester, Liverpool, Sheffield and Bristol put together. Glaswegians have always been strikingly enthusiastic about technological novelties.

St Enoch Station was the first Glasgow building lit by electric light; and later that year, 1879, electric light was installed in the head Post Office at George Square. The workers were so pleased, that the Post Office later introduced the system into their London office. The first electric street light was in Buchanan Street, a single fizzy arc lamp which blazed for a while outside the old *Glasgow Herald* building.

Glaswegians, unusually, took to this new system rather slowly. They started to electrify the trams system in 1898, but nearly 40 years later, the subway was still drawn by a continuous cable.

Glasgow had the world's first underground passenger cable line, a system which was troubled from the start and for years Glasgow's underground staggered from one sort of crisis to another.

The place it eventually won in popular affection ensured that vast sums would be spent to keep it in operation. When the revamped subway reopened to the public on April 16, 1980, it was the most modern system in the world. The old tunnels are all that remain of former workings. Modernisation not only removed the famous subway smell, but gave the system a new name: The Clockwork Orange.

Abandonment is more common than adaption. A sail up the Clyde is a salutary experience. It has become the new Necropolis, complete with cranes and rotundas. The Garden Festival site lies derelict, awaiting new occupants. The houses facing the water at Govan could be anywhere facing anything; there has been no attempt to utilise the environment; they could be in a field or previous waste ground.

The Garden Festival site was never particularly attractive and the event itself has given a jaundiced tinge to our Cultural Capital of Europe expectations. The presence of the image makers was clear indication that civic pride had joined big business in a new interpretation of our great exhibitions.

Those great Glasgow events of 1888, 1901, 1911 and 1938 had a clearly stated policy of education through entertainment. They all cost a shilling and tried to marry art and industry.

"The Musical Ride of the 15th. Hussars During the Military Tournament at the Glasgow International Exhibition, 1888", by Sir John Lavery.

St Enoch's Underground Station, supported by pillars and a concrete platform during the renovations, May 23, 1978.

THE CITY IMPROVEMENT TRUST

Glasgow's City Improvement Trust was inaugurated by Act of Parliament in 1866, with the aim of clearing away buildings and streets in some of the most congested areas of the old city around the Cross, and also in Calton and Gorbals.

The Trust embarked on the first tentative steps towards municipal involvement in house-building and ownership. Rate-payer opposition was fierce and persistent; the additional sixpenny rate imposed in 1866 cost William Blackie his office of Lord Provost. Undeterred, the Trust bought and cleared Land, often paying exorbitant prices.

Builders refused to take sites from the Trust, complaining that its prices were too high and fearing unfair competition should the Trust build subsidised housing for workers. So by 1888, the Trust was forced to begin substantial building operations, commencing in the Saltmarket, with an additional Act of 1897 extending its powers to acquire and build on a further 25 acres. Its properties ranged from the fine red sandstone tenements running up the High Street to the Barony Church to more modest houses for "the poorest class" at Haghill on the Carntyne Road.

But with rents starting at around £8 per year the real poor could never be reached; the typical tenant of a Trust property was a skilled worker, clerk, or, as critics frequently alleged, a Corporation employee. And the overall number of houses owned by the Trust (around 1,600 by the First World War, or less than one per cent of the city's total) could never even address the scale of the problem.

Nicholas Morgan

They were far from simple arbitrary happenings in what was the Workshop of the World. There were wider implications to the Exhibition movements, where civic pride overlaid a background of poor housing, post industrial squalor and the constant struggle against the decline of the monolithic industries which were proudly displayed in 1888. The people of Scotland, alongside other less favoured nations, tended to become exhibits rather than exhibitors. Chief Mekewwe and his tribe were on show in the Savage West African Stand in 1938; that Exhibition was dedicated to peace and a prosperous future and opened on the day Hitler and Mussolini met in Italy to discuss other matters.[1] Fifty years previously, in 1888, the Working Men's Dining Rooms were built safely out of sight between the Machinery Courtyard and the Dynamo Shed, where the people would doubtless feel most at home.

Something of the conditions in mid-19th century Glasgow, and consequently the reality of tenement living, can be found in the photographs of Thomas Annan, who was commissioned by the City Improvement Trust to record their work from 1868 onwards.

The Victorian passion for photography was second only to their passion for railways. The 1860s saw a railway expansion in Glasgow, which involved building new stations, and this gave the Corporation the opportunity of applying for a City Improvement Act, bankrolling the first slum clearance scheme in the country.

They demolished parts of the Trongate, the Gallowgate, Saltmarket and High Street, where as many as a thousand people lived in a single slum-ridden acre. The council's motives were not entirely philanthropic. A contemporary report says, "Hoardes of the criminal classes sheltered in the dens and caverns of dwelling houses in the narrow lanes and dark closes, rendering the localities notorious in the annals of robbery and murder."[2]

The Corporation had been buying and demolishing Glasgow's worst tenements since the middle of the 1840s and the City of Glasgow Improvement Act of 1866 was one of the most important pieces of 19th century legislation. Dr J. B. Russell was Medical Officer and throughout the Seventies and Eighties he made a series of speeches on subjects such as "Life in One Room" and "The Children of the City", where he showed that in 1880, a quarter of Glasgow's population was living in single ends and 14 per cent of these families had lodgers. Eight per cent of the population lived in a house with five rooms or more.[3]

Glasgow continued to be wracked by major epidemics, including two further major cholera outbreaks in 1848 and 1853 which claimed almost 8,000 lives between them and galvanised the Corporation into

Central Station on Fair Saturday, around 1900, photographed by Thomas Annan.

Annan's photograph of 11 Bridgegate.

1. Paul Harris, **Glasgow at War**, 1987. **2.** Quoted by Oakley in **The Second City**. **3.** ibid.

19TH CENTURY HOUSING

By the mid-19th century Glasgow had some of the worst housing conditions in Britain. Increasingly, the city's housing, good or bad, was dominated by tenements. Tenement building, in part a product of the Scottish feudal system of landholding, offered the ability to house large numbers of workers close to their place of employment.

Glasgow's largely immigrant population seemed to have preferred houses with a small number of large rooms; most lacked the wages or job security to rent anything more substantial. So even as late as the turn of the century, when many of the worst excesses of the older tenements had been cleared away, over 50 per cent of the city's housing was make up of one or two room dwellings. Many of these, one might unfashionably note, were new, well built, spacious and comfortable.

Tenements offered the potential for investment to those in the city with surplus capital; Glasgow was a landlord city, with never more than two per cent of the city's houses owner occupied. For the pragmatic artisan or middle class Glaswegian home-ownership was considered an unnecessary luxury when a slightly larger investment, backed by a mortgage, could purchase a tenement which might provide a small income for the family for years to come.

Disinterested landlords, factors working to a tight margin, tenants with little flexibility of income, buildings that lasted for ever but only at the cost of expensive maintenance; all of these factors combined to produce an unstable housing market that was to be turned upside down by the events of the First World War.

Nicholas Morgan

a further initiative. In 1857 a committee was set up to examine public health and possibilities for improvement. Cholera thrived on poor and infected water supplies taken from the polluted Clyde and infected wells could no longer be tolerated. A farsighted scheme to pipe pure water from Loch Katrine into the city was inaugurated by Queen Victoria on October 15, 1859.

Seven years later, the City Improvement Trust was created to co-ordinate a programme of slum clearance and reconstruction. Along with the slums went the Old University buildings, the original Hunterian Museum, Gorbals Castle and Mansion-House and the last of the half-timbered houses in Saltmarket and the Briggait. Along with the use of compulsory purchase orders, the Improvement Trust also introduced model lodging houses to Glasgow, which were designed to provide basic accommodation for what Messrs Bell and Paton in *Glasgow, Municipal Organisation and Administration* described as "disrobed clergymen and street bullies, decayed gentlemen and area sneaks, tramps, tinkers, labourers, sweeps, thieves and thimble-riggers."[1] Lodgers paid threepence or fourpence halfpenny a night for a wooden cubicle in a large dormitory. There was a bed, a weekly change of bedclothes, a communal kitchen and hotplate, dining hall, recreation rooms, a shop, baths, lavatories, free Bibles and improving lectures. By the 1880s, Glasgow had 23,228 "ticketed houses", which included 16,413 single apartments. A ticketed house was given a metal doorplate which limited the number of people allowed to live there. This was a measure to prevent overcrowding and was enforced by spot checks from sanitary inspectors. One seventh of Glasgow's population, around 75,000 people, lived this way.

The failure of the City of Glasgow Bank in 1878 helped to produce an economic climate where private builders were no longer willing or able to continue constructing houses for rent. By 1910 the private construction of Glasgow tenements had virtually stopped and at the end of the First World War the responsibility for working class housing was taken over by the local government.

City Improvement Trust tenements at Gorbals Cross, photographed during their construction, around 1870.

Glasgow councillors inspect the new Loch Katrine water works, around 1877.

"Mutter und Kinder in der Glasgower Slums" by Emil Orlik, 1898.

1. Published in 1896.

118 High Street by Thomas Annan, 1868.

WILLIAM YOUNG (1843–1900): THE LATER YEARS

Despite the wide notice of Glasgow Municipal Building (City Chambers) in the architectural press Young received no further major public commissions until the very end of his career. He was mainly occupied by country house alteration and restoration work but in July 1898 his influential clients secured his selection, from a list of architects nominated by the President of the Royal Institute of British Architects, to design the new War Office in London's Whitehall, adjacent to Inigo Jones' Banqueting House.

Young brilliantly solved the complexities of his irregular quadrilateral site by turning the corners with colonnaded drums, but did not live to see it beyond the foundations. After he died in 1900 at the comparatively early age of 57, the execution of the project fell to his son Clyde Young who, at the insistence of the Office of Works, worked in conjunction with Sir John Taylor, their retired chief architect.

On his death Brydon worte of Young that "no man knew the requirements of a great country house or how more effectively to carry them out". He specialised particularly in the design of great hall staircases where as A Stuart Gray has put it "guests waiting to be announced could see and be seen". His two great public buildings have the same sense of hierarchical theatre, whether it be the subtle distinction in grandeur between the elected members' and the senior officials' staircases at Glasgow Municipal Buildings or the provision for the general staff at the War Office.

David M Walker

Chapter Seventeen

A MODEL CORPORATION

Gorbals (Southern Necropolis beyond) by Oscar Marzaroli.

Ross Street Model Lodging House, early this century.

RECENT GLASGOW ARCHITECTURE

Much has been written about the "mistakes" of the building and architecture of a generation ago. The 31–storey flats at Red Road, advertised as "the highest housing in Europe", became, with all their social problems (mainly vandalised lifts), a symbol of the bold but slapdash hubris of those years, and were only just rescued from being demolished in their turn.

Yet these monoliths, built on high ground in the north of the city, should be walked up to on a dark blustery day, when they appear like a giant sculpture park. Intimidating? Glaswegians must ask themselves whether they *really* want to go back to houses with green shutters by a bonnie brier bush, as the postmodernism of the 1980s with its cute little brick boxes seems to recommend.

In the city centre, the refurbished Princes Square shopping precinct has been generally praised for its elegance, though its small scale has tempted the designers to produce a stylishness which in some aspects is dangerously parodic.

The much larger St Enoch shopping mall which has settled like a glass origami spider where railway station and hotel used to be, is brashly confident in a Glaswegian manner, and the fact that its shape and situation make it almost impossible to see as a whole renders it exploratory, mazelike, a nice complement to stark Red Road. Also refusing to be either dinky or fussy is the much criticised Forum Hotel, whose tall abstract slabs of reflective glass deliver magic effects in its urban riverine setting.

Edwin Morgan

Typical fire grate of Glasgow tenements.

Chapter Eighteen

FALLING UPWARDS

The Red Road flats, Balornock.

Glasgow has a taste for land, notably extending its boundaries in 1891 and 1912. In the mid-Twenties it acquired a further 10,000 acres. Dunbartonshire donated Scotstoun, Knightswood and Yoker while Renfrewshire gave Nitshill, Kennishead, Hurlett, Mansewood, Crookston and Cardonald, and Lanarkshire lost Lambhill, Millerston, Robroyston, Carntyne and Aitkenhead.

The Corporation began building with modest developments on greenfield sites at the edge of the city, followed by major projects at Mosspark, Riddrie, Knightswood, Carntyne and Scotstoun. Almost 30,000 people would eventually come to Knightswood, in the move to the periphery from tenements to blocks of three or four apartment houses in the 1920s. Unlike later schemes, Knightswood, by far the biggest in Scotland, was able to offer a variety of facilities, such as shops, medical services, schools and a golf course. Fifty years later the Council restored these houses to an acceptable standard, after years of decline.

Glasgow housing would never again find the room nor the time for such spaciousness either in the public or private sectors, to whom subsidies were paid for each house built. The froth of life seemed heady, with new cinemas and dance halls. Glasgow's shipbuilders, or those previously employed in heavy industry, found life tougher than it need have been. The Depression and the Means Test between them carried Victorian attitudes into the 20th century by ensuring that the poor were not only blamed for their poverty, but stigmatised as well.

For many, the main hope became a Corporation house. It may be situated miles or years away, but they could put their names down on the list.

The face of Scotland changed dramatically during the 1930s. More than half the economy was based on the construction of new housing. Desperately trying to ease the housing crisis, the slum

Bellahouston Drive, Mosspark.

THE LONG WEEKEND: GLASGOW BETWEEN THE WARS

Visitors to the Empire Exhibition in 1938 saw a smoke-blackened, busy, friendly but unlovely city with the occasional modern gleam.

Central Glasgow had changed little between the wars, save for the construction of tall, steel-framed, American inspired banks, warehouses and insurance offices; of sybarytic haunts of fun seekers such as Lang's cafe in Queen Street, Rogano restaurant off Buchanan Street; and – of course – cinemas, of which Glasgow had over 130.

The real impact of the Thirties upon Glasgow was to be seen at the periphery. Whereas in 1914, Glasgow simply stopped beyond the last tenement gable, by 1939 its spectacular surrounding countryside was covered with the measles of white semi-detached houses or virulent red brick bungalows, with spreadeagled schools, a desultory church, and the occasional Moby Dick of a suburban super cinema alongside a row of shops and a white shed garage.

The Thirties was the decade of the new man who, so long as he remained employed, had the money and leisure to go to the cinema, ice skating, dancing or out to the restaurant.

Symbolic of the period is the immense Beresford Hotel in Sauchiehall Street (now Baird Hall of Residence) built by architect W Beresford Inglis on the proceeds of selling his cinema chain to George Singleton (Mr Cosmo). The flag-capped drum towers, scarlet and black fins which streaked up the faience facade into the sky, the streamlined staircase, and the etched glass in the Reading Room were all designed in imitation of cinema architecture in order to attract custom.

The old mould had been broken, and the pattern of the future set.

Charles McKean

clearance programme continued while new estates and developments grew in places as diverse as Carntyne, Bearsden, Knightswood, Whitecraigs and Giffnock. One of the biggest developments of the Thirties was at Blackhill. The shape of the city today owes a lot to this period, as does the look of many public buildings.

There was never a serious move to bring the radical ideas or styles of the continental architects and planners to Scotland. Their influence reached us nevertheless and with it came some of the benefits and problems we still have today. Many design ideas were transferred with no regard for the differences in climate between France and Scotland. Flat roofs were perfect for sun bathing and roof gardens, but they were less practical in the wet and smoky Glasgow winters, or summers for that matter, when rain water gathered in puddles on the roof and inevitably leaked through.[1]

The occupants of Glasgow's new schemes were tempted with glowing descriptions of fitted kitchens and bathrooms, but soon found themselves isolated from their friends and essential services. Many referred to the move as the worst experience of their lives and spoke of being trapped in a hostile environment.[2]

In the early Thirties, Hogganfield and East Carntyne came under Glasgow's wing and just before the war the city extended its boundaries by a further 10,000 acres, including Drumchapel, Easterhouse, Penilee, Darnley and Summerston. The Corporation wanted to include places like Giffnock and Newton Mearns, but the Parliamentary Commissioners turned them down. This was the last great bite into the surrounding territories prior to the local government re-organisation of 1975, the city having spread itself by 24,000 acres north of the river and 15,000 acres south. Glasgow more than doubled its area between 1925 and 1938 and the planning was apparently done by four unqualified assistants in the Master of Works Office, and why not indeed.

The innovative ideas and attention to detail of such architects as Thomson, Mackintosh and Salmon were forgotten, ignored or considered irrelevant. Glasgow spread outwards with hardly any co-ordinated control. In the mid-1920s, legislation was passed to allow Corporations to subsidise "working class housing" and to offer assistance to make up mortgages. Glasgow lagged behind other Scottish cities. Three thousand of around the 50,000 houses built by 1939 were subsidised and only 428 houses were bought with assisted mortgages. The 1929 Scottish Local Government Act gave the authorities responsibility for their housing programmes and Glasgow set about a major slum clearance scheme; with subsidies

ALEXANDER "GREEK" THOMSON (1817–75)

Alexander "Greek" Thomson was Glasgow's outstanding Victorian architect yet recognition in this city, which contains most of his mature work, is still only grudging and half-hearted. His church in Caledonia Road stands a vandalised, roofless shell, while the superb warehouse in Union Street, with its unique style and decoration, is literally falling to pieces.

One of the two complete ranges of tenements, each unique in style and concept, which were his contribution to the design of flatted houses is already gone. Queen's Park Terrace, in Eglinton Street, was built between 1856 and 1860, and provided an architecturally satisfying and unified elevation while also ensuring well-proportioned and adequately lit apartments within. The rhythmic effect of the window spacing was particularly striking, and the linking horizontally of the different parts of the facade, highly novel. In particular, the north corner with its triple concave bow window, derived from the Roman temple of Venus at Baalbek, was an unusual and happy inspiration.

The other incomparable range of Thomson tenements is Walmer Crescent in Paisley Road West. Totally different in concept, it has a bold elevation, plain almost to a fault, broken up only be large blocks of rectangular bow windows. The continuous colonnade of the top floor was to influence architects for the next 50 years. Thomson declared that he was not merely a Greek Revival architect, but was using the elements of Greek design to create a new, living, contemporary Victorian style, suitable for any type of building. How well he succeeded may be judged from these two outstanding examples.

Frank Worsdall

1. Charles McKean, **The Scottish Thirties**, 1987. 2. See **Indications of Housing Satisfaction: a Castlemilk Pilot Study**, Strathclyde University, 1972, and others.

Flat roofed two and four apartment houses in Carntyne.

1937 cartoonist's vision of football in 1947, following the then anticipated rebuilding of Hampden.

Sandringham Avenue, part of Mactaggart and Mickel's Newton Mearns development.

for people removed from homes no longer fit to live in Glasgow's Housing Committee grasped the initiative.

A Government investigation, set up by the Secretary of State, found that every fifth house in Scotland could be improved "without undue cost". Glasgow, for the first time, had an officially accepted way of defining overcrowding, which ran at 40 per cent in the Clyde Valley in 1921. Twelve per cent of all Scottish houses had only one room. Working class house owners, tenants and occupiers, as well as the local authorities, now had clearly defined duties. Minimum home requirements included a separate water closet for each family, hot water, bath, larder and drying facilities wherever possible, better lighting and ventilation and a control over sub-letting.[1]

The city was short of both jobs and houses. The Depression left a slump in the Glasgow mainstays, shipbuilding and heavy engineering. That becalmed ship, number 534, symbolised the times and the crisis. Reports, pamphlets, books, surveys and many political speeches all confirmed the position: Glasgow's industry had been deteriorating since the turn of the century and there was nothing to replace it.

The dole queues dwindled through the munitions programme for the oncoming war and the building of so-called industrial estates. Hillington was first, four miles from the city centre and outside the official boundary. It successfully attracted light engineering companies.

The experiments in private housing were slightly better planned than in the public sector. Sunlight Homes at Bowling managed to incorporate Scottish design features into their cottages and though parts of Mactaggart and Mickel's Broom Estate at Whitecraigs were a bit too forward looking for Glaswegians, the more conventional home and flat-roofed bungalows sold very well. The more adventurous and, more importantly, well-heeled clients indulged the architects' pure Thirties styles. There were streamlined and ship-shaped buildings, with curtain walls, strip and corner windows, flag poles, port holes, balconies and towers. Perhaps the most prominent and successful pieces of Thirties architecture in Glasgow are the public buildings and cafés commissioned during the period.

This was the decade of the cinema; elegant, plush places, where realities could be forgotten. Glasgow, having the worst social conditions, also had some of the finest cinemas. Green's Playhouse in Renfield Street was the largest cinema in Europe. There were more than 120 picture halls across the city in 1937. The Boulevard at Knightswood and the Cosmo in Rose Street were among the new cinemas built that year.

HUGH S ROBERTON AND THE GLASGOW ORPHEUS CHOIR

The final event in the first Edinburgh International Festival in 1947 was a concert by a Glasgow choir which had long since become world famous for exceptional musicality. In an age when massed choirs were the norm and great volume the prime requirement for a chorister, the Glasgow Orpheus, under its conductor Hugh (later Sir Hugh) S Roberton, was trained to interpret its repertoire with the subtlety of a lieder singer.

Many will remember the Orpheus, formed in 1906, for its spirited renderings of Scots and other folk songs, since Roberton, as a life-long Fabian socialist, saw to it that his choir sang to audiences the length and breadth of these islands, in modest venues as well as the great halls. The Orpheus also performed all over western Europe and in Canada and the USA.

Its repertoire included Bach and Handel (on one occasion, the *Messiah* was performed complete), Mendelssohn, Brahms and Schumann, even Wagner. English composers, from Dowland to Warlock, too, were Orpheus favourites. Roberton himself was an assiduous arranger of Scots songs, and occasionally cool assessments of his choir by local musical academics stemmed from his perceived shortcomings as a composer.

The Orpheus and its conductor were inseparable. The choir voluntarily disbanded in 1951 at the moment when Roberton, at 77, felt the need to retire. The Orpheus was his self-created instrument: only the records now remain as evidence of its quality, but one recording, at least, of "The Blue Bird" by Stanford, would be hard for any modern choir to equal, let alone surpass.

Cordelia Oliver

1. Charles McKean, op. cit.

INTER-WAR HOUSING

Returns made under the 1935 Housing Act showed Glasgow with 29 per cent of houses over-crowded. The criteria placed a density of, for example, three adults to two rooms in this category. Judged by these figures the inter-war housing legislation had failed. Nonetheless, life expectancy had increased. Perhaps most striking was the decline by over 50 per cent in the number of deaths from tuberculosis, the disease most closely associated with those cramped living conditions.

1919 had witnessed the introduction of state assisted house-building. Scottish towns began the process which saw the virtual extinction of private housing markets (and the private landlord) which had dominated housing supply before the war. House styles also changed – initial subsidies were aimed at providing "Homes fit for Heroes", cottages and cottage flats based on the mode of the English Garden City movement. The new dwellings of schemes such as Mosspark and Riddrie were intended to foster new ways of living, providing both internal (parlours) and external space (gardens) for private family leisure. Many of the builders who completed local authority contracts carried these designs into private ventures.

The Corporation and the private builders who worked for it (direct labour did not gain any momentum until around 1936) were hampered by chronic shortages of materials and labour that encouraged experimentation. It was concrete in particular that Glasgow turned to in order to provide cheaper dwellings for slum clearance schemes.

The environments created in areas like Hamiltonhill and Blackhill were to be as problematic as those they replaced.

Nicholas Morgan

Glasgow got its American style commercial buildings whose solid, monumental influence still gives an air of permanence to the city centre. *The Glasgow Herald* and *Evening Times* offices in Albion Street were built in the Thirties, while the colourful and stylish extension to Templeton's mock Venetian carpet factory by Glasgow Green is still attractive and proving itself useful as a business centre.

Central Glasgow still has Thirties gems, like the Beresford Hotel at the west end of Sauchiehall Street, now Strathclyde University's Baird Hall of Residence, and the Rogano Oyster Bar, with its yellow frontage sporting a ferocious looking brilliant red lobster. The new style influenced both the sacred and profane, from The Vintners bar in Clyde Street, which still has its original frontage, to church designs like St Columba's in Maryhill or St Anne's in Dennistoun.

At best, the Thirties architects left Glasgow a legacy of graceful lines with innovative and economical designs. They did not ignore the serious housing shortage, but the politicians did not develop an approach to deal with such a wholesale crisis. The confusion was not helped by the familiar problem of a reliance on the private sector to come up with the funds and the second class status of public sector housing.

At the end of the War, Councillor James McInnes, Sub-Convener of the Housing Committee, wrote a pamphlet on *Glasgow's Housing Progress*. "Our aim is to build 100,000 houses with the maximum possible speed," he concluded, "and we are confident that if all those engaged in house building are imbued with the same desire and will render their fullest co-operation, our aim will be quickly realised."[1]

The Dunkirk spirit and a call to arms did not build Glasgow's houses when the fighting was over. Glasgow, like everywhere else, was caught up in the post-War baby boom and rather than discuss which type of home and how many rooms would be suitable for heroes, folk settled for what was available.

It wasn't till the end of the decade that the house building programme was properly productive. None the less, overspill was seriously considered and the idea of new towns discussed for the first time.

Enter East Kilbride, nine miles to the south of Glasgow and little more than a village when the New Town Development Corporation was established in 1947, with Sir Patrick Dollan, another Red Clydesider,[2] at its head. Cumbernauld, Glenrothes, Livingston and Irvine followed, taking away many of the jobs, skills and people

The Rogano.

1. Published by Glasgow Trades Council in 1946. **2.** "He had no scruples in making use of the political system towards achieving his own ends." Dr William Knox, **Scottish Labour Leaders 1918–1939**, 1984.

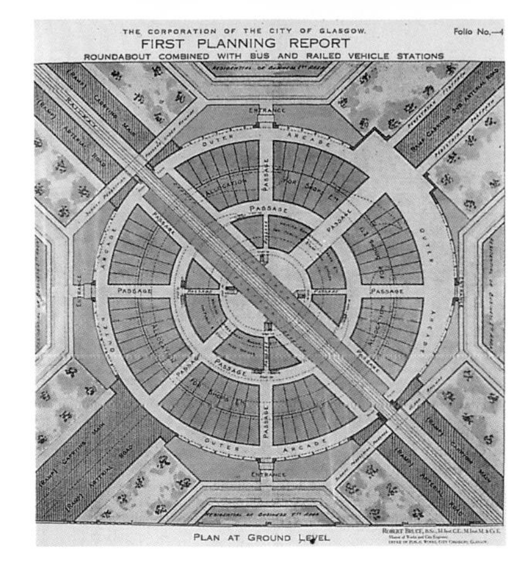

Bruce Plan.

Chapter Eighteen

FALLING UPWARDS

THE BRUCE PLAN

From the late 1930s emphasis was increasingly on the development of planned, long-term housing strategies. Glasgow's vision of the future was expressed in the two plans written by the City Engineer, the young and aggressive Robert Bruce, published in 1945 and 1946.

Bruce envisaged a city transformed over a period of around 50 years with an inner core, including a reconstructed railway network, bounded by new arterial roads. He believed housing could be provided for the city's inhabitants within the boundaries of Greater Glasgow. 172,000 houses were to be cleared from "re- development areas" where only 50,000 new homes would be built; thus the city must be allowed to build on peripheral greenfield sites. Flats were to provide the overwhelming majority of the new homes to be built by the city. The Bruce Plan jealously guarded the city's population (who through their rates provided much of its income) from the grasp of planners who had viewed Glasgow's problems in the wider context of the region.

The Clyde Valley Regional Planning team proposed the dispersal of Glasgow's overspill population (along with the concurrent development of new industries) to new towns, such as East Kilbride. Glasgow refused to sanction this but the hopelessness of the task of re-housing families within the city became only too apparent in the early 1950s. Even the boldest adventures in high-rise building could not prevent Glasgow from losing large numbers to the new towns (in addition to more traditional destinations for emigrants) in the late 1950s and 1960s.

Nicholas Morgan

Glasgow could ill afford to lose. Glasgow's city fathers had launched new towns before. Dumbarton's hopes of mercantile glory ended when Port Glasgow was built in 1667, followed by Helensburgh in 1776 and New Lanark nine years later. These places were extensions of Glasgow. New towns were a drain of people and resources.

Housing schemes and new towns face the same problem: they came from nowhere and because there was no organic development they feel wrong, even in some cases spiritually disturbing or disorientating. They produce a feeling of being in a part of the city you thought you knew and finding the buildings gone. That used to be an old man's problem, then it was a Sixties problem, now it concerns us all.

The *First Planning Report* was produced by City Engineer Robert Bruce, and published in March, 1945. It set about tidying up the city by turning it into a network of flyovers, expressways, roundabouts and railway terminals. The principal means of transport would be the helicopter, "a vehicle combining the properties of the motor car and the aeroplane".[1] Public transport would be provided by electric trains which would run along an extended, revamped system including the central reservations of the new motorways.

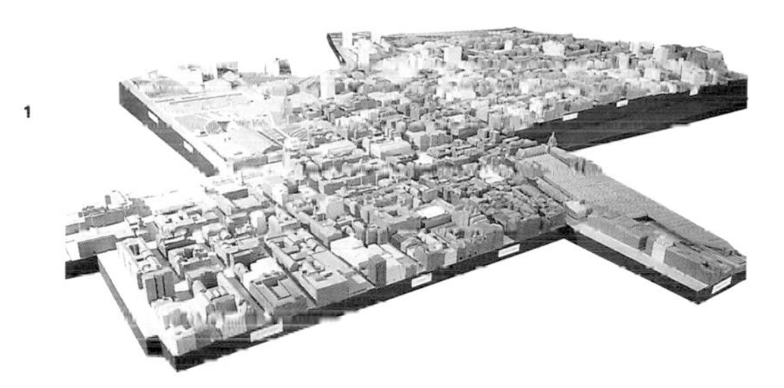

Glasgow District Council Planning Department's constantly changing model of the city centre.

Everything would go. Glasgow New Town would have its boundaries defined by main roads, all its old buildings, including the City Chambers, would be swept away and replaced by straight streets, moving logically from one central point to another. "Poor people live on dear land," said Bruce; his intention was therefore to demolish working class houses, replacing them with new commercial development and tenants who could pay realistic rents. Poor people would be moved from the city centre to a ring of new high density developments around the fringes of the city.

It would not be entirely true to say the Bruce Plan was dismissed out of hand; with a typical planners' genius for compromise, elements survived and Glasgow altered accordingly.

In the late 1940s, the Secretary of State reversed a previous decision and allowed building to begin at Castlemilk, which brought the city closer to East Kilbride. In the early Fifties permission was given to build at Drumchapel.

The overspill programme had not been a success. Movement to the new towns had been slower than anticipated and there was additional pressure from the baby boom. The redevelopment of the inner city moved people from the centre and an increasing public awareness of sub-standard properties made new houses desirable. Everyone wanted a better place to live.

The 1954 plan chose three areas for redevelopment. The intention

Bruce Plan.

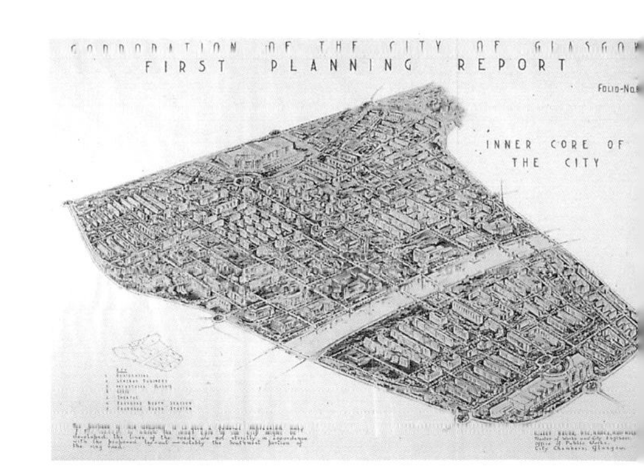

1. Robert Bruce, **First Planning Report**, 1946.

BUILDING HIGH

The first really tall buildings in Glasgow were all hotels associated with the great railway termini, the Glasgow and South Western's St Enoch's (1876) and the Caledonian's Central (1878). Opposite Central Station, Peddie & Kinnear designed the huge block at 91–115 Hope Street, the Parisian mansard attics of which enabled a total of seven storeys to be accommodated. It is difficult now to appreciate just how new buildings like these towered above everything around them in 1880s Glasgow.

J.J. Burnet's Athenaeum Theatre of 1891 was the pioneer American-type elevator building in Glasgow, built on a narrow Georgian houseplot. It provided the formula for the narrow frontage office buildings made possible by the introduction of a public electricity supply in 1893 and improved equipment at the Fire Department. Perhaps the most remarkable example of the style was Salmon and Gillespie's *Art Nouveau* sculpturesque "Hatrack" at 142a-144 St Vincent Street (1899), its eight-storey and attic frontage so narrow that its floors were cantilevered off a double row of steel columns because the luxury of load-bearing gable walls could not be afforded. At their later Lion Chambers at 172 Hope Street (1904) paper-thin concrete construction allowed eight storeys on a site only 33 feet by 46.

By a quirk of architectural patronage the earliest really large elevator blocks were the work of more conservative designers: Alexander Petrie at the huge six-storey block at the corner of St Enoch Square and Howard Street (1895); James Thomson and his sons at the six-storey Pearl at 133–137 West George Street (1897), still with Italianate elevations.

David M Walker

was to remove the slums. Everything would be demolished and rebuilt, including the roads. The three selected areas were eventually expanded to 29. One third of the city's stock and half the property not owned by the Corporation was to be demolished by compulsory purchase order and replaced by municipal housing.

The first scheme was approved in 1957. The Gorbals-Hutchesontown development was built in stages between 1958 and 1973, the first of Glasgow's Comprehensive Development Areas and the largest scheme of its type in the country, costing £13 million. The population would be reduced by 16,000 to 10,000, housed in award winning four and ten storeyed blocks. There was to be no industry; shops were reduced from 444 to 57 and instead of 46, the 10,000 new citizens of the brave new Gorbals would have nine pubs amongst them. The first phase won a Saltire Society award: "as a symbol of the new Glasgow and by contrast with its appalling surroundings. Here is new life growing out of the slums of the worst crowded city in Western Europe."[1]

In 1969 work began on the Hutchesontown E complex, using a system of site assembled industrialised building, and what became known as Hutchie E was opened by the Queen in 1972. Hutchie tenants were plagued with damp. The building system had been tested and developed in Algeria; the Glasgow problems could be averted by trying to recreate an Algerian climate, which meant constantly using the all-electric heating, a financial impossibility for most tenants. Dampness afflicted the tower blocks, designed by Sir Basil Spence. The lifts didn't work, a common enough problem in Glasgow tower blocks and a series of structural problems soon developed. Seven years after the Hutchie E complex was regally opened, the first public suggestions were made that they would have to be demolished. Structural repairs on the Spence high rises began in 1983.[2]

Back in 1960, when work on the first phase of the Gorbals development was continuing apace, it was estimated as in 1945, that Glasgow still needed 100,000 houses. Land was becoming scarcer. Much of the green belt as well as the redeveloped parts of the city now had houses. All had been built to a far greater density than was originally planned.

Around 41,000 houses were built in Summerston and Darnley over the next ten years, at even higher densities. Buildings reached upwards rather than out. The Red Road flats to the north of the city, 30 storeys into the air, were the highest steel framed towers in Europe. In the late Sixties, high rise building was extended to the periphery and by the late Seventies, Glasgow had 321 tower blocks.[3]

Glasgow Green is on the right. The second stage in development of Hutchesontown Gorbals is on the left. The year is 1961.

The demolition of Hutchie E.

1. Michael Keating, **The City That Refused To Die**, 1988. 2. ibid. 3. Many are now in the process of refurbishment.

As in 1945 and 1960, a 1970 housing review still found Glasgow needed 100,000 houses. The overspill results were disappointing, having made no sizeable dent, either in the city's congested areas or its slums. By and large, it tended to be the mobile and skilled workers, already well housed in Glasgow, who went to the new towns and the houses they left were let to the slum dwellers.

Glasgow by now had turned its attention to the country's biggest urban highway development programme, which running parallel with the Comprehensive Development Areas, was intended to transform the city by the end of the century.

The housing ideas contained in the Bruce Plan may have been rejected, but his ideas for an integrated city transport system remained in the collective mind long enough to influence highway and transport proposals. The 1963 Buchanan Report *Traffic in Towns* advocated major urban redevelopment, including traffic management and new transport plans for cities. A year later, the Greater Glasgow Transportation Study group was appointed and brought together all the major transport interests. The population and traffic projections that their study indicated were wildly exaggerated. By 1981, they predicted, 283,000 private vehicles would be owned in Glasgow; in 1981 Glaswegians owned 95,000 vehicles, well below the national average.

Public opinion organised itself. The £57 million 1975 programme of committed works included the M8 motorway across the city, the Clydeside, Great Western Road and Springburn Expressways, the Ayr, Stirling and Maryhill-Lomond Motorways. Only the M8, the north and west flanks of the ring road, the Clydeside and Springburn Expressways were completed; the latter being a particularly mysterious piece of nonsense. The road does not go anywhere and was justified because of Springburn's industrial needs. It was supposed to go through a Comprehensive Development Area and as late as 1975, the Corporation was insisting it served "two main commuter suburbs, Bishopbriggs and Lenzie." It joins the M8 at the Townhead Interchange, the nerve centre of a motorway system that is unlikely to be built. Pedestrian bridges and half-bridges which go nowhere litter motorway fringes and half-finished roads hang suspended in mid-air. A Gorbals group called itself GRIM, Glasgow Resistance to Incoming Motorways, argued that what was left of the working class communities was being threatened by destruction for the benefit of middle class commuters. The city was surprised by an argument which had not been effectively heard for a while. And in the 1988 Govan by-election, arguments centred around proposals to build a new motorway over part of that constituency.

BUILDING HIGH (AMERICAN STYLE)

Petrie and Thomson's buildings gave few hints of the iron and steel-framing within. By contrast, David Barclay's colossal Hunter Barr warehouse (now Guildhall) at 45–67 Queen Street (1899) was much more American in the frank exposure of its construction by hollow tile floors.

The most sophisticated buildings of the type were designed by the architects trained at the Paris *Beaux Arts* school. J.J. Burnet had visited America in 1896, what he saw being reflected, to take one example, in the mighty gridded facades of McGeoch's ironmongery warehouse at 28 West Campbell Street (1905). But perhaps the greatest mastery of the genre is seen in the blocks by Burnet's former partner J.A. Campbell, such as the boldly expressionist Northern Building at 84–94 St Vincent Street (1908), fully steel-framed and, like Salmon and Gillespie's Bothwell Street Mercantile Chambers, remarkable for its rear elevation of Henry Hope's steel casements.

No account of American-influenced high building in Glasgow could be complete without mention of James Miller. His distinctly American work includes the tall office slab with colonnaded upper floors at 136–148 Queen Street (1902) and the faience frontages of the Anchor Building on St Vincent Place (1906) and the Classic Cinema at 11–15 Renfield Street (1914). His Bank of Scotland at 110–120 St Vincent Street (1924–25) and the Prudential at 28–36 Renfield Street (1929) are stylistically indistinguishable from their American precursors. At six to eight storeys, they are very much lower than contemporary American structures but as high as the firemaster would allow.

David M Walker

The Bank of Scotland. Built by architect James Miller.

McGeoch's warehouse at West Campbell Street.

SIR WILLIAM BEARDMORE
(1856–1936)

In 1861 Robert Napier set up William Beardmore senior and William Rigby as partners in the Parkhead Forge.

William Beardmore senior brought with him to Glasgow his infant son William, born in Greenwich in 1856. The boy was educated in Ayr and Glasgow, and apprenticed to the Forge at the age of 14. He attended classes at Anderson's University and later at the Royal School of Mines, in London, where he was when the death of his father made him a junior partner in the Parkhead firm.

There he immediately became involved in the changeover from wrought-iron to steel. His partner, his uncle Isaac, retired in 1886, and young William diversified, first into armour plate, developing his own nickel-chrome armour in the 1890s. To ensure a market for this he had to move into shipbuilding, and in a classic sequence he then invested in iron and steel companies and in other types of engineering, including motor and aircraft manufacture.

During the First World War his company became one of the largest manufacturers of munitions in Britain, employing, it is said, about 100,000 men and women, and making guns, shells, aircrafts, ships on a vast scale.

After the war Beardmore specialised in transport (railway locomotives, motor cars, motor cycles, aeroplanes, airships and ships) but with little commercial success. Beardmore, given a peerage as Baron Invernairn of Strathnairn for his war work was forced to take a back seat when the company nearly failed in 1926, and had to leave in 1929, to live in his country estate at Flichity, in Strathnairn. He died there in 1936, and is buried by the house with the epitaph "a brain of steel and a heart of gold".

John R Hume

As motorway planning continued, Glasgow's railway developments were downgraded. A *Glasgow Planning Policy Report*, published in 1975, says railways do not redistribute income, but simply ease city centre congestion during rush hours. It does not say how this differentiates them from motorways.[1]

The region's minimal subsidies to bus services resulted in some of the highest fares in the country. Low rents were maintained at the expense of housing standards, but increased transport costs have consigned residents to a virtual imprisonment in housing schemes, isolated from services and amenities. The 1985 Transport Act is the work of free market right wingers and, despite the claims of the Scottish Office, the services of greater benefit to the customers simply never happened. Michael Keating's assessment is surely correct: "The opportunity for a fully integrated urban transport system . . . must be considered lost for ever".[2]

Other trends now look irreversible. The infamous squalor of the East End was reduced by depopulation. In 1951, 151,000 lived there. Twenty-five years later there were only 45,000.

By the middle of the last century, Glasgow's potteries were the largest survivors of the industries started by the tobacco lords and other 18th century merchants. At one time there were 25 individual potteries, as well as their associated industries, throughout the city, and most of them were located in the East End.

This was a major part of the city's powerhouse at a time when Glasgow was not only the industrial heart of the country, but also had the most diversified range of industries of any city in the British Empire, exporting across the world. Weaving was traditionally associated with the Calton, and the move to Bridgeton at the beginning of the last century, was followed by a development of manufacturing in cottons and textiles.

By the middle of the 19th century metal manufacturing and heavy engineering had spread throughout the East End. Glasgow's best known steel works was Beardmore and Company at Parkhead Forge. Today the site is a shopping centre, known as The Forge.

William Beardmore was born in 1856 in London and came to Glasgow when he was 14. A hundred years ago Parkhead was challenging Sheffield as a place where armour plating could be forged and by 1918, Beardmores were the largest concern there has ever been in Scotland. Their empire included Robert Napier's shipbuilding and marine engineering works at Govan and Lancefield.

At the height of his fame in the 1850s, Robert Napier was the leading mechanical engineer in Scotland and one of the most influential in the world. He, more than anyone else, contributed to

Frankie Vaughan and some of The Pak in Easterhouse on July 24, 1968.

The Forge Shopping Centre, Parkhead.

1. Quoted by Michael Keating in **The City That Refused To Die.** **2.** ibid.

SIR WILLIAM ARROL (1839–1913)

Born in the little village of Houston, in Ayrshire, William Arrol became a piecer in a Johnstone cotton mill at the age of nine, but moved after five years to an apprenticeship with a smith, called Reid, and followed that with several years of employment in England and in Scotland. He became a foreman at the boiler works of Laidlaw & Son, in Glasgow, at the age of 24, and after 5 years or so this was followed by the setting up of the Dalmarnock Iron Works.

From then on he concentrated largely on bridge building, starting early with the Hamilton & Bothwell branch of the North British Railway over the Clyde and soon graduating to the complex problem of passing traffic into and out of the Central Station, Glasgow; many other triumphs followed, including the 1887 reconstruction of the Tay Rail Bridge, the 1890 opening of the Forth Rail Bridge by the Prince of Wales (at which the knighting of William Arrol was announced), the 1890s Tower Bridge contract, twelve of the largest bridges over the Manchester Ship Canal, and the Wear Bridge at Sunderland. There was also much general engineering work, of almost every conceivable kind.

As W.S. Murphy said of Sir William Arrol, in 1901 "he had carried himself with a knightly grace and vigour equal to any paladin. He is of the stuff that stern adversity fashions into heroes; not a fine scholar, nor great in intellect, but a big, strong, good-natured Scot, possessing to an uncommon degree the gifts and virtues of the common man."

George Oliver

the development of steam navigation. He began in 1815 by taking over his cousin David's blacksmith's forge. By 1845 he owned the Govan shipyard, had pioneered the development of large iron ships, owned the Lancefield marine engine works, the Vulcan foundry, the Muirkirk ironworks, several coalmines and had interests in some shipping companies, notably Cunard.

The most famous Glasgow engineer at the turn of the century was William Arrol, whose company in Dalmarnock handled massive contracts for building railway bridges, as well as making the riveting machines they had patented for other shipbuilding and engineering centres throughout the world. His company constructed the Caledonian Bridge across the Clyde into Central Station, the Forth Rail Bridge, the second Tay Bridge and Tower Bridge in London, as well as the locks and viaducts for the Manchester Ship Canal.

The first all-Scottish car was based on the Daimler and produced by George Johnston, later amalgamated into the Arrol-Johnston Company. When fire destroyed their Glasgow foundry, they moved to Paisley and then Dumfries. Beardmores made a car in Arrol-Johnston's Paisley works, though Glasgow's most successful cars were by the Albion Company, founded in the last month of the previous century, and the Argyll Motor Company, founded in 1905.

At the end of the First World War, Beardmores employed almost 40,000 men and women in Glasgow, Dalmuir, Mossend, Coatbridge, Airdrie and Paisley. Apart from a flurry of activity during the Second World War, neither they nor any other engineering giant recovered from the Depression.

The real slump came in the Fifties and Sixties when more than 20,000 jobs were lost in the East End alone. Men who thought their futures secure, who assumed they would do what their fathers had done, had to rethink their lives and their families' futures as the great names of East End engineering crumbled.[1] The number of jobs lost in the subsidiary industries was as devastating as the waste of skills.

The effect on the area was catastrophic. A recent pamphlet puts it well: "Throughout the East End industrial dereliction, endemic unemployment, worsening housing and health conditions plus low education attainment were the norm. Everywhere dereliction and decay was apparent."[2] The Glasgow Eastern Area Renewal Project was launched in 1976, the first and largest scheme of its kind in Western Europe.

GEAR's arrival not only coincided with the plans for a new town at Stonehouse being scrapped, but also with the SDA being launched as a means of public investment. It came at a time when

"Steam Hammer" by James Nasmyth.

Sparks fly as the drill taps into the Clyde Iron Works Number 3 blast furnace, October 27, 1977.

1910 Albion A3 16 horse powered motor car.

1. From **The East End Experience**, Glasgow District Council, 1988. **2.** ibid.

THE MEDICIS OF MARYHILL

Patronage used to be the prerogative of princes, potentates or politicians. Similar power is now being exercised in Glasgow by groups of ordinary citizens from all backgrounds, with no training in the art. It is from this source that we are probably seeing the best of Glasgow's contemporary architecture.

Just under 20 years ago, the City began to delegate housing responsibility to local groups who formed community-based Housing Associations. Local architectural offices worked with them to create architecture by the community for the community. Preoccupied, until 1984, with the backlog of tenement repair, they then shifted the priority toward new tenements in the gap sites left over by unrealised road proposals and overhasty tenemental demolition.

In 1984, Maryhill Housing Association organised a competition for the "Tenement for the 21st century", and one of the joint winners, by McGurn Logan Duncan Opfer with Ken Macrae, is now built at Shakespeare Street. Taking the form of a gigantic, four-storey curve of flats, the building is a triumphant affirmation of the values of tenemental living in Inner Glasgow.

Patronage extends beyond buildings to the applied arts: stained glass in the bathrooms, ornamental china tiles (wally tiles again !) in the close, moulded lintels for the windows, beautifully crafted doors, fine ironwork, stone carving, decorative external tiles, and riotous decorative brickwork particularly at Queen's Cross. These new patrons accept the duty to attempt to achieve a new heritage.

The success of the new Medicis vindicates the good sense and judgement of ordinary people when offered the extraordinary challenge of determining how their community should develop.

Charles McKean

the emphasis was on the rehabilitation and improvement of existing housing stock, rather than on the pulling down of what might have been seen as sub-standard property. By the end of 1988, for example, 40 tenants had bought refurbished houses for between £22,000 and £23,500 in Barlanark, a peripheral estate. Some of these had been vacant for more than five years and a year previously none of them could have been let rent free.[1]

Another way in which public housing has come to terms with its tenants is through the burgeoning housing associations. They have tapped into Glasgow's communities and released a dormant spirit of self-help and co-operation by giving individuals inside the system the confidence to improve their lot. The previous difficulties tenants faced was legendary, both in the public and private sectors.

Tenants in Glasgow's public and private sectors have found their landlords quite happy to collect the rents but reluctant to repair the buildings. Most private property has been sub-contracted to factors, whose incompetence and rudeness would not seem out of place in a Dickens' novel. The Council's post-war housing stock became dilapidated through lack of maintenance.

Unlike similar British city schemes, Glasgow's housing associations managed to simultaneously retain the character of their areas and upgrade the houses. They did not create islands of gentrification in previously working class areas and have been highly resistant to the sale of rented properties.

Housing associations and city slogans have spread across the country. The original punchline was Glasgow's Miles Better, which was initially received with some scepticism, not to say distaste, though when compared to Edinburgh or Dundee's attempts at civic jingoism, it is the best of an infinitely forgettable bunch.[2]

Glasgow's campaign was an attempt to reverse its international image as No Mean City, where people lived in overcrowded conditions, managed by an incompetent bureaucracy. The late Roger Hargreaves' Mr Happy became the campaign mascot. Hargreaves received an undisclosed amount of money and a vast amount of free publicity when his wee yellow balloon appeared on car stickers and buses across the world and in every major city excepting Edinburgh, who refused to have their public transport bearing the legend Glasgow's Miles Better.[3] After almost a decade, the campaign's staying power alone gives it a certain amount of status.

Mr. Happy on the Berlin Wall,

1. The Scotsman, November 16, 1988. **2.** Since 1985 Dundee has called itself City of Discovery, following the return to its birthplace of Scott of the Antarctic's boat.
3. Edinburgh's civic slogan, Count Me In was masterminded by Michael Kelly's advertising agency.

Chapter Eighteen

FALLING UPWARDS

The Maryhill Housing Association's Shakespeare Street tenement, built in the late 1980s.

CHARLES WILSON (1810–63)

Like his friend Alexander Thomson, Charles Wilson had a very original and independent mind. In 1841, although only 31, Wilson was lucky enough to secure the commission for the huge asylum at Gartnavel. This was neo-Tudor, perhaps not from choice, but much more importantly it took him on a tour of mental institutions in Britain and France enabling him to visit Paris and, even if only briefly, to become familiar with the architecture of Duban and Labrouste.

Thereafter the influence of French and German round-arched neo-classicism became increasingly marked: most of his work is early Italian Renaissance but seen through French and more particularly German eyes. In 1845 he built the severely Italianate Kirklee Terrace; in 1846 he began to achieve his mature style in the Glasgow Academy (now Strathclyde Regional Headquarters) on Elmbank Street, a *cinquento* design which showed some awareness of von Klenze's Munich War Office; in 1849 the John Neilson Institution at Paisley, a square plan hilltop structure with identical elevations and a tall dome of very original, somewhat French, outline; and in 1856 his career reached its climax in the Alberti-inspired temple of the Queens's Rooms (latterly the Christian Science Church) on La Belle Place and the triple-campaniled Lombardic Trinity College on the Woodlands hilltop, the architectural expression of the Free Church's victory over the Established Church. Both these buildings lie within Wilson's Park development, the supreme example of wealthy early Victorian Glasgow urbanism, with the concentric Park Circus and Park Terrace (1854–55) crowning the hilltop.

Like Alexander Thomson's, Wilson's classical work was marked by an almost total independence of London fashions.

David M Walker

A building on the Glasgow city centre grid. The facade is being preserved and a new interior built.

GLASGOW'S CONTEMPORARY ARCHITECTURE

Glasgow is unclear whether it is a British city (which it has never been) a European city or an international city. It is particularly uncertain as to its post-industrial role.

The city divides into zones. New offices are concentrated on Blythswood Hill – indifferent glass clingwrapped blocks whose primary contribution is the reflection of their neighbours. They are almost identical, in essence, to the great red stone office blocks of the late 19th century which encumber Hope, St Vincent and West George Streets, but without their richness of carving and surface appeal.

Glaswegian institutional buildings aspire to majesty without anything like the money the Victorians made available to build the St Andrew's Halls or the City Chambers. The Royal Scottish Academy of Music and Drama presents a frigid, out of scale brick corner to Hope Street, whereas the new Concert Hall brings the upper end of Buchanan Street to an emphatic stop.

The city has unfortunately turned its back on Clydeside and the Kelvin. So preoccupied has Glasgow been to generate activity that even tedious brick boxes sporadically deposited on the riverbanks have been permitted. Perhaps the next generation will be able to link these into something genuinely urban, just as a scattering of buildings were once transformed into the Merchant City.

So far, the priority has been to knit the city together again with a lowest common architectural denominator derived from identity, scale and texture. The next step must be higher aspirations toward cultural development and architectural monuments. It will be more difficult.

Charles McKean

Chapter Nineteen

THE GRID

Glasgow would seem to be a fairly loyal place. There are about a dozen streets, places, squares and terraces featuring the word "Queen". In Victoria's day, there were more than 20, though "It by no means follows that all these are so called in honour of our present sovereign," wrote J. A. Hammerton in 1893.[1]

The best known Queen Street was Cow Loan, which was renamed in honour of Victoria's grandmother, Queen Charlotte. Victoria is still remembered in 21 streets, terraces, circuses and so on. There used to be 25, but four were cancelled. Nineteen places bore her consort's name, but now there are only eleven Albert Streets, drives and terraces, though there is still an Albert Bridge and an Albert Cross.

The royal residences have naturally found their way into the posher areas of town and the nobility are very well represented. Hamilton and Argyll seem to have done well, Lorne, Eglinton, Dundas, Montague and Bute are remembered in various lanes, streets, avenues, but not, it appears, in any closes.

Victoria's statesmen are well represented. Glasgow rose and expanded during Victoria's reign and her leaders were amongst the heroes of the age. Stanley, Grosvenor, Lansdowne, Rosebery, Salisbury, Gladstone, Peel, Granville, Shaftesbury, Palmerston and Beaconsfield still find their names on an array of streets, lanes, terraces and so on, but nothing like a hundred years ago. Holland, Derby, Cavendish, Pitt, Somerset, Dalhousie and North are still there, but Canning, Elcho, Cobden, Chatham and Hartington have gone. Parliamentary Road exists, but only just.

Balfour, Baldwin, Churchill, Chamberlain and Attlee seem to be the most recent additions to the politician's roll. There is a Wilson Street, which has nothing to do with recent parliamentary democracy, since it was called after a tobacco lord.

The real Victorian heroes were the soldiers and sailors, or rather

"Schipka Pass" by Robert Eadie.

"The City of the Circle and the Square" by Eduardo Paolozzi.

A Bird's Eye View of Glasgow from the South.

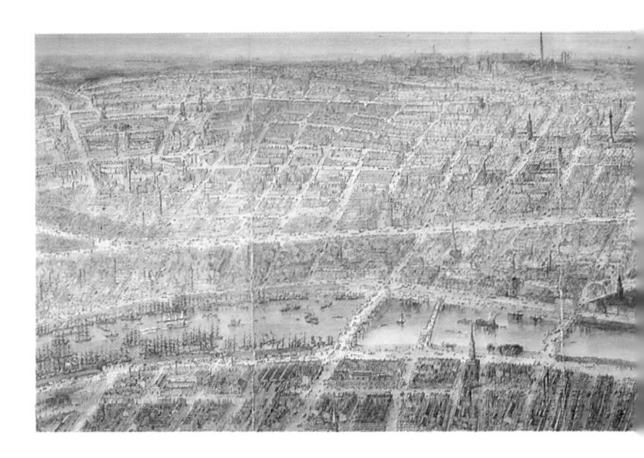

1. J.B. Hammerton, **Sketches From Glasgow**, 1893.

THE GLASGOW GRID

Even in the early medieval burgh there was a so-called *Quadrivium* at the intersection of Castle Street-High Street with Rottenrow and the Drygate. But it was not until around 1722, when with deliberate precision the north-south line of King Street and Candleriggs was laid across Trongate, that the fully geometricised pattern was established.

Thereafter the city grew to the north-west in a gridded network of streets. By the 1780s a rectilineal plan of expansion, probably the work of city surveyor, John Barry, had been confirmed as far west as Buchanan Street.

Incorporated into the planning of this 18th century Merchant City was a significant, even symbolic, variant of the cross street grid. Partly through circumstance and partly by deliberate exploitation, T-junction intersections became prime sites for *points-de-vue* – perhaps the mansions of Tobacco Lords, perhaps the institutional buildings of commercial or civic power.

By the turn of the 19th century the city's expansion westward had produced ideas for a Second New Town which would transform the rural estate of Blythswood, greatly to the financial advantage of its owners, the Campbells. Across a hilly landscape of parallel ridges and valleys, a regularised grid was feued to speculators subject to rigorous planning control and street-to-street facades of late Georgian terrace houses began to appear. That urban architecture still survives, especially on Blythswood Hill.

The 19th century grid was, above all, easy to reproduce and extend. Unconcerned to express cultural or social aspiration in the layout of the town, Glasgow, intent on growth, cast its acquisitive net of terraced or tenemented streets, north, west and south.

Frank Arneil Walker

the generals, admirals, conquerors and Empire builders. Nelson is still here with some of his victories: St Vincent, Baltic, Nile and Trafalgar. Marlborough and Blenheim continue to be remembered, so is Moore and Corunna as well as Abercromby and Aboukir. Havelock is still there, but not Lucknow, and Wolseley is still remembered, but his victories in Abyssinia and Coomassie have gone. Alma Street remains, though General Raglan lost his Maryhill address a few years ago. Cadogan and Hope have a place and a street. There is a Wellington Street and a Waterloo Street, as well as an Elba Lane. Napoleon Place went long ago.

As well as the street names there are other, more obvious memorials. Glasgow began the country's first public monument to Admiral Lord Horatio Nelson nine months after his death at Trafalgar. Nelson's Column on Glasgow Green cost £2,045. The money was raised from public subscription and the foundation stone was laid on Friday, August 1, 1806, the third anniversary of the Battle of the Nile, with an estimated crowd of more than 80,000 people attending the ceremony. The monument is 143 feet high.

At a quarter past four on the afternoon of August 5, 1810, Nelson's Monument was struck by lightning. The top 20 feet collapsed and what was left looked so shaky that soldiers kept the public at a distance. The same storm damaged the Royal Infirmary. A house in Rottenrow was also struck by lightning, the people electrocuted and their utensils melted.

Damage to the Nelson Monument made the authorities think again about lightning conductors. The thunder rod's inventor, Benjamin Franklin, had visited Glasgow in 1760 and lectured on the use of lightning conductors. The Old College alone took his advice.

A lightning conductor was fitted to the repaired Nelson Monument, in case lightning did strike twice, though the Doulton Fountain, also on the Green, was not so fortunate. The figure of Queen Victoria was struck in 1891. The fountain has been described as [1] "the most astonishing piece of earthenware ever made," when "one's instinctive dislike of the colour is overcome". Doulton of Lambeth made the piece of red terracotta for the 1888 International Exhibition in Kelvingrove Park; it was moved to Glasgow Green the following year. The Peoples of the Empire surround the fountain and Victoria stood at the top until blasted. The city fathers asked the Doulton Company for a replacement and were told such a figure came "straight from the hands of a craftsman and not from any mould". The city fathers did not like the price Doulton quoted for a replacement and decided to put an urn at the top. This would

THE WESTWARD EXPANSION

Glasgow's Second New Town, planned and promoted by the landowners of the Blythswood estate, set a pattern for the city's continued residential expansions throughout the 19th century.

New middle class suburbs began to appear on the west. There, the tightening grip of industry, already encircling the city centre on the north, east and south, had not been closed. There, too, on either side of the Kelvin valley and beyond, lay some delightful countryside with healthy air and fine prospects. Bit by bit, more than 20 estates cashed in on the growing opportunities for development and, in the 80 years or so preceding the First World War, Glasgow's distinctive West End came into being.

Each estate played its own hand in the speculative game, responding perhaps to topography in its layout and to the market in its provision of residential building types, trumping its neighbour with claims to salubrious elegance.

Despite a differing pattern of street layout, contoured crescents and circuses in Park, Dowanhill and Partickhill, gridded blocks in Hillhead, Hyndland and Broomhill, a common sequence of estate development seemed to occur. First came upmarket villas and terraces exploiting the finest locations, consistently those on higher ground or along the main westward routes. Only later as the social market broadened would tenements begin to line the streets, their predominantly red ranges linking estates together into one "extensive urbanised quarter". Even then, however, the population of the West End remained all but exclusively middle class.

Frank Arneil Walker

1. A.M. Doak and Andrew McLaren Young, **Glasgow at a Glance**, 1965.

The Doulton Fountain, Glasgow Green.

RAF photo of the 1970s, showing the Glasgow grid.

Joseph Swan's view of George Square from the east.

destroy the concept of the fountain, said Doulton, who thought it was ridiculous to have an urn presiding over the Peoples of the Empire, so he subsidised the replacement statue.

As the Second City of the Empire, Glasgow obviously commemorated the nation's great men as well as its own citizens. Five of George Square's dozen statues are to native Glaswegians; the others have fairly tenuous links with the city.

The laying of the Square was begun in 1807 and took more than 100 years to complete. The first statue, to Sir John Moore of Corunna, was erected in 1819 and the last, to William Ewart Gladstone, was unveiled by Lord Rosebery in October, 1902. It originally stood on the site of the Cenotaph, in front of the City Chambers.

Two hundred thousand Glaswegians fought in the Great War and 20,000 lost their lives. When Sir J. J. Burnet was commissioned to design a war memorial in honour of the city's dead, he was told it should not detract from the City Chambers. Something where "an attitude of reverence is secured by the eye being drawn down," was suggested. The memorial was unveiled by Earl Haig on Saturday, May 31, 1924. Public response was varied. *The Bailie* made the most telling point of all: "The women who lost their lives on active service might have been mentioned in an inscription on the memorial."[1]

Queen Victoria's statue commemorates her first visit to Glasgow in 1849. It was originally in St Vincent Place, but was moved to the Square when Prince Albert's memorial was unveiled in 1866. Victoria only paid three official visits to Glasgow. The first was in direct response to the events of March 1848 when the cotton factories were closed, the people were destitute and rioting broke[2] out in the city. Shops were looted, barricades were put up in the High Street, Saltmarket and Argyle Street and the Riot Act was read. Eventually the military were called in. Far from quelling the riots, the arrival of the 3rd Dragoons and 1st Royal Scots increased the trouble and several people, mostly innocent bystanders, were shot and killed in John Street, Bridgeton.

The poet and essayist Alexander Smith witnessed the Glasgow bread riots on March 6. He worked as a muslin pattern designer, "a mere lad" who was "in the streets at the time."[3]

"The 'Glasgow operative'", he tells us, "is, while trade is good and wages high, the quietest and most inoffensive of creatures. He cares comparatively little for the affairs of the nation. He is industrious and contented. Each six months he holds a saturnalia – one on New-year's day, the other at the Fair (occurring in July), and his excesses at these points keep him poor during the intervals."

THE FRENCH CONNECTION

It was in the 1870s and 1880s that Glasgow's links with France were closest and had the most far-reaching consequences. A fortuitous combination of circumstances saw John Burnet senior's son John James Burnet (born 1857) complete his architectural education at the *Ecole des Beaux Arts* and meet Jean-Louis Pascal whose *atelier* was much favoured by American students since he spoke good English. Burnet acquired the *Diplome du Gouvernement* in 1877. In 1880 John Archibald Campbell (born 1859), an apprentice in the Burnet office since 1877, also secured admission to Pascal's *atelier* where he remained until 1883, becoming a partner in the Burnet firm in 1886.

Robert Douglas Sandilands (with the great theorist Julien Guadet) and Alexander Nisbet Paterson and John Keppie (with Pascal) also furthered their education in France. Some very French buildings resulted, most notably Burnet's Fine Art Institute on Sauchiehall Street (1878), Clyde Trust Building (1883), the Glasgow Athenaeum and the Gustav Eiffel-inspired Edinburgh International Exhibition Building of 1886; Sandilands' giant asylum at Gartloch, begun 1883, and Govan Municipal Buildings (1897); and Keppie's Fairfield Shipyard Offices, 1890.

Perhaps the most important aspect of the Ecole connection which culminated in the appointment of Eugene Bourdon to the staff of Glasgow School of Art in 1904, was the American dimension since so many American architects had studied at the Ecole. Burnet, who made his first visit to the United States in 1896, was provided with important introductions to the best architectural practices there. From the late 1890s onwards Burnet's work carries a strongly American character.

David M Walker

1. **The Bailie**, June 1924. 2. The Chartists petitioned parliament in 1848, the year of revolution in Europe and the publication of the **Communist Manifesto**. 3. See John McDowall, **The People's History of Glasgow**, 1899 and others.

JAMES SALMON (1873–1924)

James Salmon, born and educated in Glasgow, was one of the most outstanding designers working in Scotland at the turn of the century. While his designs broadly followed the Glasgow Style, he created buildings entirely original in expression. The idiosyncratic "Hatrack" offices at 142–144 St Vincent Street (1898) with its rippling facade and convex and concave forms, and the sheer, and soaring Lion Chambers at 172 Hope Street, (1904) are among Salmon and partner John Gaff Gillespie's most uncompromising and complete designs.

However, one cannot overlook the simple Arts and Crafts detailing of the St Andrews in the East church halls, Alexandra Parade (1898) or the subtlety of the Glasgow Style coats of arms of Scotland and Glasgow to be found on the beaten relief copper panels at 79 West Regent Street, (1900).

Salmon's talents did not stop at the building exterior. He designed interior decorations and fixtures from light fittings to pepperpots and worked closely with major Glasgow Style craftsmen such as Oscar Paterson, Stephen Adam and John Crawford. The interiors of 12 University Gardens (1900) and 22 Park Circus (1900) are particularly notable.

Apart from stylistic design Salmon and Gillespie also carried out pioneering work on the use of steel casement windows and reinforced-concrete construction that significantly influenced their contemporaries.

Affectionately known as the "Wee Troot" by his many friends, Salmon had a mischievous humour and individual views. He was happy to be regarded as a "social and municipal Bolshevik".

Salmon's work more than that of any other British designer bears the closest affinity with continental *Art Nouveau* and is unparalleled within the United Kingdom.

Raymond O'Donnell

Smith soon leaves personal observation: "some of the more ingenious traders, it is said, pasting 'A Shop to Let' on their premises – that they might thereby escape the rage or the cupidity of the rioters". Within five minutes of the soldiers' arrival, not a rioter was to be seen, and evening found the Trongate with "an unwonted appearance. Troops stacked their bayonets, lighted their fires and bivouacked under the piazzas of the Tontine. Sentinels paced up and down the pavements and dragoons patrolled the streets."

Things came to a head the following day when the soldiers, "whose patience was completely exhausted, sent their shot right into the mass of people. Several were wounded, and one or more killed". A corpse was carried on a board "to madden and rouse the citizens", but "the bearers of the dead were confronted by the ominous glitter of steel. The procession paused, stopped, wavered, and finally beat a retreat, and thus the riots closed."

Victoria's official visit in August 1849 was the first by a reigning monarch since James VI came in 1617 and the first by a monarch of the United Kingdom. Ten years later, on October 14, 1859, she crossed Loch Katrine in the steamer *Rob Roy* and turned the handle which sent the water supply to Milngavie, where it was kept before being passed on to Glasgow. "Such a work is worthy of the enterprise and philanthropy of Glasgow," she said, "and I trust it will be blessed with complete success." Twelve years later the Stewart Fountain was built in Kelvingrove Park in honour of the former Lord Provost who had piloted the scheme. By the end of the century Glasgow had the best water supply in the country and a large whisky distilling industry. Victoria's last visit was in August 1888 when she opened the City Chambers and visited the Great Exhibition in Kelvingrove Park.

Sir Robert Peel and William Ewart Gladstone are in the Square as Rectors of Glasgow University and Free Traders. Glasgow's merchants took the repeal of the Corn Laws very seriously. It lifted restrictions on imported foodstuffs and abolished what were seen as prohibitive taxes. So when Peel was elected Lord Rector of the University in 1836 "the citizens of Glasgow" gave him a dinner, in January 1837, which *The Spectator* later described as "one of the greatest political marvels of all time."[1]

A wooden banqueting hall was built in what is now the foot of Buchanan Street, between Exchange Place and the Argyle Arcade. It was 127 feet long, 126 feet wide, was lined with crimson, blue, white and gold cloth and had pillars and wood carvings of Greek design. More than 4,000 people sat down to a banquet, "the like[3]

An early photograph of a City Chambers corridor.

Ingram Street looking east from the Star Inn around 1840, towards the Ramshorn Kirk and University spire.

1. James Cleland, Description of the Banquet in Honour of the Rt. Hon. Sir Robert Peel, Bart, MP, 13th January, 1837.

3. ibid.

of which for magnitude and splendour had never taken place in Scotland before."

Gladstone was one of the speakers. He was given the Freedom of the City in 1865, "to express our sense of benefits arising from his services in connection with that course of commercial legislation concisely expressed in the words 'Free Trade.'" When he was elected Lord Rector of the University in 1877, he gave his inaugural address to 2,000 students in the Kibble Palace in the Botanic Gardens. Liberals sat on the right of the platform, Tories on the left and Sir William Thomson, later Lord Kelvin, and Joseph, later Lord, Lister sat in the middle with Gladstone.

Sir Colin Campbell's statue was unveiled in 1868 and a year later he was joined in the Square by Thomas Graham, whose statue faces the south-east corner of the City Chambers. Graham, who was the Andersonian Institute's Professor of Chemistry and "Paraffin" Young's teacher, is thought to be one of the Square's unknowns, joining James Oswald, who stands at the other end of the Square, frock-coated with top hat and cane, though his statue was originally at Charing Cross.Baron Marochetti,who designed the statue as well as the effigies to Victoria and Albert and the equestrian Wellington outside Stirling's Library, would be upset to know that Oswald's inverted hat is now Glasgow's best known litter bin.

James Oswald was elected as a Whig MP in the first reformed parliament. He was one of two representatives the city of 150,000 was entitled to return; the other was a Tory named Ewing. Oswald was in Parliament from 1832-37 and again from 1839-47 and is chiefly remembered for his interest in the 1832 Reform Bill, though he is said to have been "one of the most influential Scottish members in the House of Commons".[2]

No doubting the most popular, or the best remembered statue in the Square. Robert Burns was unveiled on January 25, 1877 and more than 30,000 watched the ceremony. The statue was commissioned from public subscriptions with over 40,000 people giving a shilling each.

George Square was intended to be the centre piece of a new town development. The hope was that the prosperous merchants of the period would build themselves fine new mansions in the square. The gardens in the centre were surrounded by high railings, to keep away the riff-raff and meant for the use of residents only.

George Square soon became a mercantile centre, though Glasgow was fortunate to have a group of architects whose combined efforts made the city centre exceptional. Alexander Thomson became known as "Greek" Thomson because of his work in the classical style,

FIVE BOYS: GUTHRIE, LAVERY, HENRY AND HORNEL, CRAWHALL

In the early years of the Glasgow School James Guthrie and the Belfast-born John Lavery were at the centre of the two main groups of artists.

Lavery, the more ambitious of the two, was the first to turn away from rustic naturalism, and began to paint more saleable pictures of the middle- classes at play, rather than the rural poor at work. Guthrie followed his example in a fine series of pastels. They each began to specialise in portrait painting and became the leading society portraitists of their day, both being knighted.

George Henry began painting as a part-time student at Glasgow School of Art and then became a follower of Guthrie. Gradually his painting became influenced by the work of Arthur Melville, developing a keen sense of colour and pattern. In turn he was to impress the young E. A. Hornel. Both men had a keen interest in Japanese art and in 1894 they went there on an 18 month expedition. Henry moved from still life and figure subjects towards portraiture. Like Guthrie and Lavery he was to achieve international recognition as a portraitist, while his friend Hornel remained in Kirkcudbright, pursuing a successful career as a painter of sentimental woodland scenes populated by groups of young girls.

Joseph Crawhall grew up in Newcastle and became involved with the Glasgow Boys when his sister married a friend of James Guthrie. He was a quiet and reserved character and only came to life when painting his pictures of birds, fish and horse, which are unequalled in their freshness, intensity of colour and careful design.

Roger Billcliffe

A view of the Grand Banqueting Hall built in Buchanan Street for Sir Robert Peel's dinner.

James Oswald, with his hat outstretched on the eastern end of George Square.

1. ibid. 2. Quoted by Jack House in **The Heart of Glasgow**, 1965.

though he was strongly influenced by contemporary German architecture. Most of his mature buildings are in Glasgow, but his work has not had the appreciation it deserves. Renovation and floodlighting seems unenthusiastic and there is little sense or acknowledgement of Thomson's wonderful innovations.[1]

Lavish attention has been given to the buildings associated with Charles Rennie Mackintosh. Glasgow Art School, rises above Sauchiehall Street, round the corner from Thomson's Grecian Chambers, to the right of Scott Street.

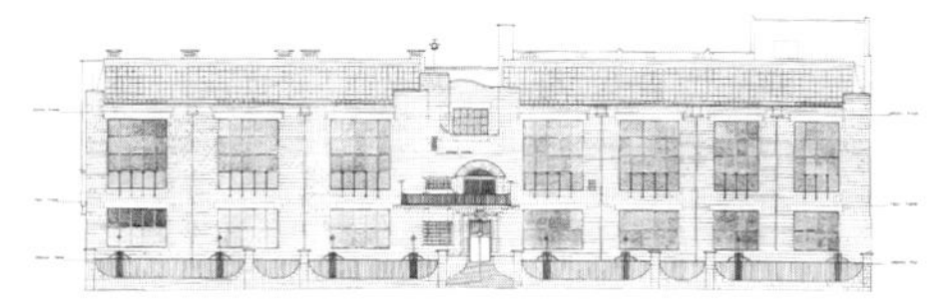

Glasgow School of Art.

The south elevation rises like a cliff face from the back of Sauchiehall Street and the east and west ends are similar in their strong use of the slope. The lines of the building lift the eye and there is almost a sense of danger that something so strong and powerful could balance on something so steep. The eastern half of the school dates from 1897 and is the result of an architectural competition. The second stage, to the west, was finished in 1909. Another exciting aspect is the way the building changes as you move around it. The huge windows to the front on Renfrew Street are designed to let as much of the northern light in as possible, while the contrast between the eastern and western ends of the building is such, that the west facade appears to have no roof while the east rises like a medieval fortress, pierced by the occasional window. There is a gently welcoming curved stone stairway leading to the front door and the relief above the doorway is the building's only decorative sculpture.

The Art School is a radical building, quite revolutionary when contrasted with contemporary Glasgow architecture. The interior is even more striking, full of elegant and graceful details and described as "a warren of discovery". On a smaller scale is the lovely door he designed for the Glasgow Society of Lady Artists at 5 Blythswood Square, round the corner from where Madeleine Smith gave her nightly dose of doctored cocoa to the hapless L'Engelier.

Madeleine featured in one of Glasgow's famous murder trials, notorious for its Not Proven verdict and the passion of her letters revealed in court. One way or another, murder has had a prominent association with the city streets, either through Percy Sillitoe and the gangs of the Thirties or the more popular image of the city as a haven of razor slashers. Glaswegians have always resented this image, preferring to highlight the social aspects of our streets and closes, often comparing the city's warmth and friendliness to that of other Scottish towns.

Until recently the prefix "Glasgow" presupposed a certain type

Madeleine Smith with her family.

MADELEINE SMITH AND OSCAR SLATER

As novelists the world over have discovered, murder can be very democratic. Glasgow's homicide records span the social classes and include a successful architect's daughter and a shady immigrant Jew. Although in both these cases, crime proved no respecter of persons, their verdicts bear witness to the enduring power of social prejudice.

On 23 March, 1857, a clerk called Emile L'Angelier died. He had consumed enough arsenic to kill 20. L'Angelier had saved 189 letters from a certain Madeleine Smith. Respectable Madeleine was engaged to a Glasgow merchant and seemed above reproach. Passionate and explicit, her letters told a different story.

Madeleine had every reason to poison a penniless lover who refused to let her marry someone else. When L'Angelier threatened to send Madeleine's father her letters, she bought arsenic and L'Angelier began to fall ill. But Madeleine walked free and L'Angelier was immortalised as a French seducer and blackmailer.

By the Spring of 1909, Madeleine's first husband had long since left her on health grounds, and Oscar Slater was on trial for murdering Marion Gilchrist. Miss Gilchrist was beaten to death in a vicious and apparently motiveless attack.

Slater was found guilty and initially sentenced to death after a trial made notable by a laughable prosecution case, primed witnesses and a hostile judge. Slater's foreign background and questionable past convinced both police and jury that, if he wasn't guilty of this crime, he deserved to hang in any case.

Glasgow policeman John Trench, Sir Arthur Conan Doyle and many others took 20 years to clear Slater's name. He spent 19 of them in prison.

Alison Kennedy

1. Thomson is by no means the only architect whose buildings have been poorly floodlit or left in the dark.

JOAN EARDLEY (1921–63)

In a tragically brief working life between 1943 when she left art school and her death from cancer exactly 20 years later Joan Eardley gained almost universal respect and admiration as one of the finest painters of her day in Scotland. Born in Sussex of an English father, she was partly Scottish, trained at the Glasgow School of Art, and lived and worked here for the whole of her adult life.

In Glasgow Eardley discovered the colourful energy of the juvenile street life around her studio at Townhead, where the insouciant, noisy, cheerful slum children against their background of dilapidated paint-peeling shop fronts gave her endless subject matter. She drew continually and the paintings which she later made in her studio retained much of this original energy.

But, just as in a student scholarship journey to Italy Eardley had divided her interest between the simple people and the landscape, so, at home, she found increasing outlet for a strong empathy with nature in its seasonal cycle. First of all at Corrie in Arran, and later from a clifftop cottage at Catterline, a little fishing village on the Kincardineshire coast, Eardley gave expression to her strong sensations in communion with nature in all its moods. The finest Catterline paintings – especially the later seascapes – will bear comparison with the best in 20th century British, not just Scottish, painting. Despite the late influence of Abstract Expressionism, used to express her consciousness of nature's endless energy and wealth, Eardley never completely lost the image of what she saw. She remained an essentially factual painter.

Cordelia Oliver

of writer and a certain type of writing. Things have changed and the city is currently home for a disparate number of individual voices whose collective ability supersedes any earlier generation.

The poetry of Edwin Morgan has shown Glasgow to be a cause for celebration, while Tom Leonard has used its speech rhythms and cadences to enhance understanding; in fiction, Alasdair Gray sees a futurist Glasgow, a city of the imagination. Between them, the close and the kailyard have given Scotland a set of popular mythologies and one of the healthiest developments of Scottish literature is that contemporary writers now have the ability to depict life as it is lived, using the language of the dispossessed.

Five boys on wall, from around the turn of the century.

The main complaint from early high rise dwellers was that the outdoor spaces were no longer suitable playgrounds. Children had to be kept indoors because their parents could not see what they were up to from their high rise windows. This was a disaster for many generations whose playgrounds were the streets. Now there is a current notion that children only play in day centres, nursery schools and the like and are only interested in BMX bikes, computers, ghetto blasters or any of the dolls and monsters they see on television. They are definitely not interested in the singing games, skipping games, clapping games, elimination and ball games. They don't play peever or chuckies, alevio, hunch-cuddie-hunch, kick-the-can or alabala. The only songs they know are in the hit parade or from the soaps and they wouldn't be seen dead with a gird.

Concerned bodies recently found pockets of resistance. There are, apparently, still weans in this city who can draw square beds or aeroplane beds and can slide a peever into boxes. They don't play on the streets any more, because of "environmental problems" but school playgrounds are the place to find tig, alevio, peevers and beds. "Cross generational" projects have been instigated in various parts of the city.[1]

Old folk and school children come together in community centres, clubs, classrooms and playgrounds where old folk taught the street games and rhymes of their childhood to another generation. Peevers, peeries, girds and cleeks were specially made for the project and rules concerning the proper way to play were drawn up.

"The first player slides her peever into Box One, hops on one foot into Box One, puts both feet down on Boxes Two and Three, then hops on one foot into Box Four, both feet in Boxes Five and

1. Strathclyde Regional Council's Community Education Service organised such a project in the Priesthill, Nitshill and Arden areas of Glasgow "to promote cross generational work between older people's clubs and the local primary schools." A pamphlet was published as a result of the project: **Old Games and Rhymes of Glasgow**, Network Scotland, undated.

GLASGOW SONGS – 20th CENTURY

The second Golden age of the Glasgow music hall supplied us with most of the best-known songs, with Will Fyffe continuing the character tradition, and Dave Willis giving new life to the "eccentric" song. A minor performer, Wullie Lindsay, wrote songs for many of the others and acted almost as a "session" comic for the recording companies when they made Scots Concert Party recordings with groups like The Troubadours.

The kilted tenors did not sing of Glasgow at all. There are few countries where the light-classical songs deal with contemporary urban life, but when it comes to singing of a romantic rural past Scotland leads the world, in terms of quantity.

As the Halls disappeared so did the singing comics. The last of them, Andy Stewart, has also dealt mainly with a rural Scotland.

Glasgow, however, has not gone unsung. The folksong revival, starting in the 1950s from a traditional base, was given an urban songwriting impetus by the political campaign against the siting of Polaris missiles on the Holy Loch. While writers like Morris Blythman and Jim MacLean confined themselves to political themes, others like Matt McGinn, Carl MacDougall, Adam McNaughtan and Jim Brown have written about all aspects of city life, and in spite of pop music's domination in recording and broadcasting, songs such as "The Red Yo-Yo", "Cod Liver Oil and the Orange Juice" and "The Jeelie Piece Song" have become widely known.

Adam McNaughtan

Six respectively, hops into Box Seven on one foot, Eight and Nine with both feet and then into Box Ten."

Which seems an awkward way of describing something which looks so effortless and graceful. Rules have been drawn up and booklets published with some of the songs. They are not only intended as an *aide memoire*. The hope is they would be the starting point for other schemes and projects.

These and similar collections have shown the need for a properly researched collection of this material which casts its net as widely as possible and puts the songs into some context rather than simply present them as curiosities. Adam McNaughtan is the best songwriter we have; he has absorbed the Glasgow folk process so well his songs are taken as part of the tradition, so varied it is difficult to imagine they are the works of a single author. His "Height Starvation Song", better known as the "Jeely Piece Song", is a city anthem for many. "Oor Hamlet" is one of the clearest analyses of the play I know, as well as being surprisingly funny. Apart from writing, he has collected many street songs and rhymes. "Where Is The Glasgow?" has been quoted, without the author, in a number of publications and has achieved some sort of status by gathering additional cack-handed verses which cosmeticise poverty and reduce hardship to shared lavatories and end with the line "Our parents had guts." McNaughtan is clearer:

[1]
Oh where is the wean that once played on the street
Wi a jorrie, a peerie, a gird wi a cleek?
Can he still cadge a hudgie and dreep aff a dyke?
Or is writin on walls noo the wan thing he likes?
Can he tell chickie mellie frae hunch cuddie hunch?

The exciting thing about these or any other folk songs is their resilience and how quickly and easily they are adapted to suit the times. It would be interesting to see how many of today's street singers would cope with songs like:

[2]
My wee laud's a sodjer,
He works in Maryhill;
He gets his pay on a Friday night
And buys a hauf a gill.
He goes tae church on Sunday,
Hauf an hour late;
He pulls the buttons aff his shirt
And flings them in the plate.

Children playing in Back Court.

Woman and child, around 1910.

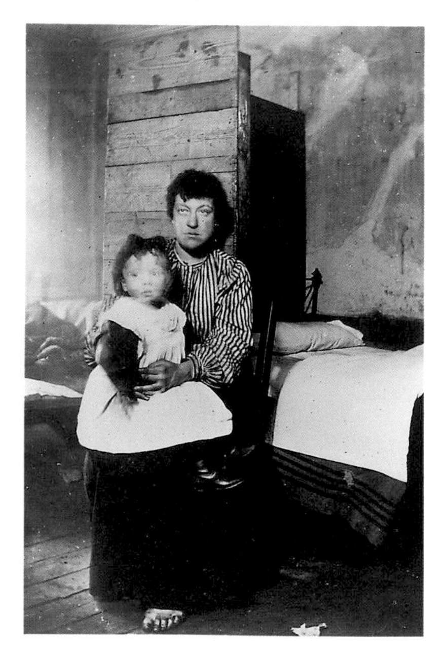

1. Norman Buchan and Peter Hall (ed.), **The Scottish Folksinger**, 1973. 2. Norman Buchan (ed.), **101 Scottish Songs, 1962.**

CHILDREN'S SONGS

Nine tenths of the songs sung in a Glasgow primary school playground come from an international repertoire of children's games. It is not, however, merely the remaining tenth that justifies the description *"Glasgow* street songs" being applied to what the girls are singing. "Ye cannae shove yer Grannie aff a Bus", "Haw Maw, Ah goat a Hammerin" and "Last Night There was a Murder in the Chip-Shoap" may be undeniably their own, but Glasgow weans have always known how to stamp any song as local.

It is not enough that the fat vowels and glottal stops of a chorus like "Rashie tashie petticoats, rashie tashie tee", issuing from the throats of two enders and ten jumpers, make it seem as aboriginally Cathurian as St Mungo's Bell; the "sailor girls" of the verse become "gallus girls", just asin other songs "Jungle Jim" became "Charlie Sim", "I spy Wallace Beery" became "Haud ma whip till Ah spin ma peerie" and Davy Crocket became a chain- swinging Gorbals teddy-boy. "Down in Yonder Meadow", played and sung in Glasgow for centuries, may be known in equally old variants in Somerset, Dublin and New York, but it can only be in this city that the bride-to-be first

Made a dumplin', she made it awfy nice,
Cut it up in slices an' gied us a' a slice.

Adam McNaughtan

Though others seem to be fine as they are and need no adaptation whatsoever:

> Does your maw drink wine?
> Does she drink it aa the time?
> Does she ever get the feeling that she's gonnae
> hit the ceiling?
> Does your maw drink gin?
> Would she drink it oot a tin?
> Does she ever get the feeling that she's gonnae
> hit the ceiling?
> Does your maw drink voddy?
> Till it dislocates her body?
> Does she ever get the feeling that she's gonnae
> hit the ceiling?

Steps in Wood Street, Port Dundas, on June 1, 1910.

1. Maureen Sinclair, **Murder, Murder Polis**, 1986, though printed versions of such pieces are not always desirable.

A piece of glassware manufactured by the Clutha company, 19th century.

Chapter Twenty

SILVER AND CLAY

Letter from Niel Fisher, in the East Indies, who went out with 300 more from Glasgow, giving a list of the names of a number of well-known young men in Glasgow, who have died from hardship, with an advice to those in this city, addressed to the heads of families; received by his mother, Mrs. Jean Fisher, head of Barrack-Street, Glasgow, 5th October, 1822.

I have sent you these few lines, by a friend to inform you, that I am in good health at present, which I bless God for, when I see the havock death has made and is making here. This is the fourth letter that I have wrote you since I left England, without having received any word from you. There is much disappointment here on account that our letters seldom or never reach their destination, when sent by the usual means. I hope that you are all in good health, and that none of my friends or acquaintance will follow my footsteps in the service, as those that come out are wrought incessantly and get nothing for it. The country is very unhealthy in the Winter season; and in Summer hundreds die on being exposed to the hot winds and perpetually drifting sand. There is a sort of mats made of grass, which they soak with water, and hang on the outside of our dwellings, to keep the inside cool, but to little effect.

The people in Glasgow will be both astonished and distressed when they learn, that the most of three hundred that came out at the same time with me are dead. I was very sorry, when I landed here, to learn, that my old comrade Mathew Campbell died at a place called Dinapore, from being exposed to the hot winds. I shall mention a few of the names of those who came out with me two years ago. Patrick Somers, M'Kenzie, James Walker, Henry Pasley, and John Cummins are all dead. Duncan Ferguson has gone into the Horse Artillery. Patrick M'Coll, M'Lean, Peter Lochrie, and James Boog, and the rest have one Pound, and seven-pence halfpenny per month, out of which they pay about two and sixpence for shoe blacking, and barber, washing and cooking. We have about a glass and a half of spirits, one pound of meat, one pound of bread, an ounce of salt and three pound of wood, daily, per man: this might do very well were we at home, but here, the [illegible] to demand a subsistance which we have not the means of affording.

We expect daily to go off for the field, which is three hundred miles up the country, where we expect to be better dealt with. Tell young men to be warned by me, and not to think of doing as we have done. There can be little doubt [illegible] friends. I would say much more if my masters would allow me. Tell them to think much of their own country. We who are here would give all we possess to set a foot on our own native heather again: We are not ashamed to shed a tear when we think on the days that can never return!

[illegible]

Letter home from Niel Fisher, warning of conditions in the East Indies, where he had gone to work.

In 1766, Captain Knight, who was later described as "the commander of a ship in the African trade", brought a cargo of slaves from Africa to Jamaica and "exposed the said cargo for sale."[1] John Wedderburn bought one of the lot, a boy of about 13, and called him Joseph Knight, after the captain who had brought him from New Guinea.

Joseph was instructed in the Christian religion, baptised and examined on his knowledge of the Holy Scriptures. Nonetheless Mr Wedderburn's chambermaid Annie Thomson had a child and Joseph was the father. Mr Wedderburn sacked Annie, while Joseph was not only "still retained as his master's domestic slave", but also given money for what was later described as "Annie's expenses, consequent upon childbed."[2] And when the child took sick, Mr Wedderburn not only paid the medical expenses, but also for the infant's burial. Joseph and Annie were then married and Joseph insisted Mr. Wedderburn should re-employ his wife as a servant. He point blank refused to let Annie cross the threshold.

According to papers lodged in the Court of Session, Joseph had been perusing the *Edinburgh Advertiser*. There he read about a slave called Somerset who had taken his case to the Court of the King's Bench in England. Somerset had successfully argued that since his master had brought him to England, he was a free man. There was no law to state that a man who was a slave in Jamaica was also a slave anywhere else in the world. From this Joseph concluded he was also free and set about quitting his master's service. He told Mr. Wedderburn as much and when Wedderburn disagreed Joseph eventually packed his bags, only to be discovered as he was about to escape.

A warrant was granted for Joseph's arrest and on November 15, 1773, he appeared before the Justices. Anonymous donations allowed him to fight a protracted legal battle. In the Court of Session on March 7, 1775, after a long debate, "the Court pronounced a

Virginia Tobacco label.

1. Senex, **Glasgow Past and Present**, 1851. 2. ibid.

GLASGOW NEWSPAPERS

Glasgow has been well served by newspapers. Its first newspaper, the *Glasgow Courant* ran for only three issues in November 1715, though staying around long enough to report the exploits of Rob Roy Macgregor. But since 1740 almost every year is covered by one or more papers out of a total of well over 100 published in the city.

The two peak periods of newspaper production were the early 1830s with the increased number of Whig papers, in support of the Reform movement, and at the height of Glasgow's prosperity around 1900 when there were more than 20 titles published. Even in the 1930s Glasgow had four morning, three evening and three Sunday papers.

Two notable productions of the press, perhaps the most lively and informative papers in Glasgow, were the *Glasgow Argus* (1833–47) described by the *Scotsman*, no less, as "distinguished for its courage in upholding Liberal principles in cases where to do so was neither popular nor profitable"; and the campaigning *North British Daily Mail*, founded in 1847 and Glasgow's first daily paper (becoming in 1901 the *Daily Record*).

And mention should be made of the phenomenon of the local newspaper. At the end of the 19th century there appeared to be an upsurge of local feeling, reflected in papers like the *Pollokshaws News* and the *Parkhead, Shettleston and Tollcross Advertiser* – the forerunners of the community newspapers of the 1970s.

Hamish Whyte

judgement in favour of Joseph on all the points at issue," and, according to Senex, who told the story, "thus he became a free man".[1]

There is no question that Glasgow merchants owned slaves, though it is uncertain as to whether they traded in slavery or not, though they were certainly no strangers to either the Caribbean or the tobacco growing areas of America, where many owned plantations.

Glasgow's merchant trade expanded in other areas. As well as dealing with the rum and sugar industries in the Caribbean, Glasgow companies traded further south, sending textiles to Buenos Aires, Rio de Janeiro and Montevideo, bringing back cotton and coffee, timber, tobacco, hides and rice. Trade with India and the Middle East expanded and Glasgow companies owned a range of properties: plantations in Dutch Guyana, copper mines in Spain, timber distributors in the Baltic, USA, Canada, South America, Indo China, and Rangoon.

Along with the growth in trade came a growth in its ancillary accomplices. The Glasgow and Ship Bank opened their doors to the world on the corner of the Saltmarket and Bridgegate, where the Ship Bank Tavern stands today, in 1750. They were the first to open in Glasgow and 26 years later they moved to the north side of Trongate, where two other finance houses were already established, to become part of a little banking enclave. Glasgow's money market was overflowing.

The merchants seemed lost when the tobacco trade dwindled and their sugar and rum concerns ran into difficulties. They were forced to sell their holdings in America and the West Indies, but bought land at home, which turned out to be a good investment when the city's industrial expansion began.

The Napoleonic wars finished Glasgow's colonial involvement, and 1793 brought the town's first financial crisis. Three banks shut up shop, another teetered without actually falling and even the great Royal Bank trembled. Only the Ship Bank carried its customers serenely through the crisis.

This was due to Robin Carrick, a joyless Scrooge of a man who lived with his niece above the bank. If anything, she was, by all accounts, even more miserable than him. She was famous for haggling with shopkeepers in King Street, trying to knock a farthing off the price of beef, and if by some miracle Robin gave a dinner she got the greengrocer to take back any left over apples or pears and deduct the price from her account.[2]

The bank itself was a dark and dingy hole with a high wooden

HENRY MONTEITH AND OTHERS

At the end of the 18th century Glasgow owed its development as an important centre of the textile industry to a small group of enterprising men, amongst whom were William Gillespie and James Monteith. These two men established handloom weaving businesses in the village of Anderston to the west of the city in the 1760s. Within 20 years they were producing "cotton stripes and checks, pulicates, shortings, jaconets, boot and maule muslim and gause spotted muslim shawls".

In 1801 John Monteith, James' eldest son, built one of the first steam-powered cotton mills in Scotland on the South Side of Glasgow at Pollokshaws. The following year his younger brother Henry took over the celebrated Glasgow dye works of David Dale at Barrowfield, founded in 1785. The plant was converted to steam to print bandana handkerchiefs.

Despite the efforts of Napoleon to keep British products out of Europe when the war with Revolutionary France resumed in 1803, Henry Monteith managed to smuggle his handkerchiefs into many continental countries. He was so successful that by the time the French were defeated at Waterloo in 1815 bandana handkerchiefs "all over the Continent . . . went under the name of Monteiths". Glasgow's cotton industry was by then substantial; it was estimated that in 1818 105 million yards of cotton cloth were made in the City.

Henry Monteith's achievement as a printer of fine calicos contributed to the West of Scotland's reputation for such craftmanship which continued well into the 20th century.

Michael S Moss

1. ibid. **2.** Robert Alison, **The Anecdotage of Glasgow**, 1892.

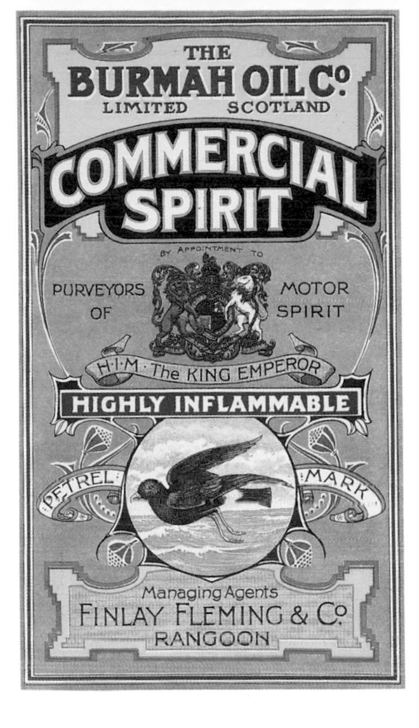

Burmah Oil Company, Finlay Fleming and Co. Rangoon.

Thomas Healey's elevation drawing of the Bank of Scotland.

partition separating the clerks from the customers. Money was placed on a shelf at the top of the partition and customers had to stand on tip-toe to bawl out their requirements. Little is known of what went on behind the screen.

Carrick apparently warmed himself up with a drink in the morning, then topped up throughout the day. His main worry, apart from money, was that the smell from his breath would ruin his respectability. If it did, nobody said, for he lived till he was 81 and left a million when he died.

Glasgow bankers were not all like him. The Royal Bank had its offices and manager's house in two tenements on St. Andrew's Square, with a couple of soldiers, loaded muskets and bayonets, to guard the place. The manager was John More, whom Robert Alison describes as "a man of dignified presence". Mr. More enjoyed the good life. On Saturdays and holidays, an elegantly equipped horse drawn carriage, complete with a black liveried footman, took the manager to his country house in Wellshot.[1]

This retreat cost Mr More £17,000 to build. It had a vinery, a flower garden, romantic walks and a bowling green on the outside and almost three quarters of a hundred weight of silver plate on the inside. Alison tells us "Mr. More became unfortunate"; whatever that means, his house was on the market for a long time, priced at £2,000, sold for a lot less and eventually tenanted by a respectable lawyer for £80 a year.

In 1825 and again in 1826 many London and provincial banks failed. The shares boom following the Napoleonic Wars was the cause, though Government blamed the banking houses. In 1826 the English Act limited and eventually banned notes under £5 and the intention was to extend this to Scotland, where the crisis was hardly felt.

There was an uproar. Sir Walter Scott wrote his wordy *Letters of Malachi Malagrowther*, where he overstates the case; no change could be made to the Scottish currency system unless Parliament was satisfied it would be to "the evident advantage of the subjects of Scotland," said the Treaty of Union, which patently meant more then than it does now. No such advantage was even suggested, said Malachi. The *Letters* worked and the "Scotch system of banking" remained untouched.[2]

The Scottish banking system owes more to Robin Carrick than John More. It was born of adversity, at a time when Scotland was a poorer place than England. Scotland's original public banks, the Bank of Scotland, which was established in 1695 and the Royal Bank, founded in 1727, encouraged the circulation of low

THE TEMPLETONS

Throughout the 19th century Glasgow was recognized as one of the leading centres of carpetmaking in Britain; due in large measure to the achievements of the Templeton family. James Templeton was born in Campbeltown in 1802. After working from some time in textile trade he patented a process for making carpets from chenille, strips of woven cloth so-named from the French for caterpillar.

The firm of James Templeton & Co was established in 1843 and within seven years was employing 400 people. James Templeton set up another enterprise in 1855 in partnership with his eldest son John Stewart to manufacture Brussels and Wilton carpets. After James Templeton's retirement in 1878 the businesses continued to prosper, extending into the production of Axminster carpets in 1887.

A magnificent new works to house Axminster looms, designed to look like the Doge's palace in Venice, began to be built facing Glasgow Green. Unfortunately it collapsed during a storm in November 1889 and was not finally completed for a further three years.

The Templetons emerged victorious from a bitter price struggle and by 1900 they were employing 1,600 men and women. Many of their carpets were supplied to Clyde shipbuilders to adorn passenger liners and paddle steamers. The Doge's Palace building is no longer a carpet factory; but has been converted into a business centre.

Michael S Moss

1. ibid. 2. Scott, The Letters of Malachi Malgrowther on the Proposed Changes in the Currency, 1826.

VICTORIAN GOTHIC

High Victorian Gothic came late to Glasgow and was only rarely adopted for secular buildings. J.T. Rochead's Park Church, built in 1858, was the first native product to abandon the cast-iron columned and galleried preaching church formula for a proper neo-medieval aisled and clerestoried plan, but stylistically it was still of the restless spiky character favoured by that architect in his neo-medieval designs.

Change came as the younger men returned to Glasgow with experience in English offices. Above all, William Leiper utilised a first-class education in the offices of J.L. Pearson and William White to design the Northamptonshire-type spire of Dowanhill UP Church (1865) and, later, the superb Normandy Gothic Camphill UP Church (1875) and the glazed tile Venetian Gothic Templeton Carpet Factory (1889) which dominates Glasgow Green. Other practices quickly joined in, most notably the elder John Burnet with his Glasgow Stock Exchange (1875) and James Sellars with his Presbyterian version of the Sainte Chapelle at Hillhead (1875–77) and his Normandy Gothic Belhaven UP Church (now St Luke's Greek Orthodox Cathedral).

In 1886, John James Burnet won the competition for Barony Church with a still finer design inspired by Dunblane Cathedral and over the next few decades a series of smaller churches with ecclesiological plans was built for both Established and Free Church congregations. Finally, in the 1890s came an outstanding series of free Arts-and-Crafts Gothic churches inspired by the work of J.D. Sedding and Harry Wilson in London of which the prime example is of course Makintosh's brilliant Queen's Cross Church (1899).

David M Walker

denomination notes, sometimes as low as a shilling, as a means of providing liquidity. Printing notes was cheaper than minting coins: in England, nothing short of a fiver could be printed. By the mid-18th century, Scotland was unique in Europe as having an almost all-paper currency: Adam Smith remarked, "The business of the country is almost entirely carried on by means of the paper of those banking companies."[1]

Such a system made them susceptible to forgery, so penalties were severe; frequent public hangings deterred most would-be forgers. It also made banks vulnerable to the over-issue of notes, so they presented themselves for a note exchange from time to time and in the main constrained themselves against hoarding a rival bank's notes and presenting huge amounts in a "raid". Everyone realised it was in their own interests to keep notes circulating, otherwise there would be a drain on the gold and silver reserves which would damage imports. Apart from being able to rely on a number of landowners and merchants, they also invented the overdraft. The Royal Bank was first to use this, a move which David Hume described as "one of the most ingenious ideas that has been executed in commerce".[2]

Scots not only invented the modern banking system, but fought long to maintain it, creating a modern economy from little or nothing. The Bank of England had a virtual monopoly, protected by laws which banned more than six men forming a bank. There was no such restrictions in Scotland and the two public banks were soon joined by others.

The system was founded on a dual need to both economise and extemporise and the freedom from restraint, except when self-interest and common sense made it worthwhile. A paper currency, small deposits, extended credit and a regulated note exchange brought plenty of criticisms, especially when, as was to happen, there was a banking collapse. But such disasters had more to do with individuals than the system.

The Western Bank of Glasgow collapsed in 1857. It had an authorised capital of £4 million, but four leading customers could not pay their debts because they were involved in an American commercial crisis and though the collapse of one of the city's biggest financial institutions had previously been unthinkable, murmurs abounded about the great City of Glasgow Bank whose directors stopped payments for a few days. There was a general panic in the city and military assistance came through from Edinburgh. Then all seemed to be well. The rumours were unfounded. The City of Glasgow Bank survived and no one foresaw its final collapse in

Glasgow Stock Exchange.

Detail of Mackintosh's Queen's Cross Church.

1. **Wealth of Nations**, 1776. 2. Quoted in **The Sunday Mail Story of Scotland**, 1988–89.

1878, later described as "the greatest disaster that has ever befallen the commercial community of Great Britain."[1]

By the middle of the last century, Glasgow's potteries were the only survivors of the industries started by the Tobacco Lords and other 18th century merchants. They extended the city's outer limits across the world, producing a range of genteel and industrial ware for a variety of locations and markets.

Without fireclay, it would have been impossible to reach the high temperatures required for production of iron, steel, glass and pottery. These were the building blocks of the new manufacturing industries. Blast, coke and gas furnaces relied on fireclay bricks, blocks and mouldings to contain the intense and sustained heat they generated.

The clay was unique in two ways. It was an unusually light buff colour which meant it could be used for ornamental pieces, such as fountains, chimney cans, garden edgings, urns and so on. More importantly, it was described as "a clay of unparalleled purity".[2] By 1833, the first full year of production at the Garnkirk works, the testimonials to its superior quality were rolling in.

The works could hardly have been better placed. All the raw materials, as well as the Glasgow-Garnkirk railway, were on the doorstep of the Garnkirk Coal Company and Fire Brick Work office. Before long they had expanded beyond the city with agents across the country, in Ireland and the prominent American cities, as well as France, Germany, Russia and even the West Indies.

In 1857 they opened a showroom at 243 Buchanan Street. The shop frontage was designed by Alexander "Greek" Thomson. The interiors of his buildings were given a similar care as his exteriors and he usually designed the cornices and fireplaces as well as lamps, railings, waterpipes and other details. His iron pieces were made at Walter MacFarlane's Saracen Foundry in Possilpark and for years his designs appeared in the firm's catalogue. Some of his chimneys were made at Garnkirk. They had a special lotus bud design, were fitted with a device to assist the draught and can still be seen on some Thomson buildings.

His association with the Garnkirk works began around 1850, when his friend, George Mossman, designed the piece now known as the Garnkirk Vase for the firm's stand at the 1888 Great Exhibition. Frank Worsdall rescued a copy of the vase from the Caledonian Road UP Church, just before fire gutted the interior in 1965. It had been smashed to around 60 fragments and though it has now been carefully restored, there is still a piece missing.[3] Thomson believed in bright decoration. Primary shades were used when a civilisation was

SARACEN FOUNDRY

Walter Macfarlane's Saracen Foundry has become the best known of Scotland's architectural ironworks. Its bandstands, ornamental cresting, gates and railways were widely exported.

The concern owed its name to its original location, in Saracen Lane, off Gallowgate and beside the Saracen's Head Inn. There young Walter Macfarlane in 1850 became the first ironfounder in Glasgow to specialise in architectural castings. The firm prospered, and in 1862 moved to Washington Street, Anderston, a splendid purpose built Gothic building. This soon proved too small and Macfarlanes removed to a greenfield site in Possilpark. By 1876 this covered seven acres, and by 1891 14. By that time more than 1,200 men were employed in what was by far the largest foundry in Scotland. Its range of products included every kind of architectural casting, from simple rainwater goods to the most elaborate examples of high Victorian art.

The fashion for such elaboration faded after the turn of the century, but the firm continued in operation until the early 1960s. The site has now been cleared, but products sent from Possilpark can still be found all over the world. Notable examples include the Durbar Hall in the Maharajah of Mysore's Palace in India, built just before the First World War, and a triumph of the ironfounder's art.

Other firms, notably in Glasgow, Kirkintilloch and Falkirk, followed Macfarlanes into the trade. Of these the most prolific was George Smith & Co, whose Iron Foundry in Townhead made many of the bandstands and other ornamental works in the West of Scotland often attributed to the Saracen Works.

John R Hume

Nautilus pottery.

Court Sketch of the trial of the Glasgow Bank Directors from the *Illustrated London News*, February 1, 1879.

Copy of the Garnkirk Vase.

1. The Bailie, January, 1849. 2. Gerald Quail, Garnkirk Fire-Clay, 1985. 3. ibid.

A ST ROLLOX APPRENTICESHIP

St Rollox works were built by the Caledonian Railway about 1850. They provided all the facilities required for the construction and repair of steam locomotives, carriages and wagons and in the steam era a St Rollox apprenticeship provided a good practical grounding in mechanical engineering practice.

Craft apprenticeships lasted from the ages of 16 to 21. Among the wide range of crafts or trades employed in the works were fitters, turners, brass-finishers, boilermakers, coppersmiths, patternmakers, moulders and blacksmiths.

The apprentice fitters spent most of their time in the fitting and erecting shops where the workforce was divided into squads. Each squad attended to specific parts of the locomotive such as motion work, brake gear, frames, boiler mountings and pipework. Apprentices moved from squad to squad so that they became familiar with the full range of work. Each apprentice worked with a journeyman fitter who was expected to instruct him in the essentials of the trade. The work was hard, physically demanding and dirty, especially in the erecting and boiler shops where the noise levels would nowadays be considered intolerable and a health risk. The apprentice fitters also worked in the machine shop, operating lathes, shaping machines and milling machines, a practice not followed in other works, but which provided the fitters with valuable additional experience.

Apprentices were encouraged to attend evening classes in mechanical engineering subjects to supplement the practical training. Attendance at such classes, generally from 7.15pm to 9.45pm three evenings per week, added to the long working day and meant that academic success was as much a test of stamina as intellect.

John Menzies

at its peak, he thought. Pastel shades were decadent. So the Garnkirk Vase was brightly painted, matching the church's interior.

By 1870 the Garnkirk Fire Clay Company employed 300 men and boys and went through 200 tons of clay and coal a day. The estate covered 35 acres and had its own railway system. The rapid growth and success of the Garnkirk works, as well as the other clay and coal pits in the area, had its effect on the village, which grew from a row of houses to a small town, whose population was almost entirely made up of Irish immigrant families. Irish labour had been used from the outset, particularly in the unskilled end of the process. By the 1850s the majority of Garnkirk's population was Irish, but most skilled jobs were still in Scots hands.[1]

Garnkirk was very much a company town. Early on there were complaints that the company's system of monthly payments meant their village store became the only place to shop. It was also claimed employees could be sacked for not using the store. Housing conditions were poor, with minimum sanitation. While the factory was producing the latest in piping and tiles for the growing luxury bathroom end of the market, their workforce were living in huts with communal toilets emptied by a man with horse and cart. There was a water pump in the middle of the village to supply all its inhabitants.

Ironically, one of Garnkirk's most important new products catered for the growing cities' newly discovered need for piped water and sanitation. Salt glazed pipes were first advertised in 1851, with a complex series of junctions and as many different bores and sizes as was considered necessary.

Paving tiles and bricks catered for the housing boom. The company also went in for mouldings, features and busts of heroes, such as James Watt and Henry Bell. They felt so secure they even supplied raw clay to other manufacturers.

The Garnkirk employees were encouraged to feel their jobs were safe. Mouldings could be produced by machine, but it was faster and more economic to make bricks by hand. A moulder and his assistant, working with wooden or brass moulds, could turn out between four and five thousand bricks a day.

The pits were eventually exhausted and the premises sold in 1901. There were still fireclay pits nearby in Cardowan, Gartcosh and Heathfield and the Garnkirk workers transferred to the nearby mines or the local distillery.

Too much of Glasgow speaks of past industry and present paralysis. Possilpark, Springburn and many similar districts are

The boiler shop, the Cowlairs railway works, Springburn.

1. ibid.

amongst the challenges to be faced if Glasgow is to achieve anything more than the sweeping of social problems under the carpet.

Much of Possilpark represents Bad Old Glasgow. And the place, maybe like the city itself, is caught between its image and the attempts the community are making to repair themselves and their territory.

In 1869 the hundred acres of Nether Possil were sold to Walter MacFarlane who cleared the site for the third incarnation of his Saracen Steel Works. The Possil Estate was completed in 1871, with £25,250 worth of additions between 1897 and 1902. The works covered 14 acres, with a rectangle block of single storey buildings and large, Gothic doorways, surmounted by the name of the company, where ornamental ironwork was much in evidence.

Possil was the perfect place for MacFarlane's business. It was near the loco works in Springburn, who used his products. The Forth and Clyde depot at Port Dundas had opened up new trading areas in and beyond the city. The road from MacFarlane's works to Port Dundas was called Saracen Street.

Possil already had some industry in the area. A mine produced "several varieties of good coal" with seams which stretched to Kelvinside, Hillhead and Partick and which threatened the West End's expansion, including the new university building at Gilmorehill, because of subsidence. Coal from this and other Glasgow mines were given the sort of names you still find occasionally in newspaper letter columns: Jewel of Giffnock, Stinking of Cowglen.[1]

The new town of Possilpark was laid out around MacFarlane's gates to house the Saracen's workforce, which was 1,200 in 1892.

Saracen castings, with their motto "Sharp, Clean and Full of Character", supplied Britain and the World with ornamental water pipes, roof terminals, gutters, grates, fountains, troughs, plumbers' and builders' castings, ventilators, sanitary appliances and a host of other useful articles. The magazine *Mechanical Engineering* said, "The productions of this well-known firm are to be found in every part of the civilised world."[2]

Many other businesses were attracted to Possilpark, though the Saracen Works was the main employer, continuing until 1965 when they were taken over by Federated Foundries. Demolition followed in 1967.

With the main employer gone, the feeder industries also left Possil and its people to fend for themselves, while Glasgow as a whole compensated for the withdrawal of the manufacturers which had been its life blood by ripping its heart out and building motorways.

THE GLASGOW BOYS

At the beginning of the 1880s a group of young painters in Glasgow set out to change public attitudes to modern painting in Scotland. Inspired by the work of James McNeill Whistler, Jean-Francois Millet and the young French painter Jules Bastien Lepage, they worked towards a new style, "naturalism".

They chose to paint direct from nature, shunning subjects contrived in the studio. Lepage's paintings were unemotional and apolitical and the Boys followed him in recording farming communities whose way of life was virtually unknown in large cities such as Glasgow.

Although almost two dozen artists are associated with the Glasgow School (they preferred to be known as "The Boys"), only about nine or ten made any real contribution to its development. Some of these trained in France, with John Lavery, while others followed James Guthrie to Cockburnspath in Berwickshire where he lived for three years.

In 1890 the group exhibited together at the Grosvenor Gallery in London. From here they were asked to show in Munich and other invitations followed from Barcelona, Paris, Berlin, St Petersburg, Vienna, Pittsburgh, Chicago and New York.

By 1895 most of the painters had left Glasgow and their work had changed considerably from the innovative painting of 1885. But they had achieved their ambition of arresting the decline of Scottish painting. The Royal Scottish Academy was forced to open its doors to them, abandoning its requirement of Edinburgh residence.

Their work and their achievement of international recognition was to inspire Scottish artists for the next 50 years or more.

Roger Billcliffe

Sketch of visit by Queen Victoria, by John Lavery.

1. C.A. Oakley, **The Second City**, 1946 2. ibid.

Nautilus Porcelain was made in the Possil Pottery, between the corners of Saracen Street and Denmark Street, facing MacFarlane's Saracen Foundry. At best, they benefited from both business acumen and a sound knowledge of pottery manufacture, a combination which was not as common as one might expect. During their time as Glasgow's only porcelain manufacturer, the Possil Pottery could match the best work from Limoges, Balleek or Worcester. Examples are highly prized by collectors, galleries and museums.[1]

The brewers J & R Tennent, who still do the business at their Wellpark Brewery, bought the premises in 1918 and Possil returned to stoneware production, mostly making beer bottles. In 1948 the pottery became a storehouse and was demolished in 1974. Today the Keppoch Nursery School occupies the site.

A Nautilus porcelain cup and saucer.

THE LIFE AND DEATH OF A RAILWAY COMMUNITY

Springburn has been the beneficiary of one transport revolution – the railway – and the victim of another – the motorway. It was once a village of weavers and miners but following the establishment of the area's four railway works speculative builders erected a city of tenements according to the classic Glasgow pattern. By 1900 there were 30,000 people living in Sprinburn. Conditions were often squalid but the highest paid skilled workers, along with doctors, clergy and teachers stayed in villas on Balgrayhill.

In a society where the only recourse during illness or poverty was the poor law, people developed a defensive culture, based on mutual help through family networks and voluntary associations. Friendly societies, trades unions and the Cowlairs Co-operative provided the thrifty with some security, and a means of taking part in local society. While the industries prospered, the magnates gave to churches and schools, promoting those aspects of co-operation they approved of, and discouraging others, such as trades unionism. The area's economic base was in decline from before the First World War and finally collapsed in the 1960s. The high unemployment undermined the community.

The Expressway built through the old centre delivered the final blow, especially galling in a place where 84 per cent of families do not own a car. It is a tribute to the people of Springburn that the spirit of the community survives, waiting for suitable soil in which to flourish.

Mark O'Neill

1. Their speciality was a reproduction of the nautilus shell, said to be as delicate as the original.

Chapter Twenty

SILVER AND CLAY

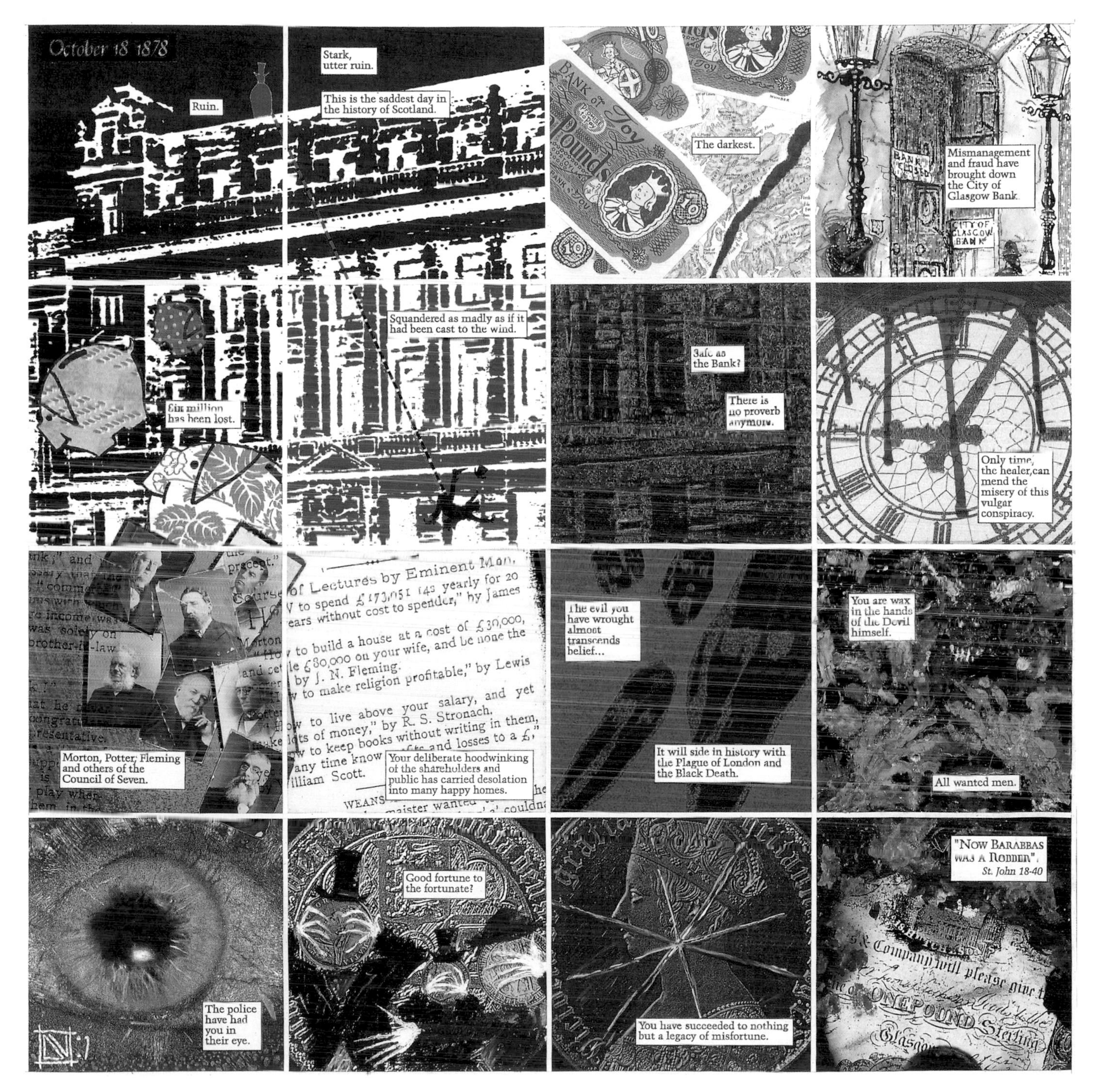

CITY OF GLASGOW BANK COLLAPSE, *by* Danny Vallely.

Highland dwelling, Morar, Invernesshire.

STAINED GLASS

The revival of the medieval art of stained-glass took place much later in Scotland than in England, chiefly because of the Calvinist attitude towards any art form in church buildings. The Catholic and Episcopal Churches imported their windows from England where any inhibitions had been broken down earlier, and where, by the 1840s, a number of firms were specialising in stained-glass and other decorative work.

However, the new art form was being popularised by such practitioners as James Ballantine in Edinburgh, and Stephen Adam and the Kiers in Glasgow, and by the 1880s it had become common for memorial windows to be erected by private donors, particularly in United Presbyterian and Church of Scotland buildings.

From the 1890s specialist stained-glass artists began to appear. They might well be considered a parallel and contemporary movement to that of the "Glasgow Boys" school of painting. In fact many of "the Boys" also made designs for stained-glass, notably David Gauld and Harrington Mann.

There are extremely good collections in Eastwood Parish Church at Pollokshaws and Shettleston Parish Church in the East End, both general in character. At Lansdowne Church, Kelvinbridge, are two outstanding large windows by Alfred Webster, full of compelling detail, and completed not long before his tragic death at the Battle of the Somme in 1915. As an example of domestic glass, there is a fascinating group of windows at 12 University Gardens in different styles, by one of the most interesting of the Glasgow artists, Oscar Paterson.

Frank Worsdall

Chapter Twenty-one

THE HEILANMAN'S UMBRELLA

The interior of a Skye black house, photographed in 1905.

St Kilda is 45 miles to the west of the most westerly point of North Uist on the Outer Hebrides. Nowadays its only human presence is an Army garrison of 40 men. When the island was evacuated in September 1930, most of its inhabitants came to Glasgow. What they made of us is not recorded, though an earlier St Kildan found the place baffling.

Martin Martin was born in Skye in 1655. He travelled extensively round the Western Isles and in May, 1697, he sailed to St Kilda in an open boat. He recounted his journeys in *A Description of the Western Islands of Scotland*, published in London in 1703. This was yet another Scottish work disliked by Dr Johnson, though he used it as a guide book for his own visit to the Highlands.

Martin had an unusual approach to Glasgow, recording the impressions the city made upon a St Kildan: "When he went through the Streets he desired to have one to lead him by the hand. Thomas Ross, a merchant, and others . . . ask'd his Opinion of the High Church? He answer'd, that it was a large Rock, yet there were some in St Kilda much higher, but that these were the best caves he ever saw . . .

"When he saw the Women's feet, he judged them to be of another shape than those of the Men, because of the different shape of their Shoes. He did not approve of the heels of Shoes worn by Men or Women; and when he observ'd Horses with shoes on their Feet, and fastened with Iron Nails, he could not forbear laughing, and thought it the most ridiculous things that ever fell under his Observation. He long'd to see his Native Country again, and passionately wish'd it were blessed with Ale, Brandy, Tobacco and Iron, as Glasgow was". [1]

Glasgow's effect on its immigrant millions may not have been so spectacular, but it was surely no less immediate. Like any city, this place has attracted its share of outsiders hoping for a future. Folk memory has preserved the notion of migratory movements

The interior of a Lewis cottage of the 1840s.

St Kildans packing their cloth.

1. Martin Martin, A Description of the Western Islands of Scotland, 1703.

THE TRANSIENT TENANT

As the pace of industrial change in 19th century Glasgow quickened so the number of people seeking temporary lodgings increased. People away from or without permanent homes included labourers seeking work, women and children put out of their homes, single women without friends and many of both sexes and all ages travelling in search of something better.

The philanthropic response – there was no municipal involvement in housing in those days – was vigorous and, according to the standards of the day, effective. The remedies provided included the Night Asylums and Lodging Houses, while a few were helped in the Poor House. The Night Asylums (f.1838) and the Lodging Houses (f.1847) became ever busier. The latter were in course of time taken over by the Corporation of Glasgow, mainly to improve standards of cleanliness.

The record of the philanthropists in providing temporary accommodation for a mobile population in Victorian Scotland was impressive. At this level of provision the relationship between the city authorities (usually acting through the police) and the philanthropic manager was close and harmonious. In Glasgow, where the problem of the houseless remained acute, the town council was responsive to demand and quickly took overall responsibility for model lodging houses.

The demand for temporary accommodation has shown no signs of slackening although the Night Asylums and the Lodging Houses have long gone. There will always be some who require temporary shelter.

Olive Checkland

stemming from the Highlands to the Lowlands, but the 1851 census shows 53 per cent of Glasgow's residents were Lowland Scots born outside the city. Migration within the country was a necessary part of the swift and total transformation of Scottish society in the 19th century. Most obvious was the rise of industry, particularly in Glasgow, which was partly sustained by the low cost of labour.

Eighteenth century migration was dominated by Lowlanders who, sharing linguistic and cultural backgrounds, assimilated far more easily than their Highland or Irish counterparts. Lowland migration into Glasgow continued until the middle of the 19th century. The common denominator of all immigrants was poverty, which forced them into the shabbiest housing.

Gorbals was the nearest Glasgow came to having a ghetto, with distinct ethnic groups settling in the area. Jewish culture was, for example, highly visible, but the community was by no means dominated by any single ethnic group. The Great Central Synagogue in Laurieston has been replaced by the Glasgow Central Mosque and Islamic Centre. Today's mythology has firmly identified the Gorbals with violent squalor, the worst housing and living conditions in Glasgow at a time when Glasgow's were the worst in Europe. All of which spread the fearful Gorbals name across the world. After the Second World War when Glasgow began its utopian redevelopment schemes, Gorbals headed the list of places to be altered or removed.

Gorbals was a 17th century burgh, laid out as a fashionable 19th century suburb and later swallowed by city expansion. In the 1930s, it was home to over 90,000 people.

When the Industrial Revolution arrived, buildings were demolished to make way for the new railway lines and the sky was lit by Dixon's Blazes. The old Main Street was cancelled and Gorbals Cross became the area's centre point. The newer Gorbals retained some of its old character. The streets were laid out in a broad design with four storeyed tenements which kept a classical influence. In the Thirties, the Gorbals had dozens of cinemas, more than 130 pubs and over 1,000 shops. It was the natural place for the new immigrant communities cramming into Glasgow. Houses were sub-divided and fell into disrepair. There was one toilet for every three houses and 94 per cent had no bath. By the Fifties most were unsuitable for human habitation.[1]

Glasgow had been trading with the Highlands and Islands since the 16th century. The first Highland Society was formed in 1727 at the Black Bull Inn. Glasgow's first Gaelic Church was established in Queen Street in 1767. The Highland evacuation continued into

DIXON'S BLAZES

The Parish of Govan stretched along the Clyde from Renfrew to Rutherglen, with a portion to the north of the river, including the village of Partick. By the late 18th century the coal in the south coast of the parish was being extensively worked to supply Glasgow. A wooden railway linked the scattered pits of Govan Colliery to a depot and point of shipment on the river at West Street.

Among those attracted to the ironmaking business by the Hot Blast process was William Dixon, of Northumbrian extraction, then owner of the Govan Colliery. He built his ironworks from 1839 on what must have been a brownfield site worked over by coal extraction beyond the southern limits of planned building in Gorbals and Hutchesontown. As was the practice at the time, his six blast furnaces were open-topped, and their flames lit up the night sky – hence the name Dixon's Blazes. It was linked to the Clyde by a Dixon-owned railway.

Dixon's Blazes continued in operation from the 1930s, in the ownership of Colvilles Ltd, until the late 1950s, when Ravenscraig came on stream. Its small blast furnaces were by that time relatively inefficient. Its coke ovens lasted a little longer, but by 1960 the site was cleared. Today the site is an industrial estate, and the housewives of the South Side do not need to worry about the red grime from one of Glasgow's most celebrated industries.

John R Hume

1. The Gorbals Heritage Trail Guide, 1988.

Old Irish couple.

Joseph Swan's view of Gorbals Chapel and the Elphinstone Tower.

Messrs Montgomery, Campbell and Allan, citizens of Glasgow, standing at the Gorbals Cross fountain, November, 1917.

the 19th century. Those who came south were originally seasonal agricultural workers, though some worked at building the canals. The Glasgow police force was a popular employer for Highland migrants after 1800 and the cotton mills, mines and heavy industry, as well as the merchant navy, were common Highland occupations. The textile industry employed men, women and children in a variety of jobs.

By 1831, there were 39,000 Highlanders resident in Glasgow, though how many survived the following year's cholera epidemic is not known. The settlement pattern was similar to other immigrants: in the cheapest housing where disease was rife, firstly in the High Street and Saltmarket slums.

Then Glasgow's Highlanders developed their affinity with the western end of the city, particularly the area around Argyle Street and Anderston. Glasgow was a magnet for West Coast Highlanders and the Islanders; East Coast Highlanders tended to gravitate to Aberdeen, Dundee or Edinburgh. Another important Highland link which developed throughout the 19th century was in the field of education, where Glasgow University became and still is, a favourite institution for Highland students. There was a huge influx of Highlanders following the famine of 1923 and 1924 and the Highlanders Institute was opened in Elmbank Street in 1925, moving to Berkeley Street and then disbanded. The Park Bar, Argyle Street, retains Glasgow's links with the north as a focal point for incoming and resident Highlanders, many of whom stay in the Finnieston and Kelvingrove hotels and guesthouses. In 1981 there were 9,500 Gaelic speakers in Glasgow.[1]

Glasgow's Highlanders were often treated in the same way as the Irish immigrants and due to their distinctive language, beautiful to our ears, were viewed as inferior, immoral subjects of ridicule. They became useful scapegoats for the indigenous population, the lot of the immigrant throughout the ages. The charge of immorality was especially double edged. In the minds of middle class Victorians, immorality was an inevitable consequence of living in an over-crowded slum, where many bodies were crammed into small rooms. Moreover, many immigrants lost their links with the church when they came to the city. For example, Irish priests are not recorded as settling in Glasgow until the 1850s. Many earlier immigrants were reported to have lost their faith in the sin-filled city, where Sunday working, which many factories and works demanded, was another road to immorality. So was the consumption of alcohol.

Evidence of Irish immigration into Glasgow can be found from the late 17th century, but in 1790 there were only 39 Roman

CHARLES MACINTOSH
(1766–1843)

Charles Macintosh's invention of the waterproof came about in a way closely integrated with social and economic change in 18th and 19th century Scotland. Macintosh's father George was a Highlander from Easter Ross. He came to Glasgow and set up as a shoemaker on a large scale, exporting to the North American colonies. In 1773 he employed 500 men. As a sideline he took over a process invented by Patrick & Cuthbert Gordon of Edinburgh for making Cudbear, a dyestuff, from lichen. He built in 1777 a "secret" works in Dennistoun, with a high wall round it, and employed only Gaelic-speaking Highlanders, who lived in the compound.

Charles after a successful career as a maker of alum and other chemicals used in dyeing succeeded his father in the Cudbear business. One of the new materials used in the process was ammonia, for which the only economic source was then fermented human urine. When gas lighting was introduced into Glasgow in 1818 the gas works produced among other by-products a liquid containing ammonia, and Macintosh experimented with this as an alternative. In doing so he isolated a light oil, naphtha, which he found would dissolve rubber.

Cloth coated with rubber solution was waterproof, but tacky when warm and hard when cold. By sticking the rubbery faces together a sandwich was produced which was entirely waterproof and much more satisfactory. This was Macintosh cloth, first made in Glasgow in 1824. His other outstanding contribution, the invention of bleaching powder, was patented by his friend Charles Tennant, and his involvement is seldom remembered.

John R Hume

1. City Profile, Facts and Figures About Glasgow, 1985, and Strathclyde Social Trends No. 2, October, 1989.

CELTIC

Celtic (founded in 1887 in St Mary's church hall, Calton and first playing in 1888) are often said to have been instituted for charitable reasons. So they were, contributing in the early years to soup kitchens in the East End. The real purpose of the middle class businessmen founders, however, was to provide a focal point of pride and achievement for the despised Irish immigrants.

The Irish have long since been assimilated but Celtic and their supporters continue to relish the image of romantic rebels. Although the first Celtic sides were formed by ruthlessly plundering the ranks of other clubs and offering illegal payments, a tradition was quickly established of rearing their own, often individualistic talents. The attackers are the most celebrated – eldritch Patsy Gallacher and prolific scorer Jimmy McGrory in the Twenties and Thirties; Kenny Dalglish and Paul McStay in modern times. Players have always been signed irrespective of religion, but the board has remained Catholic.

Celtic's greatest period has been the Sixties and early Seventies, under the management of former player and ex-miner Jock Stein. Nine successive championships were won and Celtic became the first British side to win the European Cup in 1967. That exhilarating team featured the the play-making passing of Bobby Murdoch and the heart-stopping trickery of diminutive winger Jimmy Johnstone.

The side was imperiously captained by present manager Billy McNeill. As a private limited company, Celtic principally remain in the hands of three families. It will be intriguing to see if that structure can be successfully maintained as football elsewhere is placed on a more orthodox commercial basis.

Kevin McCarra

Catholics reportedly living in Glasgow. Ireland also had a long tradition of trade and immigration with Scotland, particularly on a seasonal basis; the farmlands of Stirlingshire, Lothians and the Borders attracted landless agricultural Irish labourers, who also came to dig the canals and even today, the homes of Donegal continue to supply construction workers who return home in the summer, working until harvest.

By 1805 there were 450 Roman Catholics in Glasgow, 3,000 in 1810 and 15,000 in 1822.[1] This very rough guide is based upon the assumption that the overwhelming majority of Irish immigrants were Roman Catholics.

They came at the same time as the Highlanders and for very similar reasons, especially during the famine years in the middle of the 19th century, when steam powered ferries dramatically reduced the price of passage after 1818.

Again the slums of High Street and Saltmarket attracted the early 19th century incomers. The Briggait became a favoured Irish area, close as it was to Clyde Street and Glasgow's first post-Reformation Catholic cathedral, which was opened in 1816. The first Catholic parish since the Reformation had been established in and around the Saltmarket in 1792.

The Irish settlements crossed the water into Gorbals, especially when the core of the area was over-run with industry. The Irish also extended eastwards into the Calton, westwards to Anderston and to Cowcaddens in the north. The first Catholic schools were established in Anderston, Bridgeton and the Gorbals. In 1817, the Catholic Schools Society was formed, funded by community subscription, though it wasn't until the 1870s and 1880s that Catholic schooling developed to any great extent, following the introduction of compulsory education.

In 1831, 35,000 Glasgow residents had been born in Ireland and immigration to this country was so bad that in 1835 a Commission of Inquiry was launched into *The State of The Irish Poor in Great Britain*. Glasgow's Superintendent of Public Works James Cleland reported in 1837 that one fifth of Glasgow's paupers were Irish.[2] At the height of the famine in 1845, there were around 8,000 Irish immigrants reportedly coming to Glasgow every week. Not all stayed. Like the Highlanders, they followed a stepwise emigration pattern, using Glasgow as a stopping off point before travelling on to North America and Australasia. The majority who came were obviously destitute. They and the Highlanders must have been the main victims of Glasgow's cholera epidemics, which accounted for 4,000 deaths in four weeks of 1848 and 1849, when parishes had the

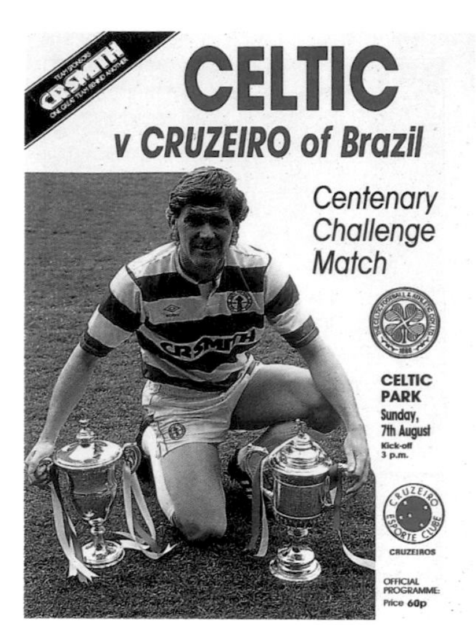

Programme for Celtic's centenary match, 1988.

A facsimile of the European Cup, which Celtic won in 1967.

1. Tom Gallagher, **Glasgow: The Uneasy Peace**, 1987. 2. See ibid.

RANGERS

Rangers, like all other clubs of the time, were formed (in 1872) simply for leisure purposes. Their origins lie amongst a group of young men who met on Glasgow Green. Despite early promise their rise to eminence really came in response to the appearance of Celtic. The often bitter feud between them has since filled the coffers of both. The term "Old Firm" was first used sardonically.

The role of Establishment club came naturally to Rangers but it was honed by William Struth, manager from 1920–54. A military discipline was imposed. At away games he would march the Rangers party, clad in overcoats and bowler hats, arms swinging in time, from the train station to the ground. Opponents were intimidated.

Rangers had the players to justify the image. From the Twenties to the Sixties they dominated Scottish football. In addition to the stalwarts like George Young, in the Fifties, and then John Greig there was always room for artists. Left winger, Alan Morton, in the Twenties, and Davie Cooper are two of the most gifted players Scotland has ever produced. The club's most glorious star was perhaps the arrogant, languid midfielder Jim Baxter in the Sixties.

Although winning the Cup Winners, Cup, in 1972, Rangers languished for a time. Then, with breathtaking boldness Lawrence Marlborough (and now David Murray) boosted expenditure, trusting that revenue would follow it upwards. Graeme Souness was attracted as manager in 1986, and a host of English internationals in his wake.

Despite its novelty and enterprise, Murray's quest is also for a return to past supremacy.

Kevin McCarra

authority to send the Irish back and around 1,000 a month were repatriated.

The Irish were also treated with suspicion and derision. The indigenous population despised the destitute incomers for requesting and receiving parish relief, accusing them of lowering wages and strike breaking. Glasgow's mid-19th century workforce was uncommonly highly skilled, so their jobs were largely insulated from the Irish, but feelings ran high, especially in the mines, where the Irish were more than willing to take on the dangerous work. Anti-Catholicism was well established in Glasgow, but the upsurge of sectarian violence in that period coincides with the influx of Ulster Protestants to the city. In 1868, 600 marched on July 12; by the 1870s 10,000 marchers assembled.[1]

Immigration from Ireland has been significantly less this century. In 1921 only 65,688 Glaswegians had been born in Ireland. Sectarianism did not stop with the lessening of the Irish immigrant boats.

Trapped by poverty, lack of skills and education, the newcomers found themselves further disadvantaged by discrimination. The coded question, "What school did you go to?" became commonplace, along with the more obvious signs of a bar on white collar jobs, including notices bearing the simple legend, "No Irish Need Apply". Surnames, Christian names, closes, streets, pubs and professions became identified along sectarian lines. Resentment against the permanent rather than seasonal Irish spilled over into the riots surrounding the 1829 Catholic Emancipation Act and reappeared whenever moves were made to increase Roman Catholic rights. The Unionist Tory Party would quickly learn to mobilise the Orange machine in its support, while the Labour Party eventually weaned the Scots Irish away from an almost obsessional interest in Ireland to a firm support of Labour in Scotland.

Slow improvements in working and living conditions, the break up of traditional Catholic and Protestant areas in the post-war rehousing drive and the simple passage of time has helped to bring down the barriers between the communities. Cynics might say the attention has now shifted to more recent and conspicuous immigrants in a Scotland which still believes it isn't racist.[2]

As Glasgow becomes increasingly paranoid lest its dirty washing be glimpsed in public, the city's sectarian past is being ignored. In a country obsessed with history and historical division, it remains to be seen how long this particular sleeping dog will lie.

When Rangers signed Maurice Johnston two days before the Twelfth of July, 1989, grown men were crying outside Ibrox.

"The Potato Diggers" by Paul Henry.

The official souvenir programme for Rangers Centenary Celebration game with Ajax in 1973.

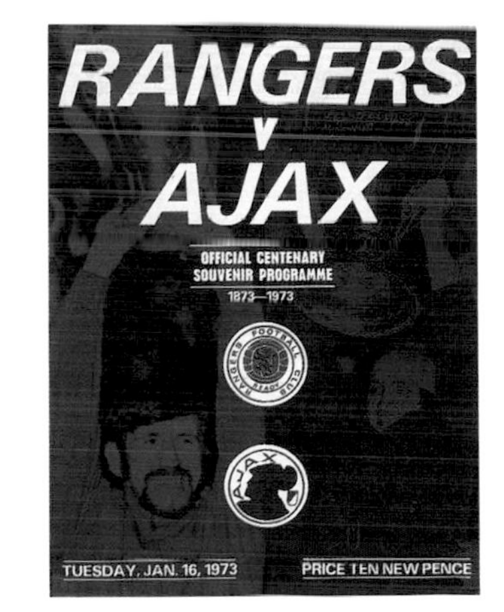

1. ibid. 2. When Glasgow Rangers signed Mark Walters some fans threw bananas onto the pitch.

The signing displeased many. Johnston is a Roman Catholic who had previously signed for Celtic in a heralded return to Scottish football, but the deal fell through over what were referred to as tax problems, but looked like greed. Television audiences were told that Maurice Johnston would not be welcomed in the Lanarkshire village of Larkhall, where Protestants outnumber Catholics by 18 to one. It was, the locals said, a sad day for the town. Outside Ibrox Stadium, angry supporters insisted that they simply did not like the man and the fact he was a Catholic had nothing to do with their feelings.

The walls of the East End of Glasgow are no strangers to graffiti: "Collaborators Can't Play Without Kneecaps", it said outside Bellgrove railway station. "Souness You Roman Bastard", appeared elsewhere. This being Glasgow, last word is given to the genius who wrote, on a motorway embankment, "Mo Surrender".

Like the Irish, European Jews had travelled to Scotland on business for centuries, though the country's first Jewish community emerged in late 18th century Edinburgh. The first reference to a Jewish settler in Glasgow concerns a burgess certificate being granted to Isaac Cohen in 1812.[1]

A High Street room and kitchen became Glasgow's first synagogue in 1823.[2] In 1831 Cleland's census found 47 Jews living in Glasgow. One of their number, a quill merchant named Joseph Levi, was the first person interred in the new Necropolis, having died in the cholera epidemic of September 1832. In 1836 a "suburb of the city of the dead" was built shortly after the Necropolis was opened. The ground of the Jews' Enclosure was bought from the Merchants' House for 100 guineas, raised by a general subscription in the synagogue. The entrance was designed after Absolom's pillar in the King's Dale, Jerusalem, with scriptural extracts and Byron's "Hebrew Melodies" below the scroll. Jewish law forbade one body to be buried on top of another, so the enclosure was soon filled, even after the wash-room, where bodies were prepared immediately before interment, had been removed. The Jews' Enclosure was filled by 1857 and the tombstones outside the enclosure are of Jews who married Gentiles.[3]

By 1850 there were 200 practising Jews in Glasgow and one of their number was the first Jewish student to enrol at Glasgow University. Asher Asher was also the first Jewish doctor to graduate from Glasgow. New synagogues had been opened behind Candleriggs and on George Street, showing the community's concentration in the old city. By 1879 sufficient numbers of the Jewish community had moved west to create a new synagogue in the Garnethill area.

The westward expansion continued throughout the late 19th and

GORBALS SYNAGOGUE LIFE

Jewish religious life in Gorbals was characterised by its vigour and colour as well as by division and disagreement. The first Gorbals synagogues date back to 1880 in small converted workshops but the influx of Jews into the area brought a need for larger places of worship. In 1898 a former Baptist Church in Oxford Street was converted for use as a synagogue. The South Portland Street synagogue (1901) accommodating 1,000 worshippers was the centre of Glasgow Jewish religious life, always open for prayer, traditional Talmudic learning and recitation of the Psalms and its basement contained a *mikva*, the Jewish ritual bath.

A split within the Oxford Street Synagogue in 1902 led to the formation of the Beth Medrash Hagodol, the "Large Study House", for many years in Govan Street before moving to Hospital Street. By the early years of the 20th century many small *shteibles*, or conventicles, were to be found around the Gorbals. Some brought together Jews who had come from the same areas of eastern Europe while others reflected trades and occupations. The Poalei Zedek in Oxford Street was known as the workingmen's synagogue while the Jewish Tailors' Union held services for the New year and Day of Atonement.

Other small prayer groups reflected different strands in Jewish religious life. The Beth Jacob in Abbotsford Place and the Nusach Ari in Oxford Street were Chassidic, or pietistic and revivalist, in outlook. The post-war decline of the once great Gorbals community, as Glasgow Jews moved out to the southern suburbs, led to various synagogue amalgamations. Eventually only South Portland Street was left but it too had to face the inevitable. Its closure in 1974 brought to an end 94 years of Jewish religious life in the Gorbals.

Kenneth Collins

Faces in the crowd at Hampden.

Collins cap-making factory in Oxford Street, Gorbals.

1. Dr Kenneth Collins, **Aspects of Scottish Jewry**, 1987. **2.** ibid. **3.** **The Glasgow Necropolis Heritage Trail Guide, 1985.**

MY SON, THE DOCTOR

As the children of the Jewish immigrants in Glasgow completed their schooling in their new land of Scotland they were encouraged to develop their intellectual potential to the full. Despite economic pressures, there were many who were prepared to make the financial sacrifices to see that at least one member of the family could get to university, above all to study medicine. The Jewish tradition encouraged the study of medicine and recognised it as an important profession. In the years after the First World War increasing numbers of Jews began to enter the three medical schools in Glasgow.

This desire to become doctors was found in every section of Glasgow Jewry. During the 1920s and 1930s Jews from all walks of life, from both the Gorbals and the West End entered the medical profession. The movement into medicine created within Glasgow Jewry its first significant professional group and marked the changing character of the community out of a dependence on the old ghetto trades.

Glasgow Jewry also developed its artistic side with the sculptor Benno Schotz leading many talented painters and writers. Avrom Greenbaum developed the modern Jewish theatrical tradition in Glasgow and the novels of Chaim Bermant and plays of C.P. Taylor have portrayed different aspects of Glasgow Jewry. Memories of the immigrant period have been evoked by Evelyn Cowan, who recalls the sentimentality of a happy Gorbals childhood, and Ralph Glasser, who has described his bitter fight to escape from the Gorbals squalor.

Kenneth Collins

early 20th century, with many Jewish families settling in Hillhead and Kelvinside. During this time an increasing number of Eastern European Jewish immigrants came to Scotland, fleeing a repressive Russian regime which controlled huge areas of Poland and the Baltic and was persecuting Jews within Russia itself. Between 1881 and 1930, an estimated four million Jews fled from Eastern Europe and 200,000 stayed in this country.

Most Eastern European Jews were destitute by the time they arrived here, gravitating to the familiar destination of the Gorbals. The Eastern European Jews spoke Yiddish and retained more of their distinctive culture than the cosmopolitan Jews who were living in the West End. In the main, the Gorbals attracted poor Jews, who found work hawking, peddling and tailoring, but also in the furniture and tobacco trades.

The first southside synagogue was established in Commerce Street in 1881; by the 1890s, the Gorbals Jewish community was larger than the northern settlement. A distress fund to help the Jews from Eastern Europe was established in Glasgow in 1891. The strength and growth of the Gorbals community is illustrated by the development of the synagogues in the area, where a Cherra Kaddish Congregation was founded in 1889. The Buchan Street Synagogue was opened in 1897, and in 1899 they acquired the site for the Great Synagogue in South Portland Street. The Great Synagogue was beset by financial troubles, which again highlighted a lack of commitment on the part of the more prosperous Jews living north of the river to the south.

The Great Synagogue was opened in 1901, the same year the Glasgow Hebrew Benevolent Society was formed to help Jews start up in business. The Jewish Institute was formed in 1900 and the Jewish Lads' Brigade, a pipe band, and the Oxford Star, a Glasgow Jewish football team, were early developments. In 1906, a Working Men's Synagogue was opened in Oxford Street. Despite the creation of a strong and significant community built on shared baking facilities, kosher food co-operatives, a network of religious and cultural societies and Jewish newspapers, suburbanisation was well underway. By the 1930s, when Jewish flights from Europe, this time mostly from Germany, were increasing, a second wave moved in to replace those Jews leaving the Gorbals. In 1933, Glasgow boycotted German goods in protest against the way Jews were being treated and in 1939, a hostel for Jewish immigrants was established in Garnethill, beside the Glasgow Refugee Centre where "friendly aliens" contributed to the war effort.[1]

Scotland and Poland have shared cultural and trade links since the

The Bedford Street entrance of the Hebrew Christian Beth Hamidrash (House of Study) in October 1917.

Jewish servicemen outside South Portland Street Synagogue in 1917.

1. Letter in the **Glasgow Herald**, November 3, 1988.

VICTORIAN GLASGOW – A MECCA FOR THE JAPANESE?

In late Victorian Glasgow you could have found a Japanese working next to you in the shipyard, sitting next to you in lecture hall or experimenting next to you in the laboratory. Why was Glasgow so popular with young Japanese engineers and shipbuilders?

The answer lies in the shipbuilding yards along the Clyde and in the lecture rooms, workshops and laboratories in College and University in Glasgow. The establishment of the University of Glasgow's Chair of Engineering in 1840, followed by the John Elder Chair of Naval Architecture (1883) together with the re-organisation of the Glasgow & West of Scotland College (1887) – later the University of Strathclyde – made Glasgow for the Japanese, and others of many nationalities, a Mecca. Further, the Japanese were good customers. Clyde shipbuilders had reason to be grateful to them. When the Japanese client made it a condition of placing the order that his own people should work as "apprentices" in the building of "his" ship it was agreed.

Some 60 Japanese attended the University of Glasgow after 1880. Some came for short courses and at the same time worked in the shipyards; others came for full degree courses. Some struggled to succeed; others distinguished themselves and won Class Prizes.

Ultimately it was the ability of those who as academics were also active in industry, which attracted the Japanese. Of these Lord Kelvin with his academic distinction, his industrial concerns and his patents was the exemplar.

Olive Checkland

Middle Ages. A Scot, Andrew Chalmers, was Mayor of Warsaw in the 16th century and by the start of the 17th 30,000 Scots were living in Poland. There was, however, little Polish emigration to Scotland until the 19th century when work in the mines and heavy industry beckoned. By 1931 several hundred Poles were resident in Glasgow and during the Second World War, their numbers were increased by soldiers and refugees. In 1942, the community became strong enough to support a school for Polish students at Dalbeath in the East End of Glasgow and in 1943, a Polish Commercial College was founded in the Cowcaddens. There were 3,000 Polish born men and women living in Glasgow in 1984, but many more second and third generation Poles live in the city.

Scotland's aristocracy has always considered the ability to speak Italian a desirable accomplishment which intensified their enjoyment of Italian art, music and literature. The rest of us, not so linguistically accomplished, converted the tongue to our own understanding; so that when the street vendors sold ice cream and said, "Ecco un poco, Signore", they became known as the Hokey Pokey men.

Excluding the Romans, Scotland has a long history of ties with Italy, particularly with the merchants of the Middle Ages. Italian street pedlars and entertainers could be found in Glasgow during the early 19th century, but the two significant waves of Italian immigration occurred towards its end and after the Second World War.

In 1890, 750 Italians were living in Scotland, though 4,500 were recorded by 1914, the bulk of them in the Glasgow area. The system was that an Italian would bring people from his native area after finding them jobs and in 1891, the Società di Mutuo Soccorso was established in this city to help establish new businesses.

Street entertaining, ice cream parlours and fish and chip shops, scattered the Italian population across the city. Hairdressing was another traditional Italian occupation imported to Glasgow with an Italian Hairdressing College opening here in 1928. An Italian Fascist Club was formed in Glasgow in 1923 and 1,400 Italians were detained at the start of the Second World War, though many later joined the British Army.

The Italian and British Ministries of Labour signed bulk labour recruitment schemes in 1951, which not only brought more Italians to Scotland, but also diversified the work they performed. As with the Polish community, the Italians were predominately Roman Catholic and were absorbed into the city's Catholic community.

The Scottish Chinese are mainly a post-War phenomenon. Chinese sailors had settled into English ports in the early 19th century, but

"My Grandmother Telling a Story on Friday Evening" by Josef Herman, a Jewish Polish refugee who came to Glasgow in 1940.

A gold medal given to Yamao Yozo who studied at the Anderson College, worked in a Glasgow shipyard and is regarded as "the father of the engineering industry in Japan".

THE GLASGOW ACCENT

It would take a linguistics expert to unpick the various strands of Lowland Scots, Highland Scots and Gaelic pronunciation, Irish, and even American influences that have produced the Glasgow accent.

It is easy enough to identify the infamous glottal stop, the lack of the sing song element of many other Scots dialects, and the shift in several vowel sounds from standard Scots, as in, for example, *wan merr boatle*. Often, the mere reception of these aural characteristics triggers various prejudices, causing many to stop listening, convinced that they cannot understand what is being slowly and clearly said. Yet the same people may watch television soap operas set in Cockney London, the north-west of England, and even Australia, in which the dialogue reflects dialects no more or less impenetrable than Glaswegian. Much is to said for simple familiarity, and most incomers to Glasgow find they can readily follow what they hear after a brief stay.

Someone who speaks naturally with a strong Glaswegian accent cannot help but say, along with his meaning, that his origins are working class. It has been argued that the culture of working class Glasgow is traditionally an oral one and it is perhaps this that informs the desire of many local writers (for example, James Kelman, Tom Leonard, Alan Spence, and Alex Hamilton) to accurately transliterate Glasgow speech. Such pains to capture the spoken work demonstrate the belief that the way people speak is as valid a carrier of their meaning as the words used.

Michael Munro

as late as 1953 there were only three Chinese families living in Glasgow.

Catering and laundry were the main Chinese occupations, though the advent of the washing machine and the launderette finished the latter business. The first Chinese carry-out opened in Govan Road in the 1930s. By 1984, Glasgow had 72 of them and 52 Chinese restaurants, as well as 3,000 people, half of Scotland's Chinese community, with language centres and Chinese shops dotted round the area. The headquarters of the United Chinese Association of Scotland is in Sauchiehall Street and Cantonese is the fourth most commonly used language in Scotland.

One of the many Chinese restaurants in Glasgow.

The term Asian covers several countries and India, Pakistan, Bangladesh and the East African Asian community have all supplied Glasgow with settlers. Again from the middle of the 19th century, Indian Sailors were frequently in Glasgow and the first Asian settler is thought to have been Mr Noor Muhammed Tanda who settled in the Broomielaw during the First World War. After a series of travels, Mr Tanda set up home and business in the Gorbals in the 1930s.

The Gorbals again became the heart of the Asian immigrant community, with the first Asian children attending Buchan Street School in 1936. The first Asian wholesale warehouse was opened in 1929, followed a year later by the first grocer's shop. A billiard hall in Oxford Street became the first Asian temple in 1944 and what remains of Gorbals Cross is nightly lit by the green minaret and dome of the Glasgow Central Mosque and Islamic Centre.

The Mosque

The Asian population grew slowly, numbering 50 in 1939 and 100 by 1947. There was a rapid growth after the Second World War when many Asians were encouraged to settle in Britain to help fill gaps in the labour supply. There were 3,000 Asians living in Glasgow in 1960 and 12,000 by 1971.

By this time the Gorbals had been evacuated and the Asian community dispersed across the city, notably to Govanhill, Pollokshields and Cessnock in the south and Woodside and Kelvingrove north of the river.

Immigrants still come to Glasgow, though no-one presently seems to be aware of how many Vietnamese or Chilean refugees are here at present. It seems our reputation for racial and social tolerance took a severe dent in the Eighties; and even though the National Front and other racially divisive political parties do not have any kind of political base in Glasgow, Strathclyde Region still felt compelled to establish a Multi Racial Action Year in 1986.

The latest survey of *Regional Trends*, shows Scotland with the [1]

1. Regional Trends 24, HMSO.

lowest population of ethnic minorities. They live in the area of Britain with the largest proportion of drink-drive prosecutions. Between 1981 and 1987 its population fell by 1.3 per cent to 5.1 million, yet in the same period the crime rate rose by 19 per cent and drug offences nearly tripled, the worst increase in the country. We have the lowest pupil-teacher ratios and 11.2 per cent of Scotland's workforce was unemployed in 1988. We are most likely to read a Sunday newspaper. The most popular is *The Sunday Post*.

'The Midgie', a Glasgow beast by Ian Hamilton Finlay.

syne
ah wis a midgie
neist a stank
foon that kin o
thankless
didjye
ever
spen
a
hail simmer
stottin
up
an
doon

GLASGOW SPEECH

The structure and content of Glasgow speech show many idiosyncratic elements that mark it out, as much as its pronunciation, from other Scots dialects, and many of these make little sense if literally translated into English. To give a few examples:

The peculiar construction *Ah'm urny*, I'm not, as in "Yous hink Ah'm stupit an Ah'm urny" if literally translated reads "I'm are not".

The use of *but*, like though, tagged on at the end of a statement to imply contradiction, as in "He's no as daft as he looks, but".

A similar, almost Germanic, tendency to leave certain verbs dangling at the tail of a sentence: "That wee boay a theirs is awfy cheeky gettin".

The use of *see* to introduce a wide range of statements, as in "See if Ah get you touchin ma Pavarotti records, you're done".

Gauny, meaning going to, used in framing a question, as in "Gauny shut that door?" A literal translation, "Going to shut that door?" smacks of the theoretical when what is meant is a strong suggestion. The negative is simply formed: "Gauny no drap yer ash on the good kerpet?" Again, the direct English equivalent "Going to not..." is merely clumsy.

The point of this is to demonstrate that Glasgow speech exhibits a structure of its own that is widely shared and understood. It cannot be dismissed as a bastardisation of Scots nor as gutter language. It has to be accepted for what it is, a contemporary urban dialect of Scots.

Michael Munro

The *Sunday Post* reporting a story outwith its normal Scottish ambit.

Coats Thread poster. A vast international concern in its hey-day.

JAMES FINLAY & COMPANY

The famous Glasgow East India merchant house of James Finlay & Co was established in the middle years of the 18th century by James Finlay, principally to export cotton goods to Europe. He died in 1790 and was succeeded by his eldest son Kirkman Finlay, one of the most prominent supporters of Free Trade in Britain in the early 19th century.

Between 1798 and 1806 he purchased three large cotton mills in the countryside near Glasgow: Ballidalloch, Catrine, and Deaston. During the Napoleonic wars he made determined efforts to smash the French blockade through a network of secret agents on the continent and by shipping his merchandise by way of Turkey. Because of these difficulties he began trading with America and India, invading the East India Company's monopoly. He soon developed an extensive enterprise, employing over 2,000 people in his three cottonmills by 1812.

After the East India Company's monopoly was broken in 1834 he started shipping tea from Canton, which he reckoned to be the most lucrative trade he had ever been involved in. He served as a Member of Parliament for Glasgow from 1812 to 1818 where he vigorously defended the interests of the city's business community. He constructed a magnificent country home appropriate to his wealth on the Firth of Clyde, Toward Castle, at the end of the Cowal peninsula overlooking Rothesay Bay. He died there in 1842 at the age of 70.

Michael S Moss

Chapter Twenty-two

EXPORTS

Lipton's shop at 105 Crown Street.

Lipton's Butter and Ham
That's the stuff you should cram
If you want to get stoot
Just tak a blaw oot
O' Lipton's Butter and Ham

It wouldn't do much today, but when Tommy Lipton opened his first shop in Stobcross Street in 1871, that jingle attracted customers.[1]

Lipton was born on May 10, 1850, on the fourth floor of a Crown Street tenement. His parents had come from County Monaghan to escape the potato famine. They opened a shop in Crown Street selling the butter and eggs they imported from Ireland.

At 17, Tommy Lipton shipped steerage to America, landing in New York. He butchered pigs on the Chicago stockyards, worked on a Virginia tobacco plantation and a rice plantation in South Carolina. He then stowed away on a cotton steamer which took him back to New York where he was eventually employed in a grocery store. He saved enough to bring himself home after four years and a particularly bad bout of homesickness, arriving back in Crown Street, 21 years old with $500 saved and presents of a barrel of flour and a rocking chair for his mother.

The main thing Tommy Lipton learned in America was how to advertise. He set about making sure everyone knew his name and associated it with food. Cartoonists painted smiling pigs going to market, squealing "Going to Liptons!" He issued Lipton's one pound notes, which resembled the real thing so closely that more than a few were passed as genuine. He imported big cheeses from America, making great statistical play on their size and weight, the amount of milk needed to make them and the number of cows required to produce the milk. The cheeses were unloaded at the docks and driven through the streets; there were competitions to

"Sir Thomas Lipton" by Sir Herbert von Herkomer.

1. Various Authors, **A Legacy of Scots**, 1988.

GLASWEGIANS IN EGYPT

When John Maxwell of Pollok visited Egypt on his Grand Tour of 1813–15, travel demanded intrepidity. Arab dress was advisable for safety and comfort, and Maxwell, in the grip of Egyptomania, loved the excuse to dress up. By the time his nephew and heir William Stirling arrived in 1842, tourists were almost commonplace and there was a flourishing expatriate society. Stirling and his dog Dusty encountered Lord Castlereagh at Abu Simbal where they all (including Dusty) left their names chiselled into one of the colossi.

In the later part of the 19th century Glasgow was exporting energetically to Egypt – Nile steamers, locomotives, even textiles made from Egyptian cotton. Commercial activities and Presbyterian fascination with the truth of the Bible supported many private obsessions with Egypt. The pyramidology of Piazzi Smyth, Astronomer Royal of Scotland, found fertile ground in Glasgow. Many religious men fell for this bewitching mixture of science and lunatic theorising about "sacred cubits" which linked the Great Pyramid with Noah's Ark. Engineers were also peculiarly susceptible.

Obelisks were another passion. When Cleopatra's Needle *en route* to England in 1877 broke loose in the Bay of Biscay it was a Glasgow ship, belonging to Burrell and Son, that repossessed it. Burrell, Sir William's father, showed his entrepreneurial mettle by asking an exorbitant £5,000 for salvage, which he would waive if the Needle were set up in Greenock. London, sadly, got the Needle, but Burrell got a lot of money.

When Britain later occupied Egypt in 1882 the local Highland Light Infantry was heavily involved. Glasgow then exported huge quantities of "Highland tea" for the soldiers, and a chain of Temperance Homes to deal with the results.

Juliet Kinchin

guess their weight and occasional sovereigns inside them. He littered Glasgow's streets with telegrams dropped from a balloon, offering rewards to the first 20 people to bring one into his shops.

Everyone knew his name. He soon had shops in every district of Glasgow, every town in Scotland, England and Ireland, moved his offices to London and in ten years had a staff of 10,000 and was a millionaire.

Lipton's Tea is still the best selling brand in America where it is reckoned more than 10 million cups are drunk every day. In 1915 he formed Thomas J Lipton Inc, which recorded a billion dollar's worth of sales in 1983.

[1] He worked enormously long hours, "The only fun is work", he said. Lipton was a teetotal, non-smoking lifelong bachelor who converted the house in Cambuslang he had bought for his parents into the Lipton Memorial Nursing Home after his mother's death. He was always a charitable man and the extent of his generosity was only known after his death. Apart from the labelled hams he gave as prizes to various charities and the presents to the policeman who patrolled Stobcross Street, he gave, in the year he won the contract to provision the Russian army, £25,000 to feed the London poor; he later donated £100,000 towards building a working class restaurant in City Road, London, where he had established his central distribution depot. In the year of his death, 1931, in the middle of the Depression, he gave £10,000 to the Lord Provost's Fund for Poor Relief in Glasgow. Most of his estate was bequeathed to the city when he died of a chill. He is buried in the Southern Necropolis on Caledonia Road, in the same lair as his parents.

His only failure was as a sportsman, where his attempts to win the America's Cup made him a household name in the United States. Americans presented him with a "loving cup" from public subscription. Utah miners made the silver base and children's pennies are supposed to have helped buy "this symbol of a voluntary outpouring of love, admiration and esteem . . . presented to the [2] gamest loser in the world of sport".

Not only Glasgow, but the same district of Glasgow gave the world its best known grocer and its first private eye. Allan Pinkerton was born in the Gorbals in 1819 and had the obligatory poor childhood of the successful Scot abroad, leaving school at the age of eight and becoming an apprentice cooper at 12. Following his father's death, he worked from dawn to dusk to support his mother and brother. The childhood incident he best remembered was his mother bringing home an egg.

ANDERSONIAN PERSONALITIES

Among the famous men of the University of Strathclyde, and its forerunners in the course of its 194 year history, are many whose inventions and discoveries changed the lot of mankind.

Thomas Graham, born in Glasgow in 1805, was a Professor of Chemistry whose work on the diffusion of liquids was to lead to the invention of the artificial kidney by Kolff in Holland. Graham moved to London to become Master of the Mint and attempted to persuade the Government to adopt the decimal system for its coinage (in 1869!). One of his pupils, James Young (from the Drygate, Glasgow) went on to develop the oil shale industry in West Lothian (which at its peak was employing 40,000 men).

Young gifted statues of Thomas Graham (George Square) and fellow student David Livingstone (outside Glasgow Cathedral). John Logie Baird of Helensburgh, a student at the "Tech" in 1912, invented television in its many forms including colour (in 1927), 3D, noctavision (transmitting pictures of people sitting in total darkness by using infra-red light) and "big-screen" TV for cinemas. A fellow student, John (later Lord) Reith, born Stonehaven, became the first Director General of the BBC.

Not everything is of the past. Wishaw-born Sir Samuel Curran, first Principal of Strathclyde University, invented the scintillation counter for measuring radioactivity; and the present Chancellor, Lord Todd (from Clarkston) is a Nobel Prizewinner. In Pharmacy, Professor John Stenlake's "Atracurium" is being used worldwide as a muscle relaxant during surgical operations. Many other outstanding academics are emerging.

Bill Fletcher

1. ibid. **2.** Lipton's press cuttings, covering every aspect of his life, were donated to Glasgow's Mitchell Library. He appears to have been genuinely liked and without a whiff of scandal about his person.

Lipton's pound note.

Sir Thomas Lipton and his yachting trophies on April 10, 1926

Alan Pinkerton (left) with Abraham Lincoln.

In 1837 he became a full member of the Coopers of Glasgow and Suburbs' Protective Association and started work as a tramp cooper, sending most of his wages home to his mother. He was active in the Chartist movement and found his name on the King's Warrant list, which forced him to go into hiding for several months and eventually made him leave the country. After a hurried marriage to Joan Carfrae, whom he met at a strikers' concert, the couple were smuggled onto a Canadian-bound boat and left the country in 1842.

They eventually settled in Chicago, where he set up his own cooperage. In 1847, his nosiness led him to uncover a counterfeiting ring, whom he had noticed meeting round a campfire every night. The next time fake bank notes appeared in the area, Pinkerton again caught the culprit and became a Chicago Sheriff on the strength of his detecting abilities.

By 1850, he had identified the new railroads' need for effective policing and the widespread corruption amongst the existing force. He took the initiative and opened his own detective agency to tackle the problems of rising vandalism and theft. His trademark, an open eye, and the slogan "We Never Sleep" earned him the nickname The Eye, which has stuck with private detectives ever since. Although he was a typical Victorian husband, who, according to his only daughter Joan, believed "women belonged in the kitchen, in bed and with the children",[1] he employed the country's first woman detective, Kate Warne. His reasons for doing so were perfectly practical; he believed her feminine wiles could "worm out secrets in many places to which it was impossible for male detectives to gain access".

Pinkerton's Agency quickly built up a reputation for integrity and efficiency; they also never collected a reward. They introduced the forerunners of police files on suspects and criminals, including detailed descriptions and crude mug-shots. His agents became masters of disguise and infiltration and though his agency enjoyed good relations with the police and always kept within the law, he had no qualms when it came to hiding escaped slaves. Both he and his wife turned their home into a runaway refuge; when the Civil War broke out he found himself on the Unionist side and used his agency to break up Rebel conspiracies.

He was also responsible for guarding President Abraham Lincoln and was called on to help with intelligence work during the Civil War. Neither his war-time exploits, nor the guarding of President Lincoln were particularly successful.

Pinkerton was the first to make extensive use of Wanted posters

WILLIAM J MACQUORN RANKINE (1820–72)

Great things may have been expected of a boy who, despite barely two years schooling, read Newton's *Principia* in Latin at the age of 14. Few though could have speculated just how great and far-reaching the achievements of William J Macquorn Rankine were to be.

As Glasgow University's second Professor of Civil Engineering and Mechanics he was to make a profound impact on the world of applied science. His introductory thesis entitled "The Harmony between Theory and Practice in the Science of Engineering" outlined the premise on which all his work was based, that general scientific principles which govern all possibilities should be applied to each individual practical situation.

The range of subjects he investigated is astounding. He published 158 papers between 1842 and 1872 on subjects as diverse as soil mechanics, thermodynamics, molecular physics and hydrodynamics. In many cases his work was so pioneering that its application accelerated the progress of technology throughout the world and there are methods and formulae bearing his name which are still in use today. Perhaps the work which had the greatest impact on science was his identification of Potential and Kinetic energy.

His output also included numerous textbooks that were among the first in their field such as *A Manual of the Steam Engine and other Prime Movers* and *Shipbuilding, Theoretical and Practical*. Their quality was such that they laid the foundations of academic engineering and remained in use for nearly a century.

All this from an ill man who lived with his parents and composed music and poetry.

Martin Bellamy

1. A Legacy of Scots, op. cit.

and made significant inroads into the lawlessness of the Wild West and the near anarchy that followed the American Civil War. He broke up a bunch of notorious train robbers, known as the Reno Gang, and chased the James Brothers. Thinking they had found the gang hideout, his men opened fire on a log cabin, killed the James' eight year old half-brother and severely wounded their mother. Jesse James swore vengeance till his dying day.

Pinkerton's men were also involved in trailing Butch Cassidy and the Sundance Kid, causing them to flee to South America, arrested two of the Wild Bunch and broke up the notorious Molly Maguires, an organisation which began as an Irish miners benevolent society, but deteriorated into an elitist organised crime syndicate.

His obsessive devotion to work left little time for his wife and family. Joan Pinkerton had six children, three of whom died, and almost no support from her husband. He was a dour, unromantic man, who treated his house as his business. Despite his early trade unionism, his firm accepted work as strike breakers.

He eventually turned the agency over to his two sons, William and Robert and though his relationship with his family mellowed with age, there were long periods of separation.

Following a stroke in 1869, he suffered rheumatics and a speech impediment even his iron will could not improve, which left him increasingly isolated from reality. The years before his death were spent in a nostalgic exercise, creating a Scotland he had never known, turning his home into a private world of larch trees imported from Scotland, grooms, stables, chandeliers and original oil paintings. The one-time Chartist died on July 1, 1884, the year the Third Reform Bill became law in this country.

Florence Street runs from the river to Old Rutherglen Road. It is the birthplace of Benny Lynch, site of the Adelphi Sporting Club, where he was discovered and trained, and the Florence Street Clinic, one of the places where Glasgow tried to tackle its frightening infant mortality rate.[1]

Benny Lynch is still a Glasgow folk hero. The city is full of old men who drank with him, saw him fight, knew him well. He was born in what was Rose Street in 1913 and became World and British Flyweight Champion at a time when the city, and the country, needed a hero. His end has endeared him in popular mythology. Benny Lynch, Champion of the World, died of alcoholism, begging for wine they say, as if that somehow reduced him, brought a hero down to their level, made his greatness understandable, raised them to a place above him. His story has been told many times to the point where one wonders why they do it; the story never gets

Benny Lynch in 1937, shortly after he beat Small Montana.

Door handle in the Mackintosh style from 68 Glencairn Drive.

MACKINTOSH THE DESIGNER

Mackintosh's interiors are very different from his architecture. Inside the buildings Mackintosh felt that he should create an environment which ignored the world outside. He set out to create a sensual world of elegance, simplicity and delight, using new materials and forms in his furniture and creating a startling contrast in his decorations between the world within and the elements outside.

Most people knew his work from the interiors he created at Kate Cranston's Tea Rooms, particularly those in Ingram Street and the Willow Tea Rooms in Sauchiehall Street. He even stipulated the flower arrangements.

Gradually he arrived at a dependence on geometric patterns, predominantly the square, and a contrast between the dark-stained woods of the furniture and the white walls and ceilings of his rooms. The Room de Luxe of the Willow Tea Rooms (1903), with its silver-painted furniture, crystal chandelier and walls covered in purple silk, was the most complete and intense of all his domestic interiors.

Obsessional in his attention to detail, Mackintosh was to design cutlery, flower vases, door handles, light shades and carpets for his clients, as well as the larger pieces of furniture.

After he settled in London in 1915, he began to design textiles for a number of manufacturers as well as book covers for Blackie's and packaging labels for Basset-Lowke models. He made a living of sorts from these but it was over 30 years after his death in 1928 that his achievement as a designer as well as architect was eventually acknowledged.

Roger Billcliffe

1. Sir Alexander McGregor in **Public Health in Glasgow, 1905–1946**, 1967, outlines various schemes to combat infant mortality. For example, in 1801 Glasgow doctors pioneered a campaign to inoculate "the children of the poor gratis" against smallpox and by 1818 31,000 children had been vaccinated.

THE PANOPTICON MEN – LAUREL AND BUCHANAN

The worn-out stone steps climbing to the old Panopticon music hall in Glasgow's Argyle Street (still visible above a shop near the Tron Steeple) could be cited in evidence for the career launching of two celebrated actors, Arthur Stanley Jefferson (later Stan Laurel of Laurel and Hardy) and Jack Buchanan, musical comedy actor.

Stan's father, Arthur Jefferson, a Tyneside, had been manager of the Metropole Theatre, once known as The Scotia, in Glasgow's Stockwell Street. Early this century Stan "stole" dad's top hat and dress suit, and made his bow as a teenage comic at A.E. Pickard's hall, to shouts of applause and laughter. A success, even to the rousing finish when, spotting Jefferson senior in the audience, he tore the precious coat to shreds in his race to escape dad's expected wrath.

Five years later young Buchanan, a stage-daft 19, also made his debut before an equally tough audience at the Panopticon, singing two comic songs and spouting the patter with enough success to be retained for a second week. It was the start of a celebrated career that took him from acting with the Glasgow Amateur Operatic Society to London and New York musicals and star parts in Hollywood. The auctioneer's son from Helensburgh, a Glasgow Academy pupil, blossomed into a British Fred Astaire.

Fittingly, this year of culture brings the centenary of Stan Laurel's birth at Ulverston, in Cumbria, on June 16, 1890. And next year (1991) marks the 100th anniversary of Jack Buchanan's birth. Their kinsfolk lie in city graveyards, Stan Laurel's songstress mother Madge Metcalfe in an (alas unmarked) plot in Cathcart Cemetery.

Gordon Irving

any better, the end is still the same, there is nothing that makes the exploitation understandable. Today he would be a footballer or a pop star, one of many; boxing made his triumphs memorable because of its individuality and Lynch's life was anything but a cliché. He died in 1946.

The outer limits of science and the city were extended by John Stewart MacArthur, born in Norfolk Street, Hutchesontown, in 1856. He was one of eight children who left school at 14 and was an apprentice chemist with the Tharsis Sulphur and Copper Company, another of Charles Tennant's many chemical interests.

Single-handedly, John MacArthur established the Witwatersrand Goldfields, making South Africa the world's premier gold producer by developing the first commercially viable method of chemical gold extraction. This helped the ailing South African mines to successfully refine up to 98 per cent of gold previously abandoned as unworkable. In the four years after 1890, his process raised the Rand Goldfields output from 286 ounces of gold to 549,781 ounces a year.

In 1911, MacArthur switched his metallurgical interests to the refining of radium which at the time was estimated to cost £1,000 for 50 milligrams. Radium was a relatively new discovery and uses were planned in the treatment of cancers and skin conditions, the production of luminous dials and various military items, excluding bombs. From Runcorn in Cheshire, then a centre of the chemical industry, MacArthur's company sent 600 milligrams of radium to the newly formed Glasgow and West of Scotland Radium Committee which was established to ensure an adequate supply was manufactured for therapeutic purposes.

He carried on his work at Balloch until his death from a stroke in 1920. His work on radium was just as pioneering as his earlier gold refining discovery and recognition of his contribution to science is long overdue, especially in his native city. He was the Institute of Mining and Metallurgy's first Gold Medal Winner and his paper on cyanidation to the Society of Chemical Industry was one of the outstanding scientific contributions to industry in the first fifty years of this century. An obituary remarked, "It is given to few men to discover a process which has had such a far-reaching effect in almost every branch of civilised life".

The story of how Scotland extended its frontiers across the world cannot be told too often, for the lesson of what happens to a place whose best export is its people is still being learned, though not perhaps understood. It is a fact that most of Glasgow's eminent men and women are buried outside the city boundary.

The Tharsis Copper Company, Spain, a Glasgow owned mining company.

At the Tharsis foundry.

DARIEN AND THEODORE ROOSEVELT

The Scotsmen who set sail in 1698 to the isthmus of Panama could not have foreseen the disastrous problems they were to encounter.

A second fleet of settlers arrived eight weeks after the original ones had left. They too were laid seige by the Spaniards and Yellow Fever. A few weeks later they set sail again. One vessel, the *Rising Sun*, travelled to America. Whilst awaiting entrance to Charleston harbour the Reverend Alexander Stobo was invited ashore to preach, the local minister having died. During his visit a hurricane wrecked his ship with the loss of all hands. The Reverend and Mrs Stobo naturally settled in the town.

That could have been the end of the story but in 1858 their great-great-great-grandson was born, Theodore Roosevelt. The Darien scheme's original progenitor, William Paterson, had talked of carrying cargoes across the isthmus from sea to sea by strings of mules and carriages. This too inspired Roosevelt though his idea was of a canal.

The same two problems remained but President Roosevelt was to succeed where Paterson failed, but not with any great subtlety. The Yellow Fever was removed by eradicating the disease-bearing insects and American gunboats solved the problem with the Spanish descendants by facilitating a revolution. The subsequent success of the Panama Canal is a fitting legacy of the original dream of Darien.

Martin Bellamy

It has been called the Scottish Diaspora and is not confined to a particular time, though emigration was greatly accelerated after the Union of 1707. Its most ruinous chapter however, began in 1695. In that year the Scots Parliament passed an Act authorising the establishment of a Company of Scotland Trading to Africa and the Indies, which was passed without King William of Orange being given the opportunity to read it. This was a "noble undertaking" whose spirit filled the country which, Andrew Fletcher of Saltoun said, seemed to be moved by a Higher Power towards the "only means to recover us from our present miserable and despicable condition".[1]

The scheme was drafted by some London Scots merchants, though mainly by the naive and creative wanderer William Paterson, who had founded the Bank of England in 1694. The first proposal was for a joint Scots and English venture, but this was stymied by the English trading companies, who also prevented a Scottish attempt to enlist the support of those towns joined by the Hanseatic League.[2]

Scotland did it alone. Four hundred thousand pounds, believed to be half the nation's available capital, was subscribed to the company from individuals, burghs, corporations and associations. The coast of Africa was originally thought to be a suitable location, but that was abandoned in favour of Darien on the Isthmus of Panama, which had been Paterson's original choice. No-one in the company had been there and they ignored an informed and sceptical would-be advisor.[3]

One of the first men to dip into his purse for a company subscription was William Arbuckle, a Glasgow merchant, wholly representative of the emergent aristocracy of wealth, a pious kirkman and political manipulator, who was able to subscribe more stock than peers whose estates spread over three shires. Throughout the spring and summer of 1696, money poured into company coffers in Glasgow and Edinburgh. The towns themselves, and many others, took out subscriptions in the name of their cities, so that, "even the poor and landless, the thieves, whores and beggars could think themselves a part of the noble undertaking".[4] The Glasgow subscription book opened on March 5 and closed on April 22 with a donation from the University. That summer William Paterson came to Glasgow to study the Clyde as far upriver as Dumbarton, looking for a run of deep water where the company ships could anchor and load. Glasgow took on an importance in other aspects of the Company plans, apart from fund raising. It was a centre for the Company's short-lived and illegal bank, with elegant, worthless

A map of New Caledonia and Darien.

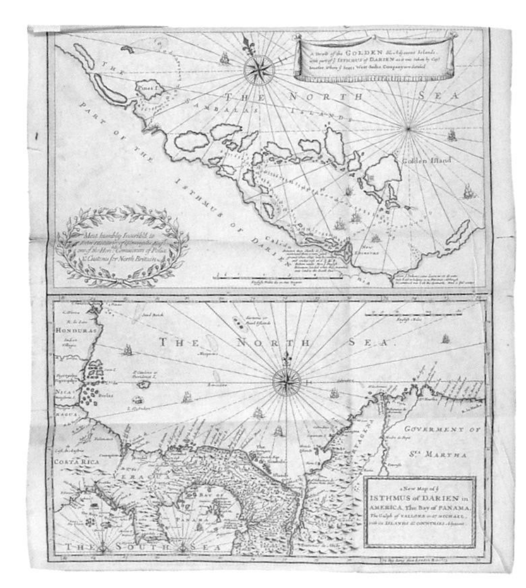

1. John Prebble's eminently readable **The Darien Disaster**, 1968, gives a complete account of the scheme and its consequences. 2. ibid. 3. ibid. 4. ibid.

GLASGOW SHIPPING LINES

In the second half of the 19th century Glasgow became the third great port of Britain, surpassed in tonnage using and registered in the port only by London and Liverpool. The world was literally at Glasgow's doorstep and it was possible to sail directly from Glasgow to virtually every country in the world. Great Empire companies like the Canadian Pacific Railway sailed from Glasgow, but Glasgow too had its own great shipping lines.

The most important were the Clan Line, the Anchor Line, the Allan Line, Burrell & Son, MacLay & McIntyre, the City Line, the Donaldson Line, and J & P Hutcheson. Together they operated some 220 vessels of more than 400,000 gross tons, about 40 per cent of all Glasgow registered vessels. While the Clan Line, Burrel & Son and MacLay & McIntyre operated mainly as cargo carriers, the Anchor Line, the Allan Line and the Donaldson Line were among the great passenger lines carrying immigrants to North America. The Donaldson Line also traded extensively with South America, and the Allan Line, largely teetotal, reflecting the Allan family practices, was the leading passenger carrier in the Canadian business.

However, not all Glasgow shipping lines were steamship-based. Even at the beginning of the 20th century, four lines, The Shire Line, Loch Line, Port Line, and County Line, still sailed the long routes to the Far East and Australasia in great steel sailing barques. As major customers of the Clyde yards, the Glasgow shipping lines were nonetheless instrumental in demonstrating the qualities of "Clydebuilt" vessels on the world's seaways.

Anthony Slaven

notes and when all was ready, a single folio sheet was posted on the walls of each Glasgow coffee house stating: "Everyone who goes on the first expedition shall receive and possess 50 acres of plantable land, and 50 foot square of ground at least in the chief city or town, and an ordinary house built thereupon by the colony at the end of 3 years".[1]

Ships had been bought, built or chartered in Holland and Hamburg and the Company filled their warehouses in Glasgow and Leith with a variety of goods to be exchanged for spices of the Orient, silks and gold. In July, 1698, five ships left Leith laden with goods, people and hope.

They made landfall in November and Paterson's wife died within a few days of her arrival. Many others died of fever and those who landed in Panama lived to regret their ambitions. The leadership quarrelled constantly, the rain was incessant and the planned towns were never more than a collection of huts.

At home, King Billy acknowledged the Spanish claim to Darien. He also ordered the English colonies in America and the Caribbean not to help the Scots, who had been attacked by the Spaniards before abandoning their settlement in fear of further skirmishes.

A second expedition, arriving in November, 1699, rebuilt and re-occupied the wilderness. Again there was dissension, fever and mutiny and again the Spaniards attacked, this time laying siege by mounting a blockade on both land and sea. The colony was abandoned on April 12, 1700, and in December the Speedy Return limped into Greenock with 40 survivors on board.

The Darien scheme has been called "perhaps the worst disaster in Scotland's history". The volatile loss of pride and money made the Union inevitable.[2] About two thirds of the money lost on the Darien venture was repaid by England after 1707; by Article XV of the Treaty of Union, the Company of Scotland was dissolved. Under the terms of the Union, Glasgow merchants could now trade with America and the West Indies.

Glasgow's vessels could complete two round trips to America without being re-provisioned; boats from Liverpool or Bristol could manage only one. In addition the Glasgow ships' insurance rates were significantly lower, since the safer northern routes they followed dispensed with the need for a pirate indemnity clause.

Glasgow's most important trading connection was with the Chesapeake. The men who controlled these lucrative commercial lanes also ran the sugar, linen and coal mining enterprises. Their influence extended outside Glasgow to their Clyde Valley estates, so that by the end of the 18th century, the Glasgow merchants

The first volume of the Journal of the Court of Directors of the Company of Scotland.

THE
Several Journals
of the
Court of Directors of the
COMPANY of SCOTLAND
Trading to
Africa and the Indies;
Together with that of the Nominees in the Act of Parliament for [illegible] Company [illegible] the 14th day of February ... 1696 and ending the 15th day of July 1698

1. ibid. 2. ibid.

THE CELLULOID MEN – GRIERSON AND McLAREN

From a bare homespun studio in the old Theatre Royal, first home of Scottish Television, John Grierson unspooled films to the nation, charming even the non-addict with a camera-eye look at genetics, the ibex, bees, the street songs of Edinburgh, greeting an audience of millions and hitting the commercial Top Ten in a ten year run of "This Wonderful World".

He was a wiry little provocative Scot, born April 26, 1898 at Deanston village on the River Teith, a schoolmaster's son who went forth from the University of Glasgow to be dubbed, worldwide, "the father of Documentary". A missionary-like zeal and a crusty style cloaked his warmth for the ordinary man. When he came to TV, at 59, he had already done sterling work for film units of the Empire Marketing Board, the GPO and in Canada, and made classics like "Drifters" and "Night Mail".

Norman McLaren, a house-painter's son, 16 years Grierson's junior, asked a Glasgow cinema to give him a worn-out 35mm print, removed the emulsion, and, with brush and coloured inks, painted directly on to the 300 feet of clear film. It was the start of a career in which McLaren made films in London and New York, then joined Grierson at the National Film Board of Canada to create an animation unit.

McLaren made animated shorts for the war effort on the dangers of gossip, the importance of savings and bonds. His recent death marked the loss of another pioneer from Glasgow's innovative past.

Gordon Irving

were also amongst the best estate improvers in some of the most neatly enclosed parts of the country.[1]

John Glassford traded with merchant houses in New York and New Jersey and his relatives, the Riddells, had been involved in New Jersey affairs almost from the very beginning. When he retired from trading, Glassford bought Netherwood Estate in Dumbartonshire, gave secure estate leases to tenants, and was credited with making "more real and substantial improvements . . . than ever was performed by any in that part of the country".[2] Similarly, Archibald Speirs, bought 18 small lairdships in Renfrewshire, which were developed with the help of his tenants.

Glasgow's merchants devised a "store system" by sending their employees to live in the colonies, purchase from the planters and warehouse the goods until the ships arrived. The promotion hopes for the Chesapeake storekeepers lay mainly in the company system, so they remained aloof from American society, biding their time till they were called back home. This made them unpopular and had its effect during and after the American Revolution.

Scotland's American links obviously expanded along the eastern seaboard out of Chesapeake Bay, and other Scottish merchants, mainly from Aberdeen and Edinburgh, expanded the trading areas. John Porterfield went to New Jersey for a Glasgow firm and bought part of Lord Melford's East Jersey Estate, following his Lordship's death. He moved into Central Jersey, set up an iron forge, a shop and a plantation. His story is typical and a colony of Scottish traders was established in New Jersey, with the families often arriving by way of New York or Philadelphia and staying awhile on the coast before moving inland.

Trade apart, it seems that Scots in America were loath to tolerate there what they had endured here. In June, 1775, Daniel Macleod petitioned the New York legislature, offering the services of himself and some newly arrived Highlanders in defence of the colony, "with the provision of having liberty to wear their own Country Dress commonly called the Highland Habit."[3] The first Scottish settlers had been discharged or deserting soldiers from the Seven Years War (1754-61). Out of the 12,000 Highlanders who enlisted, only 76 returned to Scotland and the Government in London were so alarmed at the number of Scots leaving for America that emigration there was banned in 1775.

After 1775, the Scottish emigration pattern shifted into Canada, especially Ontario, Prince Edward Island and, obviously, Nova Scotia. Scots no longer filled American political and administrative positions, nor did they hold any significant commercial influence,

Portrait of William Alexander, champion of 17th century emigration to Nova Scotia.

Anchor Line poster advertising sailings to New York.

1. J.A. Saltow, "Scottish Traders in Virginia, 1750–1775", **The Economic History Review**. 2. ibid. 3. ibid.

JAMES MCGILL (1744–1813)

James McGill was born in Glasgow in 1744. His father, also James, was a burgess and a member of the hammerman's guild, well enough off to be able to send his son to the University of Glasgow, where he matriculated in 1756.

Why or when he left Scotland is a mystery, but a short ten years later he was in Montreal *en route* for the north-west wilderness where he led the adventurous (and profitable) life of a fur trapper. Another ten years saw him back in Montreal where, abandoning the fur trade, he set up, with his brother Andrew, as a merchant in "the ordinary Colonial trade", importing tobacco, rum, molasses and sugar from the West Indies, metalware, textiles, powder and shot from Britain. Then he became involved in profitable land speculations, and soon his contemporaries "reckoned him the richest man in Montreal". Next he took a principal part in the military matters of the colony (mainly against the revolting Americans) as well as serving several terms as a trusted representative in the parliament of Lower Canada.

Starting life as a Presbyterian and marrying a Roman Catholic, he died an Anglican in 1813, leaving a bequest of £10,000 to found a college in Montreal to serve as a centre of Protestant culture. After many difficulties, mainly connected with the religious situation, McGill College was founded in 1821. Eight years later the College buildings were opened, but it was not until 1852 that the status of McGill University (as it had become) was fully established.

Joseph Fisher

but they kept coming. The 19th century saw a huge number of emigrants leaving Scotland to become lost in the general immigration into America. In the Twenties, more than 300,000 Scots sailed from Glasgow to America to avoid unemployment.

Shipping lines had been established in the 19th century: the Allan Line in 1819, the Anchor Line in 1837 and the Donaldson Line in 1879. Naturally there were those, like the extraordinary Granville Sharp Pattison, who availed themselves of the services in dramatic circumstances.

Nineteenth century Glasgow resembled an American rather than a European city. They shared the same dynamism, economics and religion. Glasgow even proved something of a model. It seemed to have found a means of dealing with the excesses of both poverty and wealth and exported its approach to America. Glasgow's philanthropic schemes were copied, as were its educational system, its sense of radicalism, especially where monopoly capitalism was concerned and its concern for the advancement of women.

Scotland exported its strongest, oldest and most potent ideal across the Atlantic. The "great Scottish Republic of the Mind" extended directly from Glasgow to America where both parties found common interests and pursuits which were of substantial mutual benefit, interests which went far beyond stale economics. There was an egalitarianism about both societies; we shared the same distaste of snobbery, arrogance, privilege and anything devoid of personal merit or social utility. Such a critical, even capricious, spirit may seem far removed from the America we know today, but they also have changed.

Amongst the notable Scots Americans with Glasgow connections (by birth or residence) are Alexander Gardener, who photographed the American Civil War and became the world's first war photographer, Stan Laurel and John Grierson. In our own time, associations with the United States have found a new form in the activities of Bill Forsyth, Bill Paterson, Tom Conti, Billy Connolly, the Glasgow Gang of artists, designers and stylists and almost all of our pop groups.

It would be difficult to think of another country which had the same impact on Canada as Scotland. Montreal's great McGill University was founded by James McGill, born in the Saltmarket, who went west, became a fur trader and left a bequest to found the university in 1821, the year after John Macdonald emigrated to Canada from Glasgow.

Macdonald was born in Glasgow in 1815 where his father was a cotton manufacturer. There were family connections in Kingston

Glaswegians engineered the CPR railway line and opened up the west of Canada.

A watercolour of Tom Conti by Ishbel McWhirter in 1986.

DAVID LIVINGSTONE (1813–73)

A "great missionary"? He made just one convert in three decades of travel in Africa, and that man lapsed. A "great healer"? Livingstone believed till the end in that primitive, false remedy, bleeding. Even as "discoverer" his credentials are questionable. The Portuguese, for example, had long known great lakes and rivers which Livingstone would claim to have "discovered".

He was never a racialist. He was even-handedly arrogant, censorious and deceitful. His optimistic or downright lying accounts of the prospects lured well meaning Britons to ghastly deaths in Africa. He was a visionary, self-aggrandizing, imperialist.

Still, he had a sheer crazy tenacity which compels attempts to understand, if not forgive, him.

He had lost his childhood and youth in a Blantyre cotton mill, working in prophetically steamy heat twelve and a half hours a day, six days a week, before attending the Company school between eight and ten in the evening. His later obsessive wanderlust was understandable. Privation never deterred him.

In 1864, he had been sacked by HM Government after the first attempt to colonise Malawi had collapsed in a welter of corpses. All he had left was the *Lady Nyassa*, a 40 foot steamer assembled from portable prefabricated parts up-river. Seeking a buyer, he and an inadequate crew brought it to Zanzibar. No takers. But with sail and courage, Livingstone (never a seaman) took it 2,500 miles to Bombay in a month and a half. As he entered the port, the monsoon began. He wandered incognito about the strange city, probably no more lonely than at every other time in his life.

Angus Calder

where John Macdonald studied law, being called to the bar when he was 21.

At the age of 29 in 1844, he was Conservative member of the Canadian Parliament for Kingston and held the seat for virtually the rest of his life. Most of Canada was owned and controlled by independent companies, the biggest of which was the Hudson's Bay Company. The land was also under threat from America, who, following their independence, extended their territorial claims, especially northwards, believing the entire continent was inevitably bound to come under their control.

In 1856, Macdonald had manoeuvred himself into the leadership of the Conservatives of Canada West and while America was occupied with the Civil War, he took the initiative, joining forces with his arch rival, the Liberal leader George Brown, to secure Canada's position as a united political entity. Between 1864 and 1867 he led negotiations with the Colonial Office and managed to unite different areas and elements in Canada behind him and persuaded the British Government to accept word for word their Bill for a new nation. On July 1, 1867, the British North America Act created the Dominion of Canada.

With the exception of four years in disgrace – following accusations of drunkenness and dubious pay-offs to his party by a railway magnate – The Old Corruptionist led the country for the rest of his life. Under Macdonald, Canada became a stable colonial democracy and as such was the model for the future development of other parts of the British Empire, such as Australia and New Zealand. As Sir John A Macdonald lay devastated by a massive stroke, the only headline needed on the morning of May 30, 1891, was HE IS DYING.

A double loop on the Canadian Pacific Railway.

Many Scots laboured in the building of the Canadian Pacific Railway.

EXPORTS

NEW LANARK, *by* Marcus Gray.

"The Thin Red Line" by Robert Gibb.

Chapter Twenty-three

THE THIN RED LINE

A Paisley pattern woodblock.

Two statues stare down Miller Street from the southern side of George Square. They represent a pair of Victorian Britain's enduring soldier heroes: Sir John Moore of Corunna and Sir Colin Campbell, Lord Clyde.

Sir John Moore is remembered as the subject of Rev Charles Wolfe's poem about his burial. He was born in the Trongate, opposite the Tron Church, on November 13, 1761 and went to the Old Grammar School in Greyfriars Wynd, off Ingram Street.

In 1808, Moore was appointed commander of the British Forces in Spain. He was given 35,000 men to remove Napoleon's troops from the Spanish Peninsula, but after the Spanish lost Madrid, 70,000 Frenchmen drove Moore to Corunna. There he was forced to fight a rearguard action, since the British fleet left him stranded for three days. During the siege of Corunna he died from a cannon shot on 16 January, 1809, giving the 19th century the second of its three Napoleonic heroes, Nelson, Moore and Wellington. His statue was cast from a bronze cannon and placed in the Square ten years after his death.

A young ensign, Colin Campbell, was part of Moore's burial party. His statue facing the Post Office is not far from where he was born in John Street on 29 January, 1792.

Campbell, a former pupil of Glasgow High School, made his name at Balaclava in 1854 against a Russian force estimated at 24,000. Campbell's Highland Brigade was only two deep. The men were ordered to hold their fire until the enemy were 600 yards away. Their fusillade brought down some of the horses and the Russian cavalry, still advancing at 200 yards, broke into confusion. The charge was halted. William Howard Russell of *The Times*, one of the world's first war correspondents, told his readers of a "thin red streak topped with a line of steel", which in time became known as the Thin Red Line.

Five months after the war had finished, on July 1, 1856 in

First World War volunteers line up outside the Glasgow Stock Exchange.

Scottish soldiers in 1641, from a German Woodcut.

GLASGOW'S REGIMENT

Glasgow's Regiment has its origins as the 73rd Highlanders, beginning life on Christmas Day 1777. Although first mustered in Elgin, Glasgow was an increasing Mecca for Highlanders before 1800 and it was only sensible to look for recruits where there were more of them to the square mile than in most areas further north. "Tom", the otherwise anonymous soldier who served in the 71st from 1806 to 1815 and wrote "Journal of a Soldier of the 71st or Glasgow Regiment, Highland Light Infantry", testifies to the number of Glasgow men in the ranks and mentions the two Paisley lassies he met in Paris in 1815, looking out for "their regiment"!

In 1881 the 71st HLI and the 74th Highlanders were linked as 1st and 2nd Battalions The Highland Light Infantry, with a permanent Depot in Hamilton, recruiting in the Glasgow area: and from 1887 the regiment was strengthened by not less than four Glasgow battalions of Volunteers, the later Territorials. In 1920 the Depot moved from Hamilton to Maryhill Barracks but, even more, the experience of the Great War and the flood of Glasgow recruits to a greatly expanded Regiment, had greatly strengthened the link between city and Regiment. In June 1923 King George V authorised the alteration of the HLI's name to Highland Light Infantry (City of Glasgow Regiment).

The link remains; the HLI's 1959 amalgamation with the Royal Scots Fusiliers producing The Royal Highland Fusiliers (Princess Margaret's Own Glasgow & Ayrshire Regiment).

Donald Mack

Glasgow City Hall, he was presented with the Freedom of the City and a "splendid sword of honour" which had been bought with the subscription of "six thousand leading Glasgow citizens".

Campbell was created Baron Clyde of Clydeside following his successful, often bloody quelling of the Indian Mutiny. He died on August 14, 1863.

The Scots had chartered a company to trade with India in 1618. It was overtaken by the English-based East India Company, which the Scots infiltrated, looking upon the sub-continent as a means of making money. When the American War of Independence ruined Thomas Munro's family, he took himself to India where he was later knighted for establishing a system of tax collection. He was born in 1761 into a Glasgow mercantile family and died in India of cholera shortly before it made an appearance in Glasgow. Throughout the 19th century, the Scots established a strong and lasting presence in India, which in turn fostered our cotton textile and jute industries. The Paisley pattern is based on an Indian design. Motherwell iron built the railways, while Glasgow engines hauled the trains and drove the ferries.

The Scots had a presence in Russia before Campbell's Crimean Highlanders, notably through the venerable Richard Smith, son of a cotton spinner. Born in Glasgow in 1824, he was apprenticed as a boilermaker, learned iron shipbuilding with Cairds of Greenock and eventually helped to build the first locomotive for the Caledonian Railway Company. He went to Russia in 1847 for the construction of the Moscow-St Petersburg railway, later used by Anna Karenina and when the Crimean War was over, in 1856, he opened an engineering company in Moscow. Smith was supposed to have been able to bend an iron bar into a horse shoe shape with his bare hands, stood over six feet tall and was one of a group of Scots who founded the Moscow Curling Club in the 1870s.

Between 1837 and 1901, not a year passed without Scottish soldiers being in action somewhere in the world, and between 1855 and 1859, the 71st Regiment took part in both the Crimean War and the Central India Campaign. In 1881 the 71st and 74th were linked to become the First and Second Battalions of the Highland Light Infantry.

The Royal Highland Fusiliers are the only regiment currently recruiting in Glasgow and are an amalgamation of two former Lowland regiments: the Highland Light Infantry, late of Maryhill Barracks and the Hallowe'en Pen, and the Royal Scots Fusiliers. The regiments were amalgamated, amid some protest, in 1959 and are now officially known as Princess Margaret's Own Glasgow and

GLASGOW MUTINIES

As a political flashpoint, Glasgow's pedigree is formidable. Paradoxically, this civil disaffection is not mirrored in the city's military past. Overshadowed by poverty, Glasgow has taken a certain pride in earning the King's shilling. The promise of glory, far from grey streets, has repeatedly left Glasgow's citizens waging wars to maintain the status quo they may have condemned in peacetime.

Glaswegians have also borne arms in causes other than their country's before now, among them the International Brigaders, but Glasgow's two military mutinies were imported phenomena.

In 1794, men of the Bredalbane Fencibles led other regiments in rioting at Candleriggs. Guaranteed service in Scotland , the Highlanders refused an attempted draught to bloody overseas campaigns and rebelled for more than two weeks during December. The affair ended with exemplary floggings and one execution.

August 1804 saw the newly formed Canadian Fencibles in revolt. Lured to Glasgow with promises of a soldier's pay and free passage to Canada for their dependants, the Highlanders received desultory subsistence and watched 50 women and children starve to death during their first five weeks of delays at Glasgow. Men deserted to find paying work and discipline collapsed. Transferred to Ayr, the ill-fated regiment was disbanded before the new year.

Government betrayals sparked both mutinies, but authorities were certain radical agitators had disaffected troops billeted on local households. Despite these fears, the military's loyalty remained firm in Glasgow during the widespread unrest of 1820. Doubts only returned in 1919 when the Highland Light Infantry were confined to their Maryhill Barracks while English troops occupied the Red Clyde's capital after the George Square riot.

Alison Kennedy

"Scottish Mercenaries landing in Romsdalen" by Adolph Tidemand and Morten Muller, 1876.

Artillery observers celebrate Armistice in George Square in 1918.

Three of the 150 women conductors who took over from men on June 3, 1940.

Ayrshire Regiment, the Royal Highland Fusiliers. The amalgamation combined two of the oldest units in Britain and the Fusiliers have more battle honours than any other regiment in the British Army.

Within two days of Britain declaring war on Germany on 4 August, 1914, the search began for 100,000 recruits. By the end of October the British Army had twelve new divisions and in one day alone 35,000 men enlisted, as many as had been recruited for the whole of 1913. By the end of August, 1914, the *Glasgow Herald* reported that 20,000 men had enlisted at the Glasgow recruiting office in the Gallowgate; 1,500 in Coatbridge, 900 in Clydebank and 940 in Dumbarton. Half a million Scots volunteered to serve in the First World War. More than 125,000 were killed in action, one sixth of the British casualty list.

At the outbreak of war, the Boys' Brigade volunteered to form a battalion of the Highland Light Infantry and when the offer was declined, the BB treasurer, David Laidlaw, approached the Cameron Highlanders, who also refused. Glasgow Corporation gave the go-ahead for the formation of a Highland Light Infantry Glasgow Tramways' Battalion, who, in their green uniforms, marched through Glasgow behind their pipe band to George Square where they offered themselves for enlistment on 7 September. Approval was given for 1,102 men to enlist and they all joined the Highland Light Infantry, becoming the 15th Battalion. Coplawhill tram depot served as recruiting hall and the new battalion was enlisted in 16 hours. In the wake of this success, the Boys' Brigade were allowed to form a 16th Battalion. There was considerable excitement in the city and a few days later another Glasgow Pals' Battalion, the 17th Highland Light Infantry, enrolled in the Lesser Hall of the Merchants' House at the instigation of the Glasgow Chamber of Commerce.

More than 500 members of the Boys' Brigade in Glasgow who had volunteered were killed when the Battle of the Somme began on July 1, 1916. Within 10 minutes of the attack on Thiepval, half the 17th Battalion of the Highland Light Infantry's strength, 1,100 men, were dead, in one of the more lethal attacks. A memorial service was held in Glasgow Cathedral on July 8. Many fell in the first few hours of the battle; others survived to die on the notorious Hohenzollern Ridge at the end of the fight. A monument to the 51st (Highland) Division looks to Beaumont Hamel, where many of the 16th Battalion of the Highland Light Infantry were killed. Its inscription is in Gaelic: *Là a' bhlàir's math na càirdean*, Friends are good on the day of battle.

THE HIGHLAND LIGHT INFANTRY IN THE TWO WORLD WARS

The outbreak of the Great War in 1914 marked a huge expansion of the British Army, an expansion far beyond that in any previous conflict. The two Regular battalions of the Highland Light Infantry were backed up by a stream of Service (ie wartime only) battalions: during the war the HLI had a total of 14 battalions on active service, the bulk of the men – all volunteers – coming from Glasgow. While many served in France and Flanders, other soldiered in Gallipoli, Palestine and Mesopotamia: the Territorial 5th, 6th and 7th, all in the 52nd (Lowland) Division were to fight in Gallipoli, Palestine and France, a veritable Cook's tour but one with some strange hotels to rest in.

1939 brought a smaller expansion of the infantry and one actually planned in advance. There was no rush of Service battalions: instead in April 1939 each Territorial battalion raised a duplicate. The HLI was down to only 3 Territorial battalions, previous reduction and reorganisation having removed the 7th and 8th Battalions. As a result the HLI sent a total of seven battalions on active service: the 11th was, alas, suddenly turned into a tank battalion of the Royal Armoured Corps and then disbanded.

Battalions served notably in Europe: remember the pipe tune, "10th HLI Crossing the Rhine", much played to this day. The 2nd Battalion, already overseas in 1939 was destined for another Cook's tour: Ethiopia, the Western Desert, Sicily and Italy, Yugoslavia and Greece. One officer of the 2nd Bn concluded in a diary that the War Office seemed determined to lose his battalion for ever this time.

Donald Mack

GLASGOW OBSERVED AT WAR

In late February 1941, there was little talk in Glasgow about the war. A butcher in Sauchiehall Street complained about the small ration of meat allowed to him to make sausages. But while most of McColl's chocolate shops were temporarily closed, lacking supplies, the rival Bisset chain still had boxes. People weren't grumbling too much. Many had the money to pay even for scarce haddock.

The exhibition of "War Artists" at Kelvingrove wasn't particularly well attended. In the Taj Mahal, Sauchiehall Street, upper-middle class women complained that the curry wasn't hot and spicey enough. Meanwhile, the restaurant's gramophone played "Pull Your Socks Up and Sing Tickety-Boo". George Formby was packing out the Empire with songs to his own banjo and a stream of *double entendres* – in his version of "Bless 'Em All", "promotion" meant "erection."

We know all this because Humphrey Pease, an Old Etonian amateur ornithologist, was up from London. He worked for Mass-Observation, a social survey organisation. He came back again in early March and sat in bars frequented by soldiers, RAF men, Polish allies, Free French sailors.

The brick "surface" shelters with concrete roofs compared well with those of other towns which Pease had visited as a "Blitz" observer. In Anderston Ward, most people would have to cram into "strutted closes" – entry passages reinforced with iron stakes and cross bars. "They're not much good", said a pubkeeper in Stobcross Street, echoing general local sentiment.

That was March 5. On the 13th, the German bombers arrived, in force.

Angus Calder

Glasgow's war effort was not confined to the battlefield. At home, the Templeton carpet factory on Glasgow Green, which had never made a blanket, supplied more than any other British firm, over four million, to the Ministry of Defence. Men and women in the shipyards, the munitions works and coal mines had a 56 hour week. Their working day began at six in the morning and finished at half past five at night, with a three-quarters of an hour breakfast break at nine o'clock and an hour for lunch at mid-day.

The Highland Light Infantry fought the Russian revolutionaries at Archangel and the Irish rebels throughout Southern Ireland in 1919. They served in Palestine, Turkey and policed the Hindu-Moslem riots in India in 1928. During the Second World War they fought in North, East and West Africa, mainly against the Italians. They landed in Sicily, fought in Yugoslavia and Greece and took part in D-Day and the Battle of the Bulge. In the late Forties they were back in Palestine, then Malta. They saw service in the Canal Zone in 1952 and Cyprus in 1956. In their new incarnation as the Royal Highland Fusiliers, they were the first Scottish regiment in Northern Ireland, moving Aden in 1960 to be deployed in Armagh, Fermanagh and Tyrone.

The Second World War was a civilians' war and everyone in Britain was affected. Full scale National Service was introduced in 1941 and by the end of the year 4,320,000 conscripts had been called up and the age limit was raised to 51. Civilians became firemen, ambulance drivers, air raid wardens and nearly 22,000 young men worked down the mines as Bevin Boys. Sixteen and a half million people registered for non-military national service.

The Second World War was photographed more than any previous war. We are now familiar with poignant photographs of children with labels on their collars, waving as they face evacuation or cuddling each other before they go; of folk waiting in the queues for coal, food, clothes or simply standing in the rubble where their homes used to be. Wartime was not easy for any city, but Glasgow's unique contribution has never been properly evaluated or appreciated.

Most of the big troop movements came through Glasgow and the Clyde was the only safe exit port for shipping. This and our heavy concentration on engineering and boat building made us a prime target for the Luftwaffe.

The Clydebank Blitz of March 1941 was intended to terrorise and dislocate an entire community. Apart from the loss of life and property, there were the obvious industrial targets: John Brown's Shipyard, the Royal Ordnance Factory, Beardmores, Arnott Young,

Susie Loftus working at Harland and Wolff during the War.

Three Glasgow grannies – Mrs Leishman, Mrs Redpath and Mrs McGinley – working on the railway during the Second World War.

GLASGOW'S GREAT SHIPS

More than 20,000 ships have been built on the Clyde in the last 200 years and Glasgow's ships led the world in innovation. After the *Comet* there was the *Sirius* of 1836, the first steamer to cross the Atlantic under continuous steampower. In 1854 the SS *Brandon* was the first vessel powered by the compound expansion engine, and 20 years later the SS *Propontis* introduced the triple expansion engine which conquered the long sea routes and made steam economic.

The finest clipper of them all, the *Cutty Sark* was built by Scott and Linton in 1869 but it was steam that won. It was the Clyde liners and naval vessels that captured the public imagination. In the 20th century, the great Cunarders take pride of place from the *Lusitania* (1906) and *Mauretania* (1907) to the *Queen Elizabeth 2* in 1967, the last of the breed. In between came the two great *Queens*, the *Queen Mary* (1934) and *Queen Elizabeth* (1938), the largest and most luxurious liners afloat which, like the *Lusitania* and *Mauretania* before this, held the Blue Riband for the fastest Atlantic crossing.

Among the great ships of war was the ill-fated HMS *Hood* launched at Clydebank in 1918, Britain's largest battle cruiser. It was believed to be invincible, but in 1943 was sunk by the *Bismack* with huge loss of life. Today the long line of great ships is almost at an end, though the famous Govan Yard has recently recaptured some of the glamour of the past with its fine cruise-ferry liner, *Norsea*, launched in 1987.

Anthony Slaven

Rothesay Docks, Tullis Engineering and Singers were all either hit, blasted or damaged by fire and millions of gallons of oil were lost at the Ministry of Defence depot at Dalnotter. When the site was cleared they counted 96 bomb craters.

Clydebank was not the only place the Germans hit and newspaper photographs of the time record a series of striking images of the damage done to the lives of those who never fought. Bomb damage ranged across the city and Glasgow's first air raid shelter in George Square, survived a shell which dropped beside it. It is impossible to imagine how anyone could have survived the mangled tram car which was directly hit on Nelson Street. Apart from the evacuations, there are pictures of rationing, queuing, the bombing and the clearing up, the gas mask drill in Sauchiehall Street shops, women porters wheeling sacks of grain and smiling girls registering at the Labour Exchange, as well as German and Italian families pushing their belongings in a handcart leaving for internment at the start of the war.

Prisoners of war made the roads and sewers for Pollok housing estate. There were perpetual troop landings and evacuations. American, Australian, New Zealand and Canadian soldiers first set foot on British soil in Glasgow, returning the way many of their forefathers left. From the survivors of the Athenia, sunk in the Atlantic the day war was declared, to those of the Bismark, the heaviest and most powerful battleship, who were carried ashore by civilians, Glasgow was a home for casualties of sea.

Glasgow was the venue for two memorable events. Rudolph Hess, who landed at Eaglesham in May 1941, was imprisoned at the Highland Light Infantry's barracks at Maryhill, before going south to await Nuremberg and Spandau. In January of that year, when things were at their worst, Churchill had made a whistle stop tour of the Civil Defence units in Glasgow, accompanied by Harry Hopkins, President Roosevelt's special envoy. He had been told to report to the President on the British war effort and to decide whether or not America should lend support. The story goes that things did not look too bright until dinner in Room 21 of the North British Hotel in George Square, when the American was reminded of his Scottish ancestry. Hopkins was visibly moved and immediately pledged American support.

During the six years of the Second World War, the Clyde built 2,000 ships and undertook 600 conversions as well as the routine servicing and repairs. Work continued after the war as vessels were adapted to, or built for, peacetime needs. Again others overtook us and overseas shipbuilders absorbed a diminishing market. By the

German aerial photograph used to target Glasgow shipyards in the Second World War.

An old man gathers his things together following a bombing raid in 1941.

PARKHEAD FORGE

When Parkhead Forge was established to make wrought-iron forgings for shipbuilding in 1836, Parkhead was a little village at some distance from Glasgow. The forge grew to be synonymous with Parkhead, and to dominate it physically. It was founded by two brothers Keoch in 1836–37, and was taken over in 1840 by David Napier, the pioneer marine engineer. He got into financial difficulties, and in 1848 it was acquired by his cousin Robert, whose sons for time managed it, greatly increasing its capacity, and making wrought-iron armour plate. In 1860–61 Robert Napier transferred the forge to William Rigby, his son-in-law, and William Beardmore, a London-based marine enginer. Under this partnership, and that of William and Isaac Beardmore, Parkhead Forge became an integrated iron (later steel) works and forge capable of making the very largest forgings for engines and shipbuilders. W & I Beardmore were among the first to make steel by the open-hearth process, in 1881.

The forge was developed by William Beardmore junior, later Sir William Beardmore, as the heart of a massive business empire. With products including armour plate and guns it prospered in times of war. It was spared when massive rationalisation destroyed most of the Beardmore empire in the early 1930s.

By concentrating on high-quality steel-making and steel forging the works survived after 1945 but succumbed to changing economic conditions in the early 1980s. Its buildings have almost all been demolished. Part of the site is now The Forge shopping centre, but Beardmore's name has disappeared from Parkhead after more than a hundred years.

John R Hume

mid-Sixties, after Fairfield collapsed, the bigger yards amalgamated into groups such as Scott Lithgow at Port Glasgow and Upper Clyde Shipbuilders in Govan. Yarrows escaped from UCS and have survived, building Royal Navy surface vessels. Kvaerner have taken over the Govan yard on the opposite bank.

September, 1940, when Glasgow had its first air raid, was a critical stage for the Battle of Britain. Archie McKellar of the 602 City of Glasgow Squadron destroyed 16 enemy aircraft, more than any other Battle of Britain pilot. He had celebrated the award of his pilot's licence by swooping over the family house and dropping a box of chocolates for his mother's birthday. He joined 602 Squadron, getting his wings in 1937.

When war broke out, 602 and 603 were assigned to the Firth of Forth area. On 16 October, 1939, Flight Lieutenant George Pinkerton and Flying Officer Archie McKellar chased a Junkers 88 around the Firth. Pinkerton fired first and the aircraft fell; McKellar had a second burst before it hit the water. This was the first enemy aircraft shot down in the Second World War, credited to George Pinkerton. Twelve days later, while investigating reports of enemy activity in the Lothians, McKellar got first shot at a Heinkel 111, which was attacked by other 602 Spitfires and finally crashed six miles south of Haddington, the first enemy aircraft brought down on British soil during hostilities.

In August, 1940, McKellar joined 605 Squadron as a Flight Lieutenant and by the end of the month had won a Distinguished Flying Cross, gaining a Bar in September. By November 1, he was dead. No-one knows precisely what happened; McKellar's plane crashed into a mansion at Mayfield.

Glasgow already had an air pioneer who can claim to have attempted powered flight four years before the Wright Brothers took off in their rickety contraption.

Percy Pilcher worked in Glasgow University's naval architecture department. Inspired by Otto Lilienthal's prototype glider, Pilcher built The Bat in 1895 and launched it near Dumbarton. It worked beautifully and was so successful, modern gliders are little different. In 1899 Pilcher fitted a petrol engine to his glider and briefly soared above. The control wire snapped, the machine turned turtle and crashed. Pilcher was killed; but four years before Frank and Orville Wright took off in Kitty Hawk, powered flight had taken place in Glasgow. So often, the future begins here.

Percy Pilcher in flight.

Perchy Pilcher landing.

THE PEACE MOVEMENT IN THE WEST OF SCOTLAND

The peace movement in Scotland, until 1914, was dominated mainly by Quakers and other religious groups. The First World War, however, brought a radical and political change, allying it more closely with emerging organisations of resistance such as the British Socialist Party, sections of the Independent Labour Party, and the No-Conscription Fellowship. John Maclean, in 1915, spoke at the first meeting of the Free Speech Committee in Glasgow, while in the same year Helen Crawfurd joined with a variety of political speakers and conscientious objectors to form the Women's Peace Crusade in Scotland. The issue of conscientious objection remained important through the inter-war years, with the formation in 1936 of the influential Peace Pledge Union. The small PPU group in Glasgow was later to become instrumental in the founding of Scottish CND.

The destruction of Hiroshima on August 6th, 1945 ushered in the cold-war freeze and a susequent decline in the peace movement. However, the explosion of Britain's first H-bomb in 1957 resulted a year later in the formation of the Campaign for Nuclear Disarmament, and the predominance of the nuclear issue in future campaigns. In Glasgow at the instigation of George MacLeod, the well- known leader of the Iona Community, Scottish CND was formed, and the first major CND march in Glasgow took place on May 2nd 1959. This campaign became increasingly militant after the 1962 Nassau Agreement to site Polaris nuclear submarines at Holy Loch.

The movement experienced another decline during the 1970s, but the 1980 decision to replace Polaris with Trident focused attention on Faslane. The Nuclear Free Scotland campaign arose in consequence.

Douglas Finnigan

Rent strike protest of 1915, featuring children.

The Bennie Railplane, Milngavie, 1939. The war and lack of investment ensured that this public transport ideal foundered.

GLASGOW AND TRANSPORT

Glasgow, like Barcelona or Chicago, belongs to a city type essentially created by the transport revolution. Even before the railways came, in the 1830s, commuters were using the canals to Paisley and the Monklands and steamers on the Clyde estuary, and when the Edinburgh and Glasgow Railway opened in 1842 it offered cheap tickets to suburbanites. But the mobility which came from the building of several hundred miles of suburban railways and tramways mainly benefited the middle classes of an overwhelmingly working class city. In Bridgeton and Govan the workers lived hard by their shipyards, engine works and cotton mills. Commuting to work by train – notably to the huge Singer factory at Clydebank – was the exception.

In the 1950s American cities tore up their railways and built urban motorways in an attempt to reconcile individual mobility and urban development. Glasgow didn't abandon its public transport network, whose decline was reversed by the electric "Blue Trains" after 1959, but in the 1960s its Labour administration went further along the American path than any other British city, and remains committed to large-scale road projects at a time when these have been abandoned in most of Europe.

The devastation of areas like Anderston by motorways, and the disadvantage caused to the non-motorised majority of Glasgow folk, whose housing schemes are frequently remote from rail links and ill-served by expensive bus services, remains the "unacceptable face" of the post-industrial city.

Christopher Harvie

Chapter Twenty-four

A DIFFICULT ART

The art of prophecy is very difficult, especially with respect to the future
Mark Twain.

The fate of Glasgow will be the fate of the world.

The changes we are capable of making to our environment are now on a scale which effectively makes us all responsible for actions and forces which may endanger the survival of our whole species.[1]

Standards of heat, light, hygienic comfort and convenience for the developed world have allowed tiny domestic actions, repeated on a massive scale, to affect the whole world. Meanwhile the developing nations want to raise their standards of living and life expectancy. Having used them as chemical dumping grounds, we are now advising that they hobble their own progress for the sake of the environment. Not surprisingly, they accuse us of self-interest.

Economically, the future for Scotland and for Glasgow does not appear to be bright. Low income, low self-esteem and low employment seem destined to dog our footsteps far into the 21st century.[2]

The Economic and Social Research Council's 1987 *Inner Cities Research Programme* Case-Study on Clydeside shows how superficial changes for the better really are. The labour force is characterised as slow to adapt and the local economy as heavily reliant on public sector intervention. Clydeside has been a Special Development Area since the end of the Second World War and has received Great Britain's highest levels of public funding. As Government support for industry becomes increasingly scarce, this will almost inevitably hit Glasgow harder than before.

It looks as though the move from manufacturing to service industries will continue, along with an overall shortage of work. In April 1989, 22.6 per cent of Strathclyde Region's labour force

Nuclear submarine HMS Churchill. Masts and periscopes by Barr & Stroud of Glasgow.

1. James E Lovelock, **Gaia: A New Look at Life on Earth**, 1979. 2. See **Glasgow 2000, Healthy Cities Project, Position Statement** and **Strathclyde Social Trends, No. 2**, October, 1989.

STALWART, SURPRISING EUROPEAN CITY OF 1990

Glasgow. City of stalwart buildings. Scots city of the world. My brief glimpse of Glasgow in three warm, silky August days has left me brighter, more hopeful of Europe, and confused.

The same 19th century entrepreneurs who went to the Empire's outposts, to India and Malaya, and built railroads, dams, and hospitals have left their staunch belief in building for permanence in the many streets of gracious, gracefully decorated buildings which surprise the visitor expecting an industrialist city. Singapore still has the MacRitchie Reservoir around whose wooded sides joggers pant each evening.

I recognised a Scots integrity, modesty, and tolerance in the way shopkeepers, writers, taxi drivers, the ordinary Glaswegians in the street spoke to me, a middle-aged Asian woman forever asking for directions. But here also are Black, Indian and Chinese children with the lilting burr that marks them as Scots. They share the earnest reserved warmth I had begun to recognise as the city's distinctive air. A multi-racial, multi-cultural city?

Going across the corner from the posh Hospitality Inn to buy the Sunday papers, I also ran into a line of young people queuing for trashy news, beer, cigarettes, and plastic bags of day-old bread. They were shabby, obviously unemployed, poorly educated; city-dwellers who had fallen through its safety nets. They reminded me of my parents, my childhood, of the cultures of poverty that also live in bright, hopeful cities.

Glasgow has tantalising stores, avant-garde dramas, dance, and music. It has a complex, vital, divided society. I only wish I had time to explore it all.

Shirley Geok Lin Lim

were looking for work. Poverty has actually increased since 1981. Then, 98,000 received Supplementary Benefit but, by May 1986 the figure had risen to 148,500. As the heritage industry gathers momentum, attractions like the Scotch Whisky Heritage Centre in Edinburgh, the Bannockburn Centre at Stirling and the proposed Emigration Centre at Greenock indicate one of the country's few growth areas. The entire country is being turned into a theme park.

The Economic and Social Research Council also highlight the risks of Scotland's reliance on foreign owned companies and even UK owned concerns with the management outside Scotland. Between 1978 and 1981 almost half the jobs in foreign owned companies were gone. In the future, a falling birth rate will help soften the effects of economic decline by reducing the possible pool of employees. Increasing longevity and a rise in the proportion of old people in the population will however bring other pressures.

As men and women remain healthier and more active longer, middle age may move towards 50, 60 and 70. Pensioners will probably live longer and stay healthier, but as their numbers increase, the demands they make on the Welfare State are set to grow to a point where they can no longer be met. Proportionately, the elderly also make an increased demand on health care and social services; an area where resources are already stretched to breaking point. Medicare in America is set to run out of funds early in the 21st century, while in Britain we may be making a choice between pensions and dole payments or family allowance, since we are unlikely to be able to afford them all.[1]

The poor living and working conditions of a lower class life contribute to ill health in old age and for all those whom later life does not treat kindly, the future may be bleak. The elderly will have more political and economic muscle and we may see them influence society and government to such an extent, that whatever remains of our welfare provision shifts its emphasis towards the over-fifties.

NHS patients can presently expect to wait up to a year for a hip joint replacement and doctors regularly have to make decisions which withdraw, or do not offer, life saving support such as kidney dialysis because of a shortage of cash.[2]

There is no reason to suppose that medical and scientific research and development will do anything further than increase in speed and effect. It is much less clear whether the benefits of much of their achievements will be distributed any more equably tomorrow than they are today. Despite Victorian public health schemes and more recent campaigns, such as Good Hearted Glasgow, the city

EARLY OUTDOORS

The young man on the West Highland Way was David Barbour. He was about 21 years of age and a recent graduate of Glasgow University. Like many of his peers, David had found that his talents and qualifications appeared to have no value. He personified a repetition of history, for it was in the last depression that working people discovered the Scottish countryside on their doorsteps.

To people who had spent their lives in foundries, steelworks and shipyards the countryside was a new world which offered respite from the sheer dehumanising dreariness of unemployment, and from the harrassments of the hated means test man. The interest in the outdoors, once established, grew apace. On Sundays in the Thirties there were six times as many trams to Milngavie as on week days. Milngavie was the great stepping off place for Carbeth, Drymen, Loch Lomond, Crianlarich, Dalmally, and for the more adventurous, Glencoe and beyond. The depression period saw the genesis of the Craigdhu Mountaineering Club, the Glasgow Wheelers, and rambling and hill walking groups, some of which survive to this day.

At the legendary Craigallion fire, week-enders gathered to swop songs and stories. They lived rough but the crack was good, and friendships were formed which were to last a lifetime. Some of the lives were short, for many signed on for the International Brigade at Craigallion Loch to fight in the Spanish Civil War, the fascist dress rehearsal for 1939.

Jimmie Macgregor

1. See **Life**, February 1989. 2. A variety of well publicised charitable events and public appeals have so far masked the real effects.

A group of mothers, children and nurses at the London Road Child Welfare Clinic, June, 1922.

Third Eye Centre Sauchiehall Street.

Children playing outside at bookie's shop on Langlands Road

and Scotland in general, has an appalling record of ill health. It will take a massive change in health provision, education and living standards to bring about a change for the better in the future.

As the developed countries are brought into almost daily contact with the detrimental effects of their ecological blunders, self-interest is finally combining with altruism. Anyone will campaign to save rainforests if it ensures them a breathable atmosphere in years to come. Previous decades have seen environmentalists painstakingly decoding specialist reports and field observations, only to have their lonely voices drowned out by big business, the state or both. Not so long ago, AIDS was beyond even the imagination of science fiction writers, ten years ago the Greenhouse Effect was a joke, 15 years ago it was romantic for people to smoke in films and 20 years ago anyone who argued for birth control on the grounds of over population were assumed to be making a religious point.

If the Green Revolution has proved nothing else, it has shown that the general public, given adequate information, can still take governments and private enterprise by surprise. Both appear to have forgotten how much they still rely on goodwill and consensus to survive. It may be that, rather than the predicted conspicuous consumption, the future will demand zero economic growth in at least the prosperous countries.

None of these issues should necessarily defeat us, anymore than the changes we have already negotiated. Glasgow, as we have seen, has always been a city of transformation. Its streets have been paved and extended by all classes of men and women in every type of employment.

Our failing has been to preserve the title Second City of the empire when the Empire itself was fragmented. Our pride was excessive and outlives its sources.

Anyone in this place will tell you we are more than the sum of our parts. Individuals like Edwin Morgan, Alasdair Gray, Liz Lochhead, Tom Leonard, James Kelman and Hamish Whyte refuse to preserve the past in a misty glow, but constantly strive to bring us face to face with the world which made us and which we continue to make.

In a time which has been singularly inauspicious for the arts, Third Eye Centre in Sauchiehall Street has never stopped expanding and diversifying, standing apart from the timidity of cultural life elsewhere in Britain by the European tenor of its sensibility. Our City of Culture accolade belongs as much to their constant efforts and to Director Chris Carrell's strivings as to any other source. He and his staff have given substance to Glasgow's new image.

THE NEW GLASGOW GANG

In the 1980s a few young Glasgow-trained painters employed figuration of a reasonably accessible kind and, predictably, captured the interest of many who disliked the feeling that much modern art demanded to be met at least halfway.

Steven Campbell and Adrian Wisniewski were the first to surface; the one with a series of large canvases, exhuberant and often humorous, in the cursory but effective manner of old fashioned scene painting; and the latter making use of a flowing, colourful, linear technique, rather like traditional, decorative peasant art applied to figuration on a large scale.

Hard on their heels came two other Glasgow-trained painters, Ken Currie and Peter Howson, embarking on a new-style "socialist realism" which, paradoxically, is far more romantic than realistic. Currie and Howson make use of increasingly formalistic methods, often on a mural scale, to express their somewhat simplistic, not to say naive, ideas about "the workers" on the one hand, and macho muscularity on the other.

A totally different seam of figurative imagery is being mined by the younger artist, Stephen Conroy, whose exceedingly clever paintings in *chiaroscuro* – again almost entirely of male figures – with their enamelled surfaces and a sense of mystery that stems from the fact that the eyes are usually hidden and that much of the content is thrown into impenetrable shadow.

Some critics have gone so far as to compare Conroy's work with that of Degas and a review of Howson ludicrously invoked Michaelangelo but such over-statements do the young artists in question no service.

Cordelia Oliver

GLASGOW FICTION IN THE 20th CENTURY

If the Glasgow novel was slow to claim its aesthetic and social rights, some of the blame could be laid on the disruptive history of the city. Frederick Niven's *Justice of the Peace* (1914) caught the flavour of Edwardian Glasgow with its story, spoiled only by an abruptly melodramatic conclusion, of a young artist trying to break away from businessman father and over-pious mother; Catherine Carswell's *Open the Door* (1920) tells a similar tale, vividly but also with a weak ending, from a woman's point of view. But these beginnings were not carried forward.

The inter-war years saw George Blake's *The Shipbuilders* (1935), a readable but not always convincing attempt to deal with unemployment and industrial decline. It is only during the second half of the century that names cluster and crowd in: Robin Jenkins and William McIlvanney, Archie Hind and Alan Sharp, George Friel and Frederic Lindsay, Alasdair Gray and Agnes Owens and James Kelman. For the first time we have not only an acute social and psychological analysis but also an awareness of the novel's potential as an art form.

The imaginative build-up and layered socio-politcal complexities of Alasdair Gray's *Lanark* (1981) and the pent, nervous, accurate, skintight angers, explosions, and hopes of James Kelman's *A Disaffection* (1989) – both of them outstanding books – come out of, pay tribute to, and enrich a steadily emerging consciousness which is not a "school" and which casts its eye over the world (or the worlds, as an Indian would say) from its well-observed Glasgow base.

Edwin Morgan

The triumvirate of Giles Havergal, Robert David MacDonald and Philip Prowse have followed similar policies with the same foresight and courage at the Citizens' Theatre.

All of which is of significant economic importance, as are the city's diversity of nimble businesses which have replaced the monoliths of previous generations. Linn Products and the California Cake & Cookie Company are two sides of the same coin, displaying an eye (to say nothing of ears and teeth) for markets which were previously invisible to others.

Glasgow is a city of story telling, but that indicates more than a simple desire to shoot the breeze. Stories try the future on for size; they tell us things do not have to be this way. Glasgow's tales are a sign of the restlessness which continually forces the city on the world's attention. First we make things up, then we make them real.

The act of imagination grows ever more precious. Scotland may seem very far from the problems of the rain forests and certainly has a more stable and sophisticated economy than Argentina or Ethiopia. Scotland's economic good health is nevertheless linked to the health of its environment and these links will become stronger rather than weaker. Excessive aforestation coupled with conifer plantation has not only altered the look of the place, it has helped acidify rivers and lochs, radically changed natural habitat and altered the amount of free water available. The spruce and pine trees closely planted with dense needles act like a filter for the sulphate and nitrates now in our atmosphere. They also concentrate aluminium sometimes to toxic levels. Whenever it rains, these deposits are washed off and eventually reach streams, rivers and lochs. This effectively poisons them by intensifying the already disastrous effects of acid rain and nitrate overspill from farmlands.

Scotland without its heather, its deer, its famous fishing rivers or its whisky, which relies on the purity of local water supplies, would be a far less appetising prospect for the tourists, whose patronage we are now told we require. Though our sea fisheries have decreased in economic importance, increasing pollution, particularly of shell and bottom-feeding fish, may deliver the death blow. As more and more people are willing to pay money to see bottle-nosed dolphins, seals, seabirds and clean beaches, our future as a developed economy will rely increasingly heavily on the purification of our air and water.

These matters are not so far removed from our local concerns. Glasgow For People, a pressure group opposed to unnecessary motorways, launched a sale of action bonds to raise money for legal action against Malcolm Rifkind, Secretary of State for Scotland,

The recently renovated Citizens' Theatre.

THE ALBION

"The Albion" outlived all its Scottish contempories, staying independent until 1952, when it was taken over by British Leyland. With consistently wise management and products of sustained quality it did not suffer the financial ups and downs of some rivals, and after 1919 continued to prosper.

Its founders, Norman Fulton and T Blackwood Murray, were engineers whose initial experience with automobiles had been gained during their time with George Johnston as he developed his dogcart after 1894. With well considered plans ready they founded the Albion Motor Car Co in December 1899, and during 1900 the first production chassis was built in their modest Finnieston Street workshop.

The rightness of its design was confirmed by a leap in output to 21 in 1901 and growing demand led to the building of a sizeable factory at Scotstoun in 1903, with later extensions. In 1914, with production concentrated on goods and bus chassis, ouput was then 591 vehicles. By then Albion was selling strongly worldwide.

Almost 6,000 32 hp lorries were supplied to the War Office during the first war and after it survivors were bought back, properly reconditioned, then sold. This wise policy (followed also by Leyland) was typical of their responsible attitude. In design, a deliberately conservative line was taken; reliability and longevity, along with high standards of care and repair, mainly through the depot system, had special priority at all times.

Between the wars bus sales grew substantially, especially to Scottish operators, and the design of a wide range of commercials kept pace with changes in users' needs and in legislation.

George Oliver

should he approve plans to build another motorway through the city centre with twin bridges across the Clyde. Not only do the proposals have a familiar ring, but Glasgow For People accused Strathclyde Regional Council of lack of consultation.

The *Glasgow Herald* of September 30, 1989, reported that a spokeswoman "claimed that the council's plans were not particularly original – they resembled old motorway proposals drawn up in 1946 by a Glasgow Corporation planner, Mr Robert Bruce.

"Former chairman of the New Glasgow Society, Mr Gordon Borthwick urged the council to follow the example of 485 major cities across the world and adopt a light rapid transit system – or modern electrified tram system – in Glasgow".

Dredging the Clyde for the twin bridges, which would be situated beside the Kingston Bridge, would not only end shipping in the area, but it has also been suggested that in a storm the north side of George Square would be flooded.

The end of petrol-fuelled transport is being taken seriously elsewhere. Motorways are being closed in other countries while we are discussing building more car parks. Traffic congestion closes our motorways. A recent ironical tail-back on the motorway and feeder roads was caused by a full car park at the Scottish Exhibition and Conference Centre where the Scottish Motor Show was in progress.[1]

Proposals to transform Glasgow Green into a £32 million "multi purpose leisure and recreation centre" have also been criticised for lack of public consultation. An £18 million water park is proposed for Fleshers' Haugh with a £5 million art gallery at Kings Drive, a £2 million horticulture centre and a £6 million redevelopment planned for the Green itself.

Glasgow is the heart attack capital of the world. It is the major cause of increased death in women. Those most at risk are young women, especially young women who smoke. There are certain well established facts: smoking brings premature wrinkles and menopause, women who smoke during pregnancy have smaller babies who are more likely to be retarded. The majority of Glasgow's women smokers between the ages of 16 and 19, those most at risk, are from low income groups.[2]

Action seems to be coming from the European Parliament, though the present British Government have been slow to implement European health and environmental recommendations. Meanwhile the Belgian Government has banned smoking in all publicly owned buildings. People find it hard to distinguish which buildings allow smoking and which do not, but the legislation is popular, so there

Smoking. Detail from "The Barras 1984" by Avril Paton.

1. Daily Record, November 18, 1989. 2. Glasgow 2000, Healthy Cities Project, Position Statement.

is a general co-operation because it actually helps. A proposal to ban smoking in all European public buildings is currently before the European Parliament. It will be law by 1992.

AIDS is the only disease composed entirely of capital letters. It is increasing in Glasgow, as elsewhere; or rather this is the general assumption, but no-one really knows, for the official figures are generally mistrusted. To save the sensibilities of the victims' families, doctors are putting causes other than AIDS on death certificates. It is generally reckoned deaths from AIDS are three times the official figures and that available resources are already overstretched. There are appalling stories of individual hardship and terror caused through public ignorance. People believe what they want to. They believe they are immune, but that they can become infected by touching an AIDS victim. They do not believe what they hear: infected prostitutes addicted to heroin, having unprophylactic sex with a punter for an extra fiver, addicts sharing the same jail cell sharing a needle with someone they know to be HIV positive, purely for a fix. There is a credibility gap between the public's perception, their own experience and the scale of the problem. AIDS is likely to affect anyone, but no-one believes it. Others say the problem is already so immense that the Government dare not release the true statistics.

Glasgow police were so concerned at the reported statistical increase, that they stepped up their raids on massage parlours and saunas and local newspapers stopped advertising their services. A recent AIDS Awareness Week in Drumchapel finished off with a Safe Sex Ceilidh. Local people are apparently still embarrassed by the word Sex, so the ceilidh was advertised as a Safe Winching Ceilidh. Winching was always considered pretty safe anyway. It is defined by Michael Munro as "to go out with a member of the opposite sex . . . to kiss and cuddle".[1]

Anti-smoking. A campaign of the Eighties.

AIDS IN GLASGOW

Up to March 31st, 1989, 259 persons are known to have HIV infection in the Greater Glasgow Health Board area. Of these, 37 per cent are homosexual, 28 per cent are drug injectors and 17 per cent became infected as a result of infected material (Factor VIII) formerly used to treat haemophilia.

Because a person infected with HIV may not have developed clinical signs of disease it is not possible to determine the true number of infected people. An estimate has been made by the Greater Glasgow Health Board in the following way:

Drug injectors – It is thought there are between 8–12,000 drug injectors in Glasgow and further estimated that there are between 225–550 infected injectors. *Homosexual men* – It is calculated that there are 150–300 infected homosexual men in the city. *Heterosexual contact* – There are not thought to be more than 50–100 people infected through heterosexual contact. *Haemophilia* – 33 patients have been infected.

Using the above assumptions the Greater Glasgow Health Board estimates that at March 31st, 1989 there were between 460 and 1,000 people in Glasgow with HIV infection. Unfortunately, predicting the number of cases likely to occur over the next few years is a difficult task but it has been calculated that around 175 cases of AIDS may require treatment by 1992; this does not include the growing number of people with HIV infection who have yet to develop symptoms.

Glasgow has had to deal with daunting epidemics of infection before. The determination once shown in the face of poliomyelitis and tuberculosis survives and augurs well in the search for a solution to the AIDS problem.

Daniel Reid

1. Michael Munro, **The Patter**, 1985.

Chapter Twenty-four
A DIFFICULT ART

Glasgow at sunset, looking west along George Street.

Postcard featuring Wee Macgreegor, the hero of J.J. Bell's popular tales early this century.

Epilogue

A WORD IN YOUR EAR

A corner of Sandyfauld Street around 1955.

In 1985, Glasgow District libraries published "A Current Guide to Glasgow Usage" and since then *The Patter* has become the best selling Scottish paperback of all time. Having sold well over 100,000 copies world-wide and with a sequel in the shops, there are no indications that the phenomenon is petering out.[1]

In his Introduction to the first volume, its compiler, Michael Munro, describes his book as "a defining guide to the language of . . . Glasgow", moving on to point out that Glasgow speech has rarely, if ever, found its way into print and that generations of Glasgow's idiosyncratic observations on life and current philosophies have been lost. Rather than categorising it as a derivative of the Queen's English, he returns it to its rightful place as a "valid regional dialect" with its own unique growth and development, to say nothing of a remarkable sense of humour.

Tom Leonard had already gone a step further; indeed, it could be argued that a climate for *The Patter*, could not have existed without Leonard's intellectual trail blazing. Insisting that language is a sound system and that our linguistic preconceptions of "good" and "bad" are class-based, he has done more than anyone to lift our everyday language away from the parochial interpretations of comedy and pawky cosmeticisation. Leonard has shown a working class form of expression to be as suitable a vehicle for poetry and serious thought as any other, giving the lie to the idea that literature and truth are reserved for those who are fluent in standard English.[2]

The word on the street is gallus and the attitude is gallusness, defined as "cocky, sharp, bold, tough, flash, nonchalant." It is, of course, all of these things and none of them; it is itself, best with the adjective dead. To be dead gallus is to be beyond reproach.

A friend would talk about "giving it the full boona." Anyone who goes to the pub after work knows there comes a time when you might as well be hung for a sheep as a lamb. "Right," said

Cumberland Street, Hutchesontown, before the demolition.

1. Rather it is spreading itself into publications such as **Electric Soup** and **The Bogie Man**.
2. See Tom Leonard, **Intimate Voices**, 1984.

"Saturday Barrows near Albert Bridge" by Muirhead Bone.

Sweeney. "Are we gonnae give it the full boona?" He meant we weren't going home immediately.

There used to be an Indian restaurant in Bank Street which offered customers "a full boona" or "a half boona" and I suppose the expression came from there, though Harry worked in the yards and I'd guess that is where it really emerged.

Another Indian restaurant used to call pakoras "Indescribables" because the waiters did not know how they were made. I recently heard a girl ask for, "Two wee Indescribables tae cairry oot, please," in a late night grocers on Great Western Road.

Munro's central point is that language is constantly changing; new meanings are continually being ascribed to familiar words or phrases, and this has generated an imaginative game of origination. Popular mythology has the well-known Glasgow term steamboats originating in the doon the watter sails by paddle steamer; drink was sold on these vessels, patrons drank it; therefore one begat the other. I find it difficult to believe that language works in such an obviously literary way. I think the word is simply a corruption of steaming, the most descriptive of the many synonyms for drunkenness to be found in *The Patter*.

You could also have a good Bayne and Ducket, on the depth charges, which would leave you bazooka'd, bladdered, birlin, or blitzed. Turn up to the work like that an you'll get the bump, probably do your bunnet and end up with a face like a Hallowe'en Cake, or even a melted wellie, in and out the Dale, or some other spinbin, generally not knowing if it's New York or the New Year.

Over the two books, the varieties of nips to be found in this city are faithfully recorded, ranging from a euphemism for seduction to, "Ah'll see if Ah can nip the brother for a ten-spot," or, "Never mind yer fag, we've no got time. Nip it and stick it behind yer ear." And, of course, the verse about Samson going along the Gallowgate picking up the nips is here, at long last correcting the Edinburgh folklorist who suggested it meant Samson was "getting free drink".

Rhyming slang disnae work but. The trouble wi rhyming slang in this place is the folk who make it up as they go along. Jiggers you. Who'd make sense of something like, "Take a jump doon the cream cookie and put a wee line on for us, son." If the line comes up, the citizen can be expected to do "a fair bit o damage", assuming, of course, others will "wear it". If the line "stots", he will be "aa cut up" and could even consider "wrapping it up" or "in", depending on where he, or she, lives.

"Gossip" by Josef Herman.

A WORD IN YOUR EAR

The Bogie Man.

There are three definitions of "a line" – betting slip, a doctor's line, or, "A special discount arrangement to be used in a designated shop or warehouse: 'A woman in the work's got a line for Goldbergs.'" Which means a line is also a cheque, maybe even a Provvy cheque.

Boots' Corner at Union Street and Argyle Street is defined as "a famous trysting place". It is also known as Dizzy Corner: "To be left alone and palely loitering here is the height of humiliation," says Munro, though anyone who doesn't get a "dizzy" has "knocked it off", dressed no doubt in "the good gear" they got with the "line", unless, of course, they'd "blagged it".

The SS, the Meanie or a Monday Book can fair rummle you up. Tans that Spam Valley team but, them that hide in the shunkie when the Meanie Man comes and have tae dive back oot when they think it's the society man or the wee tallyman. Definately BS'd, aye looking for a tap, dive bombing for douts and everything an they widnae gie ye a spear if they wur Zulus, widnae even gie ye the itch.

"I've got a mooth like a pocketful o dowts," says this yin. Worked in the yards as well. "Got a mooth like a row o condemned buildings", he tellt us eftir a claim when he was dug up and blootered by some wee chib man that was hauf scooped. Wee guy's double wide but, oot gallavantin and left without nane. Tried tae give it a B-wan and got a big Sammy Craw, bealin, so he was but, though tae hear him he's eachie-ochie.

Had tae flit tae Polomint City, roarin and greeting, Big Idleonian wi a huvtae case for a weddin; eftir livin up wi her for ages, sticks her in the plum. Just shows ye. Looked as if he's ready for a clap wi a spade, next thing he's giving it "Here Comes the Bride". What's fur ye will no go by ye.

That's your whack. This is me since yesterday.

And another thing . . .

CREDITS

The creation of *Glasgow's Glasgow*, by the educational charity 'The Words and the Stones' has been accomplished in three phases.

The first phase, from the formulation of the idea by Doug Clelland in May 1987, to the conclusion of two feasibility studies in June 1988, lasted 13 months. These studies indicated that a city centre venue, which could remain open for public assembly throughout the coming decade, could be refurbished by 1990. Equally, the idea behind the event drew widespread support and had exceptional potential to penetrate the story of Glasgow in a way likely to have popular appeal.

The second phase, from the commencement of project development in July 1988 until September 1989, when our principal patron Glasgow District Council gave their "unconditional support" for the realisation of *Glasgow's Glasgow*, lasted 14 months.

The third phase of 9 months spanned from September 1989 until April 1990, when the event was opened. This period was devoted to the technical realisation of the project and to the preparations needed to welcome the public in.

PHASE ONE: FEASIBILITY MAY 1987-JUNE 1988

STEPS

May 1987
Idea floated by Doug Clelland.

July 1987
Brief report on the idea prepared.

Aug 1987
Charity formation commences.
Meetings with Bob Palmer and Neil Wallace.
John Bampton joins the project.

Sept 1987
Research begins.

Oct 1987
First sketches and specifications.
Andrew MacMillan joins the project.
Sarah Wiscombe joins the project.

Nov 1987
An *Event* and not an *Exhibition* is the ambition.
– The *Arches* are discovered as a possible venue.
– Presentation of the idea to a group of public sector officials.

Dec 1987
Sketches and specifications for the *Arches* as venue.

Jan 1988
Glasgow and the *Epic*. The search for a way to interpret Glasgow's story in a deeply dramatic way.

Feb 1988
British Rail agree for studies to be undertaken on the *Arches* refurbishment.

Mar 1988
Business Plan begins.
Two Feasibility Studies commenced.
Alison Miyauchi joins the team.
Contact begins with all 'interested parties' in Glasgow and elsewhere.
First project office established at 2 Southpark Avenue, Glasgow.

May 1988
First explanatory brochure completed and circulated.
First detailed budget prepared.
Doug Clelland introduces the geographical analogy for the organisation of the event.

June 1988
Carl MacDougall joins the team.
Presentation of the two Feasibility Studies, one to Glasgow District Council, Strathclyde Regional Council and Glasgow Action (the *Event*) and the second to the British Rail Property Board, The Scottish Development Agency and Mitchell Car Hire (the *Arches*).

TEAM

Doug Clelland - Founder, Chairman & Managing Director
From May 1987

John Bampton - Marketing Director
From August 1987

Andrew MacMillan - Advisor
From October 1987

Sarah Wiscombe - Administrator & Assistant Project Manager
From October 1987

Alison Miyauchi - Assistant Curator, Research Co-ordinator & Caption Editor
From March 1988

Carl MacDougall - Writer
From June 1988

Siobhan MacMillan - Secretarial
From March 1998

Jaginder Kaur - Secretarial
From March 1988

Associates

Clelland Associates - Architects - Gavin Rae (Co-ordinator)
Dunsmore, Reid and Smith - Quantity Surveyors
Wallace Whittle & Partners - Mechanical & Electrical Engineers
Alastair Sidey and Associates - Structural Engineers
Mason Land Surveys - Surveyors

PHASE TWO: DEVELOPMENT JULY 1988 - SEPTEMBER 1989

July 1988
Terms of Reference established for the first development stage.
Detailed research commenced.
Working Papers circulated to a wide group.
Detailed work commenced on the refurbishment of the *Arches*.

Aug 1988
A team of six full time researchers is established.
Work begins in detail on the history/geography relationship inherent in the organising principle.
Glasgow as a "trading place" of ideas, people and things.
The first two Advisors' meetings.

Sept 1988
Interpretation Plan begins.
Alternative venues are considered due to major threats to the *Arches* as venue.
First Project Review.
Publications strategy determined.
End of "pure research".
Theatre strategy determined.
Third Advisors' meeting.

Oct 1988
Completion of *First Project Review*.
Terms of reference established for the second development stage.
Research team dedicated to the main publication.

Nov 1988
There is strong opposition to the project within specific groups.

Jan 1989
The *Arches* are discussed at a "Summit Meeting" among interested parties.
First television coverage about the event.
Conclusion of research directed to the main publication.
The research/design relationship results in a key layout of the event.
Artefact research and selection process begins.
The eighth feasibility project for the *Arches* Refurbishment proves to be acceptable to all interested parties.
Indemnity under the 1980 National Heritage Act is promoted.

Mar 1989
Presentation to representatives from a variety of Museums and Galleries.
Presentation to the Labour Group of Glasgow District Council.
Key plan of the Event.

Apr 1989
Second presentation to the Labour Group of Glasgow District Council.
Terms of Reference established for the third development stage.
Interpretation Plan and Budget Plan reach a definitive stage.

May 1989
Orientation spaces within the enclosed Midland Street are devised.
Touche Ross appointed as financial controllers and project co-ordinators represented by Ian Rae.
Transportation analysis commences for artefact movement.
Commencement of picture archive.
Brick and stone cleaning begins in the North *Arches*.

June 1989
Move project office to Washington Street.
Commence the *Big Model*.
Commence *Second Project Review*.
Loan Form Package is drafted.
Andy Arnold joins in.
Paul Sutton joins in.
Peter Wilson joins in.
Appoint Contractors to undertake the refurbishment of the *Arches*.
Analysis of research themes to be dropped.
First Loan Forms issued.

July 1989
Media are introduced to the *Arches*.
Interpretation Plan elements established and finalised.
Artefact selection complete by mid July.
Decision to name '*The Words and the Stones*' first event "*Glasgow's Glasgow*".
Contact Barry Lord in Toronto inviting him to act as Technical Curator and to participate in our *Second Project Review*.
Invited designers briefed on inner architecture.

Aug 1989
'Event Communications Ltd' participate in the *Second Project Review*.
Orientation spaces developed and the first 1:20 designs are received from the consultant designers.
All Loan Forms are sent out.
The Board of Directors unanimously agree that the project is on course.
The 'Event Communications Ltd' contribution to the *Second Project Review* is judged unhelpful.

Sept 1989
Bob Clyde and Phil Tweedy chosen to create the audio visual displays based on the Interpretation Plan.
Hugh Spencer joins in as Interpretive Planner to complete the Interpretation Plan.
Board of Directors presented with the conclusions to the *Second Project Review*. Presentation of the Project to members of the Labour Group of Glasgow District Council at Washington Street.
The "unconditional support" of Glasgow District Council is confirmed.

TEAM

Doug Clelland, John Bampton, Jaginder Kaur, Alison Miyauchi, Carl MacDougall, Sarah Wiscombe. (From Phase One).

Andy Arnold - Artistic Director
From June 1989

Mark Baines - Design Director
From February 1989

Tim Bampton - Research
From August 1989

Martin Bellamy - Research & Registrar
From August 1988

Anna Black - Housekeeper
From June 1989

Elspeth Campbell - Secretary
From June 1989

Margaret Casey - Secretary
From July 1989

Vivienne Clarke - Marketing
From October 1989

Lynn Cochrane - Research
From July 1988

Morag Cross - Research, picture research & caption research
From April 1989

John Crossland - Marketing
From October 1989

Alison Dunn - Research
From August 1988

Abigail Fields - Receptionist
From September 1989

Simon Fraser - Model Maker
From July 1989

Eleanor Harris - Events Co-ordinator
From July 1989

Linsey Irvine - P/A to Managing Director
From July 1989

Barry & Gail Lord - Curator & Deputy Curator
From August 1989

Annette MacMillan - Secretary
From July 1989

Fred MacMillan - Photographer
From July 1988

Francis McKee - Research & Interpretation
From August 1988

Ian McGuchan - Accountant
From June 1989

David Newbury - Research
From September 1988

Gerrie O'Neill - Marketing
From July 1989

Christine Neish - Marketing
From October 1989

Nick Patterson - Model Maker
From June 1989

Jill Paton - Research & Picture Archive
From August 1988

Ian Rae - Project Co-ordinator & Financial Controller
From May 1989

Hugh Spencer - Interpretation Planner
From September 1989

Paul Sutton - Design Director
From June 1989

Peter Wilson - Design & Construction Director
From June 1989

Associates

Clelland Associates - Architects - Gavin Rae (Co-ordinator); Juliet Bidgood: Dunsmore, Reid and Smith: Alastair Sidey & Associates: Wallace Whittle & Partners (from Phase One).

N.G. Bailey Ltd - Electrical Contractor
Benson & Forsyth - Architects (Area 17)
Building Co-ordination - Project Management
W.L. Chalmers Ltd - Mechanical Contractors
Paul Clarke - Architect (Area 18)
Elder & Cannon - Architects (Refurbishment and Area 6)
Gareth Griffiths - Marketing and Sponsorship
Glasgow University - Machine production
Harper - Architects (Areas 14 and 15)
Kane & Robertson - Architects (Area 9)
Kilbryde Marketing Ltd - Marketing
Lighting Design Partnership - Lighting
Colin Mackenzie - Architect (Area 10 part)
David MacMillan - Architect (Area 16 part)
McGurn, Logan, Duncan & Opfer - Architects (Area 16 part)
A. McIntyre Ltd - Joiners
Meadowline Services - Plumbing
MDW - Building Contractors
New Acoustics Ltd - Sound Consultants
Ontario Science Centre - Machine production
Page & Park - Architects (Area 16 part)
Protective Services Ltd - Flooring Contractors
Rex Stewart Advertising - Media Briefing
Simister Monaghan - Architects (Area 11)
E.J. Stiell - Electrical Contractor
Strategic Research Unit - Focus Group Surveys
Stoneguard - Stone and Brick cleaning
Thorn Security - Security Consultants
Touche Ross - Project Co-ordination & Financial Control
Robin Webster - Architect (Area 12)
Clare and Sandy Wright - Architects (Area 7)

PHASE THREE: REALISATION SEPTEMBER 1989 - APRIL 1990

STEPS

Sept 1989
Interpretation Plan and Overall Design Layout concluded.

Oct 1989
Rebriefing of the Area designers.
Selection of international loans.
Detailed specification of the Audio Visual Displays.
1,000 artefacts confirmed.
Media preview at Washington Street.
First large artefacts delivered to site.
Kevin McCarra joins in.
Arches refurbished Phase One complete.
Presentation to the Advisors at Washington Street and visit to the *Arches*.

Dec 1989
Determination of all "hands on" machines.
David Farrer appointed as Operations Director.
Determination of the extent of the electronic catalogue.

Jan 1990
Approval of the Museums and Galleries Commission on Indemnity.
1,500 artefacts confirmed.
Inner architecture contracts begin on site.
Press and Publicity campaign agreed.
TV advertisement to be created.
Detailed delivery patterns determined.
Media coverage of the arrival of the first artefacts.
Graphic panels finalised.
Final design decisions on the making of Midland Street.
2,000 artefacts confirmed.
Final scripts agreed for the AV interpretation.
Interpretative text sent to all Advisors.

Feb 1990
Installation of 2,500 artefacts begins.

Mar 1990
Installation of all AV and other building areas.
Visit by HRH Prince Philip, The Duke of Edinburgh.

Apr 1990
Rehearsal and opening.

TEAM

Doug Clelland, John Bampton, Alison Miyauchi, Carl MacDougall, Sarah Wiscombe. (From Phase One).

Andy Arnold, Martin Bellamy, Anna Black, Margaret Casey, Vivienne Clarke, Morag Cross, John Crossland, Abigail Fields, Eleanor Harris, Linsey Irvine, Barry & Gail Lord, Ian McGuchan, Francis McKee, Gerrie O'Neill, Christine Neish, Jill Paton, Ian Rae, Paul Sutton, Peter Wilson (From Phase Two).

Crawford Armstrong - Preparator
From February 1990

Gordon Black - Design Assistant
From November 1989

Celine Blair - Preparator
From March 1990

Sarah Broomhead - Preparator
From February 1990

Pamela Brown - Secretary
From January 1990

Naomi Chiswell - Preparator
From February 1990

Ellen Clarke - Preparator
From March 1990

John Dinse - Site Management
From December 1989

Laura Drysdale - Conservator
From September 1989

Amanda Farr - Preparator
From March 1990

David Farrer - Operations Director
From January 1990

Ken Gibson - Marketing
From February 1990

Anne Graham - Education Officer
From December 1989

Fiona Grieve - Preparator
From February 1990

Elizabeth Harkin - Preparator
From November 1990

Yvonne Innes - Secretary
From January 1990

Thelma Keynes - Preparator
From February 1990

Brenda Kinnaird - Preparator
From February 1990

John Kirketerp - Design Assistant
From February 1990

Myra MacDonald - Bookings
From February 1990

Susan MacLennan - Preparator
From February 1990

Claire Mason - Preparator
From February 1990

John McCafferty - Education Texts
From November 1989

Kevin McCarra - Editor
From October 1989

Lynne McCreight - Graphic Designer
From February 1990

Clare McGinley - Design Assistant & Preparator
From September 1989

Maura McKeough - Preparator
From March 1990

Ian McPhie - Design Assistant
From December 1989

Lee Mitchell - Design Assistant & Preparator
From September 1989

Alison Mills - Preparator
From March 1990

Samantha Moyes - Customer Relations
From February 1990

Anne Murray - Preparator
From February 1990

Oscar van Nieuwenhuizen, Preparator
From February 1990

Gillian Niven - Caption Research & Preparator
From January 1990

Margaret Pettigrew - Secretary
From December 1989

Julie Pottak, Preparator
From February 1990

Colin Proudfoot - Production Manager
From January 1990

Noreen Qureshi - Preparator
From February 1990

Jane Raftery - Preparator
From February 1990

William Robertson - Duty Manager
From February 1990

Onie Rollins - Preparator
From February 1990

Alison Scott - Conservation Officer
From December 1990

Sandy Scott - Driver
From February 1990

Greg Shannon - Design Assistant
From January 1990

Emma Smith - Preparator
From February 1990

Josie Stevens - Press & Publicity Officer
From January 1990

Associates

Clelland Associates - Architects - Gavin Rae (Co-ordinator); Juliet Bidgood: Dunsmore, Reid and Smith: Alastair Sidey & Associates: Wallace Whittle & Partners (from Phase One).

N.G. Bailey Ltd: Benson & Forsyth: Building Co-ordination: W.L. Chalmers: Paul Clarke: Elder & Cannon: Glasgow University: Harper Mackay: Kane & Robertson: Kilbryde Marketing Ltd: Lighting Design Partnership: Colin Mackenzie: David MacMillan: A. McIntyre Ltd: McGurn, Logan, Duncan & Opfer: MDW: Meadowline Services, New Acoustics Ltd: Ontario Science Centre: Page & Park: Protective Services: Simister Monaghan: E.J. Stiell: Strategic Research Unit: Stoneguard: Thorn Security: Touche Ross: Robin Webster: Clare and Sandy Wright. (From Phase 2).

Barlow Shopfitting - Shopfitters
Birley Electrical - Electrical Contractors
Building Co-ordination - Project Managers
Butler & Tanner - Printers
CCR - Photographic Colour Separation
Cognitive Applications - Computer Software Consultants
W.M. Display Studio - Exhibition Contractors
Dorothea Restorations - Museum Restoration Work
Joe Fisher - Book Contents Reader
Andy Gibb - Book Contents Reader
John Hewer - Typesetter
H.R.A. Heritage & Leisure - Production of Hands-on Machines
Image & Print - Text Layout and Print Service
Interactive Television Ltd - Computer Programming for A/V
Kevin Jones Associates - Technical Illustrations
John Smith & Son - Booksellers
L & R Leisure plc - Staff Training
M & M Printers - Printers
Samuel McGarva & Sons - Blacksmiths and Metal Workers
Michael Kelly Associates - Public Relations Consultants
Newton Display Group - Exhibition Contractors
Oompah Productions - Film and Sound Production for A/V
Pointsize Associates - Graphic Designers
Pullman (Scotland) Ltd - Hardware Contractors for A/V
Scottish & Newcastle Brewers - Alcohol Suppliers
Smart Graphics Ltd - Exhibition Graphics
Typographica - Design and Print
Wheatsheaf - Catering Consultants
Wide Art - Graphic Design Consultants
Wings Design Consultants - Graphic Design Consultants
Eric Young - Photographer

PRINCIPAL FILM CREDITS

Anchor Lines Ltd
François Aubry
Barclay Lennie Fine Arts
BBC Scotland
BP Exploration Ltd
Clyde Port Authority
Contemporary Films
CWS
Film Search Inc
Glasgow District Council
Glasgow Herald
Glasgow University Archives
GPO film Unit
Stuart Hepburn
Kvaerner Govan
Island Records
Island Visual Arts
Councillor Pat Lally
The Lillie Art Gallery
Kirsty MacDougall
Janet McBain - Scottish Film Archive
Susie Maguire
Movietone News Ltd
National Film Board of Canada
Neil Baxter Associates
Phonogram
Heike Rambow
Jimmy Reid
Scottish Film Library
Scottish Television plc
Sheffield Film Co-op
Windex Ltd
Frank Wordsall

THEATRE

Janie Andrews - Prop Maker
Andrew Barr - Actor
Raymond Burke - Actor
Andrew Dallmeyer - Writer
Neil Herriot - Actor
Tom Houston - Musical Arranger
Graham Hunter - Designer
Paula Macgee - Actress
Marie Claire McGuinness - Actress
Rosemary McNeill - Musician
Maggie Miller - Costumes
Ronan O'Donnell - Actor
Andi Ross - Co-ordinator Young Peoples Theatre
Mark Saunders - Actor
Julian Sleath - Theatre Consultant
Grant Smeaton - Actor
Vivian Stanshall - Music for promenades
Kath Wishart - Stage Manager

PATRONS

British Rail Community Fund
Glasgow District Council
Scottish Development Agency
Strathclyde Regional Council

BOARD DIRECTORS

Douglas Clelland
Founder Chairman and Managing Director

Mark Baines
The Mackintosh School of Architecture

John Bampton
Marketing Director

Professor Thomas Carbery, OBE., Department of Information Science Strathclyde University

Bill English
Director of Finance
Glasgow District Council

Carl MacDougall
Writer

Professor Andrew MacMillan
The Mackintosh School of Architecture

Christopher Purslow
Director of Architecture
Glasgow District Council

James Rae
Director of Planning
Glasgow District Council

Julian Spalding
Director of Museums and Galleries
Glasgow District Council

ACADEMIC ADVISORS

Archaeology
Mr Donald Farmer

Dr Lawrence Keppie
Hunterian Museum

Mr Hugh McBrien
Scottish Urban Archaeological Trust

Architecture
Mr Charles McKean, BA, FRSA, The Royal Incorporation of Architects in Scotland

Professor Andrew MacMillan
The Mackintosh School of Architecture

Professor Tom Maver
University of Strathclyde

Archive
Mr Joe Fisher
Mitchell Library

Mr Michael Moss
University of Glasgow

Cultural History
Professor David Daiches

Dr John Durkan
University of Glasgow

Economic History
Professor A Skinner
University of Glasgow

Professor Anthony Slaven
Glasgow University

Geography
Mr Andy Gibb
University of Glasgow

Historic Buildings
Mr David M Walker
Scottish Development Department

Ideas & Information
Professor Tom Carbery, OBE., Strathclyde University

Mr Edward Chisnall
Bell in the Tree Limited

Professor Blaise Cronin
University of Strathclyde

Professor Laurie Hunter
Convenor 1990 Committee

Ms Cordelia Oliver

Mr Hamish Whyte

Literature
Dr Douglas Gifford
University of Glasgow

Professor Andrew Hook
University of Glasgow

Mr Edwin Morgan

Marketing
Mr Andy Low
Strathclyde University

Mr Neil Walden
Strathclyde Unviersity

Museums & Galleries
Mr Timothy M Ambrose
Scottish Museums Council

Music
Mr Thomas Laurie, OBE

Physics & Astronomy
Professor Archie E Roy
University of Glasgow

Scottish History
Mr Angus Calder
Open University

Professor A A M Duncan
University of Glasgow

Urban History
Dr Nick Morgan
University of Glasgow

Dr Charles Oakley

LENDERS

7:84 Theatre Co.
A G Barr Plc
Aberdeen Art Gallery & Museums
Academisch Historisch Museum, Leiden
AKA Books
Altec Laboratory Services (Scotland) Ltd
An Lanntair Gallery, Stornoway
Archive of Historical Architecture, University of Strathclyde
Archives Nationales, Paris
Archives of Queen Mary & Westfield College
Argyll & Bute District Council
Armitage Shanks Ltd
Assist Architects
Auchindrain Museum, Inveraray, Argyll
Avril Paton
Bank of Scotland
Barclay Lennie
Barr & Stroud
John Bartholemew
BBC Hulton Picture Library
Bearsden & Milngavie District Council
Ben Line Group
Ben Uri Art Society
Bernard Beagan
Bet Low
BFI Stills, Posters & Designs
Blackies Publishers
Boundary Gallery
Boys Brigade
BP Exploration
British Aerospace (Commercial Aircraft) Limited, Prestwick
British Architectural Drawings Collection
British Gas Scotland
British Motor Heritage Ltd
British Telecom, West of Scotland
British Waterways
Burmah Oil Trading Limited
Burnthills Demolition Ltd
California Cake & Cookie Limited
Canadian Museum of Civilisation
Canadian Pacific Railway
Celtic Football Club
City of Edinburgh Art Centre
City of Edinburgh Art Collection
Clyde Port Authority
Clyde River Steamer Club
Clyde Ship Trust
Clyde Shipping Company
Clydebank District Museum
Coats the Thread Makers
Colin McKenzie, Hi-Fi Corner
Colonial Williamsburg Foundation
Culross Abbey Church
Cutty Sark Maritime Trust
David Edgar
David M Stewart Museum
Department of Anaesthesia, University of Glasgow
Department of Political Economy, University of Glasgow
Det Kongelige Bibliotek, Copenhagen
Donald MacCormick, Antiquarian Bookseller, Edinburgh
Dr Martin Ansell
Dugald Cameron
Dundee Art Galleries & Museums
Dunsmore Reid & Smith
Easterhouse Arts Project
Edward Chisnall
Ellan Bain
Engineering Applications Centre, University of Strathclyde
F S Insurance
Fischer Fine Art, London
Fletcher Smith Ltd

G L Watson (Naval Architects) Ltd
Gardiner's Sewing Machine Centre
George Wyllie
Gerald F Belton
Gilbert Stelter
Gillespies Landscape Architects
Gladstone Pottery Museum
Glasgow Chamber of Commerce
Glasgow District Council
Glasgow District Council, Department of Parks and Recreation
Glasgow District Council, Planning Department
Glasgow District Health Board Archives
Glasgow District Libraries
Glasgow Herald
Glasgow Humane Society
Glasgow Museums and Art Galleries
Glasgow Print Studio
Glasgow School of Art
Glasgow University Archives
Glasgow University Library
Glenbow Museum
Gray Art Gallery & Museum, Hartlepool
Greater Manchester Museum of Science and Industry
Guildhall Art Gallery, City of London
Hans Christian Andersen Museum
Heatherbank Museum of Social Work, Milngavie
Hermitage Academy, Helensburgh
Historic Buildings and Monuments
Historisches Museum der Stadt Wien
Hunterian Museum, University of Glasgow
I D Lloyd Jones
IBM
Institute of Engineers and Shipbuilders in Scotland
Iona Records
Isle of Arran Museum Trust
J S Edgar, Toronto, Canada
Jack Knox
James Howden & Co Ltd
James Reid Mackellar
Jewish Museum, London
Jimmy Boyle
John Letters & Co
Kelvin Museum, University of Glasgow
Kirk Session of Govan Old Parish Church
Kvaerner Govan
Laing's the Jewellers
Lillehammer Art Museum, Lillehammer, Norway
Limaclad Ltd
Linn Products
Lloyds Register of Shipping
Louise & Norman Naftalin
Mackintosh School of Architecture
MacTaggart & Mickel Ltd
Marquess of Lothian
Martin Bellamy
Matthew S Miller
McCall Bros, Govan
McGill University, Rare Books Department
Messrs Wartski, London
Meteorological Office
Metropolitan Toronto Reference Library
Midnight Films
Mike MacKiggan
Miss Sheila Erskine
Morris Harris
Mr Patrick Telfer Smollett
Mr Richard Carl Humphrey
Mrs A Coventry
Mrs Constance Sale
Mrs F Sutherland
Mrs I C Rogers
Mrs R Henderson Blyth
Municipal Archives of Amsterdam
Musée du Louvre
Museum of Communication
Museum of Lighting, Purves Collection
Museum of Science and Engineering, (Tyne & Wear Museum Service)
Museum of Telecommunications, London
Museum Ostdeutsche Galerie, Regensburg
National Archives of Canada
National Army Museum
National Galleries of Scotland
National Gallery of Art, Washington DC
National Library of Scotland
National Maritime Museum
National Railway Museum
National Savings Bank
National Tramway Museum, Crich, Matlock, Derbyshire
National Trust for Scotland, Hutchesons Hall
Neil MacLeod
New Lanark Conservation Trust
Nicholson & Jacobsen Architects
North Ayrshire Museum
North Down Borough Council
Notman Archives Canada
Nova Scotia Museum
Oestreichisches Museum für Angewandte Kunst
Operation Iron Horse
Palace of Westminster
Paul Harris
Pearce Institute
Physics Department, University of Glasgow
Piccadilly Gallery
Polish Social and Education Society
Precious Organisation
Presbyterian Historical Society of Ireland
Private Collection
Private Collection
Prof. Hugh Simpson, Keeper Pathological Collections,
Professor Flint
Provincial Archives of Alberta, Canada
Provincial Archives of British Columbia
Quarriers Home
Queen's Park Bowling Club
R G Hardie & Co
Radio Clyde
Rangers Football Club
Reg Barber
Regimental Museum of the Cameronians (Scottish Rifles)
RNVR Club (Scotland) S V Carrick
Robert Owen Memorial Museum, Newton, Powys
Rolls Royce
Royal Aeronautical Society
Royal College of Physicians of Edinburgh
Royal College of Physicians London
Royal Commission on the Ancient and Historical Monuments of Scotland
Royal Geographical Society
Royal Gourock Yacht Club
Royal Highland Fusiliers Museum
Royal Scottish Geographical Society
Science Museum, London
Scotch Myths Archives
Scotland Street School/Strathclyde Region Education
Scott Lithgow Ltd
Scott Polar Research Institute
Scottish Airports Authority
Scottish Catholic Archives
Scottish Film Archive
Scottish Liberal Club
Scottish Opera
Scottish Record Office
Scottish Urban Archaeological Trust
Sewing Machine & Service Centre
Smith Art Gallery & Museum
Smith International (North Sea) Ltd
Soapworks Ltd
Springburn Museum Trust
SSEB
Stained Glass Musem, Ely
Stanley K Hunter
State Library of New South Wales
State Museum of Petrodvoretz, Leningrad
State Museum of the History of Leningrad
Steven Currie, The Square Yard, The Barras
Stirling District Council
Stoddard Templeton Carpets
Strathclyde Fire Brigade
Strathclyde Police
Strathclyde Regional Archives
Strathclyde Regional Council, Department of Education
Strathclyde Regional Council, Department of Sewerage
Strathclyde Regional Council, Water Department, Lower Clyde Division
Strathclyde University Archives
STV
Tate and Lyle Plc
Tennant's Plc
Thames Police Museum
Tharsis Plc
The Archdiocese of Glasgow
The Art Museum, Princeton University
The Baron of Earlshall
The British Council
The Danish National Museum
The Dick Institute, Kilmarnock
The Governors of the Edinburgh College of Art
The Incorporation of Bakers, Glasgow
The Incorporation of Barbers, Glasgow
The Incorporation of Weavers, Glasgow
The International Stock Exchange, Scottish Region
The Iona Community
The Royal Society of London
The Scotland - USSR Society
The Scottish Maritime Museum Trust (Irvine)
The Scottish Railway Preservation Society
The State Hermitage Museum, Leningrad
The Ulster Museum, Belfast
Thor Ceramics
Thorvaldsen Museum
Tollcross Central Church
Towns Docks Museum, Hull
Trustees of E A Hornels Trust, Broughton House, Kirkcudbright
Trustees of the Imperial War Museum
Turing Institute
UIE, Scotland Ltd
Ulster Folk and Transport Museum
University of Edinburgh
University of Strathclyde
Vancouver City Archives
Victoria & Albert Museum
Walter Morris
Weir Pumps Ltd
William Hill (Scotland) Ltd
William J Guthrie (Kelvin Central Buses Ltd)
Wm Collins Sons & Co Ltd
Wm Teacher & Sons Ltd, Scottish Whisky Distillers
Wolverhampton Art Gallery

TRANSPORTATION
Wingate & Johnson

SPONSORS
Aldus (UK) Ltd
Anaplast Ltd
BP Exploration
British Gas Scotland plc
British Rail Property Board
Clyde Cablevision Ltd
Clyde Port Authority
Compaq Computer Manufacturing Ltd
Ecomax (UK) Ltd
John Woyka & Co. Ltd
Laing the Jeweller Ltd
MacRoberts
Mitchells Self Drive
Mitsubishi Electric UK Ltd
Olivetti Offices Ltd
Scottish Airports Authority
Scottish Post Office Board
Tannoy Ltd
Thorn Security Limited
Wang (UK) Ltd

IN KIND SPONSORS
British Gypsum Ltd
City Electrical Factors Ltd
Daily Record and Sunday Mail
Erco Lighting Ltd
George Boyd & Co Ltd
Gyproc Insulation Ltd
Habitat PLC
Hunting Specialised Products (UK) Ltd
International Paint Ltd
Lowland Doors Ltd
Marshalls Mono Ltd
Maxwell Exhibitions Ltd
Philips Lighting Ltd
Smart Graphics Limited
The Skillion Group
Touche Ross & Company

PROFESSIONAL ADVISORS

Advertising
Riley Advertising (Glasgow) Ltd

Company Secretary
McLachlan & Brown

Public Relations
Michael Kelly Associates

Project Management & Financial Control
Touche Ross, Glasgow

Solicitors
MacRoberts, Glasgow
Masons, London

We would also like to acknowledge the help of the following: ABSA, Ken Armstrong, Ray Ayres, Lawrence Bain, Susan Baird The Lord Provost of Glasgow, Colin Begg, Nelson Bicol, Iain S. Black, Ritsaert ten Cate, Clydeforth Office Equipment, Derek Currie, Andy Davies, Derek Dow, Lesley Dunlop, Sean Earle, GDC 1990 Festivals Unit, Graven Images, Michael Grove, Mark Hawker, Linda Hills, Neil Jamieson, Elspeth King, Fraser Laurie, Carolyn MacDonald, David MacDonald, Iain MacDonald, Jan MacDonald, John MacDonald, McIlroy Coates, Bob McKay, Alan McLean, Ken McCrae, Isi Metzstein, Kevin Murphy, Anders Nielsen, Ged O'Brien, George Oliver, Richard Orr, Sandy Page, Bob Palmer, Neal Potter, Jane Priestman, SCET, Nancy Smillie, Elizabeth Stewart, Strathclyde University Students, Mark Taylor, Neil Wallace, Ulrike Wilke, Ian Woodburn

PICTURE CREDITS

FRONT COVER:
Doug Clelland

BACK COVER:
Heike Rambow

Page 2:
University of Dundee Satellite Station

PREFACE:

Page 6:
Neil Baxter
Glasgow Herald

Page 7:
Mitchell Library
The British Council
Mitchell Library
Bartholomew's
Bartholomew's
Mitchell Library
Mitchell Library

Page 8:
Bartholomew's
Private Collection
National Gallery of Scotland
Strathclyde Regional Archives
Mitchell Library
Mitchell Library
Imperial War Museum
Glasgow Herald
Glasgow Herald
Leiden University

Page 9:
Mrs I.C. Roger
Mitchell Library
Mitchell Library
William Clyde
Mrs I.C. Roger
Mitchell Library
T & R Annan & Sons Ltd, 164 Woodlands Road, Glasgow G3 6LL
The Royal Aeronautical Society
Glasgow Herald

Page 10:
Business Archives, University of Glasgow and Scottish Record Office
Strathclyde Regional Archives
Hulton – Deutsch Collection
Fletcher Smith Ltd
Glasgow Herald
William Clyde
Glasgow Herald
Strathclyde Regional Archives

Page 11:
Water Department, Strathclyde Regional Council
Strathclyde Regional Archives
Eric Young
Eric Young
Eric Young
Strathclyde Regional Archives
William Clyde
Gillespies Landscape Architects / Scottish Development Agency

Page 12:
John Guthrie and Son

Page 13:
McGill University

Page 14:
Eric Young
Eric Young

Page 15:
Bet Low

Page 16:
Hunterian Museum, University of Glasgow

Page 17:
Dick Institute; Alan Wylie

Page 18:
Mitchell Library; Eric Young
Govan Old Parish Church; Eric Young
Mitchell Library; Eric Young

Page 19:
Mitchell Library; Eric Young
Mitchell Library; Eric Young

Page 20:
Mitchell Library; Eric Young
Glasgow Herald
Mitchell Library; Eric Young

Page 21:
Glasgow University Archives
Clyde Shipping Company
Scottish Record Office and Glasgow University Archives

Page 22:
Hunterian Museum, University of Glasgow

Page 23:
Hunterian Museum, University of Glasgow

Page 25:
Strathclyde Regional Archives

Page 26:
Wellcome Institute for the History of Medicine
Mitchell Library; Eric Young

Page 27:
Royal College of Physicians, Edinburgh

Page 28:
Special Collections, Glasgow University Library

Page 29:
Collins Gallery, Strathclyde University;
Alan Wylie
Special Collections, Glasgow University Library

Page 30:
Burmah Oil Trading Limited
BP Exploration

Page 31:
Kirkintilloch Library
Blackie & Son Ltd; Eric Young
Special Collections, Glasgow University Library

Page 32:
Special Collections, Glasgow University Library

Page 33:
'A Frieze of Famous Scots' – W B Hole, Scottish National Portrait Gallery

Page 34:
Eric Young

Page 35:
Glasgow Herald

Page 36:
Mrs I.C. Roger
Scottish Catholic Archives

Page 37:
Mitchell Library, Eric Young
Mitchell Library; Eric Young

Page 38:
Les Archives de France

Page 39:
The Burrell Collection, Glasgow Museums and Art Galleries

Page 40:
The Bridgeman Art Library/Guildhall Art Gallery

Page 41:
"A Life of Sir Titus Salt, Bt"; Eric Young
St Andrews University Library
"Preaching of John Knox. Before the Lords of the Congregation" – David Wilkie, National Gallery of Scotland

Page 42:
"James VI" att. Adrian Vanson, Scottish National Portrait Gallery
Mitchell Library; Eric Young

Page 43:
Mitchell Library, Eric Young
"Sketch of a Dead Child" – Allan Ramsay, National Gallery of Scotland
Hutchesons' Hall, The National Trust for Scotland

Page 44:
'George Buchanan', National Gallery of Scotland
British Architectural Library Drawings Collection/Royal Institute of British Architects

Page 45:
Mrs I.C. Roger

Page 46:
'History of Glasgow', R Renwick and Sir J Lindsay, Mitchell Library

Page 47:
Strathclyde Police Museum
Strathclyde Regional Archives

Page 48:
Private Collection; George Oliver
Bet Low

Page 49:
Steven Currie, The Square Yard, The Barras; Eric Young

Page 50:
The Burrell Collection, Glasgow Museums and Art Galleries
McManus Art Gallery, Dundee

Page 51:
Mitchell Library

Page 52:
Strathclyde Fire Brigade

Page 53:
Strathclyde Fire Brigade
Mitchell Library; Eric Young

Page 54:
Hulton – Deutsch Collection
Courtesy of the Scottish Film Archive
Courtesy of the Scottish Film Archive

Page 55:
Courtesy of the Scottish Film Archive
Scottish Film Archive; Alan Wylie
Courtesy of the Scottish Film Archive

Page 56:
Singleton Holdings
Courtesy of the Scottish Film Archive

Page 57:
Strathclyde Regional Archives

Page 59:
Mitchell Library
Special Collections, Glasgow University Library

Page 60:
Campbeltown Museum; Eric Young

Page 61:
"News From Scotland"
"Law and Custom of Scotland in Matters Criminal", Sir George Mackenzie

Page 62:
School of Scottish Studies

Page 63:
Nationalmuseet, Copenhagen

Page 64:
'The Constitution of the Freemasons', London, 1723.

Page 65:
'Emblemata Seu Hieroglyphica'
Special Collections, Glasgow University Library

Page 66:
Greater Glasgow Health Board; Glasgow University Archives

Page 67:
Mitchell Library; Eric Young
Mitchell Library; Eric Young
Strathclyde Regional Archives

Page 68:
Mitchell Library; Eric Young

Page 69:
Duke of Hamilton, Lennoxlove House
Polfoto

Page 70:
Special Collections, Glasgow University Library

Page 71:
Kelvingrove Art Gallery, Glasgow Museums and Art Galleries

Page 72:
British Council

Page 73:
Eric Young

Page 74:
Eric Young

Page 75:
By Permission of the Trustees of Blairs College

Page 76:
The Bridgeman Art Library/Towneley Hall Art Gallery and Museums

Page 77:
Strathclyde Regional Archives

Page 78:
"Covenanters Communion" by George Harvey, National Gallery of Scotland
"Rev. Alexander Carlyle" by Archibald Skirving, Scottish National Portrait Gallery

Page 79:
Special Collections, Glasgow University Library

Page 80:
Records Office, House of Lords

Page 81:
Trustees of the National Library of Scotland
Mrs I.C. Roger

Page 82:
Mrs I.C. Roger
Trustees of the National Library of Scotland

Page 83:
T & R Annan & Sons Ltd, 164 Woodlands Road, Glasgow G3 6LL
Service Photographique de la Réunion des Musées Nationaux
British Architectural Library Drawings Collection/Royal Institute of British Architects

Page 84:
Mitchell Library; Eric Young
Tate Gallery

Page 85:
'James Tassie' – David Allan, Scottish National Portrait Gallery
State Hermitage Museum

Page 86:
David Edgar
Hunterian Art Gallery, University of Glasgow
'Robert Burns', Alexander Nasmyth, Scottish National Portrait Gallery

Page 87:
Rijksmuseum

Page 88:
David Edgar (pistols)

Page 89:
'Charles Edward Stuart', Antonio David, Scottish National Portrait Gallery

Page 90:
'Robert Owen', Mary Ann Knight, Scottish National Portrait Gallery

Page 91:
New Lanark Conservation Trust

Page 92:
David M. Stewart Museum

Page 93:
Mitchell Library; Eric Young

Page 94:
Special Collections, Glasgow University Library

Page 95:
Stirling District Council; Alan Wylie

Page 96:
Special Collections, Glasgow University Library

Page 97:
'David Hume', Allan Ramsay, Scottish National Portrait Gallery
'James Boswell', George Willison, Scottish National Portrait Gallery

Page 98:
Mitchell Library; Eric Young
Mitchell Library; Eric Young

Page 99:
Mitchell Library, Eric Young
Mitchell Library; Eric Young

Page 100:
Mitchell Library; Eric Young

Page 101:
Mitchell Library; Eric Young

Page 102:
Museum Boerhaave, Leiden

Page 103:
Royal College of Physicians, Edinburgh
'Joseph Black', David Martin, Scottish National Portrait Gallery

Page 104:
Ann Ronan Picture Library
Wellcome Institute for the History of Medicine
Collins Gallery; Alan Wylie

Page 105:
T & R Annan & Sons Ltd, 164 Woodlands Road, Glasgow G3 6LL
McManus Art Gallery, Dundee

Page 106:
Osterreichisches Museum Fur Angewandte Kunst
Piccadilly Gallery

Page 107:
'Charles Rennie Mackintosh', Francis Newbery, Scottish National Portrait Gallery

Page 108:
Private Collection; Eric Young

Page 109:
Imperial War Museum

Page 110:
City of Edinburgh Art Centre

Page 111:
Sir John Soane's Museum
Mitchell Library; Eric Young
Royal College of Physicians and Surgeons, Glasgow

Page 112:
Strathclyde Regional Archives
Strathclyde Regional Archives
Glasgow Herald
Glasgow Herald

Page 113:
Fletcher and Stewart
Gray Art Gallery

Page 114:
The Colonial Williamsburg Foundation

Page 115:
'James Watt Devising a Major Improvement to the Newcomen Steam Engine', James E. Lauder, National Gallery of Scotland
Mitchell Library; Eric Young

Page 116:
Birmingham City Museums and Art Gallery
Mary Evans Picture Library

Page 117:
National Portrait Gallery
Eric Young

Page 118:
Eric Young
Mitchell Library; Eric Young

Page 120:
Strathclyde Regional Archives

Page 121:
Strathclyde Regional Archives
Strathclyde Regional Archives
Mitchell Library; Eric Young

Page 122:
Mitchell Library; Eric Young
Special Collections, Glasgow University Library

Page 123:
Mitchell Library; Eric Young

Page 124:
Special Collections, Glasgow University Library
Mitchell Library; Eric Young

Page 125:
Mitchell Library; Eric Young

Page 126:
Special Collections, Glasgow University Library

Page 127:
Mitchell Library; Eric Young

Page 128:
Mitchell Library; Eric Young
Mitchell Library; Eric Young

Page 129:
Mitchell Library, Eric Young

Page 130:
Special Collections, Glasgow University Library

Page 131:
The Baillie, Mitchell Library, Eric Young
Strathclyde Regional Archives

Page 132:
Kirkintilloch Library
"Courtesy of the National Railway Museum, York"

Page 133:
'The Falls of Clyde', Elizabeth Nasmyth, National Gallery of Scotland
New Lanark Conservation Trust

Page 134:
The Baillie, Mitchell Library; Eric Young

Page 136:
"Courtesy of the National Railway Museum, York"

Page 137:
Kirkintilloch Library

Page 138:
Motherwell District Library
Stock Exchange; Alan Wylie

Page 139:
Strathclyde Regional Archives
Mitchell Library; Eric Young
Strathclyde Regional Archives

Page 140:
'Collections Ulster Museum, Belfast'
Mary Evans Picture Library
Chemistry Department, University College, London

Page 141:
Mitchell Library; Eric Young
Mitchell Library; Eric Young

Page 142:
Special Collections, Glasgow University Library
Mitchell Library; Eric Young

Page 143:
Special Collections; Glasgow University Library

Page 144:
Mitchell Library; Eric Young

Page 145:
Strathclyde Regional Archives
Strathclyde Regional Archives

Page 146:
City of Edinburgh Art Centre

Page 147:
Motherwell District Library

Page 148:
Eric Young
Kirkintilloch Library

Page 149:
National Library of Australia

Page 150:
National Library of Australia
Royal Highland Fusiliers

Page 151:
Special Collections, Glasgow University Library

Page 152:
Mary Evans Picture Library
'R B Cunningham Graham';
Jacob Epstein, Scottish National Portrait Gallery

Page 154:
Strathclyde Regional Archives

Page 155:
Strathclyde Regional Archives
Rutherglen Museum, Glasgow Museums and Art Galleries

Page 156:
Glasgow Herald

Page 157:
Glasgow Herald
Glasgow Herald

Page 158:
Strathclyde Regional Archives
Mitchell Library; Eric Young

Page 159:
Trustees of the National Library of Scotland
Glasgow Herald

Page 160:
Glasgow Herald
Motherwell District Library

Page 161:
Glasgow Herald

Page 162:
Glasgow Herald
Glasgow Herald

Page 163:
Imperial War Museum
Glasgow Herald

Page 164:
Imperial War Museum
Hulton – Deutsch Collection
Glasgow Herald

Page 165:
Scottish Record Office and Glasgow University Archives
Shop Stewards, Kvaerner, Govan; Eric Young

Page 167:
Private Collection
Strathclyde Regional Archives
Strathclyde Regional Archives

Page 168:
Mary Evans Picture Library
Bet Low

Page 169:
Glasgow Herald
Strathclyde Fire Brigade
Strathclyde Fire Brigade/Glasgow Herald

Page 170:
Mitchell Library: Eric Young

Page 171:
Glasgow Herald
McManus Art Gallery, Dundee

Page 172:
T & R Annan & Sons Ltd, 164 Woodlands Road, Glasgow G3 6LL
T & R Annan & Sons Ltd, 164 Woodlands Road, Glasgow G3 6LL

Page 173:
Ostdeutsche Galerie, Regensburg
Strathclyde Regional Archives
T & R Annan & Sons Ltd, 164 Woodlands Road, Glasgow G3 6LL

Page 174:
T & R Annan & Sons Ltd, 164 Woodlands Road, Glasgow G3 6LL

Page 175:
Oscar Marzaroli, C Anne Marzaroli

Page 176:
Strathclyde Regional Archives
Strathclyde Regional Archives

Page 177:
Mitchell Library
Strathclyde Regional Archives

Page 178:
Kevin McCarra
Strathclyde Regional Archives

Page 179:
MacTaggart & Mickel Limited

Page 180:
Eric Young

Page 181:
Eric Young
Eric Young
Planning Department, Glasgow District Council

Page 182:
Strathclyde Regional Archives
Glasgow Herald

Page 183:
Mark Baines

Page 184:
Glasgow Herald
Eric Young
'Trustees of the Science Museum'

Page 185:
British Motor Industry Heritage Trust
British Steel Corporation

Page 186:
Mike MacEagan and Norman Shewan

Page 187:
Eric Young

Page 188:
Doug Clelland

Page 189:
Tate Gallery, London; Published by kind permission of the Artist
Mitchell Library; Eric Young

Page 190:
Mitchell Library; Eric Young
Eric Young

Page 191:
Royal Air Force
Mitchell Library; Eric Young
Mitchell Library; Eric Young

Page 192:
Mitchell Library; Eric Young
Mitchell Library

Page 193:
Mitchell Library; Eric Young
Eric Young

Page 194:
Glasgow School of Art
Mitchell Library; Eric Young
Mitchell Library; Eric Young

Page 195:
Strathclyde Regional Archives

Page 196:
Strathclyde Regional Archives

Page 197:
Strathclyde Regional Archives
Strathclyde Regional Archives

Page 198:
Private Collection; Eric Young

Page 199:
Special Collections, Glasgow University Library

Page 200:
The Colonial Williamsburg Foundation
Burmah Oil Trading Limited

Page 201:
British Architectural Library Drawings Collection/Royal Institute of British Architects

Page 202:
Peter Wilson
Peter Wilson

Page 203:
Pauline Jamieson Antiques; Eric Young
Frank Worsdall
Mitchell Library; Eric Young

Page 204:
Strathclyde Regional Archives

Page 205:
City of Aberdeen Art Gallery and Museums

Page 206:
Pauline Jamieson Antiques; Eric Young

Page 208:
School of Scottish Studies

Page 209:
School of Scottish Studies
School of Scottish Studies

Page 210:
Mitchell Library; Eric Young
Strathclyde Regional Archives

Page 211:
School of Scottish Studies
Clyde Shipping Company

Page 212:
Strathclyde Programme Shop
Celtic Football Club; John Cullen

Page 213:
National Gallery of Ireland
Strathclyde Programme Shop

Page 214:
Doug Clelland
Strathclyde Regional Archives

Page 215:
Strathclyde Regional Archives
Scottish Jewish Archives Centre

Page 216:
Josef Herman
The Mining and Materials Processing Institute of Japan

Page 217:
Eric Young
Eric Young

Page 218:
Ian Hamilton Finlay

Page 219:
Eric Young

Page 220:
Coats The Threadmakers

Page 221:
Strathclyde Regional Archives
Mitchell Library

Page 222:
Kelvingrove Art Gallery, Glasgow Museums and Art Galleries
Glasgow Herald

Page 223:
Hulton – Deutsch Collection

Page 224:
Hulton – Deutsch Collection
Hunterian Art Gallery, University of Glasgow

Page 225:
Tharsis Plc
Tharsis Plc

Page 226:
Special Collections, Glasgow University Library

Page 227:
Royal Bank of Scotland

Page 228:
Glasgow University Archives
'William Alexander', Scottish National Portrait Gallery

Page 229:
Special Collections, Edinburgh University Library
'Tom Conti', Ishbel McWhirter, Scottish National Portrait Gallery

Page 230:
Provincial Archives of British Columbia
Provincial Archives of British Columbia
'Trustees of the National Library of Scotland'

Page 232:
"By kind permission of Guinness PLC"

Page 233:
Daily Record

Page 234:
School of Scottish Studies
Dick Institute; Alison Miyauchi
Lillehammer Art Museum, Norway

Page 235:
Glasgow Herald
Glasgow Herald

Page 236:
Imperial War Museum
Glasgow Herald

Page 237:
Yarrow Shipbuilders Limited
Glasgow Herald

Page 238:
The Royal Aeronautical Society

Page 239:
Glasgow Herald

Page 240:
Glasgow Herald

Page 241:
Ministry of Defence

Page 242:
William Hill Ltd

Page 243:
Strathclyde Regional Archives
Eric Young
William Hill Ltd

Page 244:
Eric Young

Page 245:
Avril Paton

Page 246:
Greater Glasgow Health Board; Eric Young

Page 247:
Bill Salkeld

Page 248:
William Clyde

Page 249:
Strathclyde Regional Archives
Strathclyde Regional Archives

Page 250:
Mrs I.C. Roger
Josef Herman

Page 251:
Fat Man Press

BIBLIOGRAPHY

There is no such thing as an exhaustive Glasgow bibliography. The following titles may provide a starting point for anyone brave enough to attempt such a project. These are some of the texts we found most useful.

A

Aitken, Robert *The West Highland Way*, 1984
Alison, Robert *The Anecdotage of Glasgow*, 1892
Allen, J. Romilly *Early Christian Monuments in Scotland*, 1903
Anderson, James R. *Provosts of Glasgow, 1609–1832*, 1942
Annan, Thomas *Photographs of the Old Closes and Streets of Glasgow, 1868–1877*, 1977
Aspinall, Bernard *Portable Utopia*, 1984

B

The Bailie
Bain, Graham *John Maclean*, 1989
The Incorporation of the Bakers of Glasgow, 1958
Barke, James *The Land of The Leal*, 1939
Barr, William W. *Glaswegiana*, 1973
Barrapatter, 1983
Barrow, G.W.S. *Kingship and Unity, Scotland 1000–1306*, 1981
Barty-King, Hugh *New Flame*, 1984
Baynham, Walter *The Glasgow Stage*, 1892
Becker, Carl L. *The Heavenly City of the Eighteenth Century Philosophers*, 1932
Bell, Sir James and James Paton *Glasgow Its Municipal Organisation and Administration*, 1896
Berry, James J. *The Glasgow Necropolis Heritage Trail Guide*, 1985
Berry, Simon and Hamish Whyte *Glasgow Observed*, 1987
Bett, Norman M. *Civic Bronze*, 1983
Billcliffe, Roger *Flower Drawings*, 1977
— *Mackintosh Watercolours*, 1978
— *Charles Rennie Mackintosh, Complete Furniture, etc, 1979*
— *Mackintosh Textile Designs*, 1982
— *Mackintosh Furniture*, 1984
— *The Glasgow Boys*, 1985
— *The Scottish Colourists*, 1989
Black, C. Stewart *Glasgow's Story*, 1938
Blair, Anna *Tea at Miss Cranston's*, 1985
Blair, George *Sketches of the Glasgow Necropolis*, 1857
Blake, George *The Shipbuilders*, 1935
— *Down to the Sea*, 1937
— *Clyde Lighthouses*, 1956
Bolitho, William *Cancer of Empire*, 1924
Bone, Muirhead *Glasgow – 50 Drawings*, 1911
Borthwick, Alastair *Hallside – One Hundred Years 1873–1973*
Boyle, Jimmy *A Sense of Freedom*, 1977
The Boys' Brigade Glasgow Battalion, *Centenery Celebrations Book 1883–1983*, 1983
Bridie, James *Collected Plays*, 1934, 1938, 1940
— *One Way of Living*, 1939
Brogan, Colm *The Glasgow Story*, 1952
Broom, John *John Maclean*, 1973
Brotchie, T.C.F. *History of Govan*, 1905
— *Some Sylvan Scenes Near Glasgow*, 1910
— *Glasgow Rivers and Streams*, 1914
— *Hours in the Glasgow Art Galleries*, 1927
Brown, Andrew *History of Glasgow*, 1795
Brown, Gordon *Maxton*, 1986
Bruce, George and Paul H. Scott *A Scottish Postbag*, 1986
Bryden, Bill *Willie Rough*, 1972
— *Benny Lynch*, 1975
Burgess, Moira and Hamish Whyte (eds.) *Streets of Stone*, 1985
Burgess, Moria *The Glasgow Novel*, 1986
Burgess, Moira (ed.) *The Other Voice*, 1987
The Burmah Oil Company 1886–1986
Burnett, John *A Social History of Housing 1815–1985*, 1978 and 1986
The Burrell Collection (various authors), 1983
Butt, John, Ian L. Donnachie and John R. Hume *Industrial History in Pictures: Scotland*, 1968
Butt, John and J.T. Ward (eds.) *Scottish Themes*, 1976
Byrne, John *The Slab Boys*, 1981
— *Cutting a Rug*, 1982
— *Still Life*, 1982
— *Tutti Frutti*, 1987

C

Calder, Angus *The People's War*, 1969
— *Revolutionary Empire*, 1981
Calder, Jenni (ed.) *The Enterprising Scot*, 1986
Caldwell, John Taylor *Come Dungeons Dark*, 1988
Callant, A.G. (pseud. J.R. Russell) *St Mungo's Bells*, 1988
Cameron, Dugald *Glasgow's Own*, 1987
Cameron, Joy *Prisons and Punishments in Scotland*, 1983
Campbell, Alan B. *The Lanarkshire Miners*, 1979
Campbell, Donald *The Jesuit*, 1976
Campbell, J.D. *The Savings Bank of Glasgow*, 1985
Campbell, R.H. *The Rise and Fall of Scottish Industry, 1707–1939*, 1980
Carlyle, Alexander *Autobiography*, 1860
Carrell, Chris and Katya Young (eds.) *Our Lives*, 1988
Carslaw, Rev W.H. *Covenanting Memorials in Glasgow and Neighbourhood*, 1912
Carswell, Catherine *Open the Door!*, 1920
Castle, Colin M. *Better By Yards*, 1988
Chalmers, A.K. *The Health of Glasgow, 1818–1925*, 1930
Chalmers, John *One Hundred Hill Walks Around Glasgow*, 1988
Chapman, Robert *The Picture of Glasgow, etc*, 1818
Checkland, Olive *Philanthropy in Victorian Scotland*, 1980
Checkland, S.G. *Scottish Banking, A History 1695–1973*, 1975
— *The Upas Tree: Glasgow 1875–1975*, 1976 (revised to *1980*, 1981)
Checkland, Sydney and Olive *Industry and Ethos, Scotland 1832–1914*, 1984
Clarke, D.V., D.J. Breeze and Ghillean Mackay *The Romans in Scotland*, 1980
Cleland, James *Annals of Glasgow*, 1816
— *The Rise and Progress of the City of Glasgow*, 1820
— *Maintenance of the Poor, etc*, 1828
— *Account of the Minerals, etc in the Public Green, etc, 1836*
— *Description of the Banquet Given In Honour of the Rt. Hon. Sir Robert Peel, etc.*, 1837
Cochrane, Hugh *Glasgow – the First 800 years*, 1975
— *Impressions of Glasgow*, 1988
Conn, Stewart *At the Kibble Palace*, 1987
Collins, Kenneth *Aspects of Scottish Jewry*, 1987
Collis, Louise *A Private View of Stanley Spencer*, 1972
Coults, James *A History of the University of Glasgow, 1451–1909*, 1909
Cowan, James *From Glasgow's Treasure Chest*, 1951
Craythorne, Nancy *Tennant's Stalk*, 1973
Cronin, James E. *Labour and Society in Britain, 1918–1979*, 1984
Crowther, M. Anne and Brenda White *On Soul and Conscience*, 1988
Cullingworth, J.B. *A Profile of Glasgow Housing 1965*, 1968
Cunnison, J. and J.B.S. Gilfillan (eds.) *The Third Statistical Account of Scotland: Glasgow*, 1958
Ken Currie, 1988

D

Daiches, David *Glasgow*, 1977
Daiches, David, Peter Jones and Jean Jones *A Hotbed of Genius*, 1986
Denholm, James *History of the City of Glasgow*, 1798
Devine, T.M. (ed.) *A Scottish Firm in Virginia, 1767–1777*, 1984
Devine, T.M. *The Tobacco Lords*, 1985
Dickinson, H.W. and H.P. Vowles *James Watt and the Industrial Revolution*, 1943
Dickson, Tony (ed.) *Capital and Class in Scotland*, 1982
Doak, A.M. and Andrew McLaren Young *Glasgow at a Glance*, 1965 and 1983
Dollan, Patrick J. *The Clyde Rent War*, 1925
Donaldson, Gordon *The Scots Overseas*, 1966
Donnelly, Michael *Thomas Muir of Huntershill 1765–99*, 1975
Donnison, David and Alan Middleton (eds.) *Regenerating the Inner City, Glasgow's Experience*, 1987
Dow, Derek *The Rottenrow*, 1984
Dow, Derek with M.M. Leitch and A.F. Maclean *From Almoner To Social Worker*, 1982
Duguid, Charles *MacEwen of Glasgow*, 1957
Durkan, John *Notes on Glasgow Cathedral*, 1970
— *George Buchanan, 1506–82*
Duncan, Richard *Notices and Documents – Literary History of Glasgow*
Dunlop, Eileen and Anthony Kamm *The Story of Glasgow*, 1983

E

Eadie, Robert *Glimpses of Glasgow*
Earnshaw, John *Thomas Muir*, 1959
Eco, Umberto *Travels in Hyperreality*, 1986
Elliot, Robert David *The Glasgow Novel*, 1977 (unpublished thesis in Mitchell Library)
Ellis, P. Beresford and Seamus Mac A'Ghobhainn *The Scottish Insurrection of 1820*, 1970
The Eye of the Mind – The Scot and His Books, 1983
Eyre-Todd, George *The Book of Glasgow Cathedral*, 1898
— *The Glasgow Poets*, 1903

F

Fawcett, Richard *Glasgow Cathedral*, 1985
Fay, Charles R. *Adam Smith and the Scotland of His Day*, 1956
James Finlay and Company, 1750–1950, 1951
Finlayson, James *Maister Peter Lowe*, 1889
Fletcher, Bill *Great Scottish Discoveries and Inventions*, 1985
— *Great Scottish Feats of Engineering and Building*, 1986
Forbes, George and Paddy Meehan *Such Bad Company*, 1982
Forth and Clyde Canal Heritage Trail Guide, 1987
Foster, John and Charles Woolfson *The Politics of the UCS Work-In*, 1986
Frazer, David *The Making of Buchanan Street*, 1885
Friel, George *Mr. Alfred M.A.*, 1972

G

Gaitens, Edward *Growing Up*, 1942
Gallacher, Willie *Revolt on the Clyde*, 1936
Gallagher, Tom *Glasgow, The Uneasy Peace*, 1987
Galt, John *The Steamboat*, 1822
— *The Entail*, 1832
— *A Rich Man*, 1836
Gemmell, William *The Oldest House in Glasgow*, 1910
Gibb, Andrew *Glasgow – The Making of a City*, 1983
Gibson, John *The History of Glasgow*, 1777
Gibson, Tom *The Royal College of Physicians and Surgeons of Glasgow*, 1983
Glasgow – *AA Tour and City Guides*, 1988
Glasgow, a profile
Glasgow Art Gallery and Museum (various authors), 1987
Glasgow City Centre Architecture Heritage Trail, 1986
Glasgow City Chambers, 1988
Glasgow Delineated, 1821
Glasgow District Subway, 1979
Glasgow Green and Roundabout, 1982
Glasgow Our City, 1948
Glasgow Society of Lady Artists, 1982
The Glasgow Style, 1890–1920, 1984
Glasgow, 1919 (Introduction by Harry McShane), 1974
A Walk Through Glasgow Cathedral
Old Glasgow Club Transactions 1900–1938
Proceedings of the Royal Philosophical Society of Glasgow 1841–1951
Glasgow Women's Studies Group *Uncharted Lives*, 1983
Glasser, Ralph *Growing Up in the Gorbals*, 1986
Gomme, Andor and David Walker *The Architecture of Glasgow*, 1968 and 1987
The Gorbals Heritage Trails Guide, 1988
Gordon, Bob *Model Steam Engines*, 1987
Gordon, George and Brian Dicks (eds.) *Scottish Urban History*, 1983
Gordon, J.S.F. *Glasghu Facies*, 1872
Graham, W.S. *Collected Poems, 1942–77*, 1979
Grant, Alexander *Independence and Nationhood, Scotland 1306–1469*, 1984
Grant, Douglas *The Thin Blue Line*, 1973
Gray, Alasdair *Lanark*, 1981
— *Unlikely Stories Mostly*, 1983
Gunn, John and M.I. Newbigin (eds.) *The City of Glasgow*, 1921

H

Hale, Reginald B. *The Beloved*, 1989
Hannah, Leslie *Electricity Before Nationalisation*, 1979
Hammerton, J.A. *Sketches From Glasgow*, 1983
Handley, James *The Irish in Modern Scotland*, 1947
Hanley, Cliff *Dancing in the Streets*, 1958
Hanley, Cliff (ed.) *Glasgow, A Celebration*, 1984
Hannan, John *The Life of John Wheatley*, 1988
Harris, Paul *Glasgow at War*, 1986
Harriston, William *The Steam Boat Traveller's Remembrancer*, 1824
Harvey, W. *Chronicles of St. Mungo*, 1843
Harvie, Christopher *No Gods and Precious Few Heroes, Scotland 1914–1980*, 1981
Henderson, Margaret *Dear Allies*, 1988
Herman, Josef *Memory of Memories, The Glasgow Drawings 1940–43*, (various contributors), 1985
Hickey, Des, and Gus Smith, *Miracle*, 1978
Hind, Archie *The Dear Green Place*, 1966
Hirst, Edwin J. *Seeing Glasgow*, 1975
Holloway, James *James Tassie, 1735–1799*, 1986
Honeyman, T.J. *Art and Audacity*, 1971
House, Jack *Portrait of the Clyde*, 1969
— *Square Mile of Murder*, 1975
— *The Heart of Glasgow*, 1978
— *Music Hall Memories*, 1986
Howell, David *A Lost Left*, 1986
Hume, John R. *Industrial Archaeology of Glasgow*, 1974
Hume, John and Michael Moss *Glasgow As It Was, Vol I*, 1974; *Vol — II*, 1975; *Vol III*, 1976
— *Glasgow at War, Vol I*, 1977
— *Beardmore: the History of a Scottish Industrial Giant*, 1979
Hutchison, Gerard and Mark O'Neill *The Springburn Experience*, 1989

I/J

Irving, Gordon *The Good Auld Days*, 1977

Jacobs, Sidney *The Right to a Decent House*, 1976
Jenkins, Robin *Guests of War*, 1956
— *The Awakening of George Darroch*, 1985
Jennings, Humphrey (ed.) *Pandemonium*, 1985
Jephcott, Pearl *Time of One's Own*, 1967
— *Homes in High Flats*, 1971
Johns, Stephen *Reformism on the Clyde*, 1973
Johnston, Colin and John R. Hume *Glasgow Stations*, 1979
Johnston, Thomas *A History of the Working Class in Scotland*, 1923
Jones, Nathaniel *Directory of Useful Pocket Companion*, 1787

K

Keating, Michael *The City That Refused to Die*, 1988
Kellas, James G. *Modern Scotland*, 1980
Kellett, John R. *Glasgow's Railways*, 1964
— *Glasgow, A Concise History*, 1967
— *The Impact of Railways on Victorian Cities*, 1969
Kelman, James *Not Not While The Giro*, 1983
— *The Busconductor Hines*, 1984
— *A Chancer*, 1985
— *Greyhound for Breakfast*, 1987
Kelman, James (ed.) *An East End Anthology*, 1988
With Tom Leonard and Alex Hamilton *Three Glasgow Writers*, 1976
Kelvin, Lord *James Watt: an oration delivered in the University of Glasgow, etc.*, 1901
Kempsell, Alex *The Golden Thumb*, 1964
Kenna, Rudolph *Glasgow Art Deco*, 1985
Keppie, Lawrence *Scotland's Roman Remains*, 1986
Kernahan, Jack *The Cathcart Circle*, 1980
Kilpatrick, James *Literary Landmarks of Glasgow*, 1898
Kinchin, Juliet *Pollok House*, 1985
Kinchin, Juliet and Perrilla *Glasgow's Great Exhibitions*, 1988
King, Elspeth *The Scottish Women's Suffrage Movement*, 1978
— *Scotland Sober and Free*, 1979
— *St. Nicholas' Hospital in Glasgow*, 1984
— *The People's Palace and Glasgow Green*, 1985
— *The Strike of the Glasgow Weavers 1787*, 1987
— *St. Mungo, Patron Saint of Glasgow*
King, Jessie M. *Glasgow City of the West*, 1911
Kinghorn, Jonathan and Gerard Quail *Delftfield, a Glasgow Pottery 1748–1823*, 1986
Knight, James *Glasgow and Strathclyde*, 1930
Knox, Rt. Rev. E.A. *Robert Leighton, Archbishop of Glasgow*, 1930
Knox, William *Scottish Labour Leaders, 1918–39*, 1984
— *Maxton*, 1987

L

Larner, Gerald and Celia The Glasgow Style, 1970
Sir John Lavery R.A., 1856–1941, 1984
Leighton, John M. and Joseph Swan Select Views of Glasgow and its Environs, 1828
Lenman, Bruce An Economic History of Modern Scotland, 1660–1976, 1977
— The Jacobite Risings in Britain 1689–1746, 1980
— Integration, Enlightenment and Industrialisation, Scotland 1746–1832, 1981
Leonard, Tom If Only Bunty Were Here, 1979
— Intimate Voices, 1984
Lindsay, Frederic Brond, 1984
Lindsay, Jean The Canals of Scotland, 1968
Lindsay, Maurice The Discovery of Scotland, 1964 and 1979
— Portrait of Glasgow, 1972
Lipton, Thomas Leaves From the Lipton Log
Lister and the Lister Ward, 1927
Lochhead, Liz Memo For Spring, 1972
— Dreaming Frankenstein, 1984
Logue, Kenneth J. Popular Disturbances in Scotland, 1780–1815, 1979
Lord Provosts of Glasgow, 1883
Louden, T. The Cinemas of Cinema City, 1983
Lugton, Thomas The Old Lodgings of Glasgow, 1901
— The Story of Glasgow Cathedral, 1902
Lumsden, Henry (ed.) The Records of the Trades House of Glasgow, 1605–78, 1910

MAC

MacAskill, Moira Paddy's Market, 1987
MacDiarmid, Hugh Complete Poems, ed. Michael Grieve and W.R. Aitken, 1978
MacDiarmid, Hugh and Lewis Grassic Gibbon Scottish Scene, 1934
Macdonald, Hugh Rambles Round Glasgow, 1854
Macdonald, Ian Charles Rennie Mackintosh – His Buildings Around The City, 1968 and 1985
MacDougall, Carl Elvis Is Dead, 1986
MacDougall, Ian Labour in Scotland, 1985
MacDougall, Ian (ed.) Essays in Scottish Labour History, 1980
MacDougall, Ian (ed.) Voices From the Spanish Civil War, 1986
Macdougall, Sandra Profiles From the Past, 1982
Macfarlane, Margaret and Alastair The Scottish Radicals, 1981
MacFarlane, Fiona C. and Elizabeth F. Arthur Glasgow School of Art Embroidery, 1894–1920, 1980
MacGeorge, Andrew Old Glasgow, 1880
Macgill, Alexander Glasgow, Its Rise and Progress, 1935
Macgregor, Alexander Public Health in Glasgow 1905–46, 1967
MacGregor, George The History of Glasgow, 1881
Mackay, Donald (ed.) Scotland 1980, 1977
MacKenzie, Peter An Exposure of the Spy System, 1832
— Reminiscences of Glasgow and the West of Scotland, 1865
— Old Reminiscences and Remarkable Characters of Glasgow, 1875
— Curious and Remarkable Glasgow Characters, 1891
Mackie, Euan Scotland: an Archaeological Guide, 1975
Mackie, J.D. A History of Scotland, 1964
Mackintosh and Others, 1988
Mackintosh Flower Drawings, 1988
Charles Rennie Mackintosh, 1987
MacLean, Malcolm and Christopher Carrell As an Fhearann From The Land, 1986
Macleod, Iseabail Glasgow, the Official Guide, 1987
Macleod, Malloch D. The Book of Glasgow Anecdote, 1912
Macleod, Robert Charles Rennie Mackintosh, 1968
Macmillan, Roddy The Bevellers, 1974
— All in Good Faith, 1979
MacMillan, Hector The Sash, 1974
MacPhail, I.M.M. The Clydebank Blitz, 1974
Macquorne, Alan The Career of St. Kentigern of Glasgow
— Iona Through the Ages, 1983
McArthur, A. and H. Kingsley Long, No Mean City, 1935
McBain, Janet Pictures Past, 1985
McCallum, Neil A Small Country, 1983
McCarra, Kevin Scottish Football: A Pictorial History, 1984
McCrone, Guy Wax Fruit, 1947
McCrorie, Ian Clyde Pleasure Steamers, 1986
McDowall, John K. The Peoples' History of Glasgow, 1899
McEwan, Robert D., William Maclean and Ian L. Dunsmore Old Glasgow Weavers, 1981
McFadzean, Ronald The Life and Work of Alexander Thomson, 1979
McFarlan, Donald N. First For Boys, 1982
McFeat, William The Glasgow Directory, 1807
McGill, Jack Crisis on the Clyde, 1973
McGill, Patrick Children of the Dead End, 1914
McGinn, Matt Fry the Little Fishes, 1975
— McGinn of the Calton, 1987
McGovern, John Neither Fear nor Favour, 1960
McGrath, John The Game's a Bogey, 1975
McIlvanney, William A Gift From Nessus, 1968
McKean, Charles The Scottish Thirties, 1987
McKean, Charles, David Walker and Frank Walker Central Glasgow, 1989
McLay, Farquhar (ed.) Workers City, 1988
McLean, Iain The Legend of Red Clydeside, 1983
McNeill, Peter and Ronald Nicholson (eds.) An Historical Atlas of Scotland c400–c1600, 1975
McShane, Harry Calton Weavers' Memorial
McShane, Harry and Joan Smith Harry McShane: No Mean Fighter, 1978
McUre, John The History of Glasgow, 1736

M

Magnusson, Anna The Village, 1984
Marks, Richard Burrell: Portrait of a Collector, 1983
Marshall, James The Trial of the Glasgow Cotton-Spinners, 1837
Marshall, Rosalind K. Virgins and Viragos, 1983
Martin, Don The Garnkirk and Glasgow Railway, 1981
Marwick, Sir James Extracts from the Records of the Burghs of Glasgow, 1573–1642, 1876
— The River Clyde and the Harbour of Glasgow, 1898
— The River Clyde and the Clyde Burghs, 1909
— Early Glasgow, 1911
Marzaroli, Oscar Shades of Gray Glasgow: 1956–87, 1987
Mather, George Two Great Scotsmen, 1893
Melling, Joseph Rent Strikes, 1983
Middlemass, Robert Keith The Clydesiders, 1965
Millar, W.J. The Clyde From Its Source to the Sea, 1888
Miller, Ronald and Joy Tivy The Glasgow Region, 1958
Mills, George The Beggar's Benison, 1866
Mind These Days, 1985
Milton, Nan John Maclean, 1973 and 1979
Milton, Nan (ed.) John Maclean: In the Rapids of the Revolution, 1978
The Mitchell Library, 1977
Mitchison, Rosalind A History of Scotland, 1970
— Lordship to Patronage, Scotland 1603–1745, 1983
Mitchison, Rosalind and Leah Leneman Sexuality and Social Control, 1989
Moffat, Nan Muirhead Round the Studios, 1939, 1982
Moorehead, Alan The White Nile, 1971
Morgan, Edwin The Vision of Cathkin Braes, 1952
— The Second Life, 1968
— From Glasgow to Saturn, 1973
— Poems of Thirty Years, 1982
— Sonnets From Scotland, 1984
Moss, G.P. and M.V. Saville From the Palace to College, 1985
Moss, Michael and John R. Hume Workshop of the British Empire, 1977
Moss, Michael and Iain Russell Range and Vision, 1988
Muir, Edwin Scottish Journey, 1935
Muir, James Glasgow Streets and Places, 1899
Muir, J.H. Glasgow in 1901, 1901
Municipal Glasgow, Its Evolution and Enterprises, 1914
Munro, Michael The Patter, 1985
— The Patter, Another Blast, 1988
Munro, Neil Para Handy and Other Tales, 1980
Murray, Sarah A Companion and Useful Guide to The Beauties of Scotland, 1799 and 1803
Myerscough, John Economic Importance of the Arts in Glasgow, 1988

N

Nancarrow, F.G. Glasgow's Fighter Squadron, 1942
Napier, James Robert Napier, 1904
Newspapers, Glasgow Advertiser
— Glasgow Argus
— Glasgow Citizen
— Glasgow Courant
— Glasgow Evening Times
— Glasgow Herald
— North British Daily Mail
Newton, Kenneth The Sociology of British Communism, 1969
Nicol, Norman Glasgow and the Tobacco Lords, 1966
Nicolson, Murdoch and Mark O'Neill Springburn. Locomotive Builder the the World, 1987

O

Oakley, Charles The Second City, 1946 and 1976
Oakley, Charles (ed.) Scottish Industries, 1953
— Last Tram, 1962
— Dear Old Glasgow Town, 1975
— Our Illustrious Forbears, 1980
— These Were The Years, 1983
Oatts, L.B. The Highland Light Infantry, 1969
Oliver, Cordelia Jessie M. King, 1971
— Glasgow Citizens' Theatre, Robert David MacDonald and German Drama, 1984
— Joan Eardley RSA, 1988
Owen, Robert A Statement Regarding the New Lanark Establishment, 1812

P

Pagan, James Sketch of the History of Glasgow, 1913
— History of the Cathedral and See of Glasgow, 1897
Paisley Abbey
Palace of History, Scottish Exhibition Catalogue, 1911
Parsonage, George Glasgow Humane Society, unpublished typescript 1988
Paterson, Len Twelve Hundred Miles For Thirty Shillings, 1988
Pattison, F.L.M. Granville Sharp Pattison, 1987
Paulden, Sydney and Bill Hawkins Whatever Happened at Fairfields, 1969
Phillips, Alastair Glasgow's Herald, 1983
Porter, Roy Health For Sale, 1989
Prebble, John The Highland Clearances, 1963
— The Darien Disaster, 1968
— The Lion in the North, 1971
— Mutiny, 1975
Primrose, Rev. James Medieval Glasgow, 1913
Pringle, John Quinton, 1981
Proceedings of the Royal Philosophical Society of Glasgow

Q

Quail, Gerard Nautilus Porcelain; Possil Pottery, 1983
Quail, Gerard Garnkirk Fire-Clay, 1985
Quail, Gerard Caledonia Pottery, 1986
Quiz

R

Rae, Hugh C. Skinner, 1965
Rae, J.H. Glasgow Central Area Local Plan, 1987
Reader, W.J. The Weir Group, A Centenary History, 1971
Radford, C.A. Ralegh Glasgow Cathedral, Official Guide, 1970
The Regality Club, publications 1889–1912
Reid, J.M. Glasgow, 1956
Reid, Robert Old Glasgow and its Environs, 1864
Reid, Robert (Senex) Glasgow Past and Present, 1884
Reilly, Valerie The Paisley Pattern, 1987
Renwick, Robert Glasgow Memorials, 1908
Renwick, Robert and Sir John Lindsay History of Glasgow, 1921; continued by George Eyre-Todd, 1931 and 1934
Richardson, Ruth Death, Dissection and the Destitute, 1988
Riddell, John Clyde Navigation, 1979
Robertson, Anne S. The Antonine Wall, 1973
Robinson, Eric and A.E. Musson James Watt and the Steam Revolution, 1969
Roll, Eric The History of Economic Thought, 1937
Roxburgh, J.B. The School Board of Glasgow 1873–1919, 1971
Russell, James Burn Public Health Administration in Glasgow, 1905
Rutherglen Heritage Trail Guide, 1987

S

Saunders, Donald and others The Glasgow Diary, 1984
Scott, Walter Rob Roy, 1817 and 1829
Scottish Print Open (various artists), 1987
Shadow, (pseud. Alexander Brown) Midnight Scenes and Social Photographs, 1878, ed. Colin Harvey 1976
Sillitoe, Percy Cloak Without Dagger, 1955
Simpson, John A History of Govan, 1985
— Govan's Maritime Past, 1987
Simpson, M.A. and T.H. Lloyd Middle Class Housing in Britain, 1977
Sinclair, Maureen Murder, Murder Polis, 1986
Skillen, Brian Glasgow on the Move, 1984
Skinner, A.S. and T. Wilson Essays on Adam Smith, 1975
Smart, Aileen Villages of Glasgow Volume 1, 1988
Smith, Adam The Wealth of Nations, (edited by Andrew Skinner) 1970
Smith, Alexander City Poems, 1857
— A Summer In Skye, 1865
Smith, A. Duncan The Trial of Madeleine Smith, 1905
Smith, Sheenah Horatio McCulloch, 1805–1867, 1988
Smout, T.C. A History of the Scottish People, 1560–1830, 1969
— A Century of the Scottish People, 1830–1950, 1986
Smyth, Alfred P. Warlords and Holymen, Scotland 80–1000, 1984
Somerville, Thomas George Square, Glasgow, 1891
Springburn Heritage Trail Guide, 1988
Springhall, John, Brian Fraser and Michael Hoare Sure and Steadfast, 1983
Steven, Campbell Proud Record, 1975
Stewart, Ian Glasgow By Tram, 1977
— More Glasgow By Tram, 1978
— Round Glasgow By Tram, 1979
Stow, David The Training System, 1850
Strang, John Necropolis Glasguensis, 1831
— Glasgow and Its Clubs, 1864
The Sunday Mail Story of Scotland, 1988 and 1989

T

Tait, John Directory for the City of Glasgow, etc., 1784
Taylor, A.J.P. English History, 1914–45, 1965
William Teacher and Sons
The Tenement House, 1986
One Hundred and Forty Years of the Tennant Companies, 1797–1937
Thomas, John The Springburn Story, 1964
Thompson, E.P. The Making of the English Working Class, 1968
Thompson, Silvanus P. Lord Kelvin, 1910
Time in Motion, 1986
Jubilee Book of the Glasgow Tramways, 1922
Turton, Alison and Michael Moss The Bitter With The Sweet, 1988
Tweed, John Guide to Glasgow and the Clyde, 1872
Two Communities: Springburn and Kirkintilloch, 1983

U

Unique and Original (various artists), 1985
Urie, John Reminiscences of Eighty Years, 1908

V

Various That Land of Exiles: Scots in Australia, 1988
Vergo, Peter (ed.) Vienna 1900, 1983

W

Wade, William W. The History of Glasgow, 1821
Walker, Charles (ed.) A Legacy of Scots, 1988
Walker, Fred M. Song of the Clyde, 1984
Wallace, Andrew A Popular Sketch of the History of Glasgow, etc., 1882
Walton, Dorothy Seward The Hidden Stream, 1948
Ward, Robin Some City Glasgow, 1982
Warner, Gerald Conquering By Degrees, 1985
Waugh, Alec The Lipton Story, 1950
Waugh, Thomas M. Shettleston Past and Present, 1988
— Shettleston From Old and New Photographs, 1986
G. and J. Weir Ltd., Cathcart, Glasgow Six Years of War
Whistle Binkie, 1890
Whyte, Hamish (comp.) Glasgow Poets and Poetry, 1950–75, 1976 (unpublished typescript in Mitchell Library)
Whyte, Hamish (ed.) Four Glasgow Poems, 1981
Whyte, Hamish (ed.) Noise and Smoky Breath, 1983
Wills, Elspeth Scottish Firsts, Innovation and Achievement, 1987
Winch, Donald Adam Smith's Politics, 1978
Winter, J.M. The Great War and the British People, 1985
Wintle, Justin (ed.) Makers of Nineteenth Century Culture 1800–1914, 1982
Wintle, Justin (ed.) Dictionary of Modern Culture, 1984
Wood, John Edwin Sun, Moon and Standing Stones, 1980
Life In The Woodside Tenements, 1987
Working Lives in Woodside and North Kelvin, 1900–60, 1987
Woolfson, Charles and John Foster Track Record, 1988
Wormald, Jenny Court, Kirk and Community, Scotland 1470–1625, 1981
Worsdall, Frank The Tenement, 1979
— A Glasgow Keek Show, 1981
— The City That Disappeared, 1981
— Victorian City, 1982

Y

Young, James D. The Rousing of the Scottish Working Class, 1979
— Women and Popular Struggles, 1985

INDEX

Persons and places occurring in the preface and core text are listed in the following indexes.

PERSONS INDEX

PLACES INDEX